Frank Emmert-Streib, Salissou Moutari, and Matthias Dehm

Mathematical Foundations of Data Science Using R

Also of Interest

Data Science
Time Complexity, Inferential Uncertainty, and Spacekime Analytics
Ivo D. Dinov, Milen Velchev Velev, 2021
ISBN 978-3-11-069780-3, e-ISBN (PDF) 978-3-11-069782-7

Automata Theory and Formal Languages
Wladyslaw Homenda und Witold Pedrycz, 2022
ISBN 978-3-11-075227-4, e-ISBN (PDF) 978-3-11-075230-4

Algorithms
Design and Analysis
Sushil C. Dimri, Preeti Malik, Mangey Ram, 2021
ISBN 978-3-11-069341-6, e-ISBN (PDF) 978-3-11-069360-7

Vagueness in the Exact Sciences
Impacts in Mathematics, Physics, Chemistry, Biology, Medicine, Engineering and Computing
Edited by Apostolos Syropoulos, Basil K. Papadopoulos, 2021
ISBN 978-3-11-070418-1, e-ISBN (PDF) 978-3-11-070430-3

Smart Computing Applications
Edited by Prasenjit Chatterjee, Dilbagh Panchal, Dragan Pamucar, Sharfaraz Ashemkhani Zolfani
ISSN 2700-6239, e-ISSN 2700-6247

Frank Emmert-Streib, Salissou Moutari, and
Matthias Dehmer

Mathematical Foundations of Data Science Using R

2nd edition

DE GRUYTER OLDENBOURG

Mathematics Subject Classification 2010
35-02, 65-02, 65C30, 65C05, 65N35, 65N75, 65N80

Authors
Prof. Dr. Frank Emmert-Streib
Tampere University
Faculty of Information Technology and Communication Sciences
Tampere 33100
Finland
frank.emmert-streib@tuni.fi

Dr. Salissou Moutari
Queens University Belfast
School of Mathematics and Physics
University Road
Belfast BT7 1NN
United Kingdom
s.moutari@qub.ac.uk

Prof. Dr. Matthias Dehmer
Schweizer Fernfachhochschule
Department für Informatik
Schinerstrasse 18
3900 Brig
Schweiz
matthias.dehmer@ffhs.ch
UMIT Private Universität für Gesundheitswissenschaften
Medizinische Informatik und Technik
Eduard Wallnöfer-Zentrum 1
6060 Hall i. Tirol
Austria
matthias.dehmer@umit-tirol.at

ISBN 978-3-11-079588-2
e-ISBN (PDF) 978-3-11-079606-3
e-ISBN (EPUB) 978-3-11-079617-9

Library of Congress Control Number: 2022939964

Bibliographic information published by the Deutsche Nationalbibliothek
The Deutsche Nationalbibliothek lists this publication in the Deutsche Nationalbibliografie; detailed bibliographic data are available on the Internet at http://dnb.dnb.de.

Cover image: slabdsgn
Typesetting: VTeX UAB, Lithuania
Printing and binding: CPI books GmbH, Leck

www.degruyter.com

Preface to the second edition

In recent years, data science has gained considerable popularity and established itself as a multidisciplinary field. The goal of data science is to extract information from data and use this information for decision making. One reason for the popularity of the field is the availability of mass data in nearly all fields of science, industry, and society. This allowed moving away from making theoretical assumptions, upon which an analysis of a problem is based on toward data-driven approaches that are centered around these big data. However, to master data science and to tackle real-world data-based problems, a high level of a mathematical understanding is required. Furthermore, for a practical application, proficiency in programming is indispensable. The purpose of this book is to provide an introduction to the mathematical foundations of data science using `R`.

The motivation for writing this book arose out of our teaching and supervising experience over many years. We realized that many students are struggling to understand methods from machine learning, statistics, and data science due to their lack of a thorough understanding of mathematics. Unfortunately, without such a mathematical understanding, data analysis methods, which are based on mathematics, can only be understood superficially. For this reason, we present in this book mathematical methods needed for understanding data science. That means we are not aiming for a comprehensive coverage of, e. g., analysis or probability theory, but we provide selected topics from such subjects that are needed in every data scientist's mathematical toolbox. Furthermore, we combine this with the algorithmic realization of mathematical method by using the widely used programming language `R`.

The present book is intended for undergraduate and graduate students in the interdisciplinary field of data science with a major in computer science, statistics, applied mathematics, information technology or engineering. The book is organized in three main parts. Part I: Introduction to `R`. Part II: Graphics in `R`. Part III: Mathematical basics of data science. Each part consists of chapters containing many practical examples and theoretical basics that can be practiced side-by-side. This way, one can put the learned theory into a practical application seamlessly.

Many colleagues, both directly or indirectly, have provided us with input, help, and support before and during the preparation of the present book. In particular, we would like to thank Danail Bonchev, Jiansheng Cai, Zengqiang Chen, Galina Glazko, Andreas Holzinger, Des Higgins, Bo Hu, Boris Furtula, Ivan Gutman, Markus Geuss, Lihua Feng, Oliver Ittig, Juho Kanniainen, Urs-Martin Künzi, James McCann, Abbe Mowshowitz, Aliyu Musa, Beatrice Paoli, Ricardo de Matos Simoes, Arno Schmidhauser, Yongtang Shi, John Storey, Simon Tavaré, Kurt Varmuza, Ari Visa, Olli Yli-Harja, Shu-Dong Zhang, Yusen Zhang, Chengyi Xia, and apologize to all who have not been named mistakenly. For proofreading and help with various chapters, we would like to express our special thanks to Shailesh Tripathi, Kalifa Manjan, and Nadeesha Perera. We are particularly grateful to Shailesh Tripathi for helping us

https://doi.org/10.1515/9783110796063-201

preparing the `R` code. We would like also to thank our editor Damiano Sacco from DeGruyter Press who have been always available and helpful.

Finally, we hope this book helps to spread the enthusiasm and joy we have for this field, and inspires students and scientists in their studies and research questions.

Tampere and Brig and Belfast, August 2022

F. Emmert-Streib
M. Dehmer
Salissou Moutari

Contents

Part II: Graphics in R

1 Introduction

We live in a world surrounded by data. Whether a patient is visiting a hospital for treatment, a stockbroker is looking for an investment on the stock market, or an individual is buying a house or apartment, data are involved in any of these decision processes. The availability of such data results from technological progress during the last three decades, which enabled the development of novel means of data generation, data measurement, data storage, and data analysis. Despite the variety of data types stemming from different application areas, for which specific data generating devices have been developed, there is a common underlying framework that unites the corresponding methodologies for analyzing them. In recent years, the main toolbox or the process of analyzing such data has come to be referred to as *data science* [73].

Despite its novelty, data science is not really a new field on its own as it draws heavily on traditional disciplines [61]. For instance, machine learning, statistics, and pattern recognition are playing key roles when dealing with data analysis problems of any kind. For this reason, it is important for a data scientist to gain a basic understanding of these traditional fields and how they fuel the various analysis processes used in *data science*. Here, it is important to realize that harnessing the aforementioned methods requires a thorough understanding of mathematics and probability theory. Without such a hindsight, the application of any method is likely to be done in a blindfolded way, lacking deeper insights. This deficiency hinders the adequate usage of the methods and the ability to develop new ones. For this reason, this book is dedicated to introducing the mathematical foundations of data science.

Furthermore, in order to exploit machine learning and statistics practically, a computational realization needs to be found. This necessitates the writing of algorithms that can be executed by computers. The advantage of such a computational approach is that large amounts of data can be analyzed using many methods in an efficient way. However, this requires proficiency in a programming language. There are many programming languages, but one of the most suited programming languages for data science is `R` [154]. Hence, this book presents the mathematical foundations of data science using the programming language `R`.

That means we will start with the basics that are needed to become a data scientist with some understanding of the used methods, but also with the ability to develop novel methods. Due to the difficulty of some of the mathematics involved, this journey may take some time since there is a wide range of different subjects to be learned. In the following sections, we will briefly summarize the main subjects covered in this book as well as their relationship to and importance for advanced topics in data science.

https://doi.org/10.1515/9783110796063-001

1.1 Relationships between mathematical subjects and data science

In Figure 1.1, we show an overview of the relationships between several mathematical subjects on the left-hand side and data science subjects on the right-hand side. First, we would like to emphasize that there are different types of mathematical subjects. In Figure 1.1, we distinguish three different types. The first type, shown in green, indicates subjects that are essential for every topic in data science, regardless of the specific purpose of the analysis. For this reason, the subjects linear algebra, analysis, probability theory and optimization can be considered as the bare backbone to understand data science. The second type, shown in orange, indicates a subject that requires the data to have an additional structural property. Specifically, graph theory is very useful when discrete relationships between variables of the system are present. An example of such an application is a random forest classifier, or a decision tree that utilizes a tree-structure between variables for their representation and classification [26]. The third subject type, shown in blue, is fundamentally different to the previous

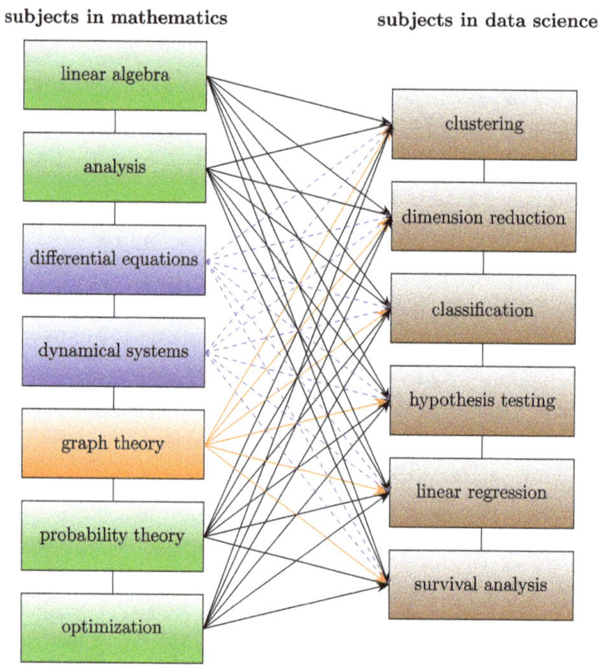

Figure 1.1: Visualization of the relationship between several mathematical subjects and data science subjects. The mathematical subjects shown in green are essentially needed for every topic in data science, whereas graph theory is only used when the data have an additional structural property. In contrast, differential equations and dynamical systems assume a special role used to gain insights into the data generation process itself.

types. To emphasize this, we drew the links with dashed lines. Dynamical systems are used to gain insights into the data-generation process itself rather than to analyze the data. In this way, it is possible to gain a deeper understanding of the system to be analyzed. For instance, one can simulate the regulation between genes that leads to the expression of proteins in biological cells, or the trading behavior of investors to learn about the evolution of the stock market. Therefore, dynamical systems can also be used to generate benchmark data to test analysis methods, which is very important when either developing a new method or testing the influence of different characteristics of data.

The diagram in Figure 1.1 shows the theoretical connection between some mathematical subjects and data science. However, it does not show how this connection is realized practically. This is visualized in Figure 1.2. This figure shows that programming is needed to utilize mathematical methods practically for data science. That means programming, or computer science more generally, is a glue skill/field that (1) enables the practical application of methods from statistics, machine learning, and mathematics, (2) allows the combination of different methods from different fields, and (3) provides practical means for the development of novel computer-based methods (using, e. g., Monte Carlo or resampling methods). All of these points are of major importance in data science, and without programming skills one cannot unlock the full potential that data science offers. For the sake of clarity, we want to emphasize that we mean *scientific* and *statistical* programming rather than general purpose programming skills when we speak about *programming skills.*

Due to these connections, we present in this book the mathematical foundations for data science along with an introduction to programming. A pedagogical side-effect of presenting programming and mathematics side-by-side is that one learns

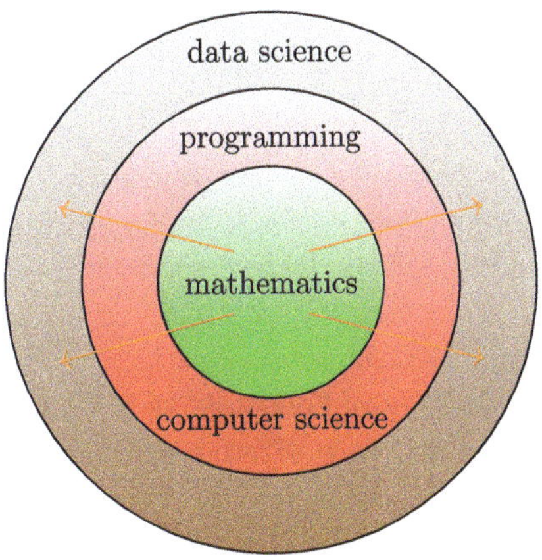

Figure 1.2: The practical connection between mathematics and methods from data science is obtained by means of algorithms, which require programming skills. Only in this way, mathematical methods can be utilized for specific data analysis problems.

naturally to think about a problem in an algorithmic or computational way. In our opinion, this has a profound influence on the reader's analytical problem-solving capabilities because it enables thinking in a guided way that can be computationally realized in a practical manner. Hence, learning mathematics in combination with a computational realization is more helpful than learning only the methods, since it leads to a systematic approach for problem solving. This is especially important for us since the end goal of mastering the mathematical foundations is for their application to problems in data science.

1.2 Structure of the book

This book is structured into three main parts. In the following, we discuss the content of each part briefly:

1.2.1 Part one

In Part one, we start with a general discussion on different programming paradigms and programming languages as well as their relationship. Then, we focus on the introduction of the programming language `R`. We start by showing how to install `R` on your computer and how to install additional packages from external repositories. The programming language itself and the packages are freely available and work for Windows, Mac, and Linux computers. Afterward, we discuss key elements of the programming language `R` in detail, including control and data structures as well as important commands. As an advanced topic, we discuss how to create an `R` package.

1.2.2 Part two

In Part two, we focus on the visualization of data by utilizing the graphical capabilities of `R`. First, we discuss the basic plotting functions provided by `R` and then present advanced plotting functionalities that are based on external packages, e. g., `ggplot`. These sections are intended for data of an arbitrary structure. In addition, we also present visualization functions that can be used for network data.

The visualization of data is very important and it can be viewed as a form of data analysis. In the statistics community, such an approach is termed *exploratory data analysis* (EDA). In the 1950s, John Tukey advocated widely the idea of data visualization as a means to generate novel hypothesis about the underlying data structure, which would otherwise not come to the mind of the analyst [97, 189]. These hypotheses can then be further analyzed by means of quantitative analysis methods. EDA uses data visualization techniques, e. g., box plots, scatter plots, and also summary statistics, e. g., mean, variance, and quartiles to get either an overview of the characteristics of the data or to generate new insights. Therefore, a first step in formulating a question, which can be addressed by any quantitative data analysis method, consists often in the visualization of the data. The Chapters 7, 8 and 9 present various visualization methods that can be utilized for the purpose of an exploratory data analysis.

1.2.3 Part three

In Part three, we start with a general introduction of mathematical preliminaries and some motivation, which highlight the merit of mathematics as the language for science. Afterward, we provide the theoretical underpinning for the programming in `R`, discussed in the first two parts of the book, by introducing mathematical definitions of computability, complexity of algorithms, and Turing machines. Thereafter, we focus on the mathematical foundations of data science. We discuss various topics including linear algebra, analysis, differential equations, dynamical systems, graph theory, probability theory, and optimization. For each of these subjects, we dedicate one chapter. Our presentation will cover these topics on a basic and intermediate level, which is enough to understand essentially most of the methods used in data science.

In addition to the discussion of the above topics, we also present worked-out examples, including their corresponding scripts in `R`. This will allow the reader to practice the mathematical methods introduced. Furthermore, at the end of some chapters, we provide some exercises that allow gaining deeper insights. Throughout the chapters, we also discuss direct applications of the methods for data science problems from, e. g., economy, biology, finance or business. This will provide answers to questions of the kind, '*what are the methods for?*'.

1.3 Our motivation for writing this book

From our experience in supervising BSc, MSc, and PhD students as well as postdoctoral researchers, we learned over the years that a common problem among many students is their lack of basic knowledge and understanding of the mathematical foundations underpinning methods used in data science. This causes difficulties in particular when tackling more advanced data analysis problems. Unfortunately, this deficiency is typically too significant to be easily compensated, e. g., by watching few YouTube videos or attending some of the many available online courses on platforms like Coursera, EdX or Udacity. The problem is actually twofold. First, it is the specific lack of knowledge and understanding of mathematical methods and, second, it is an inability to 'think mathematically'. As already mentioned above, both problems are related with each other, and the second one is even more severe because it

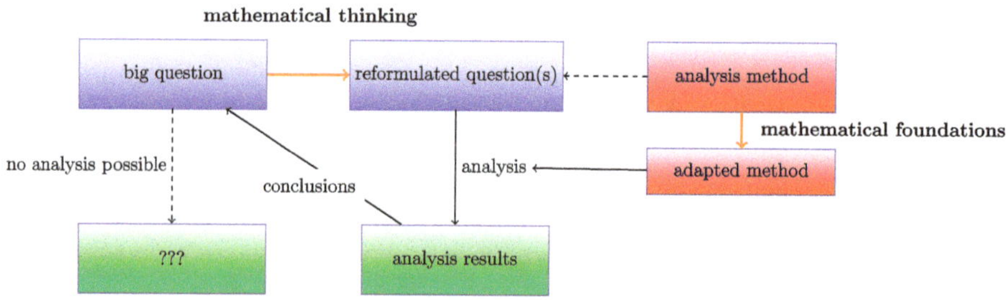

Figure 1.3: A typical approach in data science in order to analyze a 'big question' is to reformulate this question in a way that makes it practically analyzable. This requires an understanding of the mathematical foundations and mathematical thinking (orange links).

has more far-reaching consequences. From analyzing this situation, we realized that there is no shortcut in learning data science than to gain, first, a deep understanding of its mathematical foundations.

This problem is visualized in Figure 1.3. In order to answer a 'big question' of interest for an underlying problem, frequently, one needs to reformulate the question in a way that the data available can be analyzed in a problem-oriented manner. This requires also to either adapt existing methods to the data or to develop a new method, which can then be used to analyze the data and obtain results. The adaption of methods requires a technical understanding of the mathematical foundations of the methods, whereas the reformulation of the 'big question' requires some mathematical thinking skills. This should clarify our approach, which consists of starting to learn data science from its mathematical foundations.

Lastly, our approach has the additional side-effect that the learner has an immediate answer to the question, '`what is this method good for?`'. Everything we discuss in this book aims to prepare the reader for learning the purpose and application of data science.

1.4 Examples and listings

In order to increase the practical usability of the book, we included many examples throughout and at the end of the chapters. In addition, we provided many worked-out examples using `R`. These `R` based examples are placed into a dedicated environment indicated by a green header, see, e. g., Listing 1.1.

Listing 1.1: Example script for R

```
print("hallo world")
```

In addition, we provided also an environment for pseudo-code in blue, see Pseudocode 1.2, and a bash environment in gray, see Bash 1.3 below.

Pseudocode 1.2: Example for pseudocode

```
begin loop
    print("hallo world)
end loop
```

Bash 1.3: Bash environment (terminal)

```
pwd #print working directory
```

1.5 How to use this book

Our textbook can be used in many different areas related to data science, including computer science, information technology, and statistics. The following list gives some suggestions for different courses at undergraduate and graduate levels, for which selected chapters of our book could be used:

- Artificial intelligence
- Big data
- Bioinformatics
- Business analytics
- Chemoinformatics
- Computational finance
- Computational social science
- Data analytics
- Data mining
- Data science
- Deep learning
- Information retrieval
- Machine learning
- Natural language processing
- Neuroinformatics
- Signal processing

The target audience of the book is advanced undergraduate students in computer science, information technology, applied mathematics and statistics, but newcomers from other fields may also benefit at a graduate student level, especially when their educational focus is on non quantitative subjects. By using individual chapters of the book for the above courses, the lack of mathematical understanding from students can be compensated so that the actual topic of the courses becomes more clear.

For beginners, we suggest, first, to start with learning the basics of the programming language `R` from part one of this book. This will equip them with a practical way to do something hands-on. In our experience, it is very important to get involved right from the beginning rather than first reading through only the theory and then start the practice. Readers with already some programming skills can proceed to part three of the book. The chapters on linear algebra and analysis should be studied first, thereafter the order of the remaining chapters can be chosen in an arbitrary order since these are largely independent.

When studying the topics in part three of this book, it is recommended to return to part two for the graphical visualization of data. This will help to gain a visual understanding of the methods and will foster the mathematical thinking in general.

For more advanced students, the book can be used as a lookup reference for getting a quick refresher of important mathematical concepts in data science and for the programming language `R`.

Finally, we would like to emphasize that this book is not intended to replace dedicated textbooks for the subjects in part three. The reason for this is two-fold. First, we do not aim for a comprehensive coverage of the mathematical topics, but follow an eclectic approach. This allows us to have a wide coverage that gives broad insights over many fields. Second, the purpose for learning the methods in the book is to establish a toolbox of mathematical methods for data science. This motivates the selection of topics.

Part I: **Introduction to R**

2 Overview of programming paradigms

2.1 Introduction

Programming paradigms form the conceptual foundations of practical programming languages used to control computers [79, 122]. Before the 1940s, computers were programmed by wiring several systems together [122]. Moreover, the programmer just operated switches to execute a program. In a modern sense, such a procedure does not constitute a programming language [122]. Afterward, the von Neumann computer architecture [79, 122, 136] heavily influenced the development of programming languages (especially those using *imperative programming*, see Section 2.2). The von Neumann computer architecture is based on the assumption that the machine's memory contains both commands and data [110]. As a result of this development, languages that are strongly machine-dependent, such as `Assembler`, have been introduced. `Assembler` belongs to the family of so-called low-level programming languages [122]. By contrast, modern programming languages are high-level languages, which possess a higher level of *abstraction* [122]. Their functionality comprises simple, standard constructions, such as loops, allocations, and case differentiations. Nowadays, modern programming languages are often developed based on a much higher level of abstraction and novel computer architectures. An example of such an architecture is parallel processing [122]. This development led to the insight that programming languages should not be solely based on a particular machine or processing model, but rather describe the processing steps in a general manner [79, 122].

The programming language concept has been defined as follows [79, 122]:

Definition 2.1.1. A programming language is a notational system for communicating computations to a machine.

Louden [122] pointed out that the above definition evokes some important concepts, which merit brief explanation here. *Computation* is usually described using the concept of *Turing machines*, where such a machine must be powerful enough to perform computations any real computer can do. This has been proven true and, moreover, *Church's thesis* claims that it is impossible to construct machines which are more powerful than a Turing machine.

In this chapter, we examine the most widely-used programming paradigms namely, imperative programming, object-oriented programming, functional programming, and logic programming. Note that so-called "declarative" programming languages are also often considered to be a programming paradigm. The defining characteristic of an imperative program is that it expresses how commands should be executed in the source code. In contrast, a declarative program expresses *what* the program should do. In the following, we describe the most important features of these programming paradigms and provide examples, as an understanding of

https://doi.org/10.1515/9783110796063-002

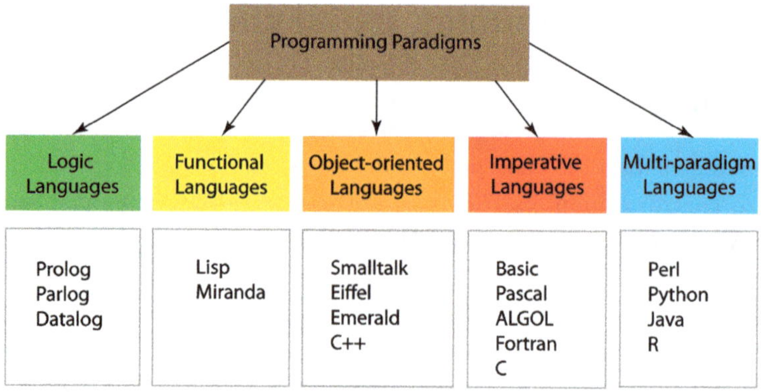

Figure 2.1: Programming paradigms and some examples of typical programming languages. `R` is a multiparadigm language because it contains aspects of several pure paradigms.

these paradigms will assist program designers. Figure 2.1 shows the classification of programming languages into the aforementioned paradigms.

2.2 Imperative programming

Many programming languages in current use belong to the imperative programming paradigm. Examples (see Figure 2.1) include `Pascal`, `C`, `COBOL`, and `Fortran`, see [122, 110]. A programming language is called imperative [122] if it meets the following criteria:

1. Commands are evaluated sequentially.
2. Variables represent memory locations that store values.
3. Allocations exist to change the values of variables.

We emphasize that the term "imperative" stems from the fact that a sequence of commands can modify the actual state when executed. A typical elementary operation performed by an imperative program is the allocation of values. To explain the above-mentioned variable concept in greater detail, let us consider the command

```
x:=x+1.
```

Now, one must distinguish two cases of `x`, see [136]. The l-value relates to the memory location, and the r-value relates to its value in the memory. Those variables can be then used in other commands, such as *control-flow structures*. The most important control-flow structures and other commands in the composition of imperative programs are [136, 168]:

- Command sequences ($\mathtt{C}_1$; $\mathtt{C}_1$; ...; $\mathtt{C}_k$).
- Conditional statements (`if`, `else`, `switch`, etc.).

- Loop structures (`while`, `while ... do`, `for`, etc.).
- Jumps and calling subprograms (`goto`, `call`)).

A considerable disadvantage of imperative programming languages is their strong dependence on the von Neumann model (i. e., the sequence of commands operates on a single data item and, hence, parallel computing becomes impossible [122]). Thus, other nonimperative programming paradigms (that are less dependent on the von Neumann model) may be useful in program design. Direct alternatives include functional and logic programming languages, which are rooted in mathematics. They will be discussed in the sections that follow.

2.3 Functional programming

The basic mechanism of a functional programming language is the application and evaluation of functions [122, 110]. This means that functions are evaluated and the resulting value serves as a parameter for calling another function.

The key feature that distinguishes functional and imperative programming languages is that variables, variable allocations, and loops (which require control variables to terminate) are not available in functional programming [122, 110]. For instance, the command `x:=x+1` is invalid in functional programming, as the above-mentioned terms, memory location, l-value, and r-value (see Section 2.2) do not carry any meaning in mathematics. Consequently, variables in functional programming are merely identifiers that are bound to values. An example that illustrates this concept is the command `x=5` as in functional programming (and in mathematics), variables stand for actual values only. In this example, the actual value equals 5. The command `x=6` would change the value of `x` from 5 to 6. In summary, variables (as explained in Section 2.2) do not exist in functional programming, but rather constants, parameters (which can be functions) and values [122] are used. The exclusive application of this concept is also referred to as *pure functional programming*.

We emphasize that loop structures, which are a distinctive feature of imperative programming, are here replaced by recursive functions. A weak point thereof is that recursive programs may be less efficient than imperative programs. However, they also have clear advantages, as functional programming languages are less machine-dependent and functional programs may be easier to analyze due to their declarative character (see Section 2.1). It is important to mention, however, that some functional programming languages, such as `LISP` or `Scheme`, nonetheless, allow variables and value allocations. These languages are called multiparadigm programming languages as they support multiple paradigms. In the case of `LISP` or `Scheme`, either purely functional or exclusively imperative features may be implemented.

The following examples further illustrate the main features of functional programming in comparison with equivalent imperative programs. The first example shows two programs for adding two integer numbers.

Using (pseudo-)imperative programming, this may be expressed as follows:

Pseudocode 2.1: Imperative version for adding two numbers

```
Proc sum (a, b);
VAR a, b, sum : Int;
begin
sum:=a+b;
end
```

In `LISP` or `Scheme`, the program is simply `(+ a b)`, but `a` and `b` needs to be predefined, e. g., as

Pseudocode 2.2: Defining constants in `Scheme`

```
(define a 4)
(define a 5)
```

The first program declares two variables `a` and `b`, and stores the result of the computation in a new variable `sum`. The second program first defines two constants, `a` and `b`, and binds them to certain values. Next, we call the function `(+    )` (a function call is always indicated by an open and closed bracket) and provide two input parameters for this function, namely `a` and `b`. Note also that `define` is already a function, as we write `(define ... )`. In summary, the functional character of the program is reflected by calling the function `(+    )` instead of storing the sum of the two integer numbers in a new variable using the elementary operation "+". In this case, the result of the purely functional program is `(+ 4 5)`=9.

Another example is the square function for real values expressed by

Pseudocode 2.3: Imperative version for squaring a number

```
Proc square (a);
VAR a, square : real;
begin
square:=a*a;
end
```

and

Pseudocode 2.4: Functional version for squaring a number

```
(define (square x)
(* x x))
```

The imperative program `square` works similarly to `sum`. We declare a real variable `a`, and store the result of the calculation in the variable `square`. In contrast to this, the functional program written using `Scheme` defines the function `(square )` with a parameter `x` using the elementary function `(* )`. If we define `x` as `(define (x 4))`, we yield `(square 4)`=16.

A more advanced example to illustrate the distinction between imperative and functional programming is the calculation of the factorial, $n! := n \cdot (n-1) \cdots 2 \cdot 1$. The corresponding imperative program in pseudocode is given by

Pseudocode 2.5: Imperative version for factorial of n

```
Proc factorial (n);
VAR b, n, square : natural;
begin
b:= 1;
while n > 0 do;
b:=n*b;
n:=n-1;
end
```

This program is typically imperative, as we use a loop structure (`while ... do`) and the variables `b` and `n` change their values to finally compute $n!$ (state change). As loop structures do not exist in functional programming, the corresponding program must be recursive. In purely mathematical terms, this can be expressed as follows: $n! = f(n) = n \cdot f(n-1)$ if $n > 1$, else $f(n) = 0$ if $n = 0$. The implementation of $n!$ using `Scheme` writes as follows [1]:

Pseudocode 2.6: Functional version for factorial of n

```
(define (factorial n)
(if (= n 0) 1
(* n (factorial (- n 1))))))
```

Calling the function `(factorial n)` (see $f(n)$) can be interpreted as a process of expansion followed by contraction (see [1]). If the expansion is being executed, we then observe the creation of a sequence of so-called deferred operations [1]. In this case, the deferred operations are multiplications. This process is called a linear recursion as it is characterized by a sequence of deferred operations. Here, the resulting sequence grows linearly with n. Therefore, this recursive version is relatively inefficient when calling a function with large n values.

2.4 Object-oriented programming

The development of object-oriented programming languages began during the 1960s, with `Simula` among the first to be developed. The basic idea in developing such a language was to establish the term *object* as an entity that has certain properties and can react to events [122]. This programming style has been developed to model real-world processes, as real-world objects must interact with one another. This is exemplified in Figure 2.2. Important properties of object-oriented programs include the reusability of software components and their independence during the design process. Classical and purely object-oriented programming languages that realize the above-mentioned ideas include, for example, `Simula67`, `Smalltalk`, and `Eiffel` (see [122]). Other examples include the programming languages `C++` or `Modula 2`. We emphasize that they can be purely imperative or purely object-oriented and, hence, they also support multiple paradigms. As mentioned above (in Section 2.3), `LISP` and `Scheme` also support multiple paradigms.

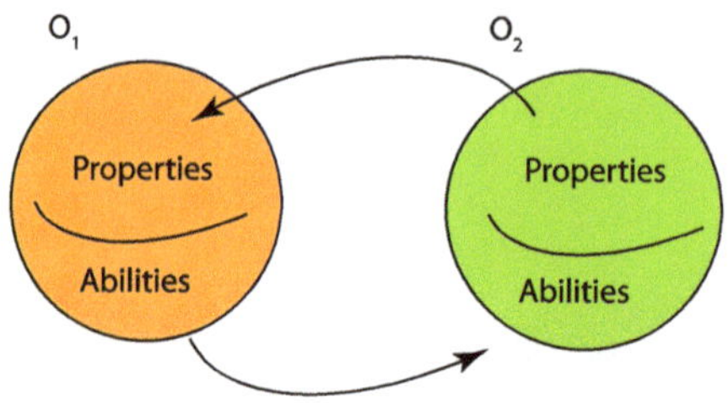

Figure 2.2: Interaction between objects.

When explaining object-oriented programming languages, concepts such as objects, classes to describe objects, and inheritance must be discussed (see [47, 111]). Objects that contain both data (relating to their properties) and functions (relating to their abilities) can be described as entities (see Figure 2.2). A class defines a certain type of object while also containing information about these objects' properties and abilities. Finally, such objects can communicate with each other by exchanging messages [47, 111]. We only explain the idea of inheritance in brief [47, 111]. To create new classes, the basic idea is to *inherit* data and methods from an already existing class. Advantages of this concept include the abstraction of data (e. g., properties can be subsumed under more abstract topics) and the reusability of classes (i. e., existing classes can be used in further programs and easily modified), see [47, 111].

The above-mentioned concepts are in contrast to imperative programming because the latter classifies data and functions into two separate units. Moreover, imperative programming requires that the user of the program must define the data before it is used (e. g., by defining starting values) and that they ensure that the functions receive the correct data when they are called. In summary, the advantages of object-oriented programming can be briefly summarized as follows [47, 111]:

- The error rate is less than that of, for example, imperative languages, as the object itself controls the data access.
- The maintenance effort can be increased compared to other programming paradigms as the objects can modify data for new requirements.

- This programming paradigm has high reusability as the objects execute themselves.

2.5 Logic programming

Before sketching the basic principles of logic programming, a short history of this programming paradigm will be provided here. We note that *formal logic* [175] serves as a basis for developing logic programming. Methods and results from formal logic have been used extensively in computer science. In particular, formal logic has been used to design computer systems and programming languages. Examples include the design of computer circuits and control-flow structures, which are often embedded in programming languages using Boolean expressions [122].

Another area in which the application of formal logic has proven useful is the description of the *semantics* of programming languages (see Section 2.8; [122, 126]). Using formal logic together with *axiomatic semantics* (see Section 2.8) has been also essential in proving the correctness of program fragments [122].

Moreover, seminal work has been conducted in theoretical computer science when implementing methods and rules from formal logic using real computers. An example thereof is *automated theorem proving* [175] which places the emphasis on proving mathematical theorems using computer programs. Interestingly, extensive research in this area led to the opposite insight, that the results of computation can be interpreted as proof of a particular problem [122]. This has triggered the development of programming languages, which are based logic expressions. A prominent example of a logic and declarative programming language is `Prolog`, developed in the seventies [95]. A concrete example is provided in the paragraph that follows.

To express logical statements formally, the so-called *first-order predicate calculus* [175], a mathematical apparatus that is embedded in mathematical or formal logic, is required. For in-depth analysis of the first-order predicate calculus and its method, see, for example, [35, 175]. A simple example of the application of the first-order predicate calculus is to prove the statement `naturalnumber(1)`. We assume the logical statements

```
naturalnumber(1)
for all n, naturalnumber(n) → naturalnumber(successor(n))
```

to be true (see also the *Peano axioms* [12]). Here, the symbol → stands for the logical implication. Informally speaking, this means that if 1 is a natural number and if `n` is a natural number (for all `n`), and that, therefore, the successor is also a natural number, then 3 is a natural number. To prove the statement, we apply the last two logical statements as so-called *axioms* [35, 175], and obtain

```
naturalnumber(1) → naturalnumber(successor(1))
 → naturalnumber(successor(successor(1)))
```

Logic programming languages often use so-called *Horn clauses* to implement and evaluate logical statements [35, 175]. Using Prolog, the evaluation of these statements is given by the following:

Listing 2.7: Logic version for natural(3) in Prolog

```
natural(0).
natural(s(X)) :- natural(X).
natural(X) :- integer(X), X >= 0.
natural(3).
yes
```

Further details of Prolog and the theoretical background of programming languages in general can be found in [34, 95, 122, 152].

2.6 Other programming paradigms

In this section, we sketch other programming paradigms and identify some typical examples thereof. To classify them correctly, we emphasize that they form sub-paradigms of those already discussed.

We begin by mentioning so-called *languages for distributed and parallel programming*, which are often used to simplify the design of distributed or parallel programs. An example thereof is the language OCCAM, which is imperative [5]. The unique feature of so-called *script languages*, such as Python and Perl, is their simplicity and compactness. Both languages support imperative, object-oriented, and functional programming. Furthermore, programs written using script languages are often embedded into other programs implemented using *structure-oriented languages*. Examples of the latter include HTML and XML, see [60]. *Statistical programming languages*, such as S and R, have been developed to perform statistical calculations and data analysis on a large scale [14, 153]. A successor of S, called the New S language, has strong similarities to S-PLUS and R, while R supports imperative, object-oriented, and functional programming. The last paradigm we want to mention are declarative *query languages*, which have been used extensively for database programming [166]. A prominent example thereof is SQL [166].

2.6.1 The multiparadigm language R

As already discussed in the last section, R is a so-called statistical programming language that supports multiple paradigms. In fact, it incorporates features from imperative, functional, and objective-oriented programming. In the following, we give some code examples to demonstrate this. The R-statements in Listing 2.8

Listing 2.8: Variable declaration in R

```
a <- 0
a <- a + 5

a
5
```

prove the existence of variables (see Section 2.2). That means, this part is imperative. Another way to demonstrate this is the procedure in Listing 2.9.

Listing 2.9: Imperative version of a sum in R

```
x=0
fun_sum_imperative <- function(n){
    for(i in 1:n){x=x+i}
    return(x)
}

fun_sum_imperative(4)
10
```

The function `fun_sum_imperative` computes the sum of the first `n` natural numbers, and is here written in a procedural way. By inspecting the code, one sees that there is a state change of the declared variable, again underpinning its imperative character. In contrast, the functional approach (see Section 2.3) to express this problem is shown in Listing 2.10.

Listing 2.10: Functional version of a sum in R

```
fun_sum_functional <- function(n){
    if(n==0){return(0)}
    else{return(n + fun_sum_functional(n-1))}
  }

fun_sum_functional(4)
10
```

This version uses the concept of recursion for representing the following formula: `sum(n)=n+sum(n-1)` (see also Section 2.3). As mentioned in Section 2.3, recursive solutions may be less efficient especially when calling a function with large values than iterative ones by using variables in the sense of imperative programming.

To conclude this section, we demonstrate the object-oriented programming paradigm in R. For this, we employ the object-oriented programming system S4 [129] and implement the same problem as above. The result is shown in Listing 2.11.

Listing 2.11: Object-oriented version of a sum in R

```
setClass("series_operation",  representation(n = "numeric"))
setGeneric("fun_sum_object_oriented",
function(n, ...)standardGeneric("fun_sum_object_oriented"))
```

```
setMethod("fun_sum_object_oriented",
    signature=c(n="series_operation"),
function(n) {t=0;for(i in 1:n at n){t=t+i }; return(t)})
k <- new("series_operation", n=4)
fun_sum_object_oriented(k)
10
```

First, we use the predefined class `series_operation` with a predefined data- type. Then, we define a prototype of the method `fun_sum_object_oriented` using the standard class `series_operation`. Using the `setMethod` command, we define the method `fun_sum_object_oriented` concretely, and also create a new object from `series_operation` with a concrete value. Finally, calling the method gives the desired result.

2.7 Compiler versus interpreter languages

In the preceding sections, we discussed programming paradigms and distinct features thereof. We also demonstrated these paradigms by giving some examples using programming languages such as `Scheme` or `Prolog`.

In general, the question as to how a programming language can be implemented concretely on a machine arises. Two main approaches exist to tackle this problem, namely by means of an *interpreter* or *compiler* (see [122, 167, 202]). We start by explaining the basic principle of an interpreter. Informally speaking, an interpreter $\mathcal{I}$ receives a program and input symbols as its input and computes an output. In mathematical terms, this can be expressed by a mapping $\mathcal{I} : L \times I \longrightarrow O$, where L is an arbitrary programming language and I and O are sets corresponding to the input and output, respectively [202]. Figure 2.3 shows the principle of an interpreter schematically.

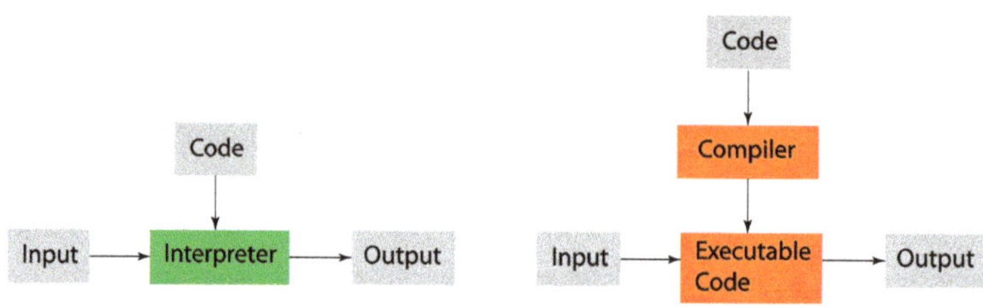

Figure 2.3: The basic principle of an interpreter (left) and compiler (right) [122].

A distinct property of an interpreter is that the program $p \in L$ and the sequence of input symbols are executed simultaneously without using any prior information [202]. Typical interpreter languages include functional programming languages, such as `Lisp` and `Miranda`, but other examples include `Python` and `Java` (see [122, 168]). A key advantage of interpreter languages is that the debugging process is often more efficient compared to that of a compiler, as the code is executed at the runtime only. The frequent inefficiency of interpreter programs may be identified as a weakness because all fragments of the program, such as loops, must be translated when executing the program again.

Next, we sketch the compiler approach to translate computer programs. A compiler translates an input program as a preprocessing step into another form, which can then be executed more efficiently. This preprocessing step can be understood as follows: A program written in a programming language (source language) is translated into machine language (target language) [202]. In mathematical terms, this equals a mapping $C : L_1 \longrightarrow L_2$ that maps programs of a programming language L_1 to other programs of programming language L_2. After this process, a target program can be then executed directly. Typical compiler languages include `C`, `Pascal`, and `Fortran` (see [122, 168]). We emphasize that compiler languages are extremely efficient compared to interpreter languages. However, when changing the source code, the program must be compiled again, which can be time consuming and resource intensive. Figure 2.3 shows the principle of a compiler schematically.

2.8 Semantics of programming languages

Much research has been conducted exploring the effect and behavior of programs using programming languages [122, 126, 168]. For example, a program's correctness can be proven mathematically using methods from so-called *formal semantics* [126]. Besides their extensive use in theory [122, 126], they have also proven useful in practice as they have positively stimulated the development of modern programming languages. Moreover, such methods have been developed as it is required to describe the effect of programming languages independently from concrete machines.

Below, we briefly sketch the three main approaches to formally describe the semantics of programming languages [122, 126, 168]:

- *Operational semantics* describes a programming language by operations of a concrete or hypothetical machine.
- *Denotational semantics* is based on the use of semantical functions to describe the effect of programs. This can be done by defining functions that assign semantical values to the syntactical constructions of a programming language.
- *Axiomatic semantics* uses logical axioms to describe the semantics of programming languages' phrases.

2.9 Further reading

For readers interested in more details about the topics presented in this chapter, we recommend [122, 126, 168].

2.10 Summary

The study of programming paradigms has a long history and is relatively complex. Nevertheless, we considered it important to introduce this fundamental aspect to show that programming is much more than writing code. Indeed, although programming is generally perceived as practical, it has a well-defined mathematical foundation. As such, programming is less practical than it may initially appear, and this knowledge can be utilized by programmers in their efforts to enhance their coding skills.

3 Setting up and installing the R program

In this chapter, we show how to install R on three major operating systems that are widely used: Linux, MAC OS X, and Windows. As a note, we would like to remark that this order reflects our personal preference of the operating systems based on the experience we gained over the years making maximum use of computers.

From our experience, Linux is the most stable and reliable operating system of these three and is also freely available. An example of such a Linux-operating system is Ubuntu, which can be obtained from the web page http://www.ubuntu.com/. We are using Ubuntu since many years and can recommend it to anyone, no matter whether it is for a professional or a private usage. Linux is in many ways similar to the famous operating system Unix, developed by the AT&T Bell Laboratories and released in 1969, however, without the need of acquiring a license. Typically, a research environment of professional laboratories has a computer infrastructure consisting of Linux computers, because of the above-mentioned advantages in addition to the free availability of all major programming languages (e. g., C/C++, python, perl, and Java) and development tools. This makes Linux an optimal tool for developers.

Interestingly, the MAC OS X system is Unix-based like Linux, and hence, shares some of the same features with Linux. However, a crucial difference is that one requires a license for many programs because it is a commercial operating system. Fortunately, R is freely available for all operating systems.

3.1 Installing R on Linux

Most Linux distributions have a centralized package repository and a package manager. The easiest installation for Ubuntu is to open a terminal and type:

Bash 3.1: Installing R using the terminal

```
sudo apt-get install r-base
```

Alternatively, one can install R by using the Ubuntu software center, which is similar to an App store. For other Linux distributions the installation is similar, but details change. For instance, for Fedora, the installation via terminal uses the command:

Bash 3.2: Installing R using Ubuntu Software Center

```
yum install -y R
```

https://doi.org/10.1515/9783110796063-003

3.2 Installing R on MAC OS X

There are two packages available to install R on a MAC OS X operating system. The first is a binary package and the second contains all source files. In the following we focus on the first type, because the second is not needed for the regular user, but the developer.

From the R web page (or CRAN), locate the newest version of R for your MAC OS X operating system. It is important to decide if you need a 64-bit or a 32-bit version. At the time of writing this book, the current R version is R 3.6.1. The installation is quite simple by double-clicking the Installer package.

3.3 Installing R on Windows

The installation for Windows is very similar to MAC OS X as described above and all files can also be found at CRAN.

3.4 Using R

The above installation, regardless for which operating system, allows you to execute R in a terminal. This is the most basic way to use the programming language. That means one needs, in addition, an editor for writing the code. For Linux, we recommend `emacs` and for MAX OS X `Sublime` (which is similar to emacs). Both are freely available. However, there are many other editors that can be used. Just try to find the best editor for your needs (e. g., nice command highlighting or additional tools for writing or debugging the code) that allows you to comfortably write code.

Some people like this vi-feeling[1] of programming, however, others prefer to have a graphical-user interface that offers some utilities. In this case, RStudio (https://www.rstudio.com/) might be the right choice for you. In Figure 3.1, we show an example how an RStudio session looks. Essentially, the window is split into four parts. A terminal for executing commands (bottom-left), an editor (top-left) to write scripts, a help window showing information about R (bottom-right) or for displaying plots, and a part displaying variables available in the working space (top-right).

3.5 Summary

For using the base functionality of R, the installation shown in this chapter is sufficient. That means essentially everything we will discuss in Chapter 5 regarding the

1 Vi is a very simple yet powerful and fast editor used on Unix or Linux computers.

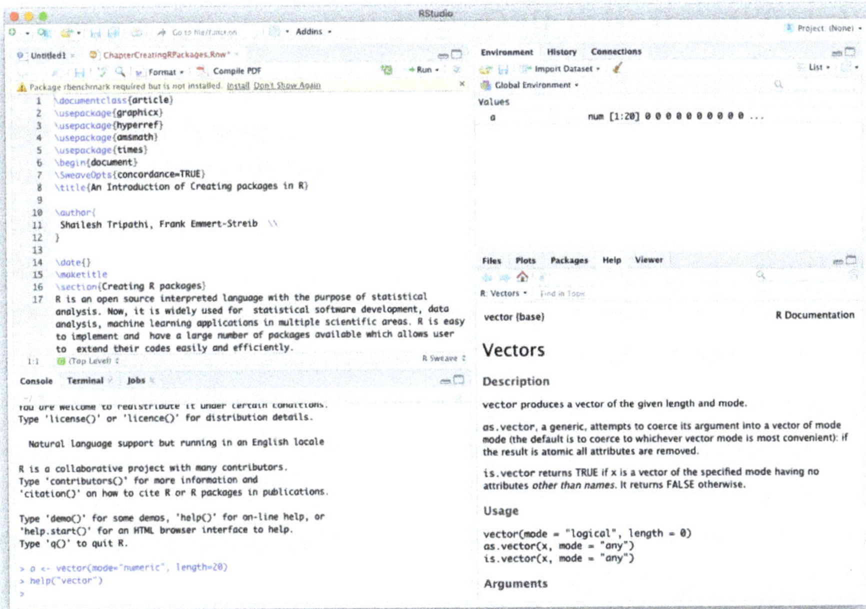

Figure 3.1: Window of an Rstudio session.

introduction to programming can be done with this installation. For this reason, we suggest to skip the next chapter discussing the installation of external packages and come back to it when it is needed to install such packages.

4 Installation of R packages

After installing the base version of R, the program is fully functional. However, one of the advantages of using R is that we are not limited to the functionality that comes with the base installation, but we can extend it easily by installing additional packages. There are two major sources from which such packages are available. One is the COMPREHENSIVE R ARCHIVE NETWORK (CRAN) and the other is BIOCONDUCTOR. Recently, GitHub has been emerging as a third major repository. In what follows, we explain how to install packages from these and other sources.

4.1 Installing packages from CRAN

The simplest way to install packages from CRAN is via the *install.packages* function.

Listing 4.1: Package installation from CRAN: general syntax

```
install.packages(pkgs = package.name)
```

Here, package.name is the name of the package of interest. In order to find the name of a package we want to install, one can go the CRAN web page (http://cran.r-project.org/) and browse or search the list of available packages. If such a package is found, then we just need to execute the above command within an R session and the package will be automatically installed. It is clear that in order for this to work properly, we need to have a web connection.

As an example, we install the bc3net package that enables inferring networks from gene expression data [45].

Listing 4.2: Package installation from CRAN: bc3net

```
install.packages(pkgs = "bc3net")
```

At the time of writing this book CRAN provided 14435 available packages. This is an astonishing number, and one of the reasons for the widespread use of R since all of these packages are freely available.

4.2 Installing packages from Bioconductor

Installing packages from Bioconductor is also straightforward. We just need to go to the web page of Bioconductor (http://www.bioconductor.org/) and search for the packages of interest. Then, on each page there is some information about how to install the package. For example, if we want do install the package graph that

https://doi.org/10.1515/9783110796063-004

provides functions to manipulate networks, one needs to execute the following commands:

Listing 4.3: Package installation from Bioconductor

```
if (!requireNamespace("BiocManager", quietly = TRUE))
    install.packages("BiocManager")

BiocManager::install("graph")
```

The first command sets the source from where to download the package, and the second command downloads the package of interest.

4.3 Installing packages from GitHub

GitHub is a website providing a home for git repositories, whereas git is a freely available and open source distributed version control system that supports software development. The general way to install a package is

Listing 4.4: Package installation from GitHub: general syntax

```
install.packages("devtools")
devtools::install_github("ID/packagename")
```

That means, first, the package `devtools` from CRAN needs to be installed and then a package from GitHub with the name `ID/packagename` can be installed. For instance, in order to install `ggplot2` one uses the command

Listing 4.5: Package installation from GitHub: ggplot2

```
devtools::install_github("tidyverse/ggplot2")
```

4.4 Installing packages manually

4.4.1 Terminal and unix commands

For the manual installation of packages, described below, on a Windows system, it is necessary to install first the freely available program Cygwin. Cygwin is an interface enabling a Unix-like environment similar to a terminal for Linux or MAC, which has this available right out of the box. In general, a terminal enables entering commands textually via the keyboard and provides the most basic means to communicate with your computer. It is interesting to note that when using your mouse and clicking a button, this action is internally converted into commands that are fed to the

Table 4.1: Essential unix commands that can be entered via a terminal.

Unix Command	Description
cd path	change to directory
clear	clear the terminal screen
cp source destination	copy files and directories
df	display used and available disk space
du	shows how much space each file uses
file filename	determine what type of data is within a file
head filename	display the beginning of a file
history	displays the last commands typed
kill pid	Stop a process
ls	list directory contents
man [command]	display help information for the specified command
mkdir directory	create a new directory.
mv [options] source destination	rename or move file(s) or directories
ps [options]	display a snapshot of the currently running processes
pwd	display the pathname for the current directory
rm [options] directory	remove file(s) and/or directories
rmdir [options] directory	delete only empty directories
top	displays the resources being used (Press q to exit)
wc file	count number of words in file

computer processor for execution. The problem is that, for what we describe below, there are no buttons available that could be clicked with your mouse. The good thing is that this is not really a problem as long as we have a terminal that allows us to enter the required commands directly.

Before we proceed, we would like to encourage the reader to get at least a basic understanding of unix commands because this gives you a much better understanding about the internal organization of a computer and its directory structure. In Table 4.1, we provide a list of the most basic and essential unix commands that can be entered via a terminal.

4.4.2 Package installation

The most basic method to install packages is to download a package to your local hard drive and then install it. Suppose that you downloaded such a package to the directory "home/new.files". Then you need to execute the following command within a terminal (and not within an R session!) from the home directory:

```
R CMD INSTALL package.name
```

4.5 Activation of a package in an R session

In order to use the functions provided by a package in R, first, one needs to activate a package. This is done by the *library* function:

Listing 4.6: Syntax for package activation in an R session

```
library(package.name)
```

Only after the execution of the above command the content of the package package.name is available. For instance we activate the package bc3net as follows:

Listing 4.7: Package activation in an R session: bc3net

```
library("bc3net")
```

To see what functions are provided by a package we can use the function *help*:

Listing 4.8: Help function for packages

```
help(package.name)
```

4.6 Summary

In this chapter, we showed how to install external packages from different package repositories. Such packages are optional and are not needed for utilizing the base functionality of R. However, there are many useful packages available that make programming more convenient and efficient. For instance, in an academic environment it is common to provide an R package when publishing a scientific article that allows reproducing the conducted analysis. This makes the replication of such an analysis very easy because one does not need to rewrite such scripts.

5 Introduction to programming in R

This chapter will provide an introduction to programming in R. We will discuss key commands, data structures, and basic functionalities for writing scripts. R has been specifically developed for the statistical analysis of data. However, here we focus on its general purpose functionalities that are common to many other programming languages. Knowledge of these functionalities is necessary for utilizing its advanced capabilities discussed in later chapters.

5.1 Basic elements of R

In R a value is assigned to a parameter by the "$<-$" operator:

Listing 5.1: Value assignment

```
a <- 4
```

In principle also, the symbol "=" can be used for an assignment, but there are cases where this leads to problems, and for this reason we suggest using always the "$<-$" operator, because it can be used in all cases.

The basic elements of R, to which different values can be assigned, are called *objects*. There are different types of objects and some of them are listed in Table 5.1.

Table 5.1: Information about basic object types in R.

Object type	Example	Description
NULL	NULL	place holder (initialized but empty)
NA	NA	missing value (non-available)
environment	a <- new.env(hash=TRUE)	an environment
logical	TRUE, FALSE	logical values
integer	$1, 2, 3, \dots$	integer values
double	1.3452	real values
character	'hallo'	a string of character values
expression	exp <- parse(text=c("x <- 2"))	an expression object
list	x <- list(3, c(5,3))	a list

The command *typeof()* provides information about the type of an object. An interesting type is NULL, which is not an actual object-type, but serves more as a place holder allowing an empty initialization. In Section 5.3.1, we will show how this can be useful. Another interesting type is NA, indicating missing values.

https://doi.org/10.1515/9783110796063-005

5.1.1 Navigating directories

When opening an R session, it may be unclear in which directory we actually are. In order to find this out one can use the get working directory function *getwd()*:

Listing 5.2: Getting the current working directory

```
getwd()
```

This will result in a character string showing the full path to the current working directory of the R session. In case one would like to change the directory, one can use the set working directory function *setwd()*:

Listing 5.3: Setting a new working directory

```
setwd(new.dir)
```

Here, **new.dir** is a character string containing a valid name of a directory you would like to set as your current working directory.

5.1.2 System functions

An important part of R and any programming language is a *system function*. A system function has a name followed by a list of arguments in parentheses. A simple example for such a function is *sqrt()*. In order to use such a function appropriately, one needs to know:

- the name of the function
- the arguments of the function
- the meaning of the function and its arguments

Let us assume that we know the name of the function, but not of its arguments. In R, there are two ways to find this out. First, one can use the function *args()* and, as an argument for this function, the name of the function with unknown arguments:

Listing 5.4: Getting arguments of a function

```
args(sqrt)
```

The information resulting from *args()* is usually only informative if one is already familiar with the function of interest, but just forgot details about its arguments. For more information, we need to use the function *help()*, which is described in detail in the next section.

In the following, we use the term "function" and "command" interchangeably, although a command has a more general meaning than a function.

5.1.3 Getting help

When there is a command that we want to use, but we are unfamiliar with its syntax, e. g., *sqrt()*, R provides a help function, which is evoked by either *help(sqrt)* or *?sqrt*:

Listing 5.5: Using the function *help()*

```
help(sqrt)
?sqrt
```

The output of either of these commands is a textual information, providing information about this function (see Figure 5.1).

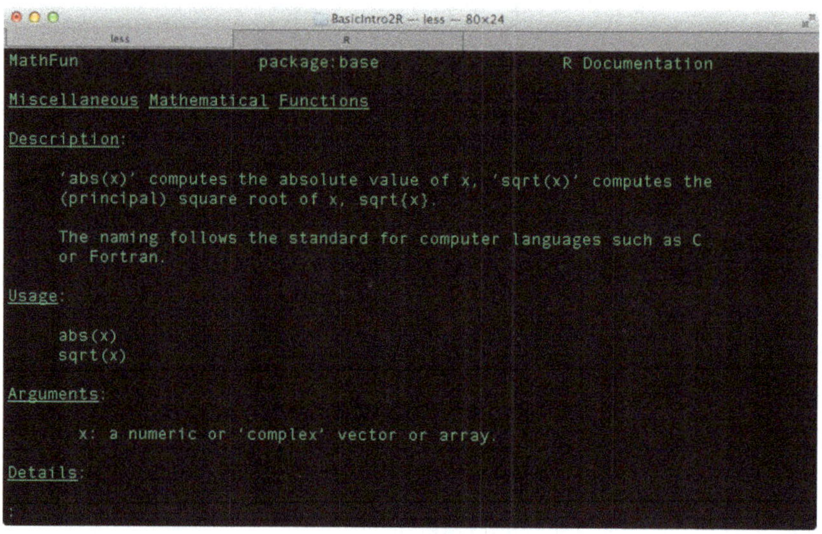

Figure 5.1: Help information provided by R for the *sqrt()* function.

At this early stage in the book, we would like to highlight the fact that R provides helpful information about functions, but this does not necessarily mean that this information will be to the extend you expect or would wish for. Instead, usually, the provided help information is rather short and not sufficient (or intended) to fully understand the very details of the complexity of the function of interest.

However, most help information comes with R examples at the end of the help file. This allows you to reproduce, at least parts, of the capabilities of the described functions by using the provided example code. It is not necessary to type these examples manually but there is a useful function available, called *example()*, that executes the provided example code automatically:

Listing 5.6: Using the function *example()*

```
example(sqrt)
```

That means you do not need to manually copy-and-paste (or type) the example code, but just apply the *example()* command to the function you wish to learn more about.

5.2 Basic programming

5.2.1 If-clause

A basic element of every programming language is an if-clause. An if-clause can be used to test the truth of a logical statement. For instance, the logical statement in the example below is: $a > 2$. If the variable a is larger than 2, then this statement is true, and the code in the first {} brackets is executed. However, if this statement is false, then the code that follows the brackets {} after else will be executed.

Listing 5.7: Using the If-clause

```
a <- 3
if(a > 2){
        print("a is larger than 2")
}
else{
        print("a is not larger than 2")
}
[1] "a is larger than 2"
```

The general form of an if-clause is given by the following structure. Here, a general logical statement is the argument of the if-clause. Depending on if this statement is true or false, the commands in part 1 or 2 are executed. That means, the outcome of the test of the provided logical statement selects the commands to be executed.

Listing 5.8: Syntax of the If-clause

```
if(logical statement){
...commands in part 1... # if the logical statement is true
}else{
...commands in part 2... # if the logical statement is false
}
```

The usage of an if-clause is very flexible, allowing the removal of the `else` clause, but also to include further conditional statements by means of the `else if` command.

Listing 5.9: Using the If-clause

```
a <- 3
if(a > 4){
        print("a is larger than 2")
}
```

Listing 5.10: Using the If-clause

```
a <- 3
if(a == 2){
        print("a is 2")
}else if(a==3){
        print("a is 3")
}else if(a==4){
        print("a is 4")
}else{
        print("a is something else")
}
[1] "a is 3"
```

We would like to note that, e. g., the statement “a=4” is not a logical statement, but an assignment, and will for this reason not work as an argument for an if-clause.

5.2.2 Switch

The *switch()* command is conceptually similar to an if-clause. However, the difference is that one can test more than one condition at the same time. For instance, in the example below, the *switch()* command tests 3 conditions, because it has 3 executable components, indicated by the “{ }” environments. If the variable “a” is 1, the first commands are executed, if “a” is 2 the second, and so on.

Listing 5.11: Using the *switch()* command

```
a <- 2
switch(a, {print("A"); print("B")},
          {print("C")},
          {print("D")})
```

For all other values of “a”, there will be no true condition and, hence, none of the above commands will be executed.

For clarity, we just want to mention that for reasons of a better readability, we split the *switch()* command in the above example into three different lines. This way one can see that it consists of 3 executable components. When you write your own programs, you will see that such a formatting is in general very helpful to get a quick overview of a program, because this increases the readability of the code.

5.2.3 Loops

In R, there are two different ways to realize a looping behavior. The first is by using a for-loop, and the second by using a while-loop. A looping behavior means the consecutive execution of the same procedure for a number of steps. The number of steps can be fixed, or variable.

5.2.4 For-loop

A for-loop repeats a statement for a predefined number of times. In the following example, i is successively assigned the values 1 to 3, and the command *print(i)* is executed 3 times, for three different values of i:

Listing 5.12: Using the For-loop

```
for(i in 1:3){
 print(i)
}
[1] 1
[1] 2
[1] 3
```

5.2.5 While-loop

Another looping function is *while()*. Its syntax is

Listing 5.13: Syntax of the While-loop

```
while(argument)
{
   statement
}
```

In contrast with a for-loop, which executes a loop a predefined number of times, a while-loop repeats a statement as long as the argument of *while()* is logically true:

Listing 5.14: Using the While-loop

```
i <- 0
while(i<3){
i <- i + 1
print(i)
}
[1] 1
[1] 2
[1] 3
```

One needs to make sure that the argument of the *while()* function becomes at some time during the looping process logically false, because otherwise the function is iterated infinitely. This is a frequent programming bug.

5.2.6 Logic behind a For-loop

Before we continue, we want to present a look behind the curtains of the logic behind a for-loop. The reader who has already some familiarity with programming can skip this section, but in our experience the following information is helpful for beginners to see in detail how a for-loop works.

The general form of a for-loop consists of a *for()* function that executes the body of the for-loop comprised of individual R commands, depending on the argument of the for-loop.

Listing 5.15: Inner working of the For-loop

```
for(argument)
{
  body
}
```

In the following, we will discuss each of the three components of the for-loop and their connections.

5.2.6.1 Argument of the For-loop

In order to keep the logic simple, let us assume that the argument of the for-loop is

$$\texttt{argument = i in 1:N} \tag{5.1}$$

This argument contains one variable and one parameter. Here `i` is the variable, because its value changes systematically with every loop that is executed, and `N` is a parameter, because its value is fixed throughout the whole loop. The values that can be assumed to `i` are determined by `1:N`, because the argument says `i in 1:N`. If you define `N=4` and execute `1:N` in an R session, you get

Listing 5.16: Inner working of the For-loop: example

```
N <- 4
1:N
[1] 1 2 3 4
```

That means `1:N` is a vector of integers of length `N`. To see this, you can define `a <- 1:N` and access the components of vector `a` by `a[1]`, e. g., for the first component.

The values that `i` can assume are *systematically* assigned according to the order of the vector `1:N`, i. e., in loop 1, `i` is equal to 1; in loop 2, `i` is equal to 2; until finally in loop `N`, `i` is equal to `N`. For this reason, the "argument" of a for-loop is—in our example—dependent on the variable `i`, i. e.,

$$\texttt{argument(i)}, \tag{5.2}$$

and in general it is dependent on the number of the loop step, i. e.,

$$\texttt{argument(loop step)}. \tag{5.3}$$

Note that this is just a symbolic writing to emphasize that the argument of a loop is connected to the step of the loop. Here, it is important to realize that the variable of the "argument" changes its value in every loop step.

5.2.6.2 Body of the For-loop

The body of the for-loop is just a list of commands provided between the curled "{}" brackets. In principle, the body can consist of one or more commands—zero commands are allowed as well, but this does not result in a meaningful action—that are executed consecutively (see the next section). In order to be precise, one needs to realize that the body is a function of the argument, i. e., symbolically we can write,

$$\texttt{body(argument)}. \tag{5.4}$$

Due to the fact that the argument itself is a function of the loop step, we have the following dependency chain:

$$\texttt{body(argument(loop step))}. \tag{5.5}$$

5.2.6.3 For-function

The third part is an actual `R` function. In `R`, you can always recognize a function by its name, followed by round brackets "()" containing, optionally, an argument. In the case of the for-function, it contains an argument, as discussed above. The purpose of the for-function is to execute the body consecutively.

To make this clear, especially with respect to the argument of the body, which depends on the number of the loop step, let us consider the following example:

Listing 5.17: Inner working of the For-loop

```
for(i in 1:3){
    a <- i + 2
    print(a)
}
```

The for-function converts this into the following consecutive execution of the body, as a function of the argument:

Listing 5.18: Inner working of the For-loop

```
#loop 1: i = 1  - change of the workspace
a <- 1 + 2
print(a)

#loop 2: i = 2 #change of the workspace
a <- 2 + 2
print(a)

#loop 3: i = 3 #change of the workspace
a <- 3 + 2
print(a)
```

First, the value of the variable `i` changes with every loop, according to the argument. In our case "`i`" just assumes the values 1, 2, 3. Then the concrete value of `i` is used in every loop, leading to different values of `a`. From a more general point of view, this means that the for-function does not only execute the body of the function consecutively, but it changes also the content of the workspace, which is the memory of an `R` session, with every loop step. This is the exact meaning of `body(argument(loop step))`.

In Figure 5.2, we visualize the general working mechanism of a for-loop by unrolling it in time. Overall, if one wants to understand what a particular For-loop does, one just needs to unroll its "body" in the way depicted in Figure 5.2, considering the influence of the "argument" on it.

This discussion demonstrates that a for-loop, or any other R function, can be quite complicated if we want to understand in more detail how it works. However, once we understand its principle working mechanism, we can fade-out these details focusing on key factors only. For the for-loop this is the systematic modification of the variable in the argument of the loop, and the consecutive execution of its body.

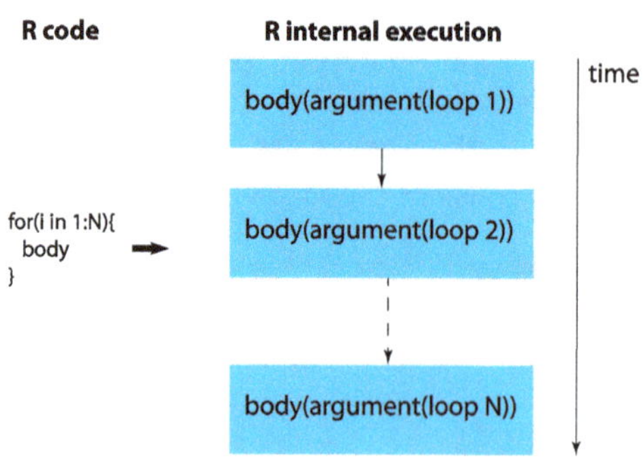

Figure 5.2: Unrolling the functional working mechanism in time of a for-loop.

5.2.7 Break

Both loop functions can be interrupted at any time during the execution of the loop using the *break()* command. Frequently, this is used in combination with an if-clause within a loop to test for a specific decision that shall lead to the interruption of the loop.

Listing 5.19: Inner working of the For-loop: example for *break()*

```
for(i in 1:3){
    print(i)
    if(i==2) break
}
```

Combining loops with if-clauses and the *break()* function allows creating very flexible constructs that can exhibit a rich behavior.

5.2.8 Repeat-loop

For completeness, we want to mention that there is actually a third type of loop in R, the repeat-loop. However, in contrast with a for-loop and a while-loop, this does not come with an interruption condition, but is in fact an infinite loop that does never stop. For this reason, the *repeat()* command needs to be used always in combination with the *break()* statement:

Listing 5.20: Using the Repeat-loop: example

```
i <- 0
repeat {
    i <- i + 1
    print(i)
    if(i > 10) break
}
```

5.3 Data structures

5.3.1 Vector

A vector is a 1-dimensional data structure. As the example below shows, a vector can be easily defined by using the combine function *c()*. This function concatenates its elements forming a vector. Individual elements can be accessed in various ways, using squared brackets.

There are many functions to obtain properties of a vector, e.g., its length or the sum of its elements. In order to make sure that the sum of its elements can be computed, the function *mode()* or *typeof()* allows determining the data-type of the elements. Examples of different types are **character**, **double**, **logical**, or NULL.

Listing 5.21: Vectors

```
a <- c(3,4,1,7,12)
a
[1]  3  4  1  7 12

a[3]
[1] 1

a[c(2,5)]
[1]  4 12

a[2:4]
[1] 4 1 7

length(a)
[1] 5

sum(a)
[1] 27

mode(a)
[1] "numeric"
```

Accessing elements of a vector can be done either individually (a[3] gives the third element of vector a) or collectively by specifying the indices of the elements (a[c(2,5)] gives the second and fifth element).

One can also assign names to elements of a vector using the command *names()*. When assessing an element with its name, one needs to make sure to use the same index. In the below example, one needs to use "C" and not C, because the latter indicates a variable rather than the capital letter itself.

Listing 5.22: Vectors

```
a <- seq(2,16,4)
a
[1]  2  6 10 14

names(a) <- LETTERS[1:4]
a
A  B  C  D
2  6 10 14

a["C"]
 C
10
```

There are also several functions available to generate vectors by using predefined functions, e. g., the sequence (*seq()*) of numbers or letters (*letters()*). A general characteristic of a vector is that whatever the type its elements, they need to be all of the same type. This is in contrast with lists, discussed in Section 5.3.3.

Listing 5.23: Vectors

```
a <- seq(2,16,2)
a
[1]  2  4  6  8 10 12 14 16

b <- letters[1:4]
b
[1] "a" "b" "c" "d"

typeof(b)
[1] "character"
```

It is also possible to define a vector of a given length and mode initiated by zeros. For example, `vector(mode = "numeric", length = 10)` results in a numeric vector of length 10, whereas each element is initialized with a 0.

It is also possible to apply a function element-wise to a vector without the need to access its elements, e. g., in a for-loop.

Listing 5.24: Vectors

```
a <- c(4,9,81,64)

sqrt(a)
[1] 2 3 9 8

a * a
[1]   16   81 6561 4096
```

Other useful functions that can be either applied to a vector or used to generate vectors are provided in Table 5.2.

If we want to add an element to a vector, we can use the command *append()*:

Listing 5.25: Vectors

```
a <- 1:3
a <- append(a, 7, after = length(a))
a
[1] 1 2 3 7
```

Here the option *after* allows specifying a subscript, after which the values are to be appended.

This command allows us also to demonstrate the usefulness of the `NULL` object type, introduced in Section 5.1.

Table 5.2: Examples of functions that can be applied to vectors or can be used to generate vectors.

Command name	Description
LETTERS	capital letters
letters	lower case letters
month.name	month names
rep("hello", times=3)	repeats the first argument n-times
sum	sum of all elements in the vector
length	length of vector
rev	reverse order of elements

Listing 5.26: Vectors

```
a <- c()
a <- append(a, 7, after = length(a))
a
[1] 7
```

Although the variable a does not contain an element with a value, it contains one initialized element as a place holder of type NULL. Repeating the above example with an uninitialized object would result in an error message.

A simplified form of the above can be written as follows:

Listing 5.27: Vectors

```
a <- c()
a <- c(a, 7)
a
[1] 7
```

5.3.2 Matrix

A matrix is a 2-dimensional data structure. It can be constructed with the command *matrix()*, see Listing 5.28.

Listing 5.28: Matrix

```
a <- matrix(c(1,2,3,4,5,6), nrow = 3, ncol = 2, byrow = TRUE)
a
     [,1] [,2]
[1,]    1    2
[2,]    3    4
[3,]    5    6

a[1,2]
[1] 2
```

```
a[1,]
[1] 1 2

a[c(1,3),]
     [,1] [,2]
[1,]    1    2
[2,]    5    6
```

Here, the option *byrow* allows controlling how a matrix is filled. Specifically, by setting it to "FALSE" (default), the matrix is filled by columns, otherwise the matrix is filled by rows. Accessing the elements of a matrix is similar to a vector by using the squared brackets. Again, this can be done either individually (`a[1,2]` giving the element in row 1 and column 2) or collectively by specifying the indices of the elements (`a[c(1,3),]` gives all the elements of row 1 and 3). It is interesting to note that by not specifying element, i. e., by using ",", all elements are selected.

There are several commands available to obtain the properties of a matrix. Some of these commands are provided in Table 5.3.

Table 5.3: Examples of functions that can be applied to matrices.

Command name	Description
`dim`	dimension of a matrix: c(nrow, ncol)
`ncol`	number of columns
`nrow`	number of rows
`length`	total number of elements

Sometimes, it is useful to assign names to rows and columns. This can be achieved by the commands *rownames()* and *colnames()*.

Listing 5.29: Matrix

```
rownames(a) <- letters[1:3]
colnames(a) <- c("white", "black")
a
  white black
a     1     2
b     3     4
c     5     6
```

Once these attributes are set, they can be retrieved by using the same command, e. g., `rownames(a)` would give you a vector of length `nrow`, including the names of the rows. The names of the rows or columns can also be used to access the rows and columns:

Listing 5.30: Matrix

```
a[,"white"]
[1] 1 3 5
```

There are alternative ways to create a matrix. For instance, by using the commands *cbind()*, *rbind()*, or *dim()*:

Listing 5.31: Matrix

```
rbind(c(2,5,3), c(4,3,4))
     [,1] [,2] [,3]
[1,]    2    5    3
[2,]    4    3    4

a <- c(2,5,6,2)
dim(a) <- c(2,2)
a
     [,1] [,2]
[1,]    2    6
[2,]    5    2
```

Also, functions can be applied to a matrix element-wise. For example, *sqrt()* calculates the square root of each element.

All basic operations known from linear algebra can be performed with a matrix, e. g., addition, multiplication, or matrix multiplication.

Listing 5.32: Matrix

```
a + a
     [,1] [,2]
[1,]    4   12
[2,]   10    4

a * a # a^2
     [,1] [,2]
[1,]    4   36
[2,]   25    4

a %*% a
     [,1] [,2]
[1,]   34   24
[2,]   20   34
```

For mathematical calculations, it is frequently necessary to “swap” the rows and the columns of a matrix. This can be conveniently achieved by the transpose function *t()*.

5.3.3 List

A list is a more complex data structure than the previous ones, because it can contain elements of different types. This was not allowed for either of the previous data structures. Formally, a list is defined using the function *list()*, see Listing 5.33.

Listing 5.33: Using a list

```
a <- matrix(c(1,2,3,4), nrow = 2, ncol = 2, byrow = TRUE)
b <- list(a, "hello", 3, c(4,2))
b
[[1]]
     [,1] [,2]
[1,]    1    2
[2,]    3    4

[[2]]
[1] "hello"

[[3]]
[1] 3

[[4]]
[1] 4 2
```

In the above example, the list b consists of 4 elements, which are different data structures. In order to access an element of a list, the double-squared brackets can be used, e. g., `b[[2]]`, to access the second element. This appears similar to a vector, discussed in Section 5.3.1. In fact, there are many commands for vectors that can also be applied to lists, e. g., *length()* or *names()*. If name attributes are assigned to the elements of a list, then these can be accesses by the "$" operator.

Listing 5.34: Accessing an element of a list

```
names(b) <- LETTERS[1:4]
b$C
[1] 3
```

In this case, the usage of double-squared brackets or the "$" operator provide the same results. It is also possible to assign names to the elements when defining a list. The following example shows that even a partial assignment is possible. In this case, the first two elements could be accessed by their name, whereas the latter two can only be accessed by using indices, e. g., `b[[3]]` for the third element.

Listing 5.35: Mixed assignment of list elements

```
a <- matrix(c(1,2,3,4), nrow = 2, ncol = 2, byrow = TRUE)
b <- list(ind1=a, ex="hello", 3, c(4,2))
> names(b)
[1] "ind1" "ex"   ""     ""
> b
```

```
$ind1
     [,1] [,2]
[1,]    1    2
[2,]    3    4

$ex
[1] "hello"

[[3]]
[1] 3

[[4]]
[1] 4 2
```

5.3.4 Array

Arrays are a generalization of vectors, matrices, and lists in the sense that they can be of arbitrary dimension and type.

Listing 5.36: Arrays

```
array(1:8, dim = c(2,2,2))
, , 1

     [,1] [,2]
[1,]    1    3
[2,]    2    4

, , 2

     [,1] [,2]
[1,]    5    7
[2,]    6    8
```

Elements of an array can be accessed using squared brackets, and the number of indices corresponds to the number of dimensions.

Listing 5.37: Arrays

```
a <- array(1:8, dim = c(2,2,2))
a[2,2,1]
[1] 4

a[,,1]
     [,1] [,2]
[1,]    1    3
[2,]    2    4
```

The components of an array can assume any type, like a list.

Listing 5.38: Arrays

```
a <- array(list("one", 1:3, matrix(0,2,2)), dim = c(2,2,2))
a
, , 1

     [,1]      [,2]
[1,] "one"     Numeric,4
[2,] Integer,3 "one"

, , 2

     [,1]      [,2]
[1,] Integer,3 "one"
[2,] Numeric,4 Integer,3
```

5.3.5 Data frame

A data frame is a generalization of a matrix and a list, allowing inheriting some of their properties. Briefly, a data frame is a rectangle data structure that allows columns (or rows) to be of a different data-type.

Listing 5.39: Data frame

```
df <- data.frame(x=1:3, y=month.name[1:3])
df
  x        y
1 1  January
2 2 February
3 3    March

df$x
[1] 1 2 3

dim(df)
[1] 3 2
```

Again the command *names()* can be used to identify the names of the elements in a data frame. Interestingly, the “$” operator can be used with `"x"` as well as `x` to access elements. Table 5.4 provides an overview of further commands for data frames.

Table 5.4: Some examples of commands that can be used with data frames.

Command name	Description
`dim`	dimension of a matrix: c(nrow, ncol)
`ncol`	number of columns
`nrow`	number of rows
`length`	total number of elements
`names`	names of the elements

5.3.6 Environment

An environment is similar to a list, however, it needs named elements. That means, the name of an element needs to be a character string. The command *ls()* provides a list of the names of all elements in an environment.

Listing 5.40: Environment

```
a <- new.env(hash=TRUE)
a$x <- c(3,4,2)

a$x
[1] 3 4 2

a$"x"
[1] 3 4 2

a[["x"]]
[1] 3 4 2

ls(a)
[1] "x"
```

Alternatively, one can use the function *assign()* to assign a new element to an environment:

Listing 5.41: Setting an element of an environment with assign()

```
assign("y", "hello", envir = a)

a$y
[1] "hello"
```

Correspondingly, the function *get()* can be used to obtain elements of an environment:

Listing 5.42: Obtaining elements from an environment with get()

```
get("y", envir = a)
[1] "hello"
```

When we are unsure about the names of elements, we can use the function *exists()* to perform a logical test, resulting in either a `true` or a `false` depending on whether the element exists in the environment or not:

Listing 5.43: Test the existence of elements in an environment

```
exists("z", envir=a)
[1] FALSE

exists("y", envir=a)
[1] TRUE
```

In order to delete elements of an environment the command *remove()* can be used:

Listing 5.44: Remove elements from an environment

```
remove(list = "y", envir = a)
```

5.3.7 Removing variables from the workspace

Sometimes it is necessary to delete variables that have been defined. In contrast to the above example for an environment, this will delete the variable from the workspace of R. This can be done by using the remove function *rm()*:

Listing 5.45: Deleting variables from the workspace

```
> a <- 4
> rm(a)
> a
Error: object 'a' not found
```

If we want to delete many variables, we need to specify the "list" argument of the command *rm()* providing a character vector naming the objects to be removed. We can also delete all variables in the current working space in the following way:

Listing 5.46: Deleting all variables in the working space

```
rm(list = ls())
```

5.3.8 Factor

For analyzing data containing categorial variables, a data structure called *factor* is frequently encountered. A *factor* is like a label or a tag that is assigned to a certain category to represent it. In principle, one could define a list containing the same information, however, the R implementation of the data structure *factor* is more efficient. An example for defining a factor is given below.

Listing 5.47: Defining a factor

```
height <- factor(c("small", "normal", "tall", "normal"))
height
[1] small  normal tall   normal
Levels: normal small tall
```

Here, we assign 4 different factors to height, but only three "values" are different. In the case of a factor, different values are actually called *levels*. The different levels of a factor can also be obtained with the command *levels()*.

In the above example, the factors were categorial variables, meaning that the levels have no particular ordering. An extension to this is to define such an ordering between the levels. This can be done implicitly or explicitly.

Listing 5.48: Defining a factor

```
height <- factor(c("small", "normal", "tall", "normal"),
ordered=T)
height
[1] small  normal tall   normal
Levels: normal < small < tall

height <- factor(c("small", "normal", "tall", "normal"),
levels=c("tall", "normal", "small"), ordered=T)
height
[1] small  normal tall   normal
Levels: tall < normal < small
```

The first example above, defines ordered factors by setting "`ordered=T`". As a result, there is an ordering between the three levels despite the fact that we did not specify this order explicitly. However, this order is not due to any semantic meaning of these words, but this is just an alphabetic ordering of the words.

If we would like defining a different order between the levels, we can include the `levels` option. Then, the resulting order will follow the order of the levels specified by this option.

5.3.9 Date and Time

For assessing the date and time of the computer system, we can use the following functions:

Listing 5.49: Date and Time

```
Sys.time()
Sys.Date()
```

Each of these functions results in an `R` object of a specific type. The first function returns an object of class `POSIXct` and the second of class `Date`. The reason for this is that objects of the same type can be manipulated in a convenient way, e. g., using subtraction, we can get the time difference between two time points or dates.

5.3.10 Information about R objects

In the above sections, we showed how to define basic `R` objects of different types. In all these cases, we knew the type of these object, because we defined them explicitly. However, when using packages, we may not always have this information. For such cases, `R` provides various commands to get information about the types of objects.

5.3.10.1 The functions *attributes()* and *class()*

The function *attributes()* gives information about different attributes an `R` object can have, including information about `class`, `dim`, `dimnames`, `names`, `row.names`, or `levels`. In case the *attributes()* function does not provide information about the class of an `R` object, one can obtain this information with the command *class()*.

5.3.10.2 The functions *summary()* and *str()*

In Chapter 2, discussed programming paradigms in detail, but we want to repeat here that every `R` object is a member of a certain class. Classes are powerful data structures that do not only have attributes, but come also with specific functions. Here, it is only important to know that this implies that behind a simple variable can be a complex structure that is not recognizable without help. `R` provides the functions *summary()* and *str()* to get information about the structure of an object, where the latter is a simplified version of the former.

5.3.10.3 The function *typeof()*

Sometimes it is important to know how an `R` object is stored internally, because this gives information about the amount of bytes that are required. The function *typeof()* gives this information and its possible outputs are `logical`, `integer`, `double`, `complex`, `character`, or `S4`.

5.4 Handling character strings

5.4.1 The function *nchar()*

There is a variety of commands available in `R` to manipulate character strings. One of the simplest functions is *nchar()*, which returns the length of a string:

Listing 5.50: Character strings

```
s <- "Hallo world!"
nchar(s)
[1] 12
```

If we use the function *length()* instead, it would not return the number of characters, but count the whole string as 1.

5.4.2 The function *paste()*

For concatenating strings together one can use the function *paste()*:

Listing 5.51: Character strings: *paste*

```
paste("Hallo", "world")
[1] "Hallo world"

paste("Hallo", "world", sep="")
"Halloworld"
```

The sep option allows specifying what separator is used for concatenating the strings; the default introduces a blank between two strings.

It is also possible to include a variable to form a new string.

Listing 5.52: Character strings: *paste*

```
i <- 3
paste("file", i, ".txt", sep="")
[1] "file3.txt"
```

This is useful if we want to read many files from a directory within a loop and their names vary in a systematic way, e. g., by an enumeration. It can also be used to create names for an environment (see Section 5.3.6), because an environment needs strings as indices for elements.

Furthermore, the function *paste()* can be used to connect more than just two strings:

Listing 5.53: Character strings: *paste*

```
paste("This", "is", "another", "example")
[1] "This is another example"
```

5.4.3 The function *substr()*

A substring of a certain length can be extracted from a string by the command *substr(x, start, stop)*:

Listing 5.54: Character strings: *substr()*

```
s <- "ABCDEFGHIJKL"
substr(s, start=3, stop=5)
[1] "CDE"

substring(s, 3) <- c("abc")
s
[1] "ABabcFGHIJKL"
```

If we want to overwrite parts of a string `s` with another string, we need to use the function *substring()* with `start`, specifying where to start overwriting. In case we just want to insert a new string without overwriting parts of the string `s`, we need to use the function *substr()*:

Listing 5.55: Character strings: *substr()*

```
s <- "ABCDEFGHIJKL"
substr(s, start=3, stop=5) <- c("abc")
s
[1] "ABabcFGHIJKL"
```

5.4.4 The function *strsplit()*

Splitting a string in one or more substrings can be done using the function *strsplit()*:

Listing 5.56: Character strings: *strsplit()*

```
s <- "A-B-C"
strsplit(s, split="-")
[[1]]
[1] "A" "B" "C"
```

The command is a bit tricky if one uses certain symbols as a split:

Listing 5.57: Character strings: *strsplit()*

```
s <- "A.B.C"
strsplit(s, split="[.]")
[[1]]
[1] "A" "B" "C"
```

The reason why a `''.''` does not work as a split symbol, but `''[.]''` does, is due to the fact that the argument `split` is a regular expression (see Section 5.4.5).

5.4.5 Regular expressions

`R` provides very powerful functions to search strings for matching patterns:

Listing 5.58: Regular expressions

```
match-object <- regexpr(pattern, text)
match-object <- gregexpr(pattern, text)
```

The first argument of the above function characterizes the `pattern` we try to find and `text` is the string to be searched.

Listing 5.59: Examples for regular expressions

```
txt <- c("This","is","just","a","test")
regexpr("is", txt)
[1]  3  1 -1 -1 -1
attr(,"match.length")
[1]  2  2 -1 -1 -1
attr(,"useBytes")
[1] TRUE

gregexpr("is", txt)
[[1]]
[1] 3
attr(,"match.length")
[1] 2
attr(,"useBytes")
[1] TRUE

[[2]]
[1] 1
attr(,"match.length")
[1] 2
attr(,"useBytes")
[1] TRUE

[[3]]
[1] -1
attr(,"match.length")
[1] -1
attr(,"useBytes")
[1] TRUE

[[4]]
[1] -1
attr(,"match.length")
[1] -1
attr(,"useBytes")
[1] TRUE

[[5]]
[1] -1
attr(,"match.length")
[1] -1
attr(,"useBytes")
[1] TRUE
```

Both functions result in similar outputs, but displayed in different ways. While *regexpr()* returns an integer vector of the same length as `text`, whose components provide information about the position of a match or no match, resulting in -1, *grepexpr()* returns a list of this information. Furthermore, both functions have the attribute `match.length` that indicates the number of elements that are actually matched. One may wonder how is it possible that the length of a match could not correspond to the length of `pattern`. This is where (nontrivial) regular expression come into play.

A regular expression is a pattern that can include special symbols, as listed in Table 5.5 below.

Table 5.5: Some special symbols that can be used in regular expressions.

Symbols	Meaning of the symbols
*	an asterisk matches zero or more of the preceding character
.	a dot matches any single character
+	a plus sign matches one or more of the preceding character
[...]	the square brackets enclose a list of characters that can be matched alternatively
{min, max}	the preceding element is matched between min and max times
\s	matches any single whitespace character
|	the vertical bar separates two or more alternatives
\t	match a tab
\r	match a carriage return
\n	match a linefeed
0 – 9	match any number between 0 and 9
A-Z	match any upper letter between A and Z
a-z	match any lower letter between a and z

For example, the regular expression `x+` matches any of the following within a string: `"x"`, `"xx"`, `"xxx"`, etc. This means that the length of the regular expression is not equal to the length of the matched pattern. By using special symbols, it is possible to generate quite flexible search patterns, and the resulting patterns are not necessarily easy to recognize from the regular expression.

To demonstrate the complexity of regular expressions, let us consider the following example. Suppose that we want to identify a pattern in a string, of which we do not know the exact composition. However, we know certain components. For example, we know that it starts with a "G" and is followed either by none or several letters or numbers, but we do not know by how many. After this, there is a sequence of number, which is between 1 and 4 elements long:

Listing 5.60: Regular expressions

```
txt <- c("ACTGGA023423GGGTGC")
m <- regexpr("G*.[0-9]{1,4}", txt)
m
[1] 4
attr(,"match.length")
[1] 7
attr(,"useBytes")
[1] TRUE
```

The above code realizes such a search and it finds at position 4 of `txt` a match that is 7 elements long.

In order to extract the matched substring of `txt`, the function *regmatches()* can be used. It expects as arguments the original string used to match a pattern and the result from the function *regexpr()*:

Listing 5.61: Regular expressions

```
regmatches(text, match-object)
```

For our above example the matched substring is "GGA0234":

Listing 5.62: Regular expressions

```
regmatches(txt, m)
[1] "GGA0234"
```

This example demonstrates that with regular expressions it is not only possible to match substrings that are exactly known, but also to match substrings that are only partially known. This flexibility is very powerful.

5.5 Sorting vectors

The elements of numerical vectors can be sorted according their size using the function *sort()*:

Listing 5.63: Sorting vectors

```
x <- sort(x, decreasing)
```

The option `decreasing` enables specifying whether the sorting should be in decreasing (TRUE) or nondecreasing (FALSE-default) order. It is important to note that the result of *sort(x)* does not directly affect the input vector `x`. For this reason, we need to assign the result of *sort(x)* to `x`, if we want to overwrite the input vector.

Listing 5.64: Sorting vectors

```
x <- c(22, 3, 7, 12, 9)
x <- sort(x)
x
[1]  3  7  9 12 22
```

If we are interested in the positions of the sorted elements in the original vector `x` we can get these indices by using the function *order()*.

Listing 5.65: Sorting vectors

```
x <- c(22, 3, 7, 12, 9)
order(x)
[1] 2 3 5 4 1
```

A somewhat related function to *order()* is *rank()*. However, *rank(x)* gives the rank numbers (in increasing order) of the elements of the input vector `x`:

Listing 5.66: Sorting vectors

```
rank(x)
[1] 5 1 2 4 3
```

In the case of ties, there are several options available to handle the situation, and one of them is `ties.method`.

5.6 Writing functions

So far, we learned how to *use* R functions either provided in the base package or in additional packages, evoked by the command *library()*. In this section, we will see how to write our own functions. First, we will focus on the definition of a function with exactly one argument and one return value. Later, we will extend this to more arguments and return variables.

5.6.1 One input argument and one output value

To write a new function, one needs to define the name, the argument, and the content of the function. The general syntax is shown in Listing 5.67.

Listing 5.67: Syntax of a function

```
fct.name <- function(argument){
    body
}
```

Here, `fct.name` is the name of the new function you want to define, `argument` is the argument you submit to this function, and `body` is a list of commands that are executed, applied to `argument`.

A new definition for a function utilizes itself an R function called `function`. If the `body` of the new function consists merely of one command, one can use the simplified syntax:

Listing 5.68: Simplified syntax of a function

```
fct.name <- function(argument) body
```

However, for reasons of clarity and readability of the code, we recommend always to define the body of the function, starting with a "{" and ending with a "}".

Let us consider an example defining a new function that adds 1 to a real number given by the argument `x`:

Listing 5.69: Example of function

```
add.one <- function(x){
   y <- x + 1
   return(y)
}
```

In this example, the name of the new function is *add.one()*. One should always pay attention to the name to not accidentally overwrite some existing function. For instance, if we would call the new function *sqrt()*, then the square root function, part of the R base package, will be overwritten.

It is good practice to finish the body with the command *return()* that contains as its argument the variable we would like to get as a result from the application of the new function. However, the following will result in the exact same behavior as the function *add.one()*:

Listing 5.70: Example of function

```
add.one.short <- function(x){
   x + 1
}
```

Here, it is important not to write `y <- x + 1`, but instead `x+1`, without assignment to a variable. We do not recommend this syntax, especially not for beginners, because it is less explicit in its meaning.

We would like to note that the above-defined function is just a simple example that does not include checks in order to avoid errors. For instance, one would like to ensure that the argument of the function, `x`, is actually a number, because otherwise operations in the body of the function may result in errors. This can be done, for instance, using the command *is.numeric()*.

The usage of such a self-defined function is the same as for a systems function, namely *fct.name(x)*. The following is an example:

Listing 5.71: Example of function

```
add.one(4)
[1] 5
```

In general, the choice of the name of a function is arbitrary as long as it consists of alphanumeric symbols, starting with a letter. Even the name of an existing function can be chosen. However, as mentioned above, in this case, this function is overwritten and no longer available in the current R season.

5.6.1.1 Merits of writing functions

Some reasons for writing your own functions are to help you to

- organize your programs
- make your programs more readable
- limit the scope of variables

The last point is very important and shall be visualized with the following example. Start a new `R` session (this is important!) and copy the following code into the `R` workspace:

Listing 5.72: Scope of a function

```
fct.test <- function(x){
          yzxv <- 2*x
          z <- 3*x
          return(z)
}

x <- 1
fct.test(x)
print(yzxv)
```

What will be the output of `print(yzxv)`? It will result in an error message, because the variable `yzxv` is defined within the scope of the function *fct.test()*, and as such, it is not directly accessible from outside the function. This is actually the reason why we need to specify with the *return()* function the variables we want to return from the function. If we could just access all variables defined within the body of a function, there would be no need to do this.

The rationale behind our recommendation to start a new `R` session is to clear any variable in the session, already defined `yzxv`; since, in this case, `print(yzxv)` would output that existing variable rather than the value calculated inside the function *fct.test()*. For the specific choice of our variable name, this may be unlikely (that is why we used `yzxv`), but for more common variable names, such as `a`, `i` or `m`, there is a real possibility that this could happen.

In general, functions allow us to separate our `R` workspace into different parts, each containing their own variables. For this reason, it is also possible to reuse the same variable name in different functions without the danger of collisions.

This point addresses the so-called scope of a variable, which is an important issue, because it is the source of common bugs in programs.

5.6.2 Scope of variables

In order to understand the full complexity of the scope of variables, let us consider the following situation. Suppose that we have just one function, then we can have three different scopes of variables depending on where and how they have been defined.

First, all variables that are defined outside the function are *global* variables. This means that the value of these variables is accessible inside the function and outside the function. Second, all variables that are defined inside the function are *local* variables, because they are only accessible inside the function, but not outside. Finally, all variables that are defined inside a function by using the super-assignment operator "<< −" are also global variables.

The following script provides an example:

Listing 5.73: Scope of a function

```
fct.test <- function(x){
          yzxv <- 2*x
          z <<- 3*x + y
          return(z)
}

x <- 1
y <- 5
fct.test(x)
print(yzxv)
print(z)
```

5.6.3 One input argument, many output values

In order to return more than one output variable, we need to apply a little trick, because an R function does not directly permit returning more than one variable with the *return* command. Instead, we need to define a single variable, which contains all the variables we want to return. The script below shows an example, utilizing a list.

Listing 5.74: Function with many output values

```
new.fct <- function(x){
  a <- matrix(c(1,2,3,4), nrow = 2, ncol = 2, byrow = TRUE)
  y <- list(a, "hello", x, c(1,2,3), 2*x)
  return(y)
}

y <- new.fct(2)
```

In this case, the list variable y serves as a container to transmit all desired variables. That means, formally, one has just one output variable, but this variable contains additional output variables that can be accessed via the components of the list. For example, we can access its third component by y[[3]].

5.6.4 Many input arguments, many output values

The case of multiple input arguments of a function is considerably easier, because R allows calling a function with more than one argument. Consider the following example:

Listing 5.75: Function with many output values

```
new.fct <- function(x1, x2, x3){
  a <- c(x1, x2)
  y <- list(a, "hello", x3)
  return(y)
}
```

R provides the useful command *args()*, which gives some information on the input arguments of a function. Try, for example, *args(matrix)*.

5.7 Writing and reading data

Writing and reading data from and to files is important in order to populate variables and data structures with, e. g., information from experiments, and to store the obtained results, as an outcome from the application of a program to such data. In some sense, this completes a programming language by providing an interface to the outside world, whereas the "world" is represented by the data.

In general, writing data to a file is much easier than reading data from a file. The reason for this asymmetry is that when writing data to a file, we do have the entire control over the format of the data to save them. In contrast, when reading data from an existing file, we need to deal with the given data format as it is, which can be very laborious and frustrating, as we will illustrate below. For reasons of simplicity, we start by discussing functions to write data to a file.

5.7.1 Writing data to a file

The easiest way to save one or more R objects from the workspace to a file is to use the function *save()*:

Listing 5.76: Saving data to a file

```
save(a, file = "filename")
```

Here, the option `file` defines the name of the file in which we want to save the data. In principle, any name is allowed, with or without extension. However, it is helpful to name this file `filename.RData`, where the extension `RData` indicates that it is a binary R data file. Here, binary file means that if we open this file within any text editor, its content is not visible because of its coding format. Hence, in order to view its content, we need to load this file again in an R workspace.

If we want to save more than one R object, two different syntax variations exist that can be used. The first way to save more than one R object is to just name these objects, separated by a comma:

Listing 5.77: Saving data to a file

```
save(a, b, c, d, file = "filename")
```

The second way is to define a list that contains the variable names as character elements:

Listing 5.78: Saving data to a file

```
e <- c("a", "b", "c", "d")
save(list=e, file = "filename")
```

If we want to save all the variables in the current workspace and not just the selected ones, we can use the function *save.image()*:

Listing 5.79: Saving data to a file

```
save.image(file = "filename")
```

This function is a short cut for the following script, which accomplishes the same task:

Listing 5.80: Saving data to a file

```
save(list=ls(all), file = "filename")
```

For the above examples, we did not need to care about the formatting of the file to which we save the data, but R makes essentially a copy of the workspace, either for selected variables or for all variables. This is a very convenient and fast way to save variables to a file. One disadvantage of this way is that these files can only be loaded with R itself, but not with other programs or programming languages. This is a problem if we plan to exchange data with other people, friends, or collaborators and we are unsure whether they either have access to R or do not want to use it, for some reason. Therefore, R provides additional functions that are more generic in this respect. In the following, we discuss three of them in detail.

There are 3 functions in the base package, namely, *write.table()*, *write.csv()*, and *write.csv2()*, that allow saving tables as a text file. All of these functions have the following syntax:

Listing 5.81: Saving data to a file

```
write.table(M, file = "filename", sep=" ")
```

Here, `M` is a matrix or a data frame, and the option **`sep`** specifies the symbol used to separate elements in `M` from each other. As a result, the data saved in **`file`** can be viewed by any text editor, because the information is saved as a text rather than a binary file as the one generated, for example, by the function *save()*. The functions *write.csv()* and *write.csv2()* provide a convenient interface to Microsoft EXCEL, because the resulting file format is directly recognized by this program. This means we can load these files directly in EXCEL.

A potential disadvantage of these 3 functions appears when the output of an `R` program is not just one table, but several tables of different size and additional data structures in the form of, e. g., lists, environments, or scalar variables. In such cases, a function like *write.table()* would not suffice, because you can only save one table. On the other hand, the functions *save()* or *save.image()* can be used without the need to combine all data structures into just one table.

5.7.2 Reading data from a file

At the beginning of this section we said that, in general, it is more difficult to read data than to save them. This is true with the exception of binary files saved with the functions *save()* or *save.image()*. Because in this case, the counterpart to read data from a file is the function *load()*:

Listing 5.82: Reading data from a file

```
load(file = "filename")
```

Since the function *save()* makes essentially a copy of the workspace, or parts of it, and saves it to a file, then the function *load()* just pastes it back into the workspace. Hence, there are no formatting problems that we need to take care of.

In contrast, if tabular data are provided in a text file, we need to read this file differently. `R` provides 5 functions to read such data, namely, *read.table()*, *read.csv()*, *read.csv2()*, *read.delim()*, and *read.delim2()*. For example, the function *read.table()* has the following syntax:

Listing 5.83: Reading data from a file

```
read.table(file = "filename", sep=" ", header=FALSE, skip=0)
```

The option **`header`** is a logical value that indicates whether the file contains the names of the variables as its first line. The option **`skip`** is an integer value indicating the number of lines that should be skipped when we start reading the file. This is useful when the file contains at the beginning some explanations about its content or general comments.

Let us consider an example:

Listing 5.84: Reading data from a file

```
infile <- "tabular_data_example.txt"
dat <- read.table(file=infile, sep=",", header=TRUE, skip=1)
```

The content of the file `infile` is shown in Figure 5.3. This file contains a comment at its beginning spanning one row. For this reason, we skip this line with the option `skip=1`. Furthermore, this file contains a header giving information about the columns it contains. By using "`header=TRUE`" this information is converted into the column names of the table we are creating using the function *read.table()*. Using `colnames(dat)` will give us this information. Most importantly, we need to specify the symbol that is used to separate the numbers in the input file. This is accomplished by setting "`sep=","`".

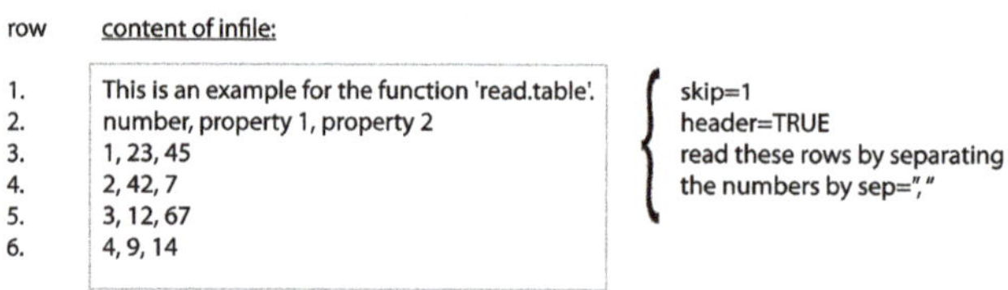

Figure 5.3: File content of `infile` and the effect the options in the command *read.table()* have on its content.

As a result, the variable `dat` will be a data frame containing the tabular data in the input file having the information about the corresponding columns as column names. We can access the information in the individual columns by using either `dat[[1]]`, e. g., for the first column or `dat$names`. Try to access the information in the second column. Is there a problem?

5.7.3 Low level reading functions

All the functions discussed so far, for reading data from a file, can be considered as high-level functions, because they assume a certain structural organization of a file that makes it relatively easy for a user to read these data into an R session. That means, the structural organization can be captured by the supplied options of these functions, e. g., by setting `sep`, `skip` etc. appropriately.

In case there is a text file that has a more complex format that cannot be read with one of the above functions, R provides a very powerful, low-level reading function called *readLines()*. This function allows reading a specified number of lines, n, from a given file:

Listing 5.85: Reading data from a file

```
readLines(con = "filename", n = -1)
```

If n is a negative value, the whole file will be read. Otherwise, the exact number of lines will be read. The advantage of this way of reading a file is that the formatting of the file can change, but does not need to be fixed.

For text files with a complex, irregular formatting it is necessary to read these files line-by-line in order to adopt the formatting separately for each line. This can be done in the following way:

Listing 5.86: Reading data from a file

```
f <- file(description = "filename", open = "r")
readLines(con = f, n = 1)
```

The function *file()* opens a connection to the file specified by the option description and the option open that we want to read the information from. Then calling *readLines()* reads exactly one line from the file. That means, if called repeatedly, for example within a for-loop, it gives one line after the other, and these can be processed individually. In this way, arbitrarily formatted files can be read and stored in variables so that the information provided by the file can be used in an R session. If we want to restart reading from this file, we just need to apply the function *file()* again.

row	content of infile:
1.	This is an example for the function 'readLInes'.
2.	number, property 1, property 2
3.	1, 23, 45
4.	2, "C", 7
5.	3, data are missing
6.	4, 9, 14

Figure 5.4: File content of infile and the effect the options in the command *read.table()* have on its content.

To demonstrate the usage of the function *readLines()*, let us consider the following example reading data from the file shown in Figure 5.4. In this case, our file contains some irregular rows, and we would either like to entirely omit some of them, such as row 5, or only use them partially, e. g., row 4. The following code reads the file and accomplishes this task:

Listing 5.87: Reading data from a file: example

```
infile <- "complex_data_example.txt"
f <- file(description = infile, open = "r")
L <- 6
cc <- 1
dat <- matrix(0, nrow=3, ncol=3)
for(i in 1:L){
  aux <- readLines(con = f, n = 1)
  aux2 <- strsplit(aux, split=",")[[1]]
  if(i==2){
    colnames(dat) <- aux2
  }
  LS <- length(aux2)
  if(i>2 & LS==3){
    dat[cc,] <- as.numeric(aux2)
    cc <- cc + 1
  }
}
```

As a result, we receive a data frame "dat" containing the following information:

Listing 5.88: Content of the read file

```
dat
     number  property 1  property 2
[1,]      1          23          45
[2,]      2          NA           7
[3,]      4           9          14
```

This corresponds to the information in the input file, skipping row 5 and omitting the second element in row 4. From this example, we can see that "low-level functions" offers some degree of flexibility, which translates into a considerable amount of additional coding that we need to do to process an input file.

There is another function similar to *readLines()*, called *scan()*. The function *scan()* does not result in a data frame, but a list or vector object. Another difference with *readLines()* is that it allows specifying the data-types to be read by setting the `what` option. Possible values of this options are, e. g., `double`, `integer`, `numeric`, `character`, or `raw`. The following code shows an example for its usage:

Listing 5.89: Reading data from a file: example

```
infile <- "complex_data_example.txt"
dat <- scan(file=infile, what=character(), sep=",", skip=0)
dat
 [1] "This is an example for the function readLines."
 [2] "number"
 [3] " property 1"
 [4] " property 2"
 [5] "1"
 [6] " 23"
 [7] " 45"
 [8] "2"
 [9] " C"
```

```
[10] " 7"
[11] "3"
[12] " data are missing"
[13] "4"
[14] " 9"
[15] " 14"
length(dat)
[1] 15
```

As one can see, the object `dat` is a vector and the components of the input file, separated according to `sep`, form the components of this vector. In our experience, the function *readLines()* is the better choice for complex data files.

We just would like to mention without discussion that the function *writeLines* allows a similar functionality and flexibility for writing data to a file in a line-by-line manner.

5.7.4 Summary of writing and reading functions

In Table 5.6, we provide a brief overview of some R functions discussed in the previous sections. Column three indicates the difficulty level in using these functions, which is directly proportional to the flexibility of the corresponding functions.

Table 5.6: Brief overview of R functions to read and write data.

Command name	File type	Usage level
save	binary file	easy
save.image	binary file	easy
write.table	text file	intermediate
write.csv	text file	intermediate
writeLines	text file	difficult
load	binary file	easy
read.table	text file	intermediate
read.csv	text file	intermediate
read.delim	text file	intermediate
readLines	text file	difficult

5.7.5 Other data formats

In addition to the R functions discussed above, which are included in the base package, there are some additional packages available that allow importing data files from other programs. In Table 5.7, we list some of the most common formats provided by other software and the corresponding package name, where one can find

Table 5.7: Reading data files from other programs.

Command name	File type	Package name
read.spss	SPSS file	foreign
read.dta	Stata file	foreign
read.systat	Systat file	foreign
sasxport.get	SAS file	Hmisc
readMat	Matlab file	R.matlab
read.octave	Octave file	foreign

the functions. This list is not intended to be exhaustive and it is recommended, if one has a data file from a well-established software or program, to search first if there is an R package available to read such data before one tries to implement a program from scratch.

5.8 Useful commands

In this section, we discuss some commands that we find particularly useful for the day-to-day applications of R.

5.8.1 The function *which()*

For identifying the indices, in a vector or a matrix, whose components have certain values, we can use the function *which()*. This function expects a logical vector or a matrix and returns the indices of the TRUE elements. A logical vector from a numerical vector v can be, e. g., obtained by an expression like v==3. This results into a logical vector that has the same length as the vector v, but its components are either TRUE or FASLE depending on whether the component equals 3 or not.

Listing 5.90: Using the function *which()*

```
v <- c(4,3,5,1)
which(v==3)
[1] 2
```

When we are interested in identifying the indices of a matrix that have a certain value, one can use the option arr.ind=TRUE to get the matrix indices:

Listing 5.91: Using the function *which()*

```
m <- matrix(c(1,2,3,4), nrow=2, ncol=2)
which(m==2, arr.ind=T)
     row col
[1,]   2   1
```

If we would set this option to **FALSE** (which is the default value), the result is just the number of **TRUE** elements, but not their indices.

5.8.2 The function *apply()*

The function *apply()* enables applying a certain function to a matrix or array along the provided dimension. Its syntax is:

Listing 5.92: Using the function *apply*

```
apply(X, MARGIN, FUN)
```

Here, X corresponds to a matrix or array, FUN is the function that should be applied to X, and MARGIN indicates the dimension of X to which FUN will be applied. The following example, calculates the sum of the rows for a matrix:

Listing 5.93: Using the function *apply()*

```
x <- 1:16
A <- matrix(x, nrow = 4, ncol = 4)
apply(A, 1, sum)
[1] 28 32 36 40
```

A similar result could be obtained by using a for-loop over the rows of the matrix A.

In the case where the variable X is a vector, there exists a similar function called *sapply()*. This function has the following syntax:

Listing 5.94: Using the function *sapply()*

```
sapply(X, FUN, simplify = TRUE)
```

There are two differences compared to *apply()*. First, no MARGIN argument is needed, because the function FUN will be applied to each component of the vector X. Second, there is an option called **simplify** resulting in a simplified output of the function *sapply()*. If set to TRUE, the result will have the form of a vector, whereas if set to FALSE the result will be a list. It depends on the intended usage, i. e., which form one might prefer, but a vector is usually most suitable for visual inspections. These results can also be obtained with the command *lapply()*.

The next example results in a vector, where each element is the third power of the components of the vector X.

Listing 5.95: Using the function *sapply()*

```
x <- 1:5
sapply(x, function(x) x^3, simplify = TRUE)
[1]   1   8  27  64 125
```

5.8.3 Set commands

A (mathematical) set is a collection of elements without duplications. This is different to a vector, which may contain duplicated elements:

Listing 5.96: Set operations

```
x <- c(1,1,2,3,3,4)
union(x, x)
[1] 1 2 3 4
unique(x)
[1] 1 2 3 4
```

The function *union()* results in a set containing all elements, without duplication, provided in the two sets of its argument.

Other commands for sets include *intersect()*, which returns only elements that are in both sets, and *setdiff()* gives only elements, which are in the first, but not in the second set, i. e., if `X = setdiff(Y, Z)`, then all the elements in the set `X` are also in the set `Y`, but not in the set `Z`. Table 5.8 provides an overview of set operations.

Table 5.8: Each of these commands will discard any duplicated values in its arguments.

Command name	Description
`union(x,y)`	combines the values in x and y
`interest(x,y)`	finds the common elements in x and y
`setdiff(x,y)`	removes the elements in x that are also in y
`setequal(x,y)`	returns the logical value true if x is equal to y and false otherwise
`is.element(x,y)`	returns the logical value true if x is a element in y and false otherwise

5.8.4 The function *unique()*

When we have a vector `x` that may contain multiple duplications of serval elements, we can use the function *unique()* to remove all such duplications:

Listing 5.97: Using the function *unique()*

```
x <- c(3,2,4,3,1,1,3)
unique(x)
[1] 3 2 4 1
```

This can be useful if we want to use the values in the vector `x` as indices, and we want to use each index only once.

5.8.5 Testing arguments and converting variables

When discussing the definition of functions in Section 5.6, we mentioned the importance of making sure that the provided arguments are of the required type. In general, R provides several useful comments for testing the nature of arguments. In Table 5.9, we give an overview of the most useful ones.

Table 5.9: Each of these commands allows testing its argument and returns a logical value.

Command name	Description
`is.numeric(x)`	returns `TRUE` if argument is numerical value (double or integer)
`is.character(x)`	returns `TRUE` if argument is of character type
`is.logical(x)`	returns `TRUE` if argument is of logical type
`is.list(x)`	returns `TRUE` if argument is a list
`is.matrix(x)`	returns `TRUE` if argument is a matrix
`is.environment(x)`	returns `TRUE` if argument is an environment
`is.na(x)`	returns `TRUE` if argument is `NA`
`is.null(x)`	returns `TRUE` if argument is of null type (`NULL`)

The above commands are complemented by conversion functions that transform arguments into a specific type. Some examples are given in Table 5.10.

5.8.6 The function *sample()*

In order to sample elements from a given vector `x`, we can use the function *sample()*. To sample just means that the vector `x` contains a certain number of elements, i. e., its components, from which we can draw a certain number according to some rules.

Listing 5.98: Using the function *sample()*

```
sample(x, size, replace = FALSE, prob = NULL)
```

Table 5.10: Each of these commands allows to convert its argument to a specific type.

Command name	Description
`as.numeric(x)`	converts the argument in a numerical value (double or integer)
`as.character(x)`	converts the argument in a character-type
`as.logical(x)`	converts the argument in a logical-type
`as.list(x)`	converts the argument in a list
`as.matrix(x)`	converts the argument in a matrix
`as.na(x)`	converts the argument to `NA`
`as.null(x)`	converts the argument to `NULL`

Here, x is a vector, from which elements will be sampled. The option **size** indicates the number of elements that will be sampled, and **replace** indicates if the sampling is with (TRUE), or without (FALSE) replacement. In the case **replace** = FALSE, the option **size** needs to be smaller than the number of elements (length of the vector) in vector x.

In Figure 5.5, we visualize the two different sampling strategies. The column x (before) indicates the possible values that can be sampled, and the column x (after) contains the elements that are "left" after drawing a certain number of elements from it. In the case of sampling with replacement, there is no difference since each element that is "removed" from x is replaced with the same element. However, for sampling without replacement, the number of elements in x decreases. It is important to note that in the case of sampling with replacement, we can sample the same element multiple times (see green ball in Figure 5.5). This is not possible without replacement.

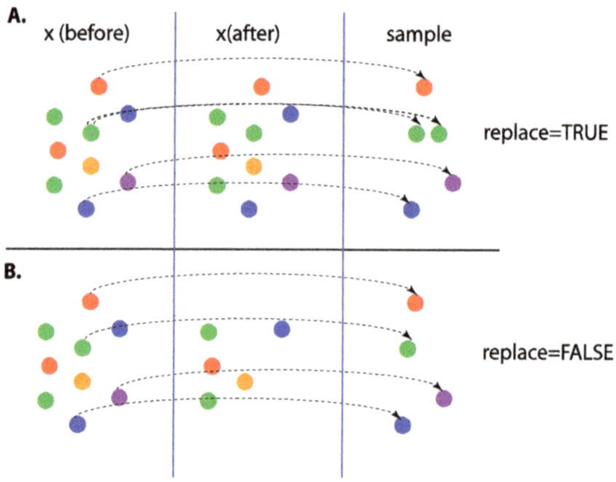

Figure 5.5: Visualization of different sampling strategies. A: Sampling with replacement. B: Sampling without replacement.

The option prob allows assigning a probability distribution to the elements of the vector x. By default, a uniform distribution is assumed, i. e., selecting all elements in x with the same probability.

Listing 5.99: Using the function *sample()*

```
sample(1:5, 20, replace = TRUE)
 [1] 5 4 5 4 1 1 4 5 4 1 1 5 2 5 1 4 3 2 5 2
```

In the case where we just want to sample all integer values from 1 to n, the following version of the function *sample()* can be used:

Listing 5.100: Using the function *sample()*

```
sample.int(n, size, replace = FALSE, prob = NULL)
```

For n=5, this realizes the same sampling function as above.

In summary, the function *sample()* allows sampling from a one-dimensional distribution prob with elements in x.

5.8.7 The function *try()*

In some cases, it may be possible that there is a command, whose execution might cause an error leading to the interruption of a program. If such a command is used within a larger program, this will of course result in the crash of the whole program. To prevent this, there is the command *try()*, which is a wrapper function to run an expression in a protected manner. That means, an expression will be evaluated and in case it would result in an error, it will capture this error, but without leading to a formal error causing the crash of a program. For example, executing sqrt("two") results in an error, because the function *sqrt()* expects a numeric argument and not a character string. However, using the following, by setting silent=T does not generate a formal error, but captures it in the object ms:

Listing 5.101: Using the function *try()*

```
ms <- try(sqrt("two"), silent=T)
```

In order to get the error message, one can execute either of the following commands:

Listing 5.102: Using the function *try()*

```
print(ms)

geterrmessage()
```

The difference between both commands is that the function *geterrmessage()* gives only the last error message in the current R session. That means, if you execute further commands that also result in an error, you cannot go back in the history of crashed functions.

In order to use the functionality of the function *try()* within a program, one can test if the output of *try()* is as expected or not. For our example above, this can be done as follows:

Listing 5.103: Using the function *try()*

```
is.numeric(ms)
```

In this way, a numeric output can be used in some way, whereas an error message, resulting in a FALSE for this test, can be handled in a different manner.

One may wonder how could it be possible that a command within a "functional" program can result in an error. The answer is that before a program is functional, it needs to be tested. And during the testing stage, there may be some irregularities, and using the function *try()* may help to find these. Aside from this, R may use an external input, e. g., provided by an input file, containing information that is outside the definition of the program. Hence, it may contain information that is not as expected in a certain context.

In addition to the function *try()*, R provides the function *tryCatch()*, which is a more advanced version for handling errors and warning events.

5.8.8 The function *system()*

There is an easy way to invoke operating system (OS) specific commands by using the command *system()*. This command allows the execution of OS commands like `pwd` or `ls` as if they would be executed from a terminal. However, the real utility of the function *system()* is that it can also be used to execute scripts.

5.9 Practical usage of R

In the previous sections, we discussed many important base functions of R. All of these can be directly executed within an R session. This works fine for exploring these functions and for playing around with their options in order to get to know them. However, this is not a good way to use R when doing serious work. Instead, it is recommended to write all the functions within a script, and then either execute the whole script, or copy-and-paste parts of the script into an R session for its execution.

In order to execute a script containing an R program, we can use the function *source()* as follows:

Listing 5.104: Using the function *source()*

```
source(file)
```

The input of the function *source()* is a character string containing the name of the file.

The advantage of writing an R program in a file and then executing it is that the results are easily reproducible in the future. This is particularly important if we are writing a scientific paper or a report and we would like to make sure that no detail about the generation of the results is lost. In this respect, it can be considered a good practice to store all of our programs in files.

Aside from this, it is also very helpful since we do not need to remember every detail of a program, which is anyway hardly possible if a program is getting more and more complex and lengthy. In this way, we can create over time our own library of programs, which we can use to look up how we solved certain problems, in case we cannot remember.

5.9.1 Advantage over GUI software

The script-wise execution of programs is actually a very important advantage of R, and any other programming language, over softwares that are based on graphical-user-interfaces (GUI). In order to understand this argument, that may even seem counterintuitive at first, let us remember how such GUI-based software, e. g., Excel or Partek, work. Usually, one selects sequentially commands from a menu and executes them. This can be seen as the sequential execution of commands directly written in an R session with exactly the same disadvantages. That means, if one would like to execute the same sequence of commands again, one needs to select them again manually from the menu. However, in contrast to R, it is not possible to save the sequence of commands so that it can be invoked automatically in an iterative manner for a future application. On the other hand, one can easily convert an R script into an R function to make it executable in any R program.

This is one argument that demonstrates the advantage of R over general GUI-based software. For fairness, we would like to add that this is only an advantage if you make use of this capability, for example when you are a developer for designing new data analysis software. If you are only interested in the application of "standard" solution methods for problems, then the usage of a GUI-based software can be very well justified.

In Chapter 2, more details about this have been presented when we introduced different programming paradigms.

5.10 Summary

In this chapter, we provided an introduction to programming with R that covered all base elements of programming. This is sufficient for the remainder of the book and should also allow you to write your own programs for a large number of different problems. A very good free online resource for getting more details about functions, options, and packages is STHDA http://www.sthda.com/english developed by Alboukadel Kassambara. For unlocking advanced features of R, we recommend the book by [46]. This is not a cookbook, but provides in-depth explanations and discussions.

6 Creating R packages

R is an open-source interpreted language with the purpose to conduct statistical analysis. Nowadays it is widely used for statistical software development, data analysis and machine learning applications in multiple scientific areas. R is easy to implement and has a large number of packages available, which allows users to extend their code easily and efficiently.

In this chapter, we show how you can create your own R package for functions you implemented. This makes your code reusable and portable. An R package is not only the most appropriate way to achieve this, but it also enables a convenient use of these functions and ensures the reproducibility of results. Furthermore, R packages enable us to easily integrate our code with other R packages.

6.1 Requirements

6.1.1 R base packages

Installation of the R environment: the first step for programming in R and developing R packages is the installation of the R software environment itself. R is an open-source programming environment, which can be downloaded free from the following address https://cran.r-project.org/.

The basic R environment provides the following core packages: **base**, **stats**, **utils**, and **graphics**.

- **base**: This package contains all the basic functions (including instructions and syntax), which allow a user to write code in R. It contains functions, e. g., for basic arithmetic operations, matrix operations, data structure, input/output, and for programming instructions.
- **utils**: This package contains all utility functions for creating, installing, and maintaining packages and many other useful functions.
- **stats**: This package contains the most basic functions for statistical analysis.
- **graphics**: This package provides functions to visualize different types of data in R.

A user can utilize the functions available in the R-based environment to create their packages rather than creating functions or objects from scratch. Below are examples to get a list of all functions in these packages.

Listing 6.1: Getting the list of functions in R-base

```
library(help = "base")
library(help = "utils")
library(help = "stats")
library(help = "graphics")
```

https://doi.org/10.1515/9783110796063-006

6.1.2 R repositories

R repositories provide a large number of packages for statistical analysis, machine learning, modeling, visualization, web mining, and web applications. A list of currently available R repositories is shown in Table 6.1.

Table 6.1: A table of repositories in R.

Repository	URL	Description	Installation
cran	cran.org	R packages for all purpose	`install.packages ("[package name]")`
Bioconductor	https://bioconductor.org/packages/	Bioconductor provides a large number of packages for high throughput genomic data analysis	Installation details are at https://bioconductor.org/install
Neuroconductor	https://neuroconductor.org	Provides packages for image analysis	`source("https://neuroconductor.org/neurocLite.R") neuro_install("aal")`
Github	https://github.com/trending/r	Githhub also provides a large number of packages. Additionally, it is also an alternative source of R packages available in other R repositories.	`install_github ("github package url")`
Omegahat	http://www.omegahat.net/	Provides different packages for statistical analysis	`install.packages (packageName, repos = "http://www.omegahat.net/R")`

6.1.3 Rtools

Rtools is required for building R packages. It is installed with R-base for Linux and MacOs, but for windows, it needs to be installed. The ".exe" file of Rtools for installation can be obtained at the following address: http://cran.r-project.org/bin/windows/Rtools/.

6.2 R code optimization

For an efficient R functioning, a developer should provide code that is efficient and fast. It is always advised to developers to perform profiling on their code to check about memory size taken by the code, execution time, and performance of each instruction in the code for making some performance improvement. The function *debug()* in R-base allows a user to test the code execution, line by line. Furthermore, the function *traceback()* helps a user to find the line where the code crashed.

6.2.1 Profiling an R script

The following Listing provides an illustration of script profiling in R:

Listing 6.2: Profiling an R script

```
sinx <- function(x, radian=T){
  if(is.null(x)){
    stop("please input numeric or integer values")
  }
  if((class(x)!="numeric") && (class(x)!="integer")){
        stop("please input numeric or integer values")
  }
  if(radian){
    x <- x*pi/180
  }
  sin(x)

}

xx <- rnorm(10000000)
Rprof(tmp <- tempfile())
y = sinx(xx)
Rprof()
summaryRprof(tmp)
```

6.2.2 Byte code compilation

From version 2.13.0, R includes the byte code compiler, which allows users to speedup their codes. In order to use the byte code compiler, the user needs to install the package `compiler`, which is available in CRAN. For the byte compilation of the whole package during the installation a user must add *ByteCompile: true* to the Description file of the package. This will avoid the use of "cmp-fun" for each function.

The following listing provides an illustration of the byte code compilation in R:

Listing 6.3: Byte code compilation in R

```
sinx <- function(x, radian=T){
  if(is.null(x)){
    stop("please input numeric or integer values")
  }
  if((class(x)!="numeric") && (class(x)!="integer")){
```

```
        stop("please input numeric or integer values")
  }
  if(radian){
    x <- x*pi/180
  }
  sin(x)

}

xx <- rnorm(100000000)
y = sinx(xx)

@

<<>>=
library(rbenchmark)
library(compiler)

xx <- rnorm(5000)
cmp_sinx <- cmpfun(sinx)

zz <- benchmark(sin(1:10),sin(xx),cmp_sinx(xx), sinx(xx),
          columns=c("test", "elapsed", "relative"),
          order="relative", replications=5000)
zz
```

6.2.3 GPU library, code, and others

Using GPU libraries, such as gpuR, h2o4gpu, gmatrix, provides an R interface to use GPU devices for computationally expensive analysis. Users can also parallelize their R code using either of the following packages: parallel, foreach, and doParallel. Furthermore, users can write scripts in C or C++ and run them in R using the package Rcpp for a faster execution of their overall code.

6.2.4 Exception handling

For a package development in R, it is essential to use error handling. R allows various error handling functions to deal with various unusual conditions, errors, and warnings that can occurred during the execution of a function or a package. Error handling provides a crisp and efficient code execution, which has the following advantages:

- Separating the main code from error-handling routines.
- Allows the complete execution of the code when the exceptions are identified and handled.
- Describing relevant errors, error types, and warnings when an error occurs.
- Preventing code or a package from crashing and recover from errors when unexpected error occurred.

This makes the debugging and profiling of complex code and packages easy. R provides two types of error handling mechanisms; the first one is *try()* or *tryCatch()*, and the second is *withCallingHandlers()*. The command *tryCatch()* registers existing handlers. When the condition is handled the control returns to the context where *tryCatch()* was called. Thus, it causes code to exit when a condition is signaled. The *tryCatch()* command is suitable to handle error conditions. The command *withCallingHandlers()* defines local handlers which are called in the same context where the condition is signaled and the control returns to the same context where the condition was signaled. Hence, it resumes the execution of the code after handling the condition. It maintains a full call stack to the code line or the segment that signals the condition. The command *withCallingHandlers()* is specifically useful to handle non-error conditions [201].

An example of exception handling is shown in the following Listing.

Listing 6.4: Exception handling

```
trgval.default <- function(x,  inv=F, ...){
      tryCatch({
      tmp <- NULL
      xrd <- x*pi/180
      if(inv){
          tmp <- sinh(xrd)
          names(tmp) <- paste0("sinh", x)
      }
      else{
          tmp <- sin(xrd)
          names(tmp) <- paste0("sin", x)
      }
      res <- list(x =x, xrd=xrd, inv=inv, val=tmp)
      }, error=function(e){
          print(e)
      })
      class(res) <- "trg"
      res
  }
```

6.3 S3, S4, and RC object-oriented systems

R utilizes functional and object-oriented features of programming. R has multiple object-oriented programming (OOP) systems, which are S3, S4, RC, and R6. However, most packages in R have been developed using the S3 OOP system.

6.3.1 The S3 class

In a S3 system, methods belong to generic functions instead of the objects of a class. A generic function checks the class of the first input object in the function argument and then dispatches a relevant method of that class. For example, *plot()* is a generic function to visualize data. Different packages inherit plot functions and develop their own functions. For instance, *plot.hclust()* is a member function, which provides visualization for dendrograms of the `hclust` class object. In the example given below, we create a generic trigonometric value (*trgval()*) function, with a default definition described by *trgval.default()* when the class of the object is unknown. To create a new function *trgval()* for the class `cosx`, we can leverage this generic function.

Listing 6.5: Illustration of the use of class S3

```
trgval <- function(x, ...)UseMethod("trgval")

# Default function function #
trgval.default <- function(x, rd=T, inv=F){
  tmp <- NULL
  if(rd){
    x <- x*pi/180
  }
  if(inv){
    tmp <- sinh(x)
    names(tmp) <- "sinh"

  }
  else{
    tmp <- sin(x)
    names(tmp) <- "sin"
  }
  tmp
}

# Extending function for class objects
trgval.cosx <- function(..., rd=T, inv=F){
    tmp <- NULL
  if(rd){
    x <- x*pi/180
  }
  if(inv){
    tmp <- cosh(x)
    names(tmp) <- "cosh"

  }
  else{
    tmp <- cos(x)
    names(tmp) <- "cos"
  }
  tmp



}

# Example 1
x <- 90
trgval(x)
```

```
# Example 2
x <- 90
class(x) <- "cosx"
trgval(x)
```

6.3.2 The S4 class

S4 works similarly to S3, but it provides a stricter definition of the object-oriented concept of programming, Hence, S3 classes allow the representation of complex data more simplistically. Below, we provide an example of class inheritance with the use of constructor and accessing a method:

Listing 6.6: Illustration of the use of class S4

```
# An example of generic function which is used by
# trg class objects.
trgval <- function(object) {

}
# create a new generic function
setGeneric"("trgval)
#class definition and return a generator
#function to create objects from the "trg" class
setClass("trg", representation(ag = "numeric",
            inv="logical", rd="logical"))
#class definition  to create objects from the
#"sinx" class which inherits the class "trg".
setClass("sinx",  contains = "trg")
#class definition  to create objects from the
#"cosx" class which inherits the class "trg"
setClass("cosx",  contains = "trg")

setMethod("trgval", signature(object = "sinx"),
  function(x) {
    tmp <- NULL
    if(object@rd){
      x@ag <- x@ag*pi/180
    }
    if(object@inv){
      tmp <- sinh(x@ag)
    }
    else{
      tmp <- sin(x@ag)
    }
    tmp
  })
setMethod("trgval", signature(object = "cosx"),
  function(x) {
    tmp <- NULL
    if(object@rd){
      x@ag <- x@ag*pi/180
    }
    if(object@inv){
      tmp <- cosh(x@ag)
```

```
    }
    else{
      tmp <- cos(x@ag)
    }
    tmp
})

aa1 <- new("sinx",ag=1, inv=F, rd=T)
aa2 <- new("cosx",ag=1, inv=F, rd=T)
trgval(aa1)
trgval(aa2)
```

6.3.3 Reference class (RC) system

The classes in the RC system provide reference semantics and support public and private methods, active bindings, and inheritance. In this system, methods belong to objects, not to generic functions. The objects are mutable. Creating RC objects is similar to creating S4 objects. The **methods** library available in R implements RC-based OOP. Also, the library R6 provides functionalities to implement RC-based OOP. An example of object mutability in the RC system is shown below.

Listing 6.7: Illustration of the use of RC

```
# Creating "trg" class using RC system
trg <- setRefClass("trg", fields=
  list(ang="numeric",
  rdn="logical", inv="logical", val="numeric"),
  methods=list(
  sinx = function(){
    if(rdn){
        ang <<- ang*pi/189
    }
    if(inv){
        val <<- sinh(ang)
    }
    else{val <<- sin(ang)}
  }
  ))
# creating an object of  trg class
s1 <- trg$new(ang = 60, rdn=F, inv=F)
s1$sinx()

# update the instance variable ""val of object s2
s2 <- s1
s2$sinx()
print(s2$val)
s2$sinx()
```

In the above example, S2 is not the copy of S1, but provides a reference of S1 so any changes on S2 will reflect on S1, and vice versa.

6.4 Creating an R package based on the S3 class system

In order to start a package generation, we first write our R program in a file with .R extension. In the next step, we call the function *package.skeleton()* with different arguments required for the package creation. Different files and folders in a package skeleton are shown in Figure 6.1.

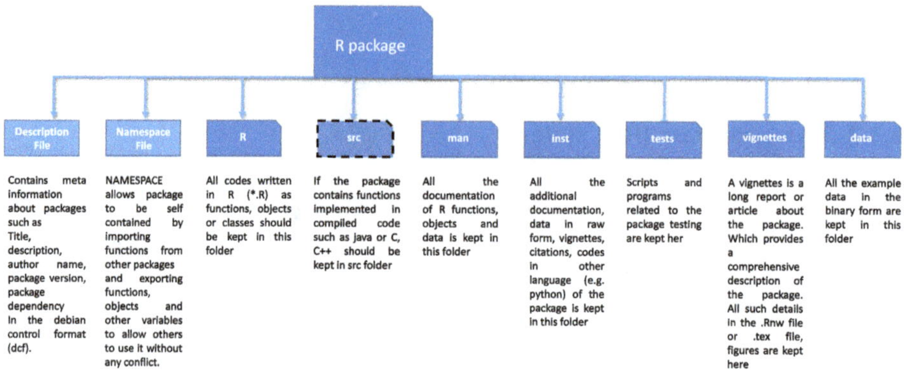

Figure 6.1: Schematic view of the file hierarchy in an R package.

6.4.1 R program file

We create an R program file named `trg.R` with the S3 system, as shown in the example below. This function creates a basic R skeleton with all the necessary folders and files required for building a package. In our example, we create a method for values of the *sin()* function. We start with our main function with a generic name *trgval()*, which calls the function *UseMethod()*. In the next step, we create a default function *trgval.default()* as well as the function *plot.trg()*.

6.4.1.1 The file trg.R

Listing 6.8: Content of the file trg.R

```
trgval <- function(x, ...)UseMethod("trgval")

# Default function function #
trgval.default <- function(x,  inv=F){
  tmp <- NULL
  xrd <- x*pi/180
  if(inv){
    tmp <- sinh(xrd)
    names(tmp) <- "sinh"

  }
```

```
  else{
    tmp <- sin(xrd)
    names(tmp) <- "sin"
  }
  res <- list(x =x, xrd=xrd, inv=inv, val=tmp)
  class(res) <- "trg"
  res
}

# Creating plot function for plotting the  "trg" class

plot.trg <- function(trg, wave=T,minang=-450,maxang=450,...){
   theta <- trg$x

     if(!wave){

     x <- sort(runif(10000, min=-1, max=1))
     r = 1
     y <- sqrt(1-x^2)
     tmp <-cbind(x = c(x,rev(x)), y=c(y,rev(-y)))
     plot(tmp, type="l", lwd=2, cex=.1)
     points(cos(theta*pi/180), sin(theta*pi/180),
       pch=20, col=20, cex=2)
     segments(0, 0, x1 = cos(theta*pi/180),
       y1 = sin(theta*pi/180))
     segments(-1, 0, x1 = 1, y1 = 0)
     segments(0, -1, x1 = 0, y1 = 1)
     segments(0, -1, x1 = 0, y1 = 1)
     segments(cos(theta*pi/180), sin(theta*pi/180),
       cos(theta*pi/180), 0, col="blue")
     segments(0, 0, cos(theta*pi/180),0, col="blue")

     rin <- .1
     for(i in theta){
         x1 <- rin*cos(c(0:i)*pi/180)
         y1 <- rin*sin(c(0:i)*pi/180)

         mn1 <- mean(x1)
         mn2 <- mean(y1)

         x11 <- cos(i*pi/180)/2
         y11 <- sin(i*pi/180)/2
         lb1 <-  parse(text=(paste0("theta[",i,"]")))
         lb2 <-  parse(text=(paste0("theta[",i,"]")))

         text(cos(i*pi/180)-.12, sin(i*pi/180)/2, "sin")
         text(cos(i*pi/180), sin(i*pi/180)/2, lb1)
        text(cos(i*pi/180)/2-.12,-.1,  "cos")
         text(cos(i*pi/180)/2, -.1, lb2)

         lb <- parse(text=(paste0("theta[",i,"]")))
         points(x1, y1, pch=20, col=20, cex=.1)
         text(mn1, mn2, lb)
         if(rin!=1){
             rin = rin+.1
         }

     }
     }
     else{
```

```
        plot(sin(c(minang:maxang)*pi/180), type="l",
        lwd=2, xaxt="n", ylab="sin (x)", xlab="")
        abline(h=0,lwd=2)
        tmp <- c(minang:maxang)
        k <- which(tmp==0)
         points(theta+k, sin(theta*pi/180), col="blue", pch=20, cex=2)
         abline(v=theta+k)

         tt <- which(abs(tmp)%%90==0)
         aa <- tmp[tt]/90
         lbn <- sapply(1:length(tt),
             function(x)parse(text=(paste0("pi"))))
         axis(1, at=which(abs(tmp)%%90==0), labels=lbn, tick=TRUE)
         axis(1, at=which(abs(tmp)%%90==0)-15, labels=aa/2, cex=.5,
             tick=FALSE)
   }

   }
```

6.4.1.2 Package skeleton

Listing 6.9: Generating the package skeleton

```
# R function to create package skeleton
#package.skeleton("trgpkg",code_files = ["path to the R file"] )
package.skeleton("trgpkg",code_files = "trg.R" )
```

Once the package skeleton is created, we need to edit the DESCRIPTION, NAMESPACE, and the package description files in the folder man. The content of the edited files are shown in Section 6.7.1. The folder trgpkg contains the following files and folders:

Description: This file contains some basic information of the package, for example: version, author, description, and package dependency.

Man: This folder contains documentation of functions and data of the package in .Rd format; the developer needs to edit these files to describe their function's inputs, output, and examples.

Data: If a package contains any data-set, those files should be kept in the data folder. These data files should be R-objects such as matrix, vector, data frame, and saved in the folder Data.

6.4.2 Building an R package

Now we need to check, compile, and build the package. First, we go to the command prompt and change to the directory, where the package is kept and run the command R CMD build [package name] to build the package tarball. We can also use the same command in R calling it inside the system function of R. Below we provide an example.

Listing 6.10: Building an R package

```
if(dir.exists("trgpkg")){
  system("R CMD build trgpkg")
}
```

Now we get the tarball of package, which is named `trgpkg_1.0.tar.gz`.

6.5 Checking the package

In order to check errors and warnings before installing a package, it needs to be debugged properly. A package is checked by the commands shown below.

Bash 6.11: Checking an R package from the terminal

```
R CMD check [package name]
# Example
R CMD check trgpkg_1.0.tar.gz
```

The `check` command creates a folder with the package name and `.Rcheck` extension. All the error logs and warning files are created inside this folder. The user can check all these files to evaluate the package.

Listing 6.12: Checking an R package from R

```
if(dir.exists("trgpkg")){
   system("R CMD check trgpkg_1.0.tar.gz")
}
```

6.6 Installation and usage of the package

When a package is built and checked properly, and all errors and warnings have been addressed, then it is ready for installation in R. The following command is used to install a package in R:

Bash 6.13: Installing an R package from the terminal

```
R CMD INSTALL [package name] #general syntax
R CMD INSTALL trgpkg_1.0.tar.gz
```

Listing 6.14: Installing an R package from R

```
if(file.exists("trgpkg_1.0.tar.gz")){
   system("R CMD INSTALL trgpkg_1.0.tar.gz")
}
```

6.7 Loading and using a package

When the package is installed, we can easily load it, call its functions and load data associated with the package.

Below, we provide some examples of using functions in the package built in the previous section (i. e., the package **trgpkg**.)

Listing 6.15: Using an R package

```
    library("trgpkg")    #loading the library

    data(angls)  #loading the data in the package
    angls

# calculating sin value of the data
    data(angls)
    zz <- trgval(angls)

# plotting the output values
    rm(trgval)
    library("trgpkg")
    data(angls)
    zz <- trgpkg::trgval.default(angls)
    plot(zz)

    library("trgpkg")

    data(angls)
    zz <- trgpkg::trgval.default(c(30,60))

    ## plotting on a circle of unit radius
    plot.trg(zz, wave=FALSE)
```

6.7.1 Content of the files edited when generating the package

Content of the file "DESCRIPTION"

```
Package: trgpkg
Type: Package
Title: Example package for package creation
Version: 1.0
Date: 2019-01-20
Author: Shailesh Tripathi and Frank Emmert Streib
Maintainer: Shailesh Tripathi <shailesh.tripathy@gmail.com>
Description: This provides simple example for package creation in R
License: GPL (>= 2)
LazyLoad: yes
```

Content of the file "NAMESPACE"

```
exportPattern("^[[:alpha:]]+")
export(plot.trg, trgval)
importFrom("graphics", "abline", "axis", "plot",
           "points", "segments", "text")
importFrom("stats", "runif")
```

Content of the file "man/plot.trg.Rd"

```
\name{plot.trg}
\alias{plot.trg}
\title{
    Plots the sin function and the input value of "trg" class.
 }
\description{
  Plots the sin function and the input value of "trg" class.
}
\usage{
   plot.trg(trg, wave = T, minang = -450,
  maxang = 450, ...)
}
\arguments{
\item{trg}{
  this is a "trg" class object generated using "trgval" function.
}
\item{wave}{
  It is a logical value. If true gives a wave plot of sin function.
}
\item{minang}{
  the minimum value of the domain of sin function for visualizing
  sin function on the x-axis.
}
\item{maxang}{
   maximum value of domain of sin function for
  visualizing sin function on x- axis.
}
 \item{\dots}{
  all other input type as available in "plot" function
}
}
\value{
  Provides a graphic view of the sin function
```

```
}

\author{
   Shailesh Tripathi and Frank Emmert Streib}

\seealso{
   \code{\link{plot}}
}

\examples{
   zz <- trgval(90)
   plot(zz)
   plot(zz, wave=FALSE)
}
```

Content of the file "man/trgval.Rd"

```
\name{trgval}
\alias{trgval}
%- Also NEED an '\alias' for EACH other topic documented here.
\title{
   A generic function which is used to calculate
   trigonometric values.
}
\description{
   A generic function which is used to calculate
   trigonometric values.}
\usage{
   trgval(x, ...)
}
\arguments{
   \item{x}{
       is a numeric value or vector}
   \item{\dots}{
 }
}

\value{
   returns a "trg" class object
}

\author{
```

```
   Shailesh Tripathi and Frank Emmert-Streib}

\seealso{
   plot.trg, trgval.default}

\examples{
     zz <- trgval(c(30, 60, 90))
   plot(zz)
   plot(zz, wave=FALSE)
 }
```

6.8 Summary

In this chapter, we provided a brief introduction how to create an R package. This topic can be considered advanced and for the remainder of this book it is not required. However, in a professional context the creation of R packages is necessary for simplifying the usage and exchange of a large number of individually created functions.

Nowadays, many published scientific articles provide accompanying R packages to ensure that all obtained results can be reproduced. Despite the intuitive clarity of this, the reproducability of results has recently sparked heated discussions, especially regarding provisioning the underlying data [70].

Part II: **Graphics in** R

7 Basic plotting functions

In this chapter, we introduce plotting capabilities of R that are part of the base installation. We will see that there is a large number of different plotting functions that allow a multitude of different visualizations.

7.1 Plot

The most basic plotting tool in R is provided by the *plot()* function, which allows visualizing y as a function of x. The following script gives two simple examples (see Figure 7.1 (A) and (B)):

Listing 7.1: Examples for basic plotting, see Figure 7.1

```
# A
x <- seq(from=0, to=2*pi, length.out = 50)
y <- sin(x)
plot(x, y)

# B
x <- seq(from=0, to=2*pi, length.out = 50)
y <- sin(x)
plot(x, y, type="l")
```

In this example, we first define the elements of vector x as a sequence of points ranging from 0 to 2π with 50 intermediate values. That means, vector x contains 50 equally-spaced points from 0 to 2π. The elements of vector y correspond to a sinus evaluated at the 50 points provided by x.

The first example, shown in Figure 7.1 (A), plots each element in the vector x against each element in the vector y. That means, the plot function visualizes always pairs of elements in x and y, i. e., (x_i, y_i) for all $i \in \{1, \ldots, 50\}$. In contrast, Figure 7.1 (B) shows the same result, but with the **line** option for the type of the visualization. The difference is that in this case, the 50 pairs of points are connected by *smooth* line segments that result in a smooth line visualization.

At first glance, Figure 7.1 (B) may appear as the natural visualization of a sinus function, because we know it is a smooth function. However, it is important to realize that a computer graphics is always pixel-based, i. e., a line is always a sequence of points. But what is then the difference to a point-based graphics? It is the spacing between consecutive points (and their size). In this sense, Figure 7.1 (B) is realized, internally by R, as a sequence of points that are very close to each other so that the resulting plot *appears* as a continuous line.

For instance, change the value of the option **length.out** in the **seq** command to see what consequence this has on the resulting plot.

https://doi.org/10.1515/9783110796063-007

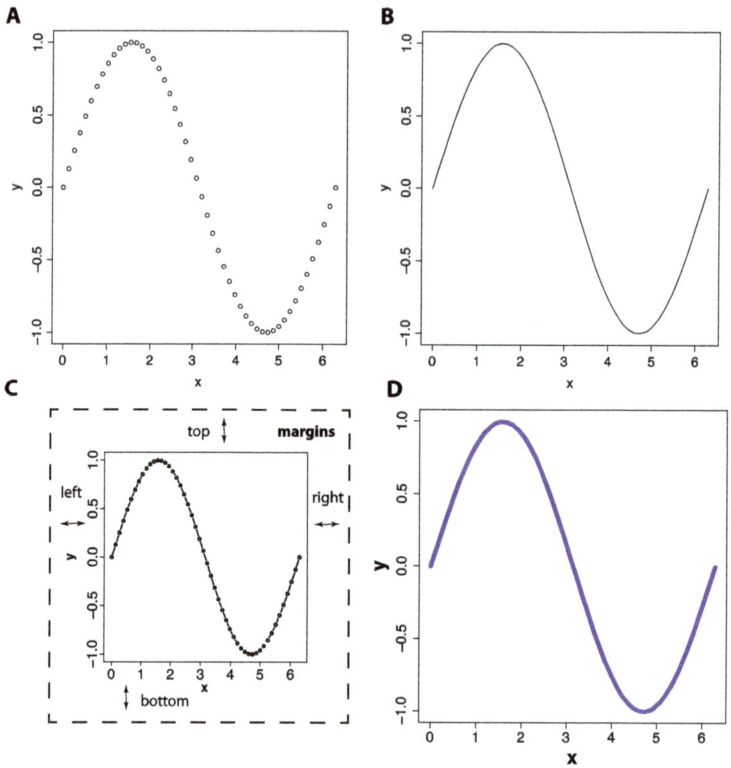

Figure 7.1: Examples for the basic plotting function *plot()*.

The two examples shown in Figure 7.1 (A) and (B) demonstrate just a quick visualization of the functional relation between x and y. However, in order to improve the visual appearance of these plots, usually, it is advised to utilize additional options. Below we show two further examples, see Figure 7.1 (C) and (D), that use different options.

Listing 7.2: Examples of basic plotting see Figure 7.1

```
# C
x <- seq(from=0, to=2*pi, length.out = 50)
y <- sin(x)
par(mar=c(5,5,1,1))
plot(x, y, type="b", cex.axis=1.6, cex.lab=2.2, font.lab=2,
lwd=4.0)

# D
x <- seq(from=0, to=2*pi, length.out = 50)
y <- sin(x)
par(mar=c(5,5,1,1))
plot(x, y, type="l", cex.axis=1.6, cex.lab=2.2, font.lab=2,
lwd=8.0, col="blue")
```

The type option allows specifying if we want points (p), lines (l), or both (b) options, to be used simultaneously. The option cex allows changing the font size of the axis (cex.axis) and the labels (cex.lab), and font.lab leads to a bold face of the labels. Finally, the line width can be adjusted by setting the lwd to a positive numerical value, and col specifies the color of the lines or points.

There is one further command in the above examples (par) that appears unimpressive at first. However, it allows adjusting the margins of the figure by setting mar. Specifically, we need to set a four-dimensional vector to set the margin values for (bottom, left, top, right) (in this order). This command is important, because when setting the font size labels larger than a certain value, it can happen that the labels are cut-off. For preventing this, the mar option needs to be set appropriately.

In the following, we will always modify a basic plot by setting additional options to improve its visual appearance.

7.1.1 Adding multiple curves in one plot

There are two functions available that enable adding multiple lines or points into the same figure, namely **lines** and **points**. Two examples for the script below are shown in Figure 7.2 (A) and (B). In order to distinguish different lines or points from each other, we can specify the line-type (lty) or point-type (pch) option.

Listing 7.3: Multiple curves in one plot, see Figure 7.2

```
# A
x <- seq(from=0, to=2*pi, length.out = 50)
y1 <- sin(x)
y2 <- sin(x+0.4)
par(mar=c(5,5,1,1))
plot(x, y1, type="l", cex.axis=1.6, cex.lab=2.2, font.lab=2,
lwd=4.0, lty=1)
lines(x, y2, lwd=4.0, lty=2)

# B
x <- seq(from=0, to=2*pi, length.out = 50)
y1 <- sin(x)
y2 <- sin(x+0.4)
par(mar=c(5,5,1,1))
plot(x, y1, type="p", cex.axis=1.6, cex.lab=2.2, font.lab=2,
lwd=4.0, pch=1)
points(x, y2, lwd=4.0, pch=2)
```

This can be extended to multiple **lines** or **points** commands as shown for the next examples; see Figure 7.2 (C) and (D). Here, we add in a legend to the figures that allows a better identification of the different lines with the parameters that have been used. The **legend** command allows specifying the position of the legend within the figure. Here, we used **bottomright** so that the legend does not overlap

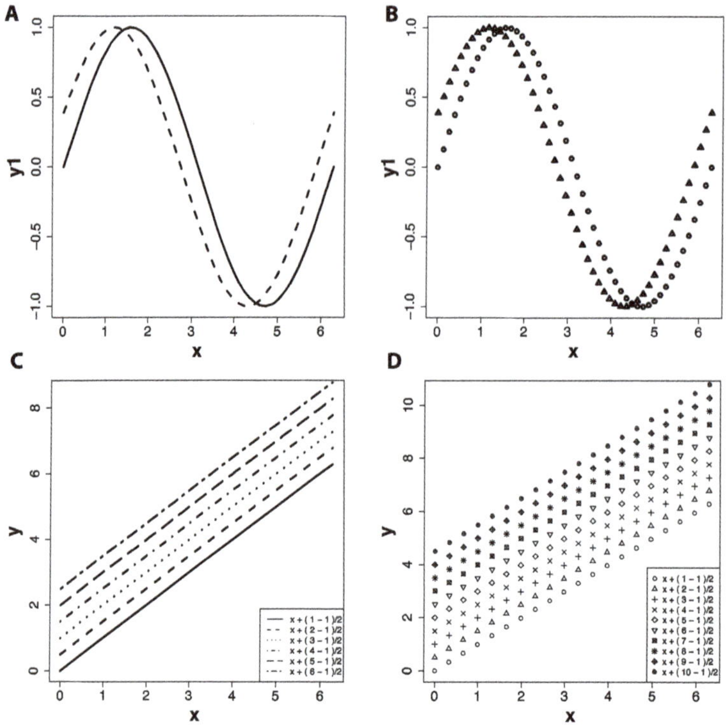

Figure 7.2: Examples for multiple plots in one figure.

with the lines or points. Further, we need to specify the text that shall appear in the legend and the symbol, e. g., `lty` or `pch`. There are more options available, but these provide the basic functionality of a legend.

For the above example, we used the `xlab` and `ylab` option to change the appearance of the labels of the x- and y-axis. In the previous examples, we did not specify them explicitly. For this reason, R uses as default names for the labels the names of the variables that have been used in the function *plot()*.

Listing 7.4: Multiple curves in one plot, see Figure 7.2

```
# C
n <- 6
x <- seq(from=0, to=2*pi, length.out = 50)
y <- matrix(0, nrow = n, ncol = 50)
for(i in 1:n){
  y[i,] <- x + (i-1)/2
}
par(mar=c(5,5,1,1))
plot(x, y[1,], type="l", cex.axis=1.6, cex.lab=2.2,
font.lab=2, lwd=4.0, lty=1, ylim=c(0,8.5), ylab="y", xlab="x")
for(i in 2:n){
  lines(x, y[i,], lwd=4.0, lty=i)
}
```

```
legend("bottomright", paste("x + (", 1:n, "- 1 )/2"),
lty=1:n, lwd = 2)

# D
n <- 10
x <- seq(from=0, to=2*pi, length.out = 20)
y <- matrix(0, nrow = n, ncol = 20)
for(i in 1:n){
  y[i,] <- x + (i-1)/2
}
par(mar=c(5,5,1,1))
plot(x, y[1,], type="p", cex.axis=1.6, cex.lab=2.2,
font.lab=2, lwd=2, pch=1, ylim=c(0,10.5), ylab="y", xlab="x")
for(i in 2:n){
  points(x, y[i,], lwd=2.0, pch=i)
}
legend("bottomright", paste("x + (", 1:n, "- 1 )/2"), pch=1:n)
```

7.1.2 Adding horizontal and vertical lines

We can also add straight horizontal and vertical lines on the graph using the function *abline()*. Depending on the option used, i. e., `h` or `v`, horizontal or vertical lines are added to a figure at the provided values. Also this command allows changing the line-type (`lty`) or color (`col`). In Figure 7.3, we show an example that includes one horizontal and one vertical line.

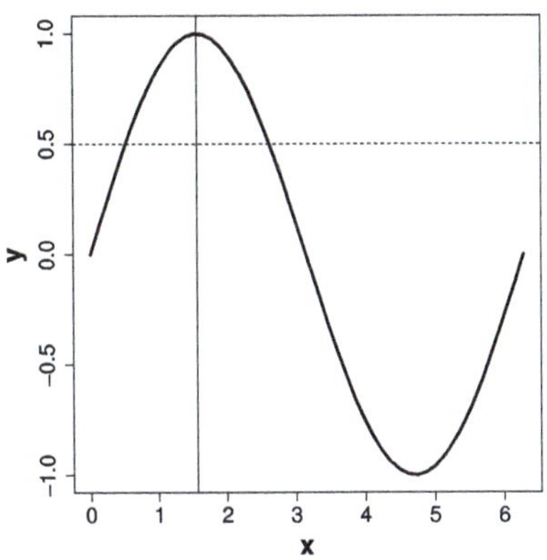

Figure 7.3: Example for adding horizontal and vertical lines to a plot using the function *abline()*.

Listing 7.5: Add horizontal and vertical lines to a plot, see Figure 7.3

```
x <- seq(from=0, to=2*pi, length.out = 50)
y <- sin(x)
par(mar=c(5,5,1,1))
plot(x, y, type="l", cex.axis=1.6, cex.lab=2.2, font.lab=2,
lwd=4.0)
abline(v=pi/2)
abline(h=0.5, lty=2)
```

7.1.3 Opening a new figure window

In order to plot a function in a new figure by keeping a figure that is already created, one needs to open a new plotting window using one of the following commands:
- X11(), for Linux and Mac if using R within a terminal
- macintosh(), for a Mac operating system
- windows(), for a Windows operating system

If these commands are not executed, then every new *plot()* command executed will overwrite the old figure created so far.

7.2 Histograms

An important graphical function to visualize the distribution of data is *hist()*. The command *hist()* shows the histogram of a data set. For instance, we are drawing $n = 200$ samples from a normal distribution with a mean of zero, a standard deviation of one, and saving the resulting values in a vector called x, see the code below. The left Figure 7.4 shows a histogram of the data with 25 bars of an equal width, set by the option breaks. Here, it is important to realize that the data in x are raw data. That means, the vector x does not provide directly the information displayed in Figure 7.4 (Left), but indirectly. For this reason, the number of occurrences of values in x, e. g., in the interval $0.5 \leq x \leq 0.6$, need to be calculated by the *hist()* function. However, in order to do that one needs to specify what are the boundaries of the intervals to conduct such calculations. The function *hist()* supports two different ways to do that. The first one is to just set the total number of bars the histogram should contain. The second one is by providing a vector containing the boundary values explicitly.

Listing 7.6: Plotting histograms, see Figure 7.4

```
# Left
n <- 200
x <- rnorm(n, mean=0, sd=1)
hist(x, breaks=25, col="lavender", main="", cex.lab=2.0,
cex.axis=1.4)

# Right
b <- c(-5,-2,-1.5,-1,-0.5,seq(-0.4, 0.4, 0.2),0.5,1,1.5,2,5)
hist(x, breaks=b, col="lavender", main="", cex.lab=2.0,
cex.axis=1.4, freq=F)
```

An example for the second way is shown in Figure 7.4 (Right). Here, the boundary values are provided by the vector b. Also, in this case we set the option freq to TRUE, which results in a histogram of densities. In contrast, Figure 7.4 (Left) shows the frequencies for each bar corresponding to the number of x-values that fall in the boundaries of one bar.

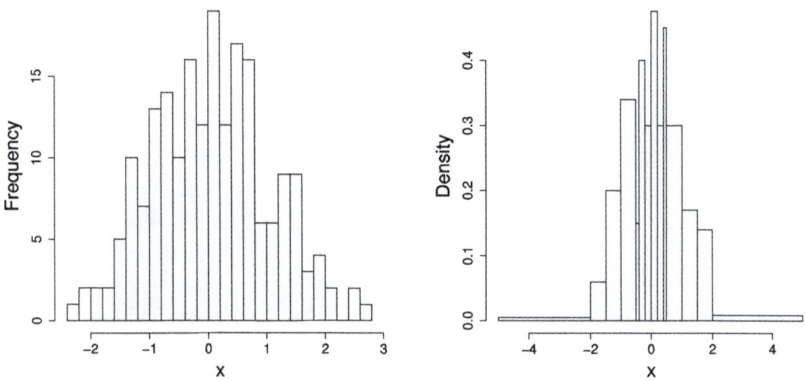

Figure 7.4: Examples for histograms. Left: Providing the total number of bars. Right: Providing the boundary values.

7.3 Bar plots

If the bin information of the individual cells is already available, one can use the command *barplot()*. In the following example, we assign to each of the $n = 10$ bars a color randomly. We do that by using the command *color()*, which provides a vector of 667 defined color names available in R. In order to select the colors randomly, we use the *sample()* command to sample n integer values between 1 and 667 randomly without replacement. Here, randomly means that each element has the same probability to be selected, namely $p = 1/667$.

Listing 7.7: Plotting bar charts, see Figure 7.5

```
# Left
n <- 10
x <- runif(n, 0, 10)
ind <- sample(1:667, n, replace=F)
barplot(x, xlab="x", ylab="Frequency", legend=1:n,
names.arg=1:n, cex.axis=1.4, cex.lab=2.0, font.lab=2,
col=colors()[ind])
```

In Figure 7.5 (Right), we show a second example for a bar plot that splits each bar into individual contributing components. Such plots are called stacked bar charts. For instance, suppose we have 3 factors that contribute to the outcome of a variable that is measured for 5 different conditions indexed by the letters A–E. Then, for each condition, the outcome of a variable can be broken down into its constituting 3 values.

In the example below, we use two new options. The first one is `space` allowing to adjust the spacial distance between adjacent bars. The second one is `names.arg`, which allows specifying the labels that appear below each bar. For specifying the labels, we use the function *LETTERS()* to conveniently assign the first 5 capital

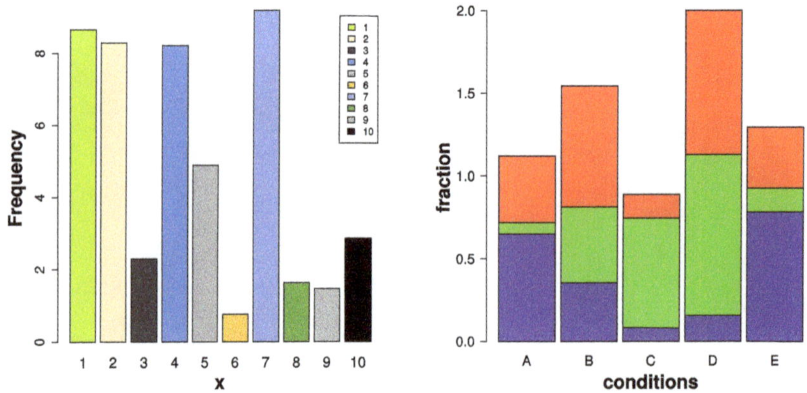

Figure 7.5: Examples for a normal bar chart (Left) and a stacked bar chart (Right).

letters of the alphabet to `names.arg`. Alternatively, the function *letters()* can be used to generate lowercase letters.

Listing 7.8: Plotting stacked bar charts, see Figure 7.5

```
# Right
n <- 5; m <- 3
par(mar=c(5,5,1,1))
mat <- matrix(runif(m*n), nrow=m, ncol=n)
barplot(mat, main="", ylab="fraction", xlab="conditions",
col=c("blue","green","red"), space=0.1, cex.axis=1.4, las=1,
names.arg=LETTERS[1:5], cex.lab=2, font.lab=2, cex.names=1.4)
```

7.4 Pie charts

An alternative visualization to a bar plot is a pie chart, also called circle chart. In a pie chart, the arc length of each slice is proportional to the quantity which it represents.

Listing 7.9: Plotting pie charts, see Figure 7.6

```
n <- 5
x <- runif(n, 0, 10)
pie(x, col = gray(seq(0.0,1.0,length=n)), cex=2)
```

7.5 Dot plots

For the visualization of a large number of single-valued entities, a dot plot can be useful. A dot plot is like a graphical version of a table that makes it easier to recognize the relative differences between the values of the different entities.

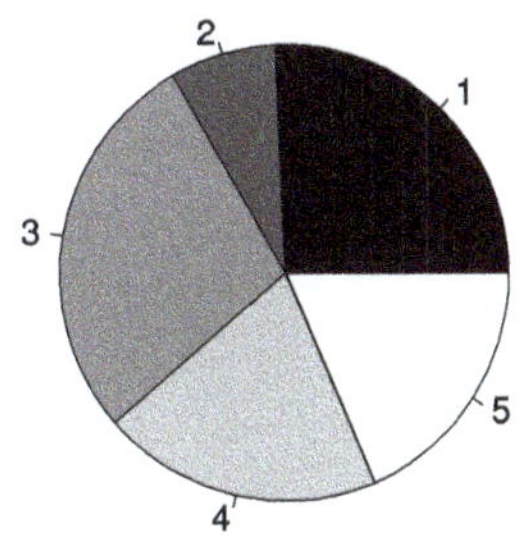

Figure 7.6: A simple pie chart.

In Figure 7.7, we show an example visualizing the mortality of cancer in European countries normalized per 100,000 people. The information is taken from the World Health Organization (WHO) data for the year 2013. These data are provided in the file `WHO.RData`.

In Figure 7.7, the average number of cancer deaths (averaged over gender) is alphabetically ordered according the country names. Overall, the information about the 53 countries and the range of all possible values is easy to grasp, making a dot plot an attractive graphical alternative to a table.

In the following code, we first identify all European countries in the data frame `dat.who.ave`, because it contains also information about non-european countries. Then, we use the *dotchart()* function specifying the entries which shall be visualized `dat.who.ave$deaths[ind]` and the labels (`dat.who.ave[ind,1]`) that should be used to identify the corresponding rows in the dot plot.

Listing 7.10: Example of dot plots, see Figure 7.7

```
aux <- "Europe"
ind <- which(dat.who.ave[,3]==aux)
dotchart(dat.who.ave$deaths[ind], labels=dat.who.ave[ind,1],
cex=0.5, cex.lab=2.0, cex.main=2.0, font.lab=2,
main="Mortality by european country",
xlab="Cancer deaths per 100,000")
```

As usually, there is more than one way to visualize a data set in a meaningful way, depending on the perspective. In the following, we present just one alternative representation of the same data set by sorting the mortality values of the countries.

In Figure 7.8, we ordered the mortality values and grouped the countries into three categories. Each of these categories is highlighted in a different color by specifying the option `color`. The category of a country is specified with the `groups` option by providing a vector of factors. If visualized in this way, subgroups within the data set can be highlighted additionally. Of course, there are further modification one could conduct, e. g., the alphabetic organization of the countries within the subgroups or subdividing the subgroups, e. g., highlighted by specifying different symbols using the `gpch` option.

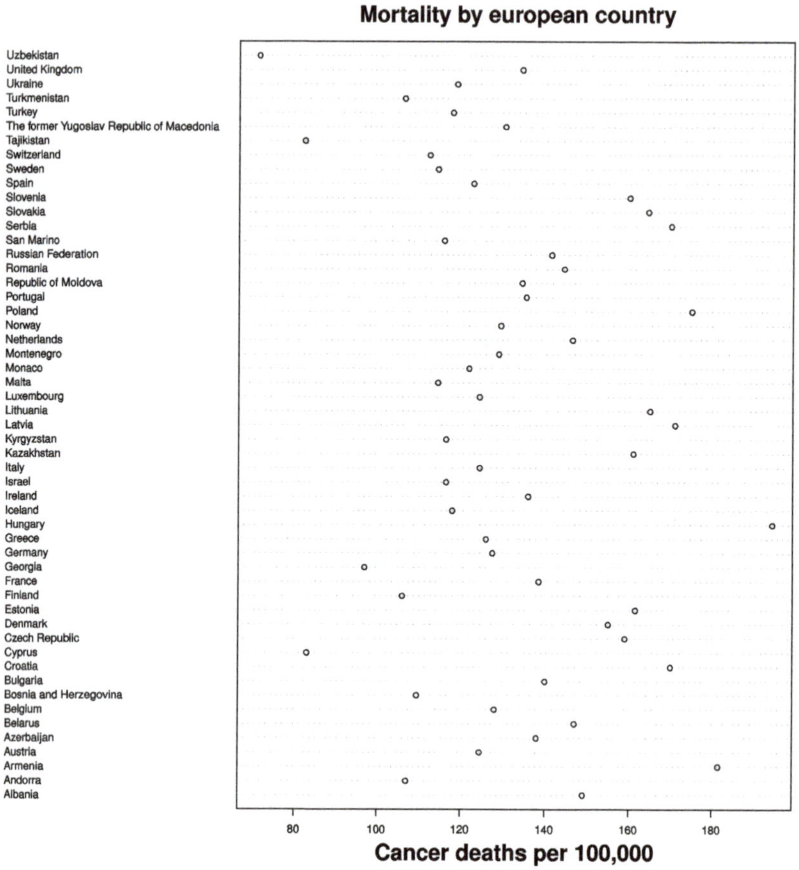

Figure 7.7: Information about cancer mortality in Europe taken from the World Health Organization (WHO) data for the year 2013.

Listing 7.11: Example of dot plots, see Figure 7.8

```
aux <- "Europe"
ind <- which(dat.who.ave[,3]==aux)
ind2 <- order(dat.who.ave[ind,2])
L <- length(ind)
n <- round(L/3)
country.col <- c(rep("blue2", n), rep("green3", n),
rep("purple2", (n-1)))
country.g <- factor(c(rep("3", n), rep("2", n),
rep("1", (n-1))))

dotchart(dat.who.ave$deaths[ind[ind2]],
labels=dat.who.ave[ind[ind2],1], cex=0.5, cex.lab=2.0,
cex.main=2.0, font.lab=2,
main="Mortality by european country - ordered",
xlab="Cancer deaths per 100,000",
groups=country.g, color=country.col)
```

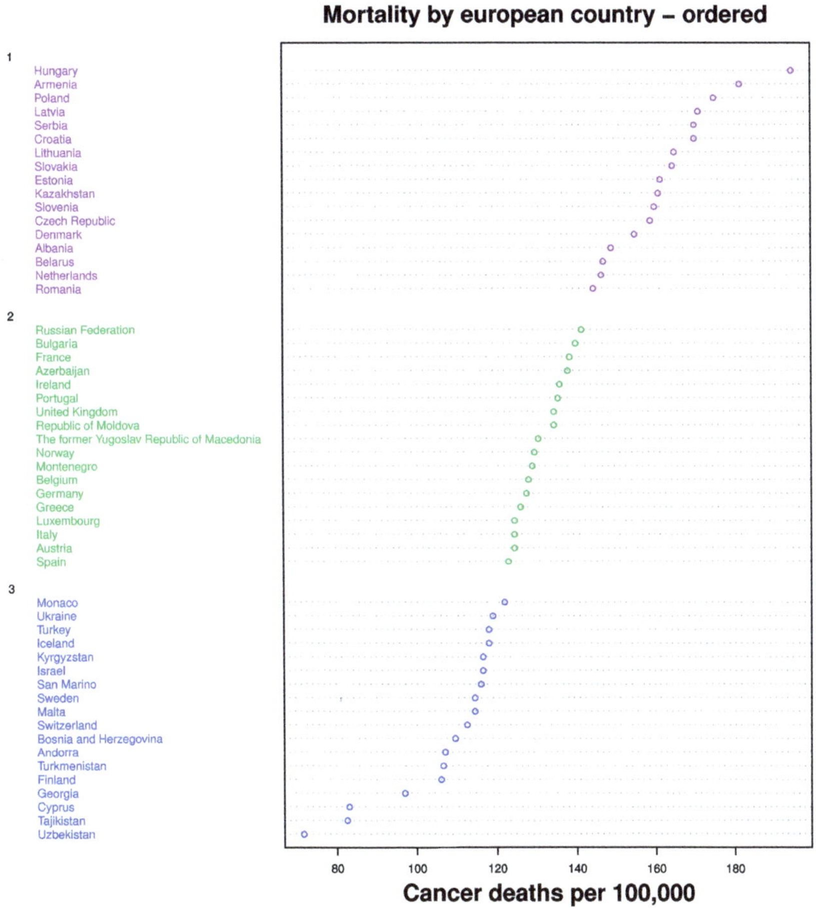

Figure 7.8: Ordered information about the cancer mortality in Europe. Same data as in Figure 7.7.

Finally, we would like to note that a dot plot is also called a Cleveland dot plot, because William Cleveland pioneered this kind of visualization.

7.6 Strip and rug plots

Another plotting style, which is also due to Cleveland, is called a strip plot. It can be used to visualize one-dimensional data along a line, plotting each data point to its corresponding spot. In R, the *stripchart()* function allows the application of this style, and in Figure 7.9 we show three examples (corresponding to the green, red, and blue data points).

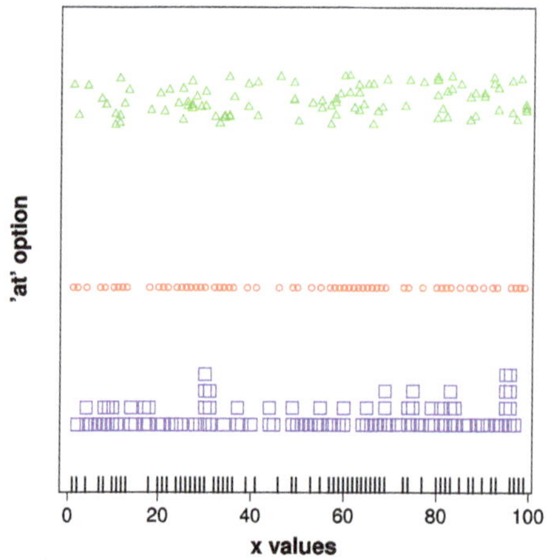

Figure 7.9: Examples for strip plots (corresponding to the green, red, and blue data points) and a rug plot.

For these examples, we generated 100 integer values from the interval 1 to 100. The example shown by the red data points corresponds to the base form of this plot function that overwrites the data points, as specified by the option **method**. Alternatively, the data points can be stacked leading to a kind of histogram (in blue), although the height does not exactly reflect the count values, but is merely proportional to the relative density of the **x values** within a certain region. Finally, the data points can be *jittered* by applying a small offset between data points of the same **x-value**.

Listing 7.12: Example of strip and rug plots, see Figure 7.9

```
n <- 100
x <- round(runif(n, 1, 100))

par(mar=c(5,5,1,1))
stripchart(x, method="stack", at=0.2, cex=2, offset=0.5,
xlab="x values", ylab="'at' option", font.lab=2, cex.lab=2.0,
cex.axis=1.4, col = "blue", ylim=c(0,1.8))
stripchart(c, method="overplot", at=0.75, col="red", pch=1,
add=T)
stripchart(c, method="jitter", at=1.5, col = "green3", pch=2,
add=T)
rug(c, lwd=2.5)
```

In addition to a strip plot, there is the *rug()* function available in R, which we included also in Figure 7.9. The function *rug* is similar to the function *stripchart()*; however, the difference is that the *rug* function does not provide an option similar to at for *stripchart()*, allowing to shift the rug of data points along the y-axis. Also, there is no option to specify the symbol to be displayed as a data point, instead, data points are shown as vertical lines.

7.7 Density plots

The next visualization style we will discuss is the density plot. A density plot can be seen as an extension of strip plots and histograms. The idea of a density plot is to convert the density of the data points within certain *sensible* regions into relative height values so that a summation over all density values adds up to one.

The example in the previous section for *stripchart()*, with the option `method="stack"`, is almost a density plot, according to the above description. However, instead of converting regions of **x-values** into relative height values, individual data points are stacked if they are identical. Furthermore, height values are merely the number of identical data points and, hence, these values would not sum up to one. However, summation over all data points and division of the stacked heights normalizes the resulting values giving, in principle, a valid density plot. Also, if we are creating a histogram with a certain bin size and normalize the resulting height values by the total sum over all bins, we obtain another valid density plot.

Despite the fact that these simple modifications of a strip plot and a histogram lead to density plots, there are two characteristics missing that enable general density plots. These characteristics are (1) to average over overlapping regions, and (2) weighted regions of the data points by application of a sliding window.

In order to understand these two characteristics, we show in Figure 7.10 some examples. The data in these examples are again the average cancer mortalities from the WHO, however, this time also for non-European countries. In the top row, we show an example that averages over overlapping regions, but does not apply a weighting to these regions. This corresponds to a sliding window of a fixed size that counts for each position of the window the number of data points within this window, and discards all other data points outside. In `R`, this can be obtained by using the function *density()* and specifying `rectangular` for the option `kernel`. The size of the window is specified by the option `bw` (band width). One can see that for `bw=0.5`, the resulting density plot is much more rugged than for `bw=5`, hence, this option allows a smoothing of the plot.

In the bottom row in Figure 7.10, we show examples, which additionally invoke a weighting of the data points. For these examples, we used a normal distribution (`kernel="gaussian"`). In Figure 7.11, we depict the principle idea that underlies the weighted averaging. In this figure, a normal distribution with a mean value of $\mu = m.k = 175$ and a standard deviation of $\sigma = sd.k = 10$ (given formally by

$$f(x) = \frac{1}{\sqrt{2\pi}\sigma} \exp\left(-\frac{(x-\mu)^2}{2\sigma^2}\right), \quad -\infty \leq x \leq \infty, \tag{7.1}$$

and discussed in detail in Chapter 17) is shown. The mean value $m.k$ is highlighted by the red vertical line to indicate the current position of the averaging. The averaging itself involves all data points, however, the weight is proportional to the density of the normal distribution for the given values of $m.k$ and $sd.k$.

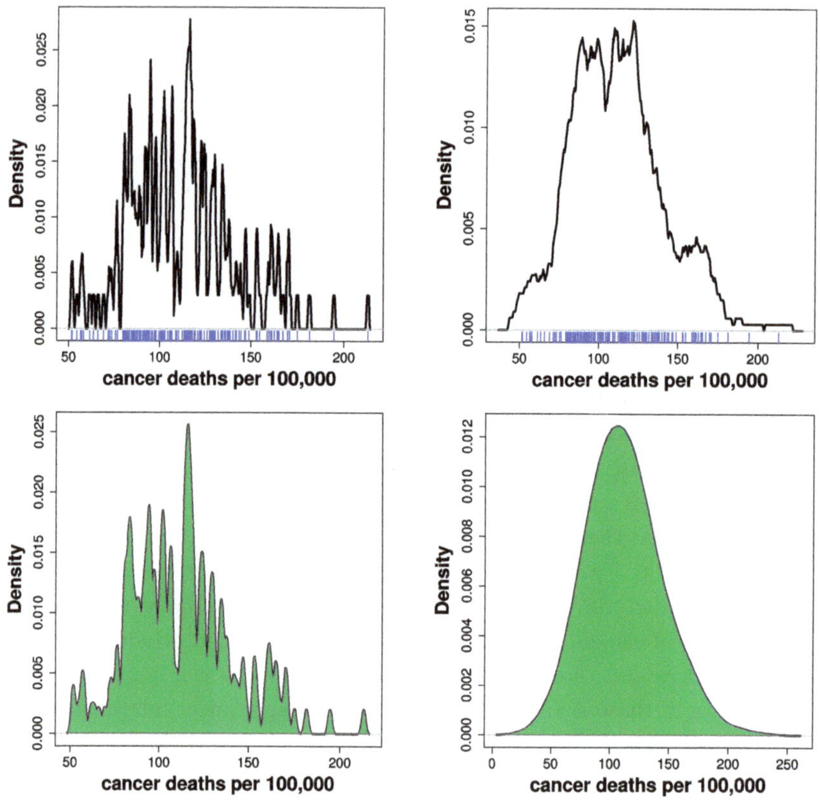

Figure 7.10: Density plots for cancer mortality worldwide. Data are from the WHO. Top row: Averaged over overlapping regions. Bottom row: Averaged and weighted over overlapping regions.

Listing 7.13: Example of density plots, see Figure 7.10

```
num <- dat.who.ave[,2]
# Top row, Left
d <- density(num, kernel="rectangular", bw=0.5)
h <- hist(num, 20, plot=F)
par(mar=c(5,5,1,1))
plot(d, main="", xlab="cancer deaths per 100,000", font.lab=2,
cex.lab=2.0, cex.axis=1.4, lwd=4)
rug(num, lwd=2, col="blue")
# Top row, Right
d <- density(num, kernel="rectangular", bw=5)
h <- hist(num, 20, plot=F)
par(mar=c(5,5,1,1))
plot(d, main="", xlab="cancer deaths per 100,000", font.lab=2,
cex.lab=2.0, cex.axis=1.4, lwd=4)
rug(num, lwd=2, col="blue")
# Bottom row, Left
num <- dat.who.ave[,2]
d <- density(num, kernel="gaussian", bw=1)
par(mar=c(5,5,1,1))
```

```
plot(d, main="", xlab="cancer deaths per 100,000", font.lab=2,
cex.lab=2.0, cex.axis=1.4, lwd=4)
polygon(d, col="green", border="gray50")
# Bottom row, Right
num <- dat.who.ave[,2]
d <- density(num, kernel="gaussian", bw=16)
par(mar=c(5,5,1,1))
plot(d, main="", xlab="cancer deaths per 100,000", font.lab=2,
cex.lab=2.0, cex.axis=1.4, lwd=4)
polygon(d, col="green", border="gray50")
```

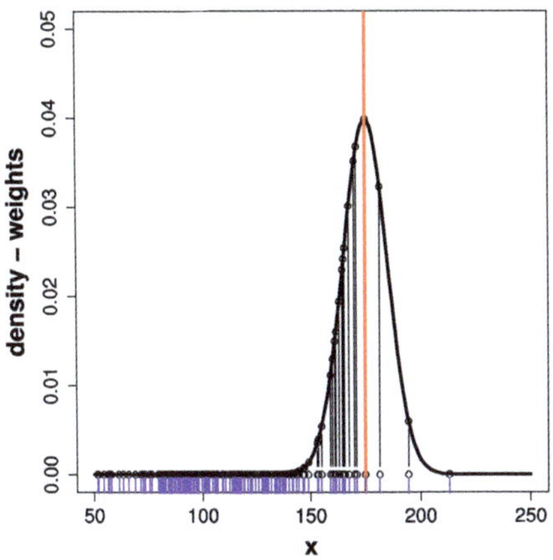

Figure 7.11: Principle idea of the sliding window assigning weights to data points.

In order to emphasize that different data points contribute differently, we added vertical lines of different length, according to the density values above these data points. Hence, the value for $m.k$ is proportional to the sum of all values weighted by the density at the data points, resulting in

$$v(m.k) = \sum_{i}^{L} f\big(\text{num}(i); m.k, sd.k\big). \tag{7.2}$$

Here, L is the total number of data points and $num(i)$ is the number of data points in window i. In this way, for each position along the x-axis, the value $v(m.k)$ is evaluated by changing the values of $m.k$.

The corresponding results are shown in the Figure 7.10 (bottom row). Again, depending on the value of the band width (`bw`), the obtained density plots can be smoothed. For the normal distribution, the parameter `bw` changes the standard deviation, making the normal distribution broader for larger values.

We would like to finish this section by mentioning that the above discussion focused on the graphical meaning of density plots and their underlying idea. However, it is important to note that the quantitative estimation of the probability density of a given data set is an important statistical problem in its own right.

Listing 7.14: Example of density plots, see Figure 7.11

```
num <- dat.who.ave[,2]
L <- length(num)
x <- seq(50, 250, 1)
m.k <- 175
sd.k <- 10
y <- dnorm(x, m.k, sd.k)
d.rnorm <- dnorm(num, m.k, sd.k)

plot(x, y, type="l", lwd=4, ylim=c(0,0.05),
ylab="density - weights", font.lab=2, cex.lab=2.0,
cex.axis=1.4)
for(i in 1:L){
  lines(c(num[i],num[i]), c(0,d.rnorm[i]), type="b")
}
abline(v=m.k, lwd=4, col="red")
rug(num, lwd=2, col="blue")
```

7.8 Combining a scatterplot with histograms: the layout function

R provides a very powerful command that allows to combine different plot functions with each other. This command is the *layout()* function. Basically, the function *layout()* enables the partition of a figure into different sections where different plots can be places. The option `mat` allows to define such a separation by choosing an integer number for each section where we want to place a plot in. In the example below, we split the whole figure into 4 regions, but we would like to put plots in only 3 of them. The integer number corresponds to the order in which these regions are plotted. In our example, the first plot is placed in the bottom-left region.

In addition to the partitioning of the figure itself, we need also to specify what width and height these regions should have. For instance, in the example below, we use a relative width of 3 to 1 for regions $(2, 1)$ to $(0, 3)$. By using the function *layout.show(lla)*, we can display the defined regions explicitly in order to see if the ratios are as desired.

Finally, we needs to make sure that the different plots we uses do actually go over the same range of the x-axis. Here, we guarantee this by providing the break points of the histograms explicitly.

Listing 7.15: Combining a scatterplot with histograms, see Figure 7.12

```
n <- 1000; v1 <- -3.1; v2 <- 6;nb <- seq(v1,v2,0.2)
x <- rnorm(n,1,1); y <- x + rnorm(n,0,0.4)
hx <- hist(x, breaks=nb, plot=F)
hy <- hist(y, breaks=nb, plot=F)
mc <- max(c(hx$density, hy$density))
lla <- layout(mat=matrix(c(2,1,0,3),ncol=2,nrow=2),
widths=c(3,1), heights=c(1,3), respect=T)
plot(x, y, xlim=range(x), ylim=c(v1,v2), xlab="x", ylab="y",
```

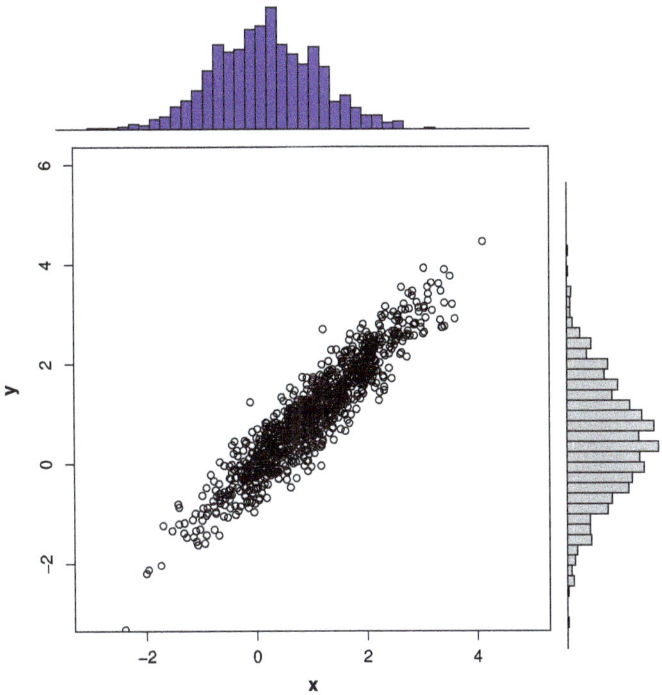

Figure 7.12: Combining a scatterplot with histograms of its x- and y-components.

```
cex.lab=2.2, cex.axis=1.4, font.lab=2)
par(mar=c(1,3,0,0))
barplot(hx$density, axes=F, ylim=c(0,mc), space=0, col="blue")
par(mar=c(3,1,1,1))
barplot(hy$density, axes=F, xlim=c(0,mc), space=0, horiz=T)
```

In this way, we can create very complex figures that carry a lot of information.

7.9 Three-dimensional plots

The visualization capability of R is not limited to one- and two-dimensional plots. It is also possible to create three-dimensional visualizations. The example below shows an application of the command *persp()* for visualizing the density of a two-dimensional normal distribution.

Listing 7.16: Three-dimensional basic plot, see Figure 7.13

```
n <- 2; L <- 50; v <- 1.5
S <- matrix(0, nrow=n, ncol=n)
diag(S) <- v^2
S.i <- solve(S)
x <- seq(-5, 5, length = L); y <- x
```

```
z <- matrix(0, nrow=L, ncol=L)
for(i in 1:L){
  for(j in 1:L){
    z[i,j] <- 1/(sqrt((2*pi)^2 * det(S))) *
exp(- c(x[i],y[j]) %*% S.i %*% c(x[i],y[j])/2)
  }
}
par(mar=c(3,3,0,0))
persp(x, y, z, theta = 30, phi = 30, expand = 0.5,
col = "purple", ltheta = 120, shade = 0.75,
ticktype = "detailed", xlab = "X", ylab = "Y",
zlab = "Z - density", cex.lab=1.9, font.lab=2)
```

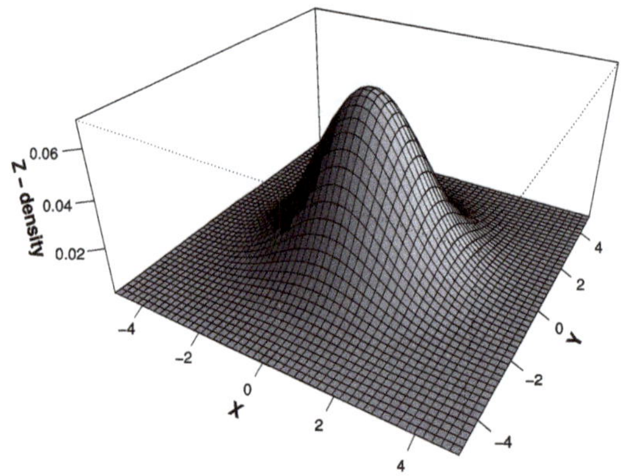

Figure 7.13: A three-dimensional visualization of the two-dimensional normal distribution.

7.10 Contour and image plots

Alternatives to three-dimensional plots, available in R, include *contour maps* and *image plots*. Such plots are projects of thee-dimensional plots to a two-dimensional canvas.

Listing 7.17: Contour and image plots, see Figure 7.14

```
# Left
z2 <- z + matrix(rnorm(L*L, 0, 0.001), nrow=L, ncol=L)
par(mar=c(5,5,1,1))
contour(x, y, z2, xlab = "X", ylab = "Y", cex.lab=1.9,
font.lab=2, levels=seq(0, 1, by=0.01), col=rainbow(10))

# Right
par(mar=c(5,5,1,1))
image(x, y, z2, col=terrain.colors(10), xlab = "X",
ylab = "Y", cex.lab=1.9, font.lab=2)
```

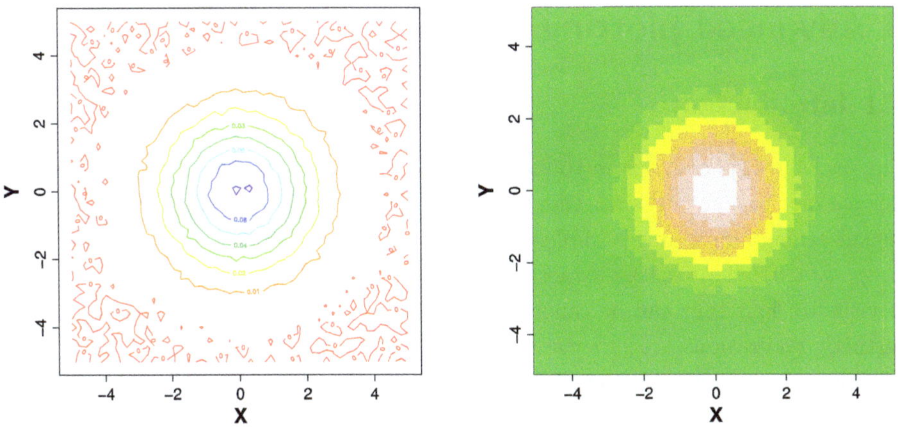

Figure 7.14: Examples for a contour (Left) and an image plot (Right) of a normal distribution.

7.11 Summary

Despite the fact that all of the commands discussed in this chapter are part of the base installation of R, they provide a vast variety of options for the visualization of data, as we have seen in the last sections. All extension packages either address specific problems, e. g., for the visualization of networks, or for providing different visual aesthetics.

8 Advanced plotting functions: ggplot2

8.1 Introduction

The package **ggplot2** was introduced by Hadley Wickham [200]. The difference of this package to many others is that it does not only provide a set of commands for the visualization of data, but it implements Leland Wilkinson's idea of the *Grammar of Graphics* [204]. This makes it more flexible, allowing to create many different kinds of visualizations that can be tailored in a problem-specific manner. In addition, its aesthetic realizations are superb.

The **ggplot2** package is available from the CRAN repository and can be installed and loaded into an R session by

Listing 8.1: Installing the package ggplot2

```
install.packages("ggplot2")
library("ggplot2")
```

There are two main plotting functions provided by the **ggplot2** package:

- *qplot():* for quick plots
- *ggplot():* allows the control of everything (grammar of graphics)

In this chapter, we discuss both of these plotting functions.

8.2 *qplot()*

The function *qplot()* is similar to the basic plot function in R. The q in front of plot stands for "quick", in the way that it does not allow getting access to the full potential provided by the package **ggplot2**. The full potential is accessible via **ggplot**, discussed in Section 8.3.

To demonstrate the functionality of *qplot()*, we use the penguin data provided in the package **FlexParamCurve**.

Listing 8.2: Installing the package FlexParamCurve and loading the data

```
install.packages("FlexParamCurve")
library("FlexParamCurve")
data(penguin.data)
```

The **penguin.data** data frame has 2244 rows and 11 columns of the measured masses for little penguin chicks between 13 and 74 days of age (see [33]).

In Figure 8.1, we show the basic functionality of *qplot()*, generating a scatter plot using the following script:

https://doi.org/10.1515/9783110796063-008

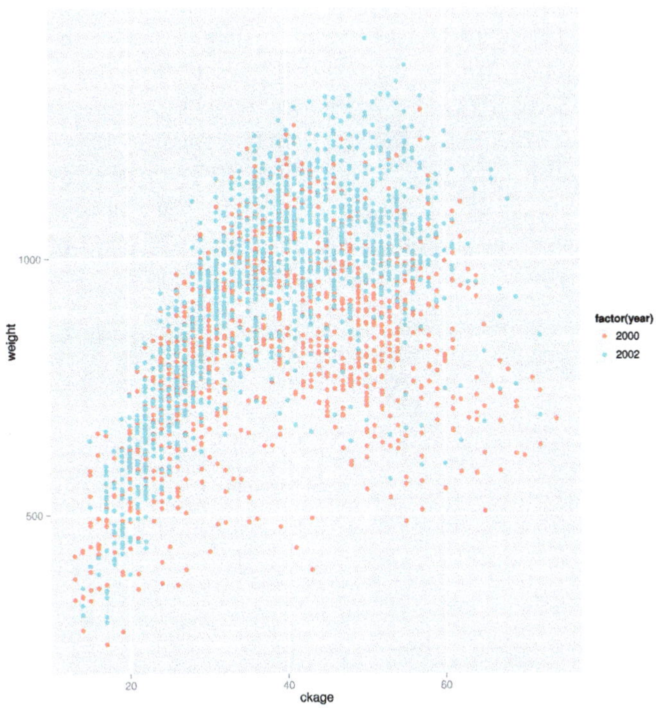

Figure 8.1: Example of a scatter plot for multiple data sets using *qplot()*.

Listing 8.3: Simple example for *qplot()*, see Figure 8.1

```
qplot(ckage, weight, data = penguin.data,  geom=c("point"),
     color=factor(year))
```

Similar to the base plot function in R, we first specify the values for the x and y coordinates using the column names in the data file penguin.data. The geom option defines the geometry of the object. Here, we chose "point" to produce a scatter plot for all data points (x_i, y_i). Other options are given in Table 8.1. The last option we

Table 8.1: Examples for different options for qplot.

Option for geom	Description
point	scatterplot
line	connects ordered data points by a line
smooth	smoothed line between data points
path	connects data point by a line in the order provided by data
step	step function
histogram	histogram
boxplot	boxplot

use is `color` to allow different colors for the observation points depending on the year the observation has been made. We use the function "factor" to indicate that the values of the variable "year" are only used as categorical variable. The aesthetics command `I()` can be used to set the color of the data points manually.

In order to further distinguish data points from each other, one can use the `shape` option using the factor `ck` for the hatching order. Because this can lead to a crowded visualization, *qplot()* offers the additional option `facets`. The effect of this option is shown in Figure 8.2.

Listing 8.4: An example for the usage of facets, see Figure 8.2

```
qplot(ckage, weight, data =penguin.data,  geom=c("point"),
    color=factor(year), facets = ~ck)
```

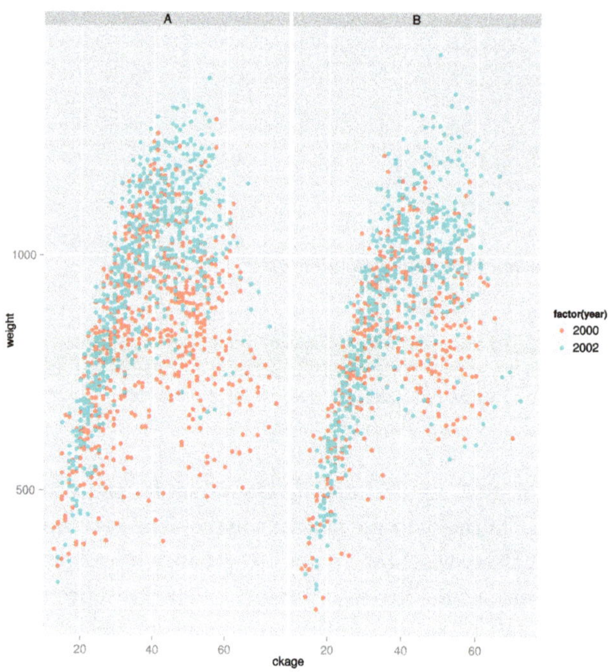

Figure 8.2: An example for the usage of facets.

The two columns in Figure 8.2 are labeled **A** and **B**, corresponding to the factors of the `ck` variable indicating first hatched (**A**), and second hatched (**B**).

Next, we visualize the effect of the option value `smooth` for `geom`.

Listing 8.5: An example for smoothing data, see Figure 8.3

```
qplot(ckage, weight, data =penguin.data[1:10,],  geom=c("point",
    "smooth"))
```

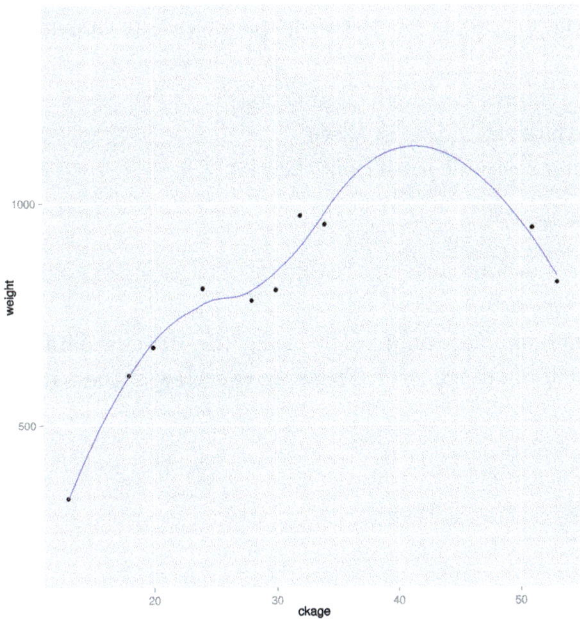

Figure 8.3: An example for smoothing data with *qplot()*.

For this, we use only the first 10 observation points. As we can see in Figure 8.3, in addition to these 10 data points, there is a smooth curve added as a result from the smoothing function. We would like to note that here, we used a vector to define the option `geom`, because we wanted to show the data points in addition to the smooth curve.

Similar to the base plot function in `R`, there are options available to enhance the visual appearance of a plot. Table 8.2 shows some additional options to enhance plots.

8.3 *ggplot()*

The underlying idea of the function *ggplot()* is to construct a figure according to a certain grammar that allows adding the desired components, features, and aspects

Table 8.2: Further options to improve the visual appearance of a plot for *qplot()*.

`Option`	**Description**
`xlim, ylim`	limits for the axes, e. g., xlim=c(-5, 5)
`log`	character vector indicating logged axes, e. g., log="x" or log="xy"
`main`	main title for the plot
`xlab, ylab`	labels for the x- and y-axes

to a figure and then generate the final plot. Each of such components is added as a layer to the plot.

The base function *ggplot()* requires two input arguments:

- `data`: a data frame of the data set to be visualized
- `aes()`: a function containing aesthetic settings of the plot

8.3.1 Simple examples

In the following, we study some simple examples by using the **`Orange`** data set containing data about the growth of orange trees. To get an overview of these data, we show the first lines.

```
> head(Orange)
Grouped Data: circumference ~ age | Tree
  Tree  age circumference
1    1  118            30
2    1  484            58
3    1  664            87
4    1 1004           115
5    1 1231           120
6    1 1372           142
```

The data set contains only three variables (tree, age, and circumference), whereas the variable "Tree" is an indicator variable for a particular tree.

Listing 8.6: Example of a data plot with `ggplot`, see Figure 8.4 (Left)

```
data(Orange)
ggplot(data=Orange, aes(age, circumference)) + geom_point()
```

In order to plot any figure, we need to use the *ggplot()* command, and specify how we want to plot these data by providing information about the geometry. In the above case, we just want to plot the circumference of the trees as a function of their age by means of points, see Figure 8.4 (Left). The same result can be obtained by splitting the whole command into separate parts as follows:

Listing 8.7: A simple point plot with `ggplot()`, see Figure 8.4 (Left)

```
p <- ggplot(data=Orange, aes(age, circumference))
p + geom_point()
```

In order to demonstrate the working principle of the different layers, we improve the visual appearance of the above plot by setting a variety of different options.

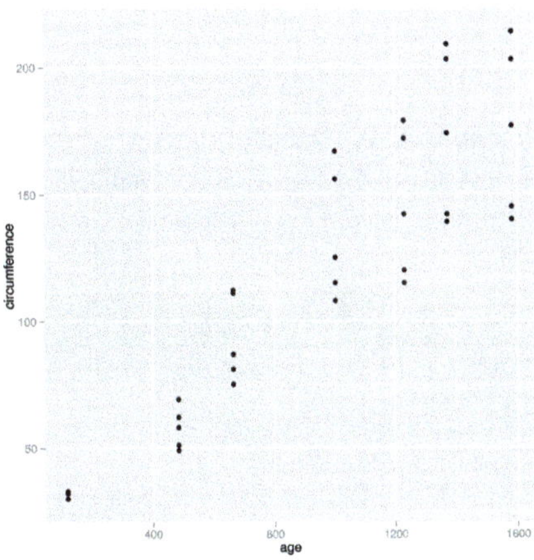

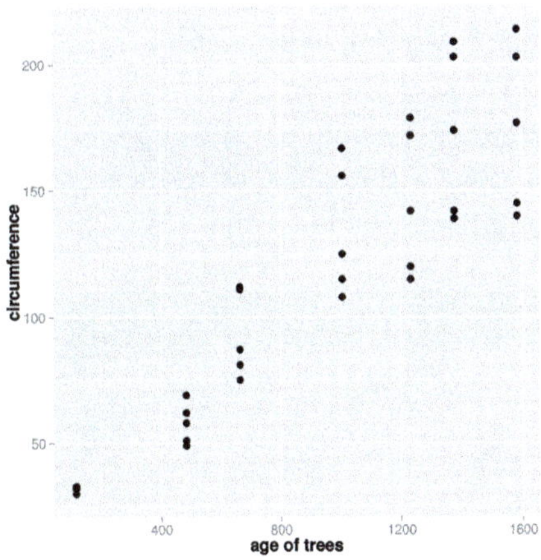

Figure 8.4: Examples for point plots. Left: Base functionality without setting options. Right: Modified point size.

Listing 8.8: Improved point plot with ggplot, see Figure 8.4 (Right)

```
p <- ggplot(Orange, aes(age, circumference))
p <- p + geom_point(size=3) + scale_x_continuous(name="age of
    trees")
p <- p + theme(axis.text.x=element_text(size=12),
    axis.title.x=element_text(size=15, face="bold"))
p <- p + theme(axis.text.y=element_text(size=12),
    axis.title.y=element_text(size=15, face="bold"))
p
```

The corresponding result is shown in Figure 8.4 (Right). For this plot we involved three different layers, namely

- `geoms`: controls the geometrical objects
- `scales`: controls the mapping between data and aesthetics
- `themes`: controls nondata components of the plot

by setting options for the following functions:

- *geom_point()*
- *scale_x_continuous()*
- *theme()*

The meaning of the available options is rather intuitive, if we know all options available. This information can be acquired from the manual of *ggplot()*, which is quite extensive.

8.3.2 Multiple data sets

Beyond the simple usage of *ggplot()* demonstrated above, the combination of many options within different layers becomes quickly involved. In Figure 8.5, we show two additional examples that highlight the presence of multiple data sets.

Listing 8.9: A plot with multiple points, see Figure 8.5 (Left)

```
p <- ggplot(Orange, aes(age, circumference, color=Tree))
p <- p + geom_point(size=3, aes(shape=Tree)) +
    scale_x_continuous(name="age of trees")
p <- p + theme(axis.text.x=element_text(size=12),
    axis.title.x=element_text(size=15, face="bold"))
p <- p + theme(axis.text.y=element_text(size=12),
    axis.title.y=element_text(size=15, face="bold"))
p
```

By adding the option `color` to the function *aes()* in *ggplot()*, different colors will be assigned to different factors, as given by `Orange$Tree`, and a figure legend will be automatically generated. Specifying the types of the `shape` for the data points will, in addition, assign different point shapes corresponding to the different trees.

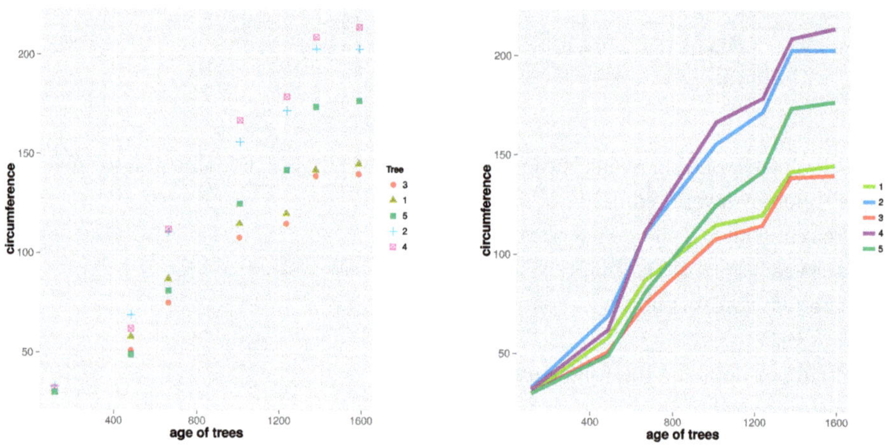

Figure 8.5: Examples of multiple data sets plotted using *ggplot()*.

In Figure 8.5 (Right), we provide an example using *geom_line()* instead of *geom_point()*. This displays the connected points in form of different lines for the different trees.

Listing 8.10: A plot with multiple lines, see Figure 8.5 (Right)

```
ind <- order(as.numeric(levels(Orange$Tree)))
```

```
Tree2 <- factor(Orange$Tree, levels=levels(Orange$Tree)[ind],
    ordered=T)
df <- data.frame(Orange, Tree2)
p <- ggplot(df, aes(age, circumference, color=Tree2))
p <- p + geom_line(size=2, aes(shape=Tree2))
p <- p + scale_x_continuous(name="age of trees")
p <- p + theme(axis.text.x=element_text(size=12),
    axis.title.x=element_text(size=15, face="bold"))
p <- p + theme(axis.text.y=element_text(size=12),
    axis.title.y=element_text(size=15, face="bold"))
p <- p + scale_colour_manual("", values = c("1" = "olivedrab3", "2"
    = "dodgerblue1", "3" = "indianred2", "4" = "purple", "5" =
    "mediumseagreen"))
p
```

Furthermore, we rearranged the 5 trees in the legend in their numerical order. This is a bit tricky, because there is no option available that would allow to do this directly. Instead, it is necessary to provide this information for the different factors, by generating a new factor `Tree2` that contains this information.

Before we continue, we would like to comment on the logic behind *ggplot()* used to add either multiple points or lines to a plot. In contrast to the basic plotting function *plot()* discussed in Chapter 7.1.1, which adds multiple data sets successively by, e. g., using the *lines()* command, *ggplot()* can accomplish this by setting an option (shape). However, this requires the data frame to contain information about this in the form of an indicator variable (in our case "Tree"). Hence, the simplification in the commands for multiple lines needs to be compensated by a more complex data frame. This can be in fact nontrivial.

The good news is that it is possible to use *ggplot()* in the same logical way as the basic plotting function. An example for this is shown in Listing 8.11.

Listing 8.11: Using multiple data frames to plot multiple lines.

```
df1 <- data.frame(X = Orange[1:7,2], Y = Orange[1:7,3])
df2 <- data.frame(X = Orange[8:14,2], Y = Orange[8:14,3])

gg <- ggplot()
gg <- gg + geom_line(data=df1, aes(x=X,y=Y), size=1.5,
    color='purple')
gg <- gg + geom_line(data=df2, aes(x=X,y=Y), size=1.5,
    color='green')

print(gg)
```

For the shown example in Listing 8.11, there is certainly no advantage in using *ggplot()* in this way, because a data frame with the required information exists already. However, if one has two separate pairs of data in the form $D_i = \{(x_i, y_i)\}$ available, the advantage becomes apparent.

8.3.3 *geoms()*

There is a total of 37 different *geom()* functions available to specify the geometry of plotted data. So far, we used only *geom_point()* and *geom_line()*. In the following, we will discuss some additional functions listed below.

In Table 8.3, we list *geom()* functions with their counterpart in the R base package.

Table 8.3: Functions associated with *ggplot()* and *geom()* and their corresponding counter parts in the R base package.

ggplot function	Base plot function
geom_point()	*points()*
geom_line()	*lines()*
geom_curve()	*curve()*
geom_hline()	*hline()*
geom_vline()	*vline()*
geom_rug()	*rug()*
geom_text()	*text()*
geom_smooth(method = "lm")	*abline(lm(y x))*
geom_density()	*lines(density(x))*
geom_smooth()	*lines(loess(x, y))*
geom_boxplot()	*boxplot()*

Additional ***geom*** functions include:
- *geom_bar()*
- *geom_dotplot()*
- *geom_errorbar()*
- *geom_jitter()*
- *geom_raster()*
- *geom_step()*
- *geom_tile()*

For adding straight lines into a plot, we can use the functions *geom_abline()* and *geom_vline()*, see Figure 8.6 (Left). Because a straight line is fully specified by an intercept and a slop, these two options need to be set for *geom_abline()*. If we use a zero slop, we obtain a horizontal line. For adding vertical lines, the function *geom_vline()* can be used, specifying the option `xintercept`. In addition, both functions allow setting a variety of additional options, to change the visual appearance of the lines. For example, valid `linetype` values include `solid`, `dashed`, `dotted`, `dashdot`, `longdash`, and `twodash`.

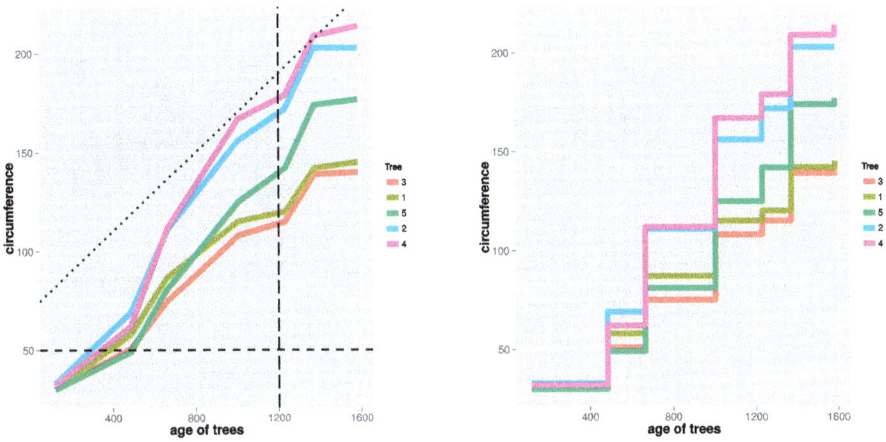

Figure 8.6: Examples using *geom_abline()* and *geom_vline()* (Left) and *geom_step()* (Right).

Listing 8.12: Additional modifications of a multiline plot, see Figure 8.6 (Left)

```
p <- ggplot(Orange, aes(age, circumference, color=Tree))
p <- p + geom_line(size=3) + scale_x_continuous(name="age of trees")
p <- p + theme(axis.text.x=element_text(size=12),
   axis.title.x=element_text(size=15, face="bold"))
p <- p + theme(axis.text.y=element_text(size=12),
   axis.title.y=element_text(size=15, face="bold"))
p <- p + geom_abline(intercept=70, slope=0.1, size=1,
   linetype="dotted")
p <- p + geom_abline(intercept=50, slope=0, size=1,
   linetype="dashed")
p <- p + geom_vline(xintercept=1200, size=1, linetype="longdash")
p
```

In Figure 8.6 (Right), we show an example for the *geom_step()* function. This function connects the data points by horizontal and vertical lines making it easier to recognize horizontal and vertical jumps.

Listing 8.13: An example for step functions, see Figure 8.6 (Right)

```
p <- ggplot(Orange, aes(age, circumference, color=Tree))
p <- p + geom_step(size=3) + scale_x_continuous(name="age of trees")
p <- p + theme(axis.text.x=element_text(size=12),
   axis.title.x=element_text(size=15, face="bold"))
p <- p + theme(axis.text.y=element_text(size=12),
   axis.title.y=element_text(size=15, face="bold"))
p
```

In Figure 8.7, we show examples for boxplots using the function *geom_boxplot()*. For these examples, we do not distinguish the different trees, but we are rather interested in the distribution of the circumferences of the trees at the 7 different time points of their measurement.

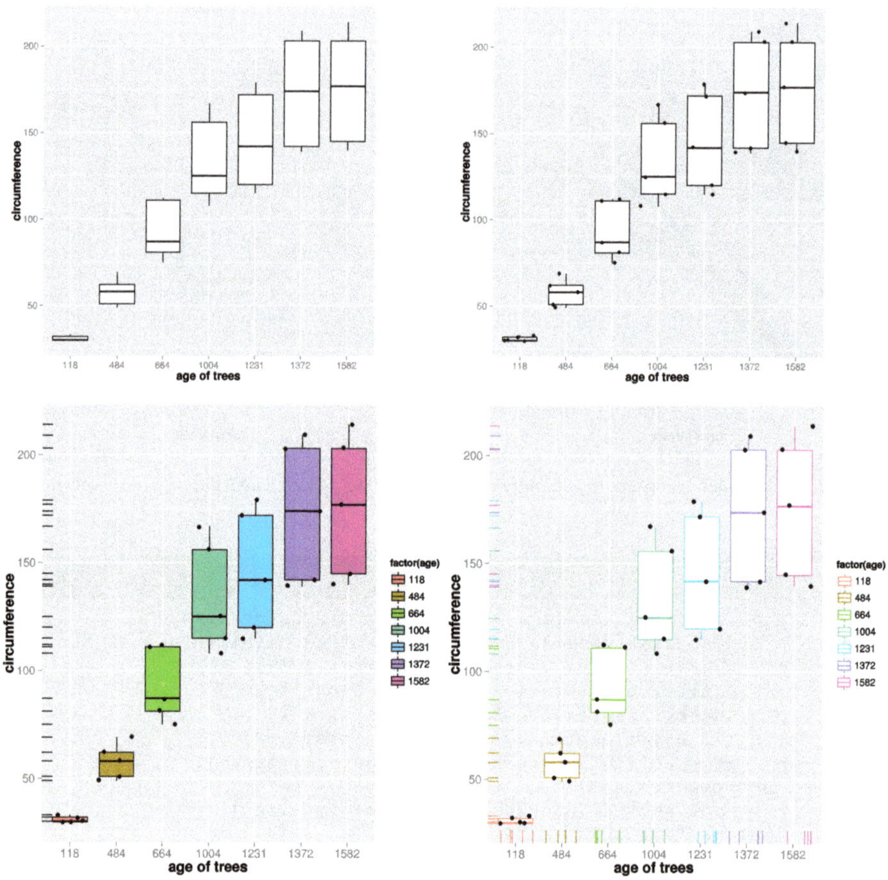

Figure 8.7: Different examples for boxplots.

In Figure 8.7 (Top row, Right), we added the original data points, for which the boxplots are assessed. In order to avoid a potential overlap between the data points, the function *geom_jitter()* can be used to introduce a slight horizontal shift to the data points. These shifts are randomly generated and, hence, different executions of this function lead to different visual arrangements of the data points.

Listing 8.14: Examples for boxplots shown in Figure 8.7 (Top row)

```
# Top-Left
p <- ggplot(Orange, aes(factor(age), circumference))
p <- p + geom_boxplot() + scale_x_discrete(name="age of trees")
p <- p + theme(axis.text.x=element_text(size=12),
    axis.title.x=element_text(size=15, face="bold"))
p <- p + theme(axis.text.y=element_text(size=12),
    axis.title.y=element_text(size=15, face="bold"))
p
```

```
# Top-Right
p <- p + geom_jitter()
p
```

Furthermore, it can be informative to add projections of the data points next to the coordinate axes. By using the function *geom_rug()*, this information can be added. Specifying the option **sides** allows to include these projections in form of dashed lines to the left (l), right (r), bottom (b) or the top (t) of the plot; see Figure 8.7 (bottom-left). Also, it is possible to color these lines according to the color of the boxplots; see Figure 8.7 (bottom-right).

Listing 8.15: Examples for boxplots shown in Figure 8.7 (Bottom row)

```
# Bottom-Left
p <- ggplot(Orange, aes(factor(age), circumference))
p <- p + geom_boxplot(aes(fill=factor(age))) +
    scale_x_discrete(name="age of trees")
p <- p + geom_jitter()
p <- p + geom_rug(sides="l")
p <- p + theme(axis.text.x=element_text(size=12),
    axis.title.x=element_text(size=15, face="bold"))
p <- p + theme(axis.text.y=element_text(size=12),
    axis.title.y=element_text(size=15, face="bold"))
p

# Bottom-Right
p <- ggplot(Orange, aes(factor(age), circumference,
    color=factor(age)))
p <- p + geom_boxplot() + scale_x_discrete(name="age of trees")
p <- p + geom_jitter(color="black")
p <- p + geom_rug(sides="bl", position='jitter')
p <- p + theme(axis.text.x=element_text(size=12),
    axis.title.x=element_text(size=15, face="bold"))
p <- p + theme(axis.text.y=element_text(size=12),
    axis.title.y=element_text(size=15, face="bold"))
p
```

8.3.4 Smoothing

In this section, we demonstrate the application of statistical functions for data smoothing. In Figure 8.8 (Top), we show two examples using the function *stat_smooth()*. For both figures, we used the "loess" method as the smoothing method. This method averages over a sliding window along the x-axis to obtain averaged values for the outcome variable, depicted by the blue line. The purpose of the application of a smoothing function is to provide a graphical regression, which summarizes data points. The option **se** corresponds to the standard error, which we disable in the left figure by setting **se=F**.

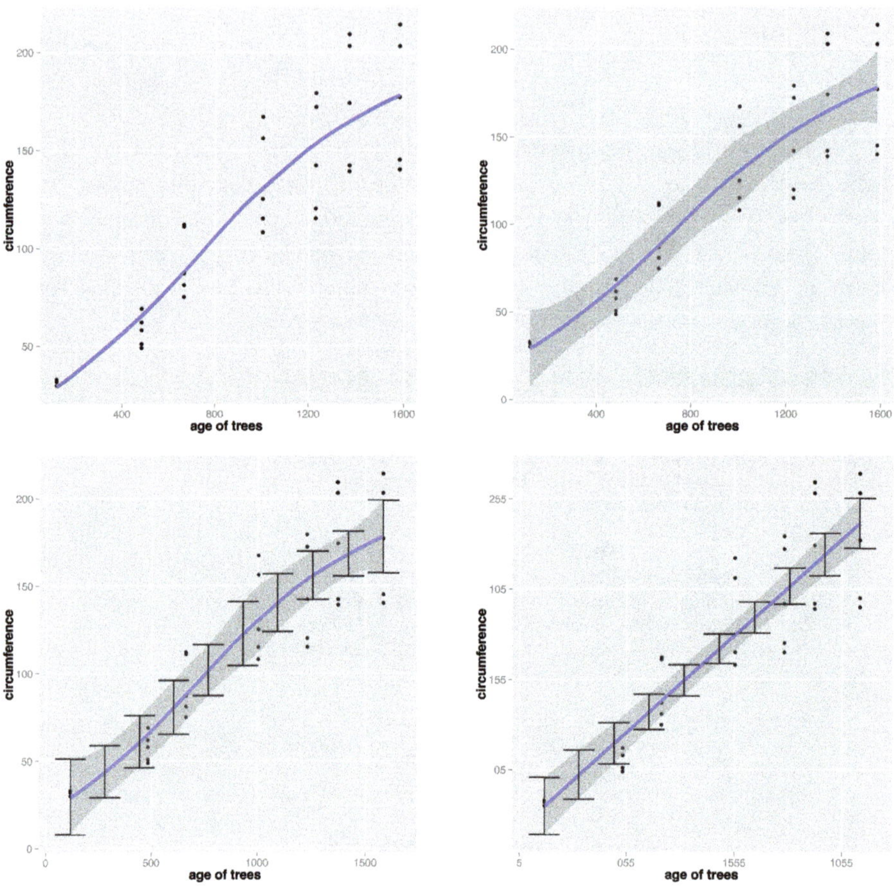

Figure 8.8: Examples for smoothing functions.

On the right figure, we add the information of the standard error in form of a gray band that underlies the loess curve. Furthermore, we set the color of this band with the `fill` option. We want to point out that by not specifying this option, the default value is to use a transparent background. Unfortunately, our experience is that this can cause problems, depending on the operating system. For this reason, setting this option explicitly is a trick to circumvent potential problems.

Listing 8.16: Some examples for data smoothing, see Figure 8.8 (Top row)

```
# Top-Left
p <- ggplot(Orange, aes(age, circumference))
p <- p + geom_point(size=2) + scale_x_continuous(name="age of
   trees")
p <- p + stat_smooth(method = "loess", se=F, size=2)
p <- p + theme(axis.text.x=element_text(size=12),
   axis.title.x=element_text(size=15, face="bold"))
```

```
p <- p + theme(axis.text.y=element_text(size=12),
    axis.title.y=element_text(size=15, face="bold"))
p

# Top-Right
p <- ggplot(Orange, aes(age, circumference))
p <- p + geom_point(size=2) + scale_x_continuous(name="age of
    trees")
p <- p + stat_smooth(method = "loess", se=T, fill="grey60", size=2)
p <- p + theme(axis.text.x=element_text(size=12),
    axis.title.x=element_text(size=15, face="bold"))
p <- p + theme(axis.text.y=element_text(size=12),
    axis.title.y=element_text(size=15, face="bold"))
p
```

Next, in Figure 8.8 (bottom-left), we add to the color band explicit error bars by using the `geom` option for *stat_smooth()*. Since we have a continuous x-axis, we need to specify the number `n` of error bars we want to add to the smoothed curve.

Finally, in Figure 8.8 (bottom-right), we show an example for a different smoothing function. In `ggplot2`, the available options are `lm` (linear model), `glm` (generalized linear model), `gam` (generalized additive model), `loess` and `rlm` (robust linear model) and in this figure we use `lm`. A linear model means that the resulting curve will be restricted to a straight line obtained from a least-squared fit.

Listing 8.17: Some examples for data smoothing, see Figure 8.8 (Bottom row)

```
# Bottom-Left
p <- ggplot(Orange, aes(age, circumference))
p <- p + geom_point(size=2) + scale_x_continuous(name="age of
    trees")
p <- p + stat_smooth(method = "loess", fill="grey60", size=2)
p <- p + stat_smooth(method="loess", geom = "errorbar", size=0.75,
    n = 10)
p <- p + theme(axis.text.x=element_text(size=12),
    axis.title.x=element_text(size=15, face="bold"))
p <- p + theme(axis.text.y=element_text(size=12),
    axis.title.y=element_text(size=15, face="bold"))
p

# Bottom-Right
p <- ggplot(Orange, aes(age, circumference))
p <- p + geom_point(size=2) + scale_x_continuous(name="age of
    trees")
p <- p + stat_smooth(method = "glm", fill="grey60", size=2)
p <- p + stat_smooth(method="glm", geom = "errorbar", size=0.75, n =
    10)
p <- p + theme(axis.text.x=element_text(size=12),
    axis.title.x=element_text(size=15, face="bold"))
p <- p + theme(axis.text.y=element_text(size=12),
    axis.title.y=element_text(size=15, face="bold"))
p
```

8.4 Summary

The purpose of this chapter was to introduce the base capabilities offered by `ggplot2` and to highlight some aesthetic extensions it offers over the basic `R` plotting functions. It is clear that the *Grammar of Graphics* offers a very rich framework with incredibly many aspects that is continuously evolving. For this reason, the best way to learn further capabilities is by following online resources, e. g., https://ggplot2.tidyverse.org/ or http://moderngraphics11.pbworks.com/f/ggplot2-Book09hWickham.pdf.

9 Visualization of networks

9.1 Introduction

In this chapter, we discuss two R packages, igraph and NetBioV [42, 187]. Both have been specifically designed to visualize networks. Nowadays, network visualization plays an important role in many fields, as they can be used to visualize complex relationships between a large number of entities. For instance, in the life sciences, various types of biological, medical, and gene networks, e. g., ecological networks, food networks, protein networks, or metabolic networks serve as a mathematical representation of ecological, molecular, and disease processes [9, 71]. Furthermore, in the social sciences and economics, networks are used to represent, e. g., acquaintance networks, consumer networks, transportation networks, or financial networks [74]. Finally, in chemistry and physics, networks are used to encode molecules, rational drugs, and complex systems [20, 55].

All these fields, and many more, benefit from a sensible visualization of networks, which enables gaining an intuitive understanding of the meaning of structural relationships between the entities within the network. Generally, such a visualization precedes a quantitative analysis and informs further research hypotheses.

9.2 igraph

In Chapter 16, we will provide a detailed introduction to networks, their definition, and their analysis. Here, we will only restate that a network consists of two basic elements, nodes and edges, and the structure of a network can be defined in two ways, by means of:

- an edge list or
- an adjacency matrix

An edge list is a two-dimensional matrix that provides, in each row, information about the connection of nodes. Specifically, an edge list contains exactly two columns and its elements correspond to the labels of the nodes. The following script provides an example:

Listing 9.1: Basic network generation

```
library(igraph)
el <- matrix(c(1,2,2,3), nrow=2, ncol=2, byrow=T)
g <- graph.edgelist(el, directed=F)

V(g)
Vertex sequence:
[1] 1 2 3
```

https://doi.org/10.1515/9783110796063-009

```
E(g)
Edge sequence:
[1] 2 -- 1
[2] 3 -- 2
```

The second command defines an edge list (`el`). The function *graph.edgelist()* converts the matrix `el` into an `igraph` object `g` representing a graph. Calling the functions ***V*** and ***E***, with `g` as argument, provides information about the vertices and the edges in the graph `g`. This is an example of a simple graph consisting of merely three nodes, labeled as 1, 2, and 3. This graph contains only two edges between the nodes 1 and 2, and nodes 2 and 3. By using the function *plot()*, the `igraph` object `g` can be visualized.

Listing 9.2: Basic network visualization, see Figure 9.1 (Top-left)

```
plot(g)
```

In Figure 9.1 (Top-left), the output of the above plot function is shown. In order to understand the effect of the option `directed` in the function *graph.edgelist()*, we show in Figure 9.1 (Top-right) an example for setting this option `TRUE`.

Listing 9.3: Basic network visualization, see Figure 9.1 (Top-right)

```
g <- graph.edgelist(el, directed=T)
plot(g)

E(g)
Edge sequence:
[1] 1 -> 2
[2] 2 -> 3
```

The result is that the edges have now arrows, pointing from one node to another. Specifically, for `directed=T`, the first column of the edge list contains information about the nodes from which an edge points toward the nodes contained in the second column.

An alternative definition of a graph can be obtained by an adjacency matrix. The following script produces exactly the same result as in Figure 9.1 (Top-left):

Listing 9.4: Basic network generation and visualization

```
am <- matrix(c(0,1,0,1,0,1,0,1,0), nrow=3, ncol=3, byrow=T)
g <- graph.adjacency(am, mode="undirected")
plot(g)
```

By setting the option `mode="directed"`, we obtain the graph in Figure 9.1 (Top-right).

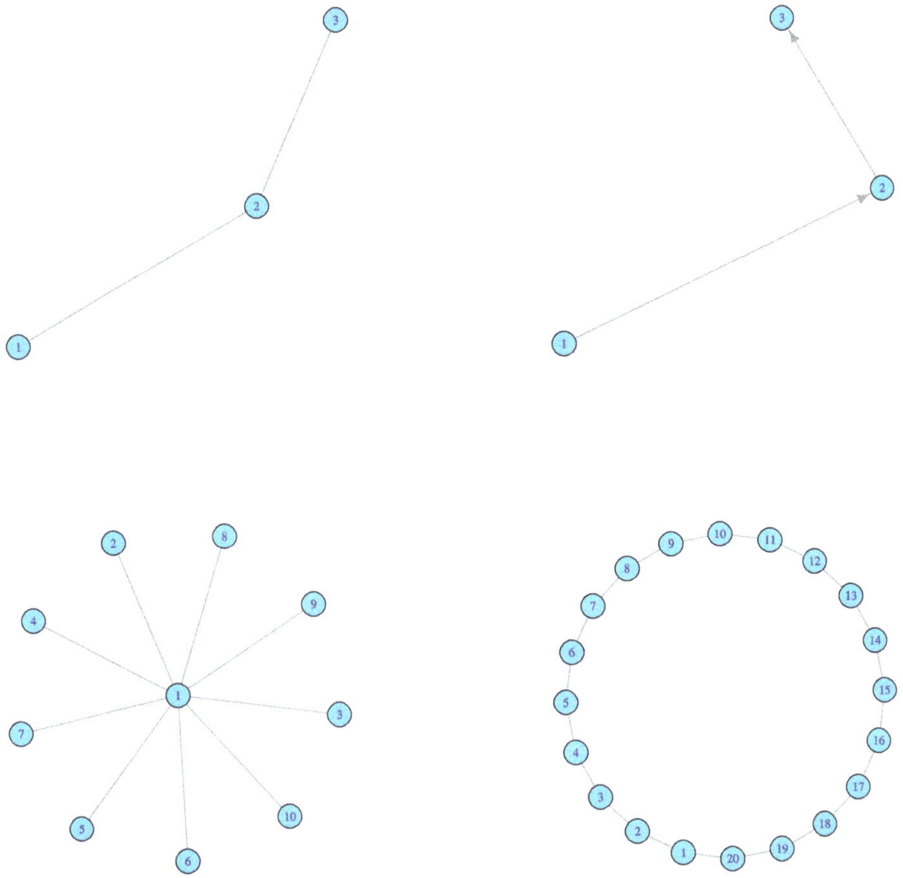

Figure 9.1: Some examples for network visualizations with `igraph`.

Here, an adjacency matrix is a binary matrix containing only zeros and ones. If node i is connected with node j, then the corresponding element (i, j) is one, otherwise it is zero. The adjacency matrix is a square matrix, meaning that the number of rows is the same as the number of columns. The number of rows corresponds to the number of nodes of the graph.

9.2.1 Generation of regular and complex networks

For the examples above, we defined the structure of a graph manually, either by defining an edge list or its adjacency matrix. However, the `igraph` package provides also a large number of functions to generate networks with certain structural properties. In Tables 9.1 and 9.2, we list some of these.

In Figure 9.1 (Bottom), we show two such examples.

Table 9.1: Examples of different regular network-types provided by `igraph`.

Type	Syntax
star	`graph.star(n, mode = c("in", "out", "mutual", "undirected"))`
lattice	`graph.lattice(length, dim, nei = 1, directed = F, mutual = F, circular = F)`
ring	`graph.ring(n, directed = F, mutual = F, circular=T)`
tree	`graph.tree(n, children = 2, mode="out")`

Table 9.2: Examples of different complex network-types provided by `igraph`.

Type	Syntax
random network	`erdos.renyi.game(n, p.or.m, type=c("gnp", "gnm"), directed = F, loops = F)`
scale-free network	`barabasi.game(n, power = 1, m)`
small-world network	`watts.strogatz.game(dim, size, nei, p, loops = F, multiple = F)`
geometric random network	`grg.game(nodes, radius, torus = F, coords = F)`

This functionality for generating such networks is very convenient because implementing network generation algorithms can be tedious.

9.2.2 Basic network attributes

There is a variety of options to change the attributes of vertices and edges. In Tables 9.3 and 9.4, we list the most important ones. Basically, the appearance of each vertex and edge can be set independently for most options. This gives a large flexibility with respect to the graphical appearance of networks, allowing to adjust a network individually.

Table 9.3: Basic vertex attributes that can be modified.

Option	Data structure	Description
`vertex.size`	numeric vector	components set the size of each vertex
`vertex.label`	character vector	components set the lable of each vertex
`vertex.label.dist`	numeric vector	components set the distance of the labels from the vertex
`vertex.color`	character vector	components set the color of each vertex
`vertex.shape`	character vector	components set the shape of each vertex

Table 9.4: Basic edge attributes that can be modified.

Option	Data structure	Description
edge.color	character vector	components set the color of each edge
edge.width	numeric value	same width for every edge
edge.lty	numeric vector	0 ("no line"), 1 "solid", 2 ("dashed"), 3 ("dotted"), 4 ("dotdash"), 5 ("longdash"), 6 ("twodash")
edge.label	character vector	components set the label of each edge
edge.label.cex	numeric value	size of the edge labels
edge.label.color	character vector	components set the color of each edge
edge.curved	logic or numeric vector	if logic values, "true" draws curved edges; if numeric values specify the curvature of the edge, zero curvature means straight edges, negative values mean the edge bends clockwise, whereas positive values mean the opposite
edge.arrow.mode	numeric vector	0 (no arrow), 1 (backward arrow), 2 (forward arrow), 3 (both)

Figure 9.2 illustrates the outputs from network visualization when modifying the vertex and edge attributes.

Although, in principle, the attributes for each vertex and edge can be set independently by specifying a numeric or character vector, this is not necessary in the case where the attributes have to be identical for all vertices or edges. Then, it is sufficient to provide a scalar numeric or character value to set the option throughout the network.

Listing 9.5: Advanced network visualization, see Figure 9.2

```
L <- 10 # length(shapes())
g <- graph.ring(L)

# Top-left
vs <- round(seq(1, 2*L, length.out=L))
vc <- heat.colors(L)
plot(g, vertex.size=vs, vertex.label=as.character(vs),
    vertex.label.dist=1.3, vertex.color=vc)

# Top-right
vsh <- c(rep("circle", L-2), rep("pie", 2))
v.pie <- as.pairlist(rep(0, L))
v.pie[[L-1]] <-c(3,2,6); v.pie[[L]] <- c(5,3,5,2,5)
v.pie.col <- list(c("black", "blue", "red", "green", "yellow"))
plot(g, vertex.size=vs, vertex.label=as.character(vs),
    vertex.label.dist=1.3, vertex.color=vc, vertex.shape=vsh,
    vertex.pie=v.pie, vertex.pie.color=v.pie.col)

# Bottom-left
v.shapes <- vertex.shapes()
plot(g, vertex.shape=v.shapes, vertex.label=v.shapes,
    vertex.label.dist=1.2,
```

```
        vertex.size=20, vertex.color="green",
        vertex.pie=lapply(shapes(), function(x) if (x=="pie") c(1,4,2)
            else 0), vertex.pie.color=list(heat.colors(5)))

# Bottom-right
el <- as.character(1:L)
elc <- seq(1,5, length.out=L)
elcol <- terrain.colors(L)
ec <- sample(c(0,-0.5, 0.5), replace=T, L)
eam <-  sample(c(0,1,2,3), replace=T, L)
plot(g, vertex.label="", edge.label=el, edge.label.cex=elc,
    edge.label.color=elcol, edge.curved=ec, edge.arrow.mode=eam)
```

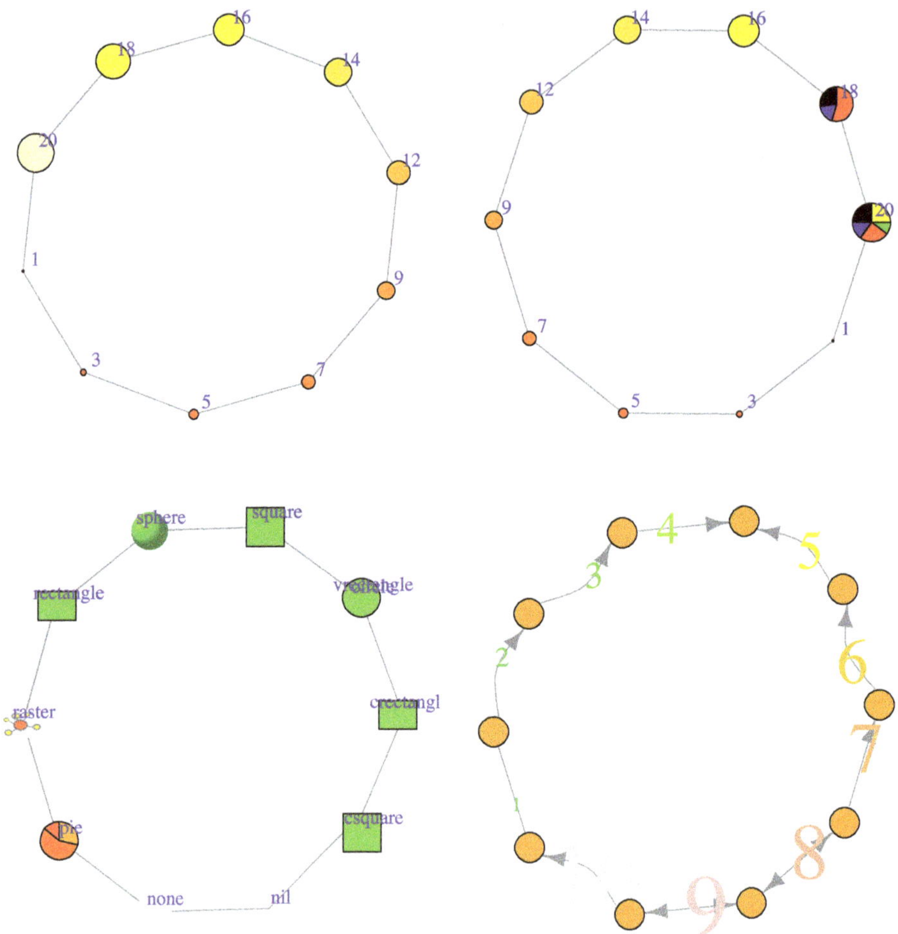

Figure 9.2: Examples demonstrating vertex and edge attributes.

9.2.3 Layout styles

It is important to realize that a network is a topological object, and not a geometric one. That means, by defining an edge list or an adjacency matrix of a network, its structure is defined. However, this does not provide any information regarding the graphical visualization of the networks. Therefore, for a given adjacency matrix, the spacial coordinates of the nodes of a network are not part of the definition of a network, but they are part of its graphical visualization. In order to make this important point more clear, we provide, in Figure 9.3, four different graphical visualizations of the same network.

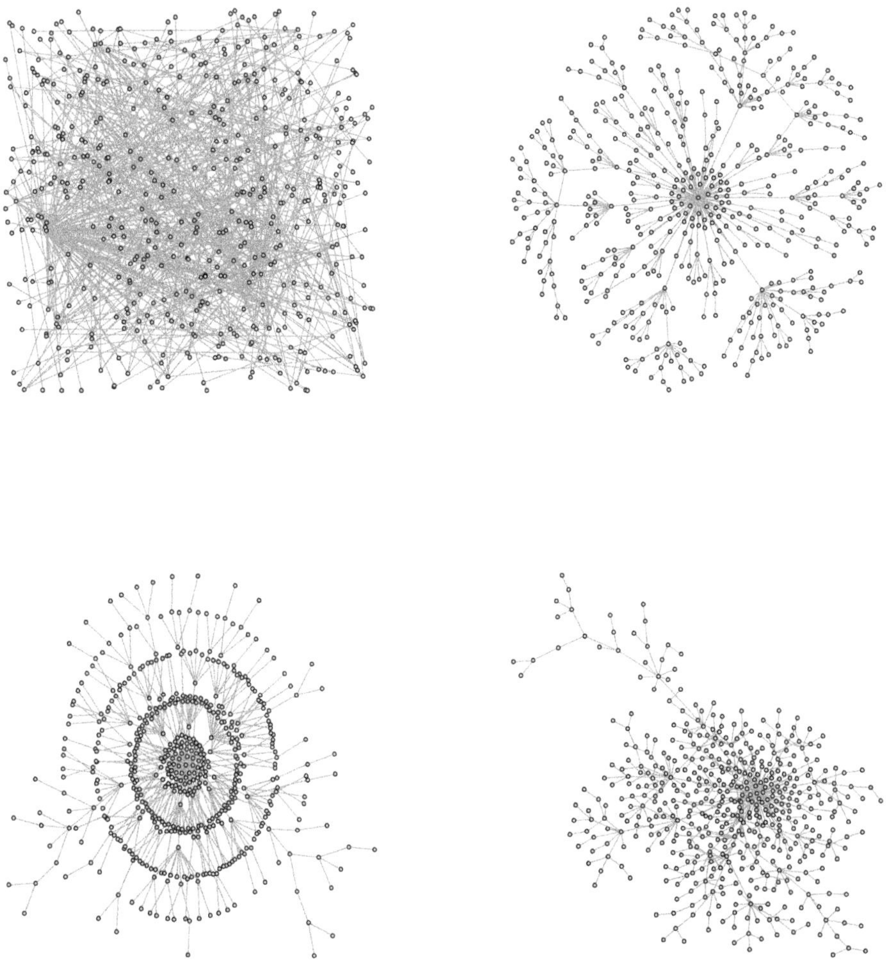

Figure 9.3: Effect of different layout functions to generate the cartesian coordinates of the nodes of a network. Importantly, for all cases the same network is used.

Specifically, we generate a scale-free network with $n = 500$ nodes and use four different layout functions to generate the cartesian coordinates for the nodes of this network.

Listing 9.6: Effect of network layouts, see Figure 9.3

```
n <- 500
m <- 1
g <- barabasi.game(n, power = 1, m, directed=F)

la1 <- layout.random(g)
plot(g, vertex.size=2, vertex.label=NA, layout=la1)

la2 <- layout.fruchterman.reingold(g)
plot(g, vertex.size=2, vertex.label=NA, layout=la2)

la3 <- layout.kamada.kawai(g)
plot(g, vertex.size=2, vertex.label=NA, layout=la3)

la4 <- layout.lgl(g)
plot(g, vertex.size=2, vertex.label=NA, layout=la4)
```

It is clear from Figure 9.3, that depending on the used algorithm to generate the cartesian coordinates, the same network "looks" quite different. The coordinates, contained in `la1` to `la4`, are represented in the form of a matrix with n rows (the number of nodes) and 2 columns (corresponding to the x and y coordinates of a node). That means, the x- and y-coordinates of the nodes are used to place the nodes of the network onto a 2-dimensional plane, as shown in Figure 9.3.

The reason why all four layout styles result in different coordinates is that any layout style is in fact an optimization algorithm. And each of these optimization algorithms uses a different optimization function. For example, `layout.fruchterman.reingold` and `layout.kamada.kawai` are two force-based algorithms proposed by Fruchterman & Reingold and Kamada & Kawai [82, 106] that optimize the distance between the nodes in a way similar to spring forces. In contrast, `layout.random` chooses random positions for the x- and y-coordinates. Hence, it is the only layout style among those illustrated that is not based on an optimization algorithm.

An important lesson from the above examples is that for a given network, the graphical visualization is not trivial, but requires additional work to select a layout style that corresponds best to the intended expectations of the user.

9.2.4 Plotting networks

There are two possible ways to plot an `igraph` object `g` representing a graph. The first option is to use the function *plot()*. This option has been used in the previous examples. The second option is to use the function *tkplot()*. In contrast with the function *plot()*, the function *tkplot()* allows the user to change the position of the vertices interactively by providing a graphical user interface (GUI). Hence, this can be done by means of the computer mouse.

Listing 9.7: Alternative plotting functions

```
plot(g)
tkplot(g)
```

At first glance, the function *tkplot()* function may appear superior, because of its interactive capability. However, for large networks, i. e., networks with more than 50 vertices, it is hardly possible to adjust the position for each vertex manually. That means, practically, the utility of *tkplot()* is rather limited because only small networks can be adjusted. A second argument against the usage of *tkplot()* is that due to the involvement of a graphical user interface, there may be operating system specific problems caused by the usage of TK libraries. Basically, such TK libraries are freely available for all common operating systems, however, some systems may require these libraries to be installed when they are not available.

9.2.5 Analyzing and manipulating networks

In addition to the visualization of networks, the `igraph` package offers a variety of functions to analyze and manipulate networks quantitatively. For instance, one can easily find shortest paths, the minimum spanning tree or study the modularity of a community structure of a graph. In Chapter 16, we will discuss some of these methods, e. g., finding shortest paths or the depth-first search, in more detail.

9.3 NetBioV

`NetBioV` is another package for visualization networks. It provides three main layout architectures, namely global, modular, and layered layouts [187]. These layouts can be used either separately or in combination with each other. The rationale behind this functionality is motivated by the fact that a network should be visualized not only using one layout, but through many perspectives. Furthermore, since many real-world networks are generally acknowledged to have a scale-free, modular, and hierarchical structure, these three categories of layouts enable the highlighting of, e. g., specific biological aspects of the network. Moreover, `NetBioV` includes an additional layout category, which enables a spiral-view of the network. In the spiral view, the nodes' placement can be made using force-based algorithm, or using network measures for nodes. Overall, this provides a more abstract view on networks.

The `NetBioV` package has been implemented in the `R` programming environment and is based on the `igraph` library. For this reason, it can be seen as complementing `igraph` by providing more advanced visualization capabilities.

A list of its main functions used for different layout architectures available in `NetBioV` is shown in Table 9.5. In the subsequent sections, we provide a brief description of the different types of layouts offered by `NetBioV`.

9.3.1 Global network layout

Real-world networks, e. g., biological or social networks are usually not planar. That means, they have edges crossing each other if a graph is displayed in a two-dimensional plane. However, for a more effective visualization, the crossing of edges should be minimized. The global network layouts of `NetBioV` aim to minimize such crossings.

The most important features that can be highlighted via a global layout include the backbone of the network, the spread of information within the network, and the properties of the nodes, e. g., using various network measures. For instance, for highlighting the backbone structure of a network `NetBioV` applies the following strategy. In the first step, we define the backbone of a network. For this, we use the minimum spanning tree (MST) algorithm to extract a subnetwork from a given network. In the second step, we obtain the coordinates for the nodes by applying a force-based algorithm to the subnetwork consisting of the MST. In the third step, we assign a unique color to the MST edges whereas the remaining edges are colored according to the distance between the nodes.

9.3.2 Modular network layout

Most networks have a modular characteristics, that means there are groups of nodes that are more strongly connected with each other than the rest of the nodes. Depending on the origin of the network, such modules serve a different purpose. For instance, in biology, these modules can be thought of as performing a specific biological function for the organism.

The modular network layouts in `NetBioV` allow to highlight the individual modules by using standard graph-layout algorithms. The principle approach to this works as follows. In the first step, we determine the relative coordinates of the nodes within each module. In the second step, we optimize the coordinates for each module using standard-layout algorithms, and then we place the modules according to these positions. In general, modules can be identified with module detection algorithms. However, in specific application areas also other approaches are possible. For instance in biology, modules can be defined by gene-sets defined via biological databases, such as gene ontology [6] or KEGG [107].

Table 9.5: An overview of different layouts provided by NetBioV.

Layout categories	Functions in R	
Global layout	mst.plot, mst.plot.mod	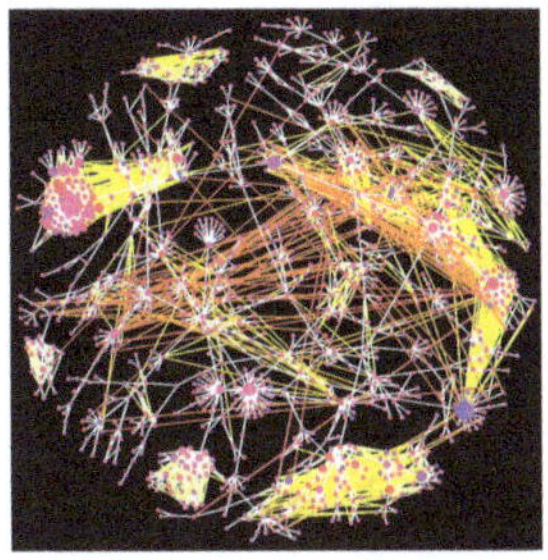
Modular layout	plot.modules, plot.abstract.modules, plot.abstrat.nodes, splitg.mst	
Layered layout	level.plot	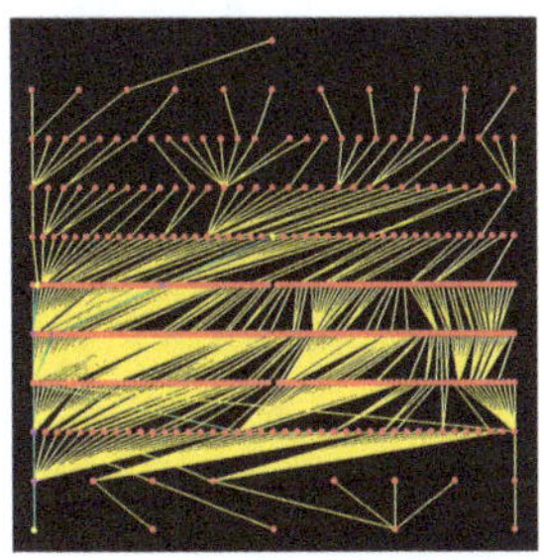
Spiral layout	plot.spiral.graph	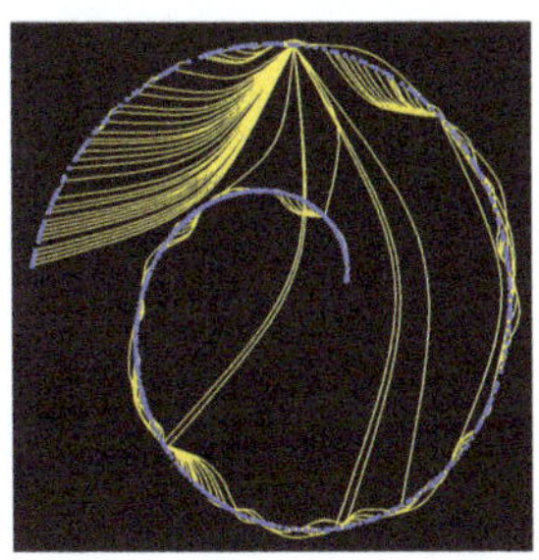

As an additional feature, the nodes in a module can be colored based on the rank assigned to the nodes, e. g., ranks assigned according to their node degree. Alternatively for biological networks one could utilize, e. g., gene expression values.

9.3.3 Layered network (multiroot) layout

In order to emphasize the hierarchy in a network, `NetBioV` provides a layered network layout. This algorithm organizes the nodes by hierarchy levels that are directly obtained from the distance between nodes. The layered network layout function assumes an initial subset, N, of nodes in a graph G. That means the resulting hierarchical graph does not need to have a unique root node but can have multiple roots. Starting from this initial set, the distances to all other nodes are determined and the nodes are plotted on their corresponding hiearchy level.

9.3.4 Further features

9.3.4.1 Information flow

For visualizing the spread of information within a network, `NetBioV` provides an algorithm which highlights either the shortest paths between modules or the nodes in the modular and layered network layouts. Highlighting such information is useful for visualizing key connections between nodes or modules that may play an important role in exchanging information. More specific interpretations depend on the nature of the underlying network.

9.3.4.2 Spiral view

The spiral layout included in the `NetBioV` package provides the user with some options to visualize networks in different spiral forms. The aestetics of the spirals can be influenced by setting a tuning parameter for the angle of the spiral. In addition, a wide range of color options is provided as an input to highlight, e. g., the degrees of nodes. In addition, the placement of nodes can be either determined by standard layout functions or by a user-defined function.

9.3.4.3 Color schemes, node labeling

`NetBioV` provides many options to color edges, vertices, and modules either based on different properties of the network, or based on user input. For the global network layouts, the edges corresponding to the backbone of the network (MST) are shown in one color, and the remaining edges are colored according to a range of colors reflecting the distance between nodes. The vertices or nodes of the network can be highlighted using a range of colors and sizes. For instance, the expression values of nodes representing genes or proteins can be shown with shades of colors from high- to low-expression values or vice versa. One can also assign ranks to the nodes based on network-related measures, which are visualized by the size of the nodes.

Also for the modular graph layout functions a variety of color options are available. The default color scheme for modules is a heat map of colors, where nodes with a high degree are assigned dark colors, whereas low-degree nodes are represented by light colors in a module. The nodes in a graph can also be colored individually in two ways. The first coloring option is based on the global rank in the network, whereas the second coloring option is based on local ranks in the modules. The ranks are determined by the different properties of nodes, such as the degree or expression value observed from, e. g., experimental data. The global rank describes the rank of an individual node with respect to all other nodes in the network, whereas the local rank of a node in a module is obtained with respect to the nodes from the same module. Edges for different modules can be colored differently so that the connectivity of individual modules can be highlighted. Additionally, the node-size can be used to highlight the rank of the nodes in the network. Moreover, for each module, an individual graph layout can be defined as a parameter vector as argument for a modular layout function.

For the layered network layout, the color scheme is defined as follows. For a directed network, the levels of the network are divided into three sections, namely the lower, the initial, and the upper section. Importantly, only the initial section and the upper section are used for undirected networks. A user can assign different colors to different levels. For a directed network, if edges connect nodes with a level difference greater than one, then edges are colored using two colors for two opposite directions (up and down). If edges connect nodes on the same level, then the edges are shown in a curved shape and in a unique color.

9.3.4.4 Interface to `R` and customization

The availability of `NetBioV` in `R` enables it to make use of various additional packages to enhance a visualization. For instance, various biological packages related to gene ontology (GO, TopGO) can be utilized to include information about the enrichment of biological pathways. Such information is particulary useful for the visualization of modules.

Furthermore, information obtained about genes, proteins, and their interactions, as well as network measures from many external `R` libraries, e. g., available in CRAN and Bioconducor, can be used as a part of the visualization of a network.

9.3.5 Examples: Visualization of networks using `NetBioV`

In this section, we demonstrate the capabilities of `NetBioV` by visualizing various networks with different layout and plotting options. The applications of the `NetBioV` functions are provided for some example networks. Some details about the investigated networks are shown in Table 9.6.

Listing 9.8: Loading network data for the examples

```
#Loading the NetBioV package
 library("netbiov")

#Loading the artificial network with $5,000$ nodes
```

Table 9.6: Examples of networks available in the NetBioV package.

Networks	Number of vertices	Number of edges
Artificial network	5000	23878
B-Cell lymphoma network	2498	2654
PPI (Arabidopsis thaliana)	1212	2574

```
 data("artificial2.graph")

#Loading the B-Cell lympoma network and module information
 data("gnet_bcell")
 data("modules_bcell")

#Loading the Arabidopsis Thaliana network and module information
 data("PPI_Athalina")
data("modules_PPI_Athalina")
```

Listing 9.9: Global network layouts, see Figure 9.4

```
# Left
data("gnet_bcell")
mec <- "white"
ecls <- rgb(r=0, g=1, b=1, alpha=.2)
exp <- abs(rnorm(vcount(g1)))
xx <- mst.plot(g1,layout.function=layout.fruchterman.reingold,
mst.edge.col=mec,colors=ecls,expression=exp, v.size=1.75)

# Right
mec <- "green"
vc <- rgb(r=1, g=0, b=0, alpha=.7)
ecls= rgb(r=.5, g=.5, b=1, alpha=.3)
id<-mst.plot.mod(g1,layout.function=layout.fruchterman.reingold,
mst.edge.col=mec,vertex.color=vc,colors=ecls, v.size=1.5)
```

Listing 9.10: Modular network layouts, see Figure 9.5

```
# Left
data("PPI_Athalina")
data("modules_PPI_Athalina")
cl <-rgb(r=0, g=0, b=1, alpha=.55)
lc <- "white"
ecl <- "gold"
xx <- plot.abstract.nodes(g1,mod.list=lm,nodes.color=cl,
edge.colors=ecl,layout.function=layout.fruchterman.reingold,
v.sf=-30,lab.color=lc, lab.cex=1, lab.dist=5)

# Right
data("PPI_Athalina")
data("modules_PPI_Athalina")
clx <- rgb(red=0,green = .6, blue = .6, alpha = 0.4)
cl <- rep(clx, 28);
lb <- names(lm)
lb[c(1:24)[-c(1,5,17,21)]] <- ""
```

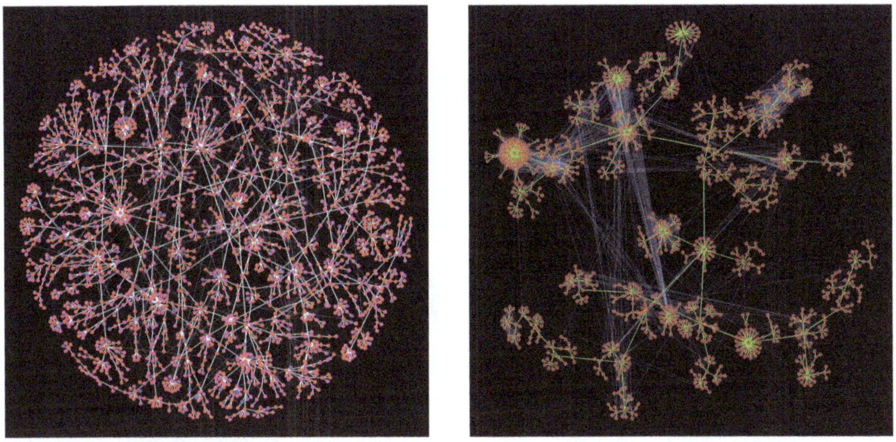

Figure 9.4: Global network layouts using different options available in NetBiov. Left: Coloring vertices of the B-cell lymphoma network based on external information, such as expression value (red to blue—smaller to higher expression value). Right: Edges of the MST are shown in "green" and the remaining edges in "blue".

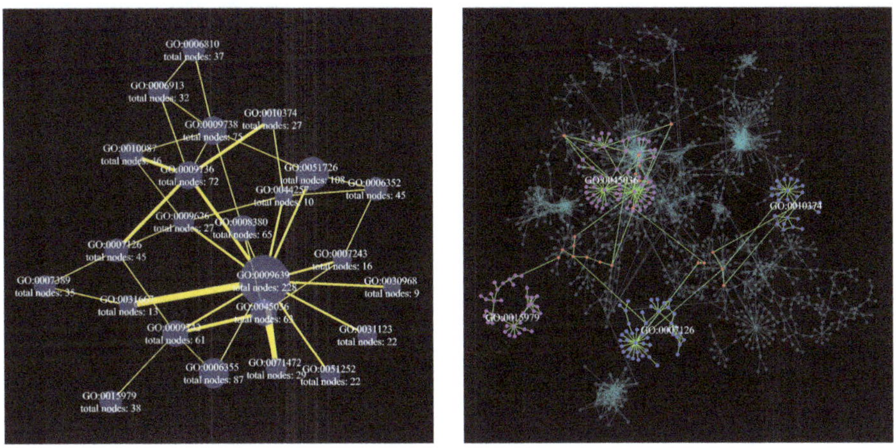

Figure 9.5: Modular layouts using different options available in NetBiov: Left: Abstract modular view of A. thaliana; each module is labeled with the most significant enriched GO-pathway. Edge width is proportional to the number of connections between modules. Right: Information flow in A. thaliana network by highlighting shortest paths between nodes of modules 1, 5, 17 and 21.

```
names(lm) <- lb
id  <- plot.modules(g1,mod.list=lm,layout.function =
layout.fruchterman.reingold,
modules.color =cl,mod.edge.col=c(clx),ed.color= c(clx),sf=-20,
nodeset=c(1,5,17,21),col.s1="blue",  col.s2="purple",
nodes.on.path="red", mod.lab=TRUE,lab.color="white",
v.size.path=1.5, v.size=1.2)
```

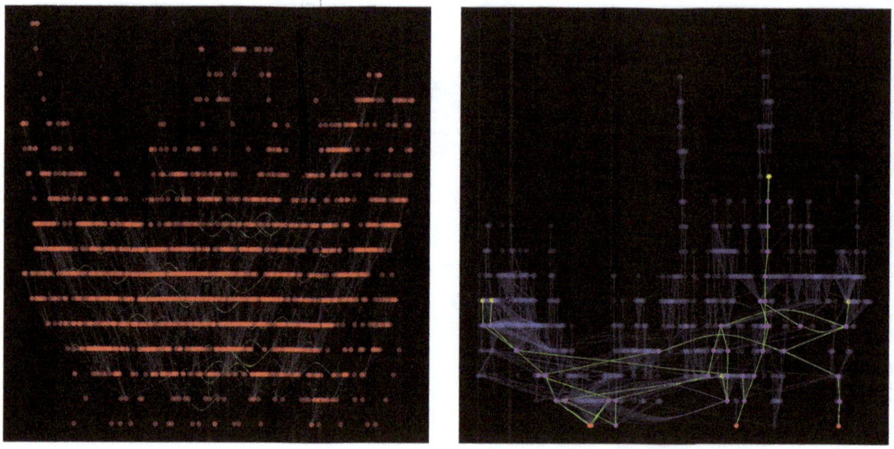

Figure 9.6: Layered network layouts. Left: The B-cell lymphoma network is shown. Right: The protein-protein interaction (PPI) network of *Arabidopsis thaliana* is shown.

Listing 9.11: Layered network layouts, see Figure 9.6

```
# Left
data(gnet_bcell)
clx <- rgb(red=1,green = 0, blue = 0, alpha = 0.5)
cl1  <- rgb(r=.5, g=.5, b=.5, alpha=.3)
cl2  <- rgb(r=0,g=1, b=0, alpha=1)
ec = c(cl1, cl1, cl2, cl1 )
id  <- level.plot(gnet, layout=layout.fruchterman.reingold,
vertex.colors=c(clx,clx,clx),edge.col=ec,e.size=.3,e.curve=1.2,
init_nodes=20,order_degree=NULL)

# Right
data(PPI_Athalina)
clx <- rgb(red=.3,green = .3, blue = 1, alpha = 0.2)
id  <- level.plot(g1, layout.function=layout.reingold.tilford,
vertex.colors=c(clx,clx,clx),edge.col=c(clx,clx,clx,clx),
e.size=.3,e.curve=.4, initial_nodes=c(1,5,7,12,101,125),
nodeset=list(c(1,5,7,101), c(501, 701, 801,901,1001)),
order_degree=NULL, )
```

9.4 Summary

Networks from biology, chemistry, economy or the social sciences can be seen as a data-type. For the visualization of such networks, we provided in this chapter an introduction for `igraph` and `NetBioV`. Overall, `igraph` provides many helpful base commands for the generation, manipulation, but also visualization of graphs, whereas `NetBioV` focuses on high-level visualizations from a global, modular, and layered perspective.

In contrast to conventional data-types from measurements, e. g., from sensors that provide direct numerical data, network data are considerably different. For this reason dedicated plots for their visualization have been developed that allow to gain a more intuitive understanding of the meaning of the provided networks.

Part III: Mathematical basics of data science

10 Mathematics as a language for science

10.1 Introduction

In data science, all problems will be approached computationally. For this reason, we started this book with an introduction to the programming language R.

Since most of the models for data analysis are based on mathematics and statistics, the next step will focus on the understanding of mathematical background needed to formulate and build these models. However, before we present, in the subsequent chapters, the mathematical basis of data science, we want to emphasize in this chapter a more general point concerning the mathematical language itself. This point refers to the abstract nature of data science.

In Figure 10.1, we visualize a generic framework that holds for every data analysis problem. The key point here is that every data analysis is conducted via a computer program that represents methodological ideas from statistics and machine learning, and every computer program consists of instructions (commands) that enable the communication with the processor of a computer to perform computations electronically. Since every data analysis is conducted via a computer program that contains instructions in a programming language, a good data scientist needs to "*speak*" fluently a programming language. However, the basis of *any* programming language for data analysis is mathematics, and its key characteristic is *abstractness*. For this reason, a simplified message from the above discussion can be summarized as follows:

> *Thinking in abstract mathematical terms makes you a better programmer and, hence, a better data scientist.*

This is also the reason why mathematics is sometimes called the language of science [185, 188], as noted by Galileo.

Before we proceed, we would like to add a couple of notes for clarification. First, by a programmer we mean actually a *scientific programmer* i. e., someone who is concerned with the conversion of statistical and machine learning ideas into a computer program rather than a general programmer who implements graphical user interfaces (GUIs) or websites. The crucial difference is that the level of mathematics needs for, e. g., the implementation of a GUI is minimal comparable to the implementation of a data analysis method. Also, such a way of programming is usually purely deterministic and not probabilistic. On the other hand, the nature of a data analysis is to deal with measurement errors and other imperfections of the data. Hence, probabilistic and statistical methods cannot be avoided in data science since they are integral pillars of the topic.

Second, although it is certainly not necessary to implement *every* method for conducting a data analysis, a good data scientist *should be capable* to implement

https://doi.org/10.1515/9783110796063-010

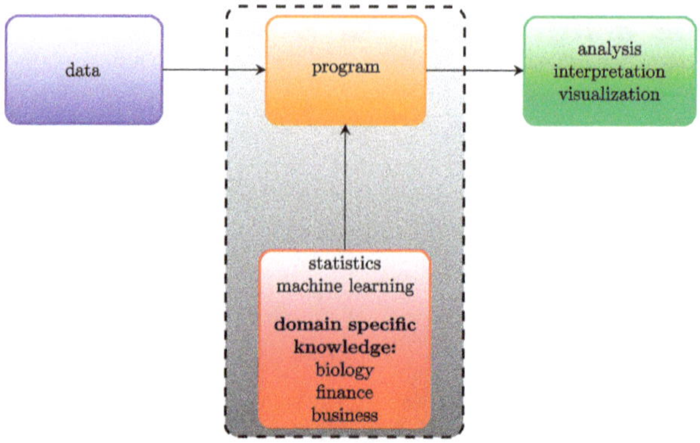

Figure 10.1: Generic visualization of any data analysis problem. Data analysis is conducted via a computer program that has been written based on statistical- and machine-learning methods informed with domain-specific knowledge, e. g., from biology, medicine, or the social sciences.

any method required for the analysis. Third, the natural language we are speaking, e. g., English, does not translate equally well into a computer language like R, but there are certain terms and structures that translate better. For instance, when we speak about a "vector" and its components, we will not have a problem to capture this in R, as shown in Chapter 5. Furthermore, in Chapter 12, we will learn much more about vectors in the context of linear algebra. This is not a coincidence, but the meaning of a vector is informed by its mathematical concept. Hence, whenever we use this term in our natural language, we have an immediate correspondence to its mathematical concept. This implies that the more we know about mathematics, the more we become familiar with terms that are well defined mathematically, and such terms can be swiftly translated into a computer program for data analysis.

We would like to finish this section by adding one more example that demonstrates the importance of "language" and its influence on the way humans think. Suppose, you have a twin sibling and you both are separated right after birth. You grow up in the way you did, and your twin grows up on a deserted island without civilization. Then, let say after 20 years, you both are independently asked a series of questions and given tasks to solve. Given that you both share the same DNA, one would expect that both of you have the same potential in answering these questions. However, practically it is unlikely that your twin will perform well, because of basic communication problems in the first place. In our opinion the language of "mathematics" plays a similar role with respect to "questions" and "tasks" from a data analysis perspective.

In the remainder of this chapter, we provide a discussion of some basic abstract mathematical symbols and operations we consider very important to (A) help formulating concise mathematical statements, and (B) shape the way of thinking.

10.2 Numbers and number operations

In mathematics, we distinguish five main number systems from each other:

- natural numbers: $\mathbb{N}$
- integers: $\mathbb{Z}$
- rational numbers: $\mathbb{Q}$
- real numbers: $\mathbb{R}$
- complex numbers: $\mathbb{C}$

Each of the above symbols represents a set of all numbers that belong to the corresponding number system. For instance, $\mathbb{N}$ represents all natural numbers, i. e., $1, 2, 3, \ldots$; $\mathbb{Z}$ represents all integer number, i. e., $\ldots, -2, -1, 0, +1, +2, \ldots$; $\mathbb{Q}$ represents all rational numbers $\frac{a}{b}$ with a and b being any integer number; and $\mathbb{R}$ is the set of all real numbers, e. g., 1.4271.

There is a natural connection between these number systems in the way that

$$\mathbb{N} \subset \mathbb{Z} \subset \mathbb{Q} \subset \mathbb{R} \subset \mathbb{C}. \tag{10.1}$$

That means, e. g., every integer number is also a real number, but not every integer number is a natural number. Furthermore, the special sets $\mathbb{Z}_+$ and $\mathbb{R}_+$ denote the set of all positive integers and positive reals.

Intervals

When defining functions, it is common to limit the value of numbers to specific intervals. One distinguishes finite from infinite intervals. Specifically, finite intervals can be defined in four different ways:

$$[a, b] = \{x \mid a \le x \le b\} \quad \text{closed interval,} \tag{10.2}$$

$$[a, b) = \{x \mid a \le x < b\} \quad \text{half-closed interval,} \tag{10.3}$$

$$(a, b] = \{x \mid a < x \le b\} \quad \text{half-closed interval,} \tag{10.4}$$

$$(a, b) = \{x \mid a < x < b\} \quad \text{open interval.} \tag{10.5}$$

Similarly, infinite intervals can be defined as follows:

$$[a, \infty) = \{x \mid a \le x < \infty\}, \tag{10.6}$$

$$(a, \infty) = \{x \mid a < x < \infty\}, \tag{10.7}$$

$$(-\infty, b] = \{x \mid -\infty < x \le b\}, \tag{10.8}$$

$$(-\infty, b) = \{x \mid -\infty < x < b\}, \tag{10.9}$$

$$(-\infty, \infty) = \mathbb{R}. \tag{10.10}$$

The difference between a closed interval and an open interval is that for a closed interval the end point(s) belong to the interval, whereas this is not the case for an open interval.

Modulo operation

The modulo operation gives the remainder of a devision of two positive numbers a and b. It is defined for $a \in \mathbb{R}_+$ and $b \in \mathbb{R}_+ \setminus \{0\}$ by

$$a \mod b = \text{modulo}(a, b) = a - n \cdot b = r. \tag{10.11}$$

Here, $n \in \mathbb{N} \cup \{0\}$ is a natural number, and $r \in \mathbb{R}_+$ is the remainder of the division of a by b. For programming, the modulo operation is frequently used for integer numbers a and b, because a cyclic mapping can be easily realized, i. e., $N + 1 \to 1$ can be obtained by

$$\text{modulo}(N + 1, N). \tag{10.12}$$

In R, the module operation is carried out using the following code:

Listing 10.1: Modulo Operation

```
a %% b       # modulo(a, b)
```

Example 10.2.1. We calculate $17 \mod 4 = \text{modulo}(17, 4)$ and $3 \mod 7 = \text{modulo}(3, 7)$. In these examples, a and b are integers. Therefore, we use the fact that in case we determine $\frac{a}{b}$, we always find $q, r \in \mathbb{Z}$ such that $a = b\dot{q} + r$, see [199].

We start with $17 \mod 4$ and see that $17 = q \cdot 4 + r$. Hence, $q = 4$, and $r = 1$. Thus, $17 \mod 4 = 1$. If we consider $3 \mod 7$, we find $3 = q \cdot 7 + r$. Thus, $q = 0$, and $r = 3$. This yields to $3 \mod 7 = 3$.

Rounding operations

The floor and ceiling operations round a real number to its nearest integer value up or down. The corresponding functions are denoted by

$$\lfloor x \rfloor \quad \text{floor function,} \tag{10.13}$$

$$\lceil x \rceil \quad \text{ceiling function.} \tag{10.14}$$

As an example, the value of $x = 1.9$ results in $\lfloor x \rfloor = 1$ and $\lceil x \rceil = 2$.

In contrast, the command round(x), rounds the value of the real number x to its nearest integer value. For instance, round(0.51) = 1. In R, the value 0.5 is rounded toward the lower integer value, e. g., round(−3.5) = −4.

Finally, the truncation function, $\mathrm{trunc}(x)$, of a real number x is just the integer digits of the number x without the fractional digits i.e., the numbers after the decimal point. For instance, $\mathrm{trunc}(3.91) = 3$.

Listing 10.2: Rounding operations, sign function and absolute value

```
floor(x)        # ⌊x⌋
ceiling(x)      # ⌈x⌉
round(x)        # round(x)
trunc(x)        # truncation(x)
sign(x)         # sign of x
abs(x)          # absolute value of x
```

Sign function

For any real number $x \in \mathbb{R}$, the sign function, $\mathrm{sign}(x)$, is given by

$$\mathrm{sign}(x) = \begin{cases} +1 & \text{if } x > 0; \\ 0 & \text{if } x = 0; \\ -1 & \text{if } x < 0. \end{cases} \tag{10.15}$$

Absolute value

The absolute value or the modulus of a real number $x \in \mathbb{R}$ is given by

$$\mathrm{abs}(x) = |x| = \begin{cases} +x & \text{if } x \geq 0; \\ -x & \text{if } x < 0. \end{cases} \tag{10.16}$$

10.3 Sets and set operations

In the following, we introduce sets and some of their basic operations. In general, a set is a well-defined collection of objects. For instance, $\mathcal{A} = \{1, 2, 3\}$ contains the three natural numbers 1, 2, and 3, $\mathcal{B} = \{\triangle, \circ\}$ is a set consisting of two geometric objects,

$$\mathcal{C} = \{♔, ♛, ♘, ♝, ♙\} \tag{10.17}$$

is the set containing chess pieces, and $\mathcal{D} = \{\mathcal{A}, \mathcal{C}\}$ is a set of sets. From these examples, one can see that an object is something very generic, and a set is just a container for objects. Usually, the objects of a set are enclosed by the curly brackets "{" and "}".

The symbol $\in$ denotes the *membership relation* to indicate that an object is contained in a set. For instance, $2 \in \mathcal{A}$, and $\circ \in \mathcal{B}$. Here, the objects 2 and $\circ$ are also called elements of their corresponding sets. The symbol $\in$ is a *relation,* because it establishes a connection between an object and a set and, hence, relates both with each other.

If we have two sets, A_1 and A_2, and every element in A_1 is also contained in A_2, but there are also elements in A_2 that are not in A_1, we write $A_1 \subset A_2$. In this case A_1 is called a subset of A_2. In contrast, if every element in A_1 is also contained in A_2, and there are *no* additional elements in A_2, we write $A_1 = A_2$, because both sets contain the same elements. Finally, if every element in A_1 is also contained in A_2, and there is at least one additional element in A_2, we write $A_1 \subsetneq A_2$. In this case A_1 is a *proper subset* of A_2.

A special set is the empty set, denoted by $\emptyset$, which does not contain any element. $|A|$ is the cardinality of A, i. e., the number of its elements. It is possible that a set contains a finite or infinite number of elements. For instance, for the above set $\mathcal{B}$, we have $|\mathcal{B}| = 2$, and for the set of natural numbers we have $|\mathbb{N}| = \infty$.

The set $A_1 \cup A_2 = \{x : x \in A_1 \vee x \in A_2\}$ is called the *union* of A_1, and A_2. $A_1 \cap A_2 = \{x : x \in A_1 \wedge x \in A_2\}$ is called the *intersection* of A_1 and A_2. For the definition of these sets, we used the colon symbol ":" within the curled brackets. This symbol means "*with the property*". Hence, the set $\{x : x \in A_1 \vee x \in A_2\}$ can be read explicitly as every x that is element in A_1 or every x that is element of A_2 is a member of the set $A_1 \cup A_2$. Alternatively, sometimes the symbol "|" is used instead of ":".

In Figure 10.2, we show a visualization of the union and the intersection. It is important to realize that both operations create new sets, i. e., $B = A_1 \cup A_2$, and $C = A_1 \cap A_2$ are two new sets. If $A_1 \cap A_2 = \emptyset$, then A_1, A_2 are called *disjoint* sets.

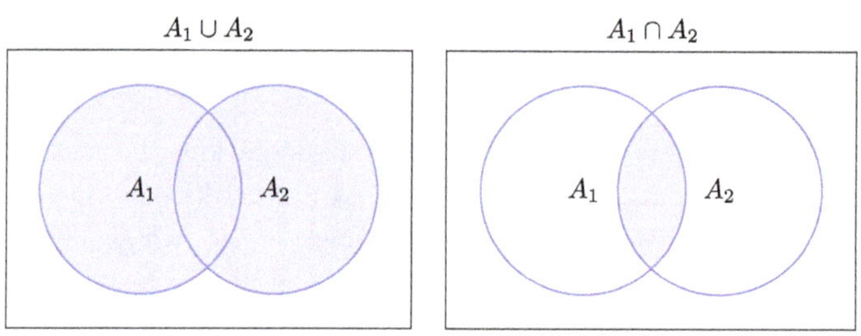

Figure 10.2: Visualization of set operations. Left: The union of two sets. Right: The intersection of A_1 and A_2.

An alphabet Σ is a finite set of atomic symbols, e. g., $\Sigma = \{a, b, c\}$. That means, Σ contains all elements for a given setting. No other elements can exist.

$\Sigma^\star$ is the set of all words over Σ. For example if $\Sigma = \{b\}$, then $\Sigma^\star = \{\epsilon, b, bb, bbb, bbbb \dots\}$. Here ϵ is the empty word.

There are three quantifiers from predicate logic that allow a concise description of properties of elements of sets.

Definition 10.3.1. The expression $\forall$ means *for all.* For example if $A = \{a_1, a_2, a_3\}$, then by $\forall x \in A$, we mean all elements in set A, i. e., a_1, a_2, a_3.

Definition 10.3.2. The expression $\exists$ means *there exits.* For example if $B = \{-1, 2, 3\}$, then by $\exists x \in B : x < 3$, we mean that in set B there exists an element, which is less than 3. Possibly, there is more than one such element, as is the case for B.

Definition 10.3.3. The expression $\exists!$ means *there exits only one.* For example: $\exists! x \in B : x < 2$ means that in the set B there exists only one element, which is less than 2.

10.4 Boolean logic

The operators $\vee$ and $\wedge$ are the logical *or* and *and*, respectively. They form logical operators to combine logical variables $v, q \in \{1, 0\}$. Sometimes the logical variables are expressed as $\{\text{true}, \text{false}\}$. By using operations from the set

$$\mathcal{O} := \{\neg, \wedge, \vee, ()\}, \tag{10.18}$$

of logical operators, we can easily construct logical formulas. For instance, the formulas

$$v \vee q,\ (v \vee q),\ (v \vee q) \wedge \neg(v \vee q) \tag{10.19}$$

represent valid logical formulas as they are derived by using the operators in (10.18). However, according to this definition, the formulas

$$(v \vee q)qq,\ (v\,q) \tag{10.20}$$

are not valid (their meaning is undefined).

Suppose that S_1, S_2, S_3 are logical expressions (statements) derived by using the elements of the set operators $\mathcal{O}$, similar to the ones given in equation (10.19). The following statements about logical formulas hold:

Theorem 10.4.1 (Commutative laws [98]).

$$S_1 \wedge S_2 \iff S_2 \wedge S_1 \tag{10.21}$$

$$S_1 \vee S_2 \iff S_2 \vee S_1 \tag{10.22}$$

Theorem 10.4.2 (Associative laws [98]).

$$(S_1 \wedge S_2) \wedge S_3 \iff S_1 \wedge (S_2 \wedge S_3) \tag{10.23}$$

$$(S_1 \vee S_2) \vee S_3 \Longleftrightarrow S_1 \vee (S_2 \vee S_3) \tag{10.24}$$

Theorem 10.4.3 (Distributive laws [98]).

$$S_1 \vee (S_2 \wedge S_3) \Longleftrightarrow (S_1 \vee S_2) \wedge (S_1 \vee S_3) \tag{10.25}$$

$$S_1 \wedge (S_2 \vee S_3) \Longleftrightarrow (S_1 \wedge S_2) \vee (S_1 \wedge S_3) \tag{10.26}$$

Theorem 10.4.4 (Rules of de Morgan [98]).

$$\neg(S_1 \vee S_2) \Longleftrightarrow \neg S_1 \wedge \neg S_2 \tag{10.27}$$

$$\neg(S_1 \wedge S_2) \Longleftrightarrow \neg S_1 \vee \neg S_2 \tag{10.28}$$

Theorem 10.4.1 says that the logical arguments can be switched for the logical operators *and* and *or*. Theorem 10.4.2 says that we may successively shift the brackets to the right. Similarly, when expanding expressions over the reals, for instance $x(x+1) = x^2 + x$, Theorem 10.4.3 gives a rule for expanding logical expressions.

The rules of de Morgan given by Theorem 10.4.4 state that a negation applied to the single expressions flips the logical operator. Note that these rules can be formulated for sets accordingly.

Theorem 10.4.5 (Rules of de Morgan for sets [100]).

$$\overline{A \cup B} = \overline{A} \cap \overline{B} \tag{10.29}$$

$$\overline{A \cap B} = \overline{A} \cup \overline{B} \tag{10.30}$$

The resulting statements (or forms) are called *normal forms,* and important examples thereof are the *disjunctive normal form* and *conjunctive normal form* of logical expressions, see [98].

Definition 10.4.1 (Disjunctive normal form (DNF) [98]). A logical expression S is given in disjunctive normal form if

$$S = S_1 \vee S_1 \vee \cdots \vee S_k, \tag{10.31}$$

where

$$S_i = S_{j_1} \wedge S_{j_2} \wedge \cdots \wedge S_{j_{k_j}}. \tag{10.32}$$

The terms S_{j_i} are literals, i. e., logical variables or the negation thereof.

Two examples for logical formulas given in disjunctive normal form are

$$(v \wedge q) \vee (\neg v \wedge \neg q) \tag{10.33}$$

or

$$v \vee (v \wedge q). \tag{10.34}$$

Here we denote the literals by using the notations v and q for logical variables.

Definition 10.4.2 (Conjunctive normal form (DNF) [98]). A logical expression S is given in conjunctive normal form if

$$S = S_1 \wedge S_1 \wedge \cdots \wedge S_k, \tag{10.35}$$

where

$$S_i = S_{j_1} \vee S_{j_2} \vee \cdots \vee S_{j_{k_j}}. \tag{10.36}$$

The terms S_{j_i} are literals.

Examples for logical formulas given in conjunctive normal form are

$$(v \vee q) \wedge (\neg v \vee \neg q) \tag{10.37}$$

or

$$v \wedge (v \vee q). \tag{10.38}$$

In practice, the application of Boolean functions [98] has been important to develop electronic chips for computers, mobile phones, etc. A logic gate [98] represents an electronic component that realizes (computes) a Boolean function $f(v_1, \ldots, v_n) \in \{0, 1\}$; v_i are logical variables. These logic gates use the logical operators $\wedge$, $\vee$, $\neg$ and transform input signals into output signals. Figure 10.3 shows the elementary logic gates and their corresponding truth tables.

We see in Figure 10.3 that the OR-gate is based on the functionality of the operator $\vee$. That means, the output signal of the OR-gate equals 1 as soon as one of its input signals is 1.

The output signal of the AND-gate equals 1 if and only if all input signals equal 1. As soon as one input signal equals 0, the value of the Boolean function computed by this gate is 0.

The NOT-gate computes the logical negation of the input signal. If the input signal is 1, the NOT-gate gives 0, and vice versa.

10.5 Sum, product, and Binomial coefficients

For a given set $A = \{a_1, \ldots, a_n\}$, the sum and product of its components can be conveniently summarized by the sum operation ($\sum$) and the product operation ($\prod$).

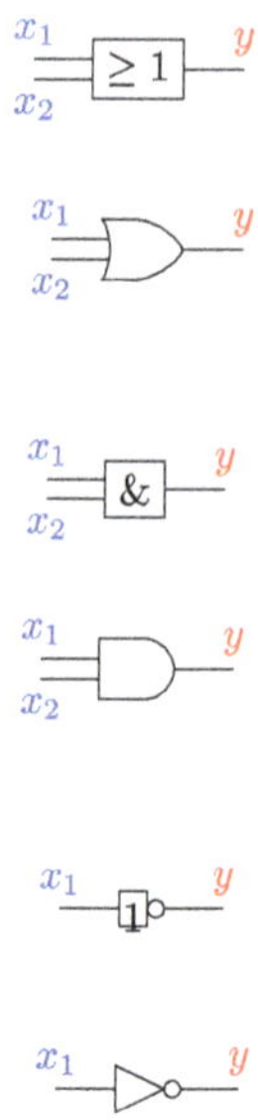

logic OR gate

x_2	x_1	y
0	0	0
0	1	1
1	0	1
1	1	1

logic AND gate

x_2	x_1	y
0	0	0
0	1	0
1	0	0
1	1	1

logic NOT gate

x_1	y
0	1
1	0

Figure 10.3: Elementary logic gates of Boolean functions and their corresponding truth table. The top symbol corresponds to the IEC, and the bottom to the US standard symbols.

Sum

The sum, $\sum$, for the numbers a_i involving the integer indices $i_l, i_l + 1 \ldots, i_u \in \mathbb{N}$ is defined by

$$\sum_{i=i_l}^{i_u} a_i = a_{i_l} + a_{i_l+1} + \cdots + a_{i_u}. \tag{10.39}$$

Here the index "l" indicates "lower" whereas "u" indicates "upper", and they are used to denote the start and end of the sequence of indices. For $i_l = 1$, and $i_u = n$, we obtain the sum over all elements of A, $\sum_{i=1}^{n} a_i = a_1 + \cdots + a_n$. Alternatively, the sum can also be written using a different notation for the index of the sum symbol, namely

$$\sum_{i \in \{i_l, i_l+1, \ldots, i_u\}} a_i = a_{i_l} + a_{i_l+1} + \cdots + a_{i_u}. \tag{10.40}$$

The latter form is more convenient when the summation concerned a subset of the indices. For instance, suppose that $I = \{2, 4, 5\}$ is a subset containing the desired indices for the summation then

$$\sum_{i \in I} a_i = \sum_{i \in \{2,4,5\}} a_i = a_2 + a_4 + a_5. \tag{10.41}$$

Product

Similar to the sum, the product, $\prod$, for the numbers a_i involving the integer indices $i_l, i_l + 1 \ldots, i_u \in \mathbb{N}$ is defined as follows.

$$\prod_{i=i_l}^{i_u} a_i = a_{i_l} \cdot a_{i_l+1} \cdot \cdots \cdot a_{i_u}; \tag{10.42}$$

$$\prod_{i \in \{i_l, i_l+1 \ldots, i_u\}} a_i = a_{i_l} \cdot a_{i_l+1} \cdot \cdots \cdot a_{i_u}. \tag{10.43}$$

Remark 10.5.1. In the above discussions of the sum and product, we assumed integer indices for the identification of the numbers a_i, i. e., $i \in \mathbb{N}$. However, we would like to remark that, in principle, this can be generalized to arbitrary "labels". For instance, for the set $A = \{a_\triangle, a_\circ, a_\otimes\}$, we can define the sum and product over its elements as

$$\sum_{i \in \{\triangle, \circ, \otimes\}} a_i = a_\triangle + a_\circ + a_\otimes; \tag{10.44}$$

$$\prod_{i \in \{\triangle, \circ, \otimes\}} a_i = a_\triangle \cdot a_\circ \cdot a_\otimes. \tag{10.45}$$

Hence, from a mathematical point of view, the nature of the indices is flexible. However, whenever we implement a sum or a product with a programming language, integer values for the indices are advantageous, because, e. g., the indexing of vectors or matrices is accomplished via integer indices.

In R, the most flexible way to realize sums and products is via loops. However, if one just wants a sum or a product over all elements in a vector A, from $i_l = 1$ to $i_u = N$, one can use the following commands:

Listing 10.3: Sum and product

```
sum(A)            # sum of all elements in vector A
prod(A)           # product of all elements in vector A
```

Binomial coefficients

For all natural numbers $k, n \in \mathbb{N}$ with $0 \leq k \leq n$, the binomial coefficient, denoted $C(n, k)$, is defined by

$$C(n,k) = \binom{n}{k} = \frac{n!}{k!(n-k)!}. \tag{10.46}$$

It is interesting to note that a binomial coefficient is a natural number itself, i. e., $C(n, k) \in \mathbb{N}$.

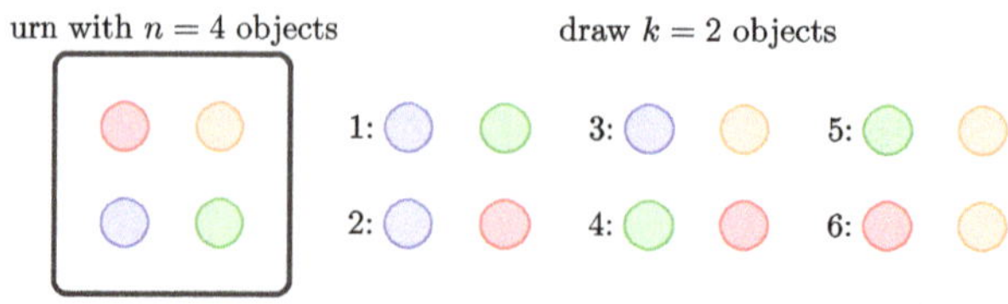

Figure 10.4: Visualization of the meaning of the Binomial coefficient $C(4, 2)$.

For the definition of a binomial coefficient, the factorial of a natural number, denoted by the symbol "!", is used. The factorial of an natural number n is just the product of the numbers from 1 to n, i. e.,

$$n! = \prod_{i=1}^{n} i = 1 \cdot 2 \cdot \dots \cdot n. \tag{10.47}$$

The binomial coefficient has the combinatorial meaning that from n objects, there are $C(n, k)$ ways to select k objects without considering the order in which the objects have been selected. In Figure 10.4, we show an urn with $n = 4$ objects. From this urn, we can draw $k = 2$ objects in 6 different ways.

Also, the factorial $n!$ has a combinatorial meaning. It gives the number of different arrangements of n objects by considering the order. For instance, the objects $\{1, 2, 3\}$ can be arranged in $3! = 6$ different ways:

$$(1,2,3) - (1,3,2) - (2,3,1) - (2,1,3) - (3,1,2) - (3,2,1). \tag{10.48}$$

Listing 10.4: Factorial and Binomial coefficients

```
factorial(k)        # factorial of the natural number k
choose(n, k)        # binomical coefficient C(n,k)
```

Properties of Binomial coefficients

The binomial coefficients have interesting properties. Some of these are listed below.

$$C(n,0) = \binom{n}{0} = 1, \tag{10.49}$$

$$C(n,n) = \binom{n}{n} = 1, \tag{10.50}$$

$$\binom{n}{k} = \binom{n}{n-k}, \tag{10.51}$$

$\forall n \in \mathbb{N}$, and $0 \leq k \leq n$.

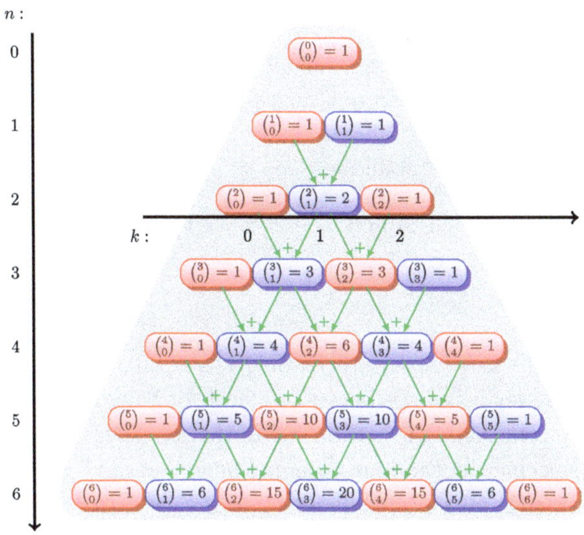

Figure 10.5: Pascal's triangle for Binomial coefficients. Visualized is the recurrence relation for Binomial coefficients in equation (10.52).

The following recurrence relation for binomial coefficients is called *Pascal's rule*:

$$\binom{n+1}{k+1} = \binom{n}{k} + \binom{n}{k+1}. \tag{10.52}$$

In Figure 10.5, we visualize the result of Pascal's rule for $n \in \{0, \dots, 6\}$. The resulting object is called *Pascal's triangle.*

10.6 Further symbols

Let us again assume we have a given set $A = \{a_1, \dots, a_n\}$, where its elements a_i are numbers.

Minimum and maximum

The minimum and the maximum of the set A are defined by

$$a^*_{\text{min}} = \min_{i=1,\dots,n} \{A\} = \{a_i \mid a_i \in A \text{ and } a_i \leq a_j \ \forall j \neq i\}; \tag{10.53}$$

$$a^*_{\text{max}} = \max_{i=1,\dots,n} \{A\} = \{a_i \mid a_i \in A \text{ and } a_i \geq a_j \ \forall j \neq i\}. \tag{10.54}$$

If there is more than one element that is minimum or maximum, then the corresponding sets a^*_{min} and a^*_{max} contain more than one element.

Argmin and Argmax

There are two related functions to the minimum and maximum that return the indices of the minimal/maximal elements instead of their values:

$$i^*_{\text{min}} = \underset{i=1,\dots,n}{\operatorname{argmin}}\{A\} = \{i \mid a_i \in A \text{ and } a_i \leq a_j \ \forall j \neq i\}; \tag{10.55}$$

$$i^*_{\text{max}} = \underset{i=1,\dots,n}{\operatorname{argmax}}\{A\} = \{i \mid a_i \in A \text{ and } a_i \geq a_j \ \forall j \neq i\}. \tag{10.56}$$

Logical statements

A logical statement may be defined verbally or mathematically, and take one of the values *true* or *false*. For simplicity, we define the Boolean value 1 for true, and 0 for false. One can show that the set $\{\text{true}, \text{false}\}$ is isomorphic to the set $\{0, 1\}$.

The Boolean value of the statement "*The next autumn comes for sure*" equals 1 and, hence, the statement is true. From a probabilistic point of view, this event is certain and its probability equals one. Therefore, we may conclude that this statement does not contain any information, see also [169]. The following inequalities and equations

$$i = -5, \tag{10.57}$$

$$100 = 50 + 20 + 30, \tag{10.58}$$

$$-1 \geq 5, \tag{10.59}$$

$$1 < 2, \tag{10.60}$$

$$\sum_{j=1}^{n} j = \frac{n(n+1)}{2}, \quad n \in \mathbb{N}, \tag{10.61}$$

are mathematical statements, which are true or false. The first equation is false, as $i = \sqrt{-1}$, where i is the imaginary unit of a complex number $z = a + ib$. The second equation is obviously true, as $50 + 20 + 30$ equals 100. For the third statement, a negative number cannot be greater or equal than a positive number and its Boolean value is therefore false. The fourth statement represents an inequality too, and is true. Strictly speaking, the fifth equation is a *statement form* (Sf) over the natural numbers, as it contains the variable $n \in \mathbb{N}$.

In general, statement forms contain variables and are true or false. In case of equation (10.61), we can write $\langle \text{Sf}(n) \rangle = \langle \sum_{j=1}^{n} j = \frac{n(n+1)}{2} \rangle$. This statement form is true for all $n \in \mathbb{N}$ and can be proven by induction. Another example of a statement form is

$$\big\langle \text{Sf}(x) \big\rangle = \langle x + 5 = 15 \rangle > . \tag{10.62}$$

For $x = 10$, $\langle \text{Sf}(x) \rangle$ is true. For $x \neq 10$, $\langle \text{Sf}(x) \rangle$ is false.

Generally, we can see that the statement changes if the variable of the statement form (Sf) changes. Once we define statements (or statement forms), they can be combined by using logical operations. We demonstrate these operations by first assuming that S_1 and S_2 are logical statements. The statement $S_1 \wedge S_2$ means that S_1 *and* S_2 hold. This statement may have the value true or false, see Figure 10.3. For instance, $S_1 := 2+2=4 \wedge S_2 := 3+3=6$ is true, but $S_1 := 2+2=4 \wedge S_3 := 3+3=9$ is false. Similarly, $S_1 \vee S_2$ means that S_1 *or* S_2 holds. Here, $S_1 := 2+2=4 \vee S_2 = 3+3=6$ is true, but $S_1 := 2+2=4 \vee S_3 := 3+3=9$ is true as well. The logical negation of the statement S is usually denoted by $\neg S$. The well-known triangle equation,

$$|x_1 + x_2| \leq |x_1| + |x_2|, \quad x_1, v_2 \in \mathbb{R}, \tag{10.63}$$

holds true, but not

$$\neg(|x_1 + x_2| \leq |x_1| + |x_2|). \tag{10.64}$$

This means

$$|x_1 + x_2| > |x_1| + |x_2| \tag{10.65}$$

is generally false.

Statement: ⇒

The logical implication $S_1 \Longrightarrow S_2$ means that S_1 *implies* S_2. Verbally, one can say S_1 “logically implies” S_2, or if S_1 holds, then follows S_2.

Statement ⇔

The statement $S_1 \Longleftrightarrow S_2$ is stronger, because S_1 holds *if and only if* S_2 holds.

For the above statements, it is important to note that to go from the left statement to the right one, or vice versa, one needs to apply logical operators ($\neg$, $\wedge$, $\vee$) or algebraic operations (+, −, /, etc.). For instance, by assuming the true statement $n^2 \geq 2n$, $n > 1$, we obtain the implications

$$n^2 \geq 2n \Longrightarrow n^2 - 2n \geq 0 \Longrightarrow n^2 - 2n + 1 = (n-1)^2 \geq 0. \tag{10.66}$$

Finally, we want to remark that a false statement may imply a true statement; $i^2 = 1$ (false as $i^2 = -1$) implies $0 \cdot i^2 = 0 \cdot 1$ (true).

10.7 Importance of definitions and theorems

In order to develop and formulate precise mathematical concepts and ideas, we need a concise language. For instance, if we want to define a mathematical term, we first need to understand what a mathematical *definition* is. In general, a definition is a concept formation of a mathematical term that is (possibly) based on other (mathematical) terms, which are either immediately clear or which have already been defined. Put simply, a definition is used to give a precise meaning to a new term.

It is important not to confuse a *definition* with a *theorem*. As mentioned above, a definition is just a concept formation, and not a statement and, therefore, it cannot be proven, but it is assumed to be true. In contrast, a theorem is a mathematical statement that needs to be proven by using other statements. In the following, we give some examples of definitions:

Definition 10.7.1. Let $a, b \in \mathbb{R}$. The sum of these two real numbers are defined by

$$\mathrm{sum}(a, b) := a + b. \tag{10.67}$$

Definition 10.7.1 defines the sum of two real numbers based on the trivial definition of the symbol "+".

Definition 10.7.2. Let $a, b \in \mathbb{R}$. The function $f_L : \mathbb{R} \longrightarrow \mathbb{R}$, given by

$$f_L(x) := ax + b, \tag{10.68}$$

defines a linear function or a linear mapping.

The next statement can be formulated as a theorem based on the previous definition.

Theorem 10.7.1. *The unique solution of the equation*

$$f_L(x) = 0 \tag{10.69}$$

is given by $x = -\frac{b}{a}$.

The proof of Theorem 10.7.1 is very simple, as $f_L(x) := ax+b = 0$ leads directly to $x = -\frac{b}{a}$ by performing elementary calculations. Specifically, the first elementary calculation is subtracting b from $ax+b = 0$. Second, we divide the resulting equation by a and obtain the result.

Another example is the famous binomial theorem.

Theorem 10.7.2. *Let* $a, b \in \mathbb{R}$ *and* $n \geq 1$. *Then,*

$$(a + b)^n = \sum_{k=1}^{n} \binom{n}{k} a^{n-k} b^k. \tag{10.70}$$

Theorem 10.7.2 can be proven by induction over n.

Sometimes, one uses the term *lemma* instead of theorem. Also a lemma is a statement that needs to be proven, however, it is not as important as a theorem. An example of an important theorem is the well-known *fundamental theorem of Algebra* [127], stating that any complex-valued polynomial with degree n has exactly n zeros. To give a function-theoretic proof, one needs several lemmas to conclude this theorem, see, e. g., [49].

10.8 Summary

In general, the mathematical language is meant to help with the precise formulation of problems. If one is new to the field, such formulations can be intimidating at first, and verbal formulations may appear as sufficient. However, with a bit of practice one realizes quickly that this is not the case, and one starts to appreciate and to benefit from the power of mathematical symbols. Importantly, the mathematical language has a profound implication on the general mathematical thinking capabilities, which translate directly to analytical problem-solving strategies. The latter skills are key for working successfully on data science projects, e. g., in business analytics, because the process of analyzing data requires a full comprehension of all involved aspects, and the often abstract relationships.

11 Computability and complexity

This chapter provides a theoretical underpinning for the programming in R that we introduced in the first two parts of this book. Specifically, we introduced R practically by discussing various commands for *computing* solutions to certain problems. However, *computability* can be defined mathematically in a generic way that is independent of a programming language. This paves the way for determining the complexity of algorithms. Furthermore, we provide a mathematical definition of a Turing machine, which is a mathematical model for an electronic computer. To place this in its wider context, this chapter also provides a brief overview of several major milestones in the history of computer science.

11.1 Introduction

Nowadays, the use of information technologies and the application of computers are ubiquitous. Almost everyone uses computer applications to store, retrieve, and process data from various sources. A simple example is a relational database system for querying financial data from stock markets, or finding companies' telephone numbers. More advanced examples include programs that facilitate risk management in life insurance companies or the identification of chemical molecules that share similar structural properties in pharmaceutical databases [170, 54].

The foundation of computer science is based on theoretical computer science [163, 164]. Theoretical computer science is a relatively young discipline that, put simply, deals with the development and analysis of abstract models for information processing. Core topics in theoretical computer science include formal language theory and compilers [121, 160], computability [22], complexity [37], and semantics of programming languages [126, 167, 122] (see also Section 2.8). More recent topics include the analysis of algorithms [37], the theory of information and communication [40], and database theory [124]. In particular, the mathematical foundations of theoretical computer science have influenced modern applications tremendously. For example, results from formal language theory [160] have influenced the construction of modern compilers [121]. Formal languages have been used for the analysis of automata. The automata model of a Turing machine has been used to formalize the term *algorithm*, which plays a central role in computer science. When dealing with algorithms, an important question is whether they are computable (see Section 2.2). Another crucial issue relates to the analysis of algorithms' complexity, which provides upper and lower bounds on their time complexity (see Section 11.5.1). Both topics will be addressed in this chapter.

https://doi.org/10.1515/9783110796063-011

11.2 A brief history of computer science

In this section, we briefly sketch the history of computer science with respect to the most important milestones for its theoretical foundations [89, 32, 146]. As early as 1100 BC, the first mechanical calculators were constructed. The abacus, for example, is over 3000 years old. In approximately 300 BC, Euclid contributed to the development of computational methods by calculating the greatest common divisor (GCD). Another milestone was achieved in approximately 820 AD by Al-Khwarizmi, who explored the fundamental aspects of computing methods. The term *algorithm* is derived from the Latinization of his name: Algorithmi. From about 1518, the scientist Adam Riese developed algorithms with the aim of establishing the decimal system.

Further milestones in computer science were achieved in the seventeenth century (see [89, 32]). Pascal (approx. 1641) developed a patent for his calculator, *Pascaline*, which was used for accounting and tax calculations. Leibniz (approx. 1673) developed a calculating machine to perform the four fundamental arithmetic operations. In 1679, Leibniz was also the first to develop the dual system, which uses only the digits 0 and 1. Its development had a fundamental influence on modern computers, as well as processors.

The development of mechanic calculating machines controlled by programs was advanced in the nineteenth century [89, 32]. The idea was to use control-based programming to perform more complex calculations than were possible using the simple machines described above. A highlight was the seminal work by Babbage (1822), who developed the concept of a computer called the *analytical engine*. A contribution with significant impact on modern computer science was achieved by Boole in 1854. He developed the mathematical foundations of so-called Boolean logic, based on logic operations. Another breakthrough, attributable to Hollerith in 1886, was the development of a system for data processing using card-to-tape calculations. This system was used until the second half of the twentieth century, and contributed greatly to modern information processing.

Turing developed the concept of the so-called *Turing machine* in the 1930s [89, 32]. This automaton-based model has had a considerable influence on modern (theoretical) computer science, and nowadays serves as a theoretical foundation for computers. Zuse, in 1941, was among the pioneers who contributed to the development of electronic calculating machines. He developed the program-controlled computer *Z3* together with a programming language called *Plankalkül*. The first fully electronic computer, developed by Eckert and Mauchly (1946), was called *ENIAC* (for electronic numerical integrator and computer), and industrial production of computers started since the 1950s.

Another computer science pioneer was John von Neumann, who developed the so-called *Von Neumann architecture* published in 1945, as a basis for computing machines that are programmable from memory. We wish to emphasize that, besides the above-mentioned developments and findings, mathematical principles from information theory, signal processing, computer linguistics, and cybernetics have also influenced the development of modern electronic computers.

11.3 Turing machines

The search for a precise definition of an algorithm has challenged mathematicians for several decades [37]. In fact, the quest to resolve this problem began at the beginning of the twentieth century during the search for solutions to complex computational problems. Hilbert's tenth problem, which addressed the question of whether an arbitrary diophantine equation [30] possesses a solution, is an example of this. Various methods were developed in the attempt to solve this problem; however, it was disproven in 1970. Interestingly, the quest to solve such computational problems also led to questions about the computability of algorithms (or functions). This will be discussed in greater detail in Section 11.4.

Turing machines constituted an important contribution to the above-mentioned developments. A Turing machine is a *mathematical machine* with relatively primitive operations and constraints that mimics a real computer. Since a Turing machine is a mathematical model, its memory can be infinite (e. g., given by an infinite strip or tape that is sub-divided into fields; see Figure 11.1). Formally, a Turing machine is defined as follows:

Definition 11.3.1 (Turing machine). A deterministic Turing machine is a tuple $\mathrm{TM} = (S, \Sigma, \Gamma, \delta, s_0, \$, F)$ consisting of the following:

$$S,\ |S| < \infty \text{ is a set of states.} \tag{11.1}$$

$$\Sigma \subset \Gamma \text{ is the input alphabet.} \tag{11.2}$$

$$\Gamma \text{ is the alphabet of the strip (tape).} \tag{11.3}$$

$$\begin{aligned} &\delta : S \times \Gamma \longrightarrow S \times \Gamma \times \{l, r\} \text{ is called the transition function, where} \\ &l \text{ and } r \text{ denote left shift and right shift, respectively} \end{aligned} \tag{11.4}$$

$$s_0 \in S \text{ is the initial state.} \tag{11.5}$$

$$\$ \in \Gamma - \Sigma \text{ is the blank symbol.} \tag{11.6}$$

$$F \subset Z \text{ is the set of final states.} \tag{11.7}$$

Given an alphabet Σ, one can print only one character $c \in \Gamma$ in each field. A special character (e. g., \$) is used to fill the empty fields (blank symbol).

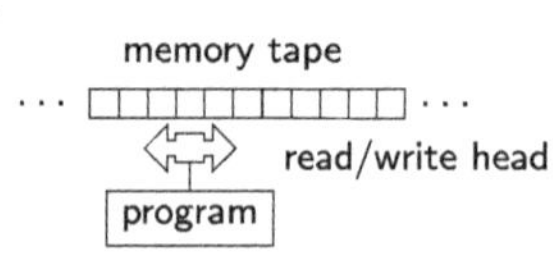

Figure 11.1: Illustration of the principle behind a Turing machine.

The transition function δ is crucial for the control unit, and encodes the program of the Turing machine (see Figure 11.1). The Turing table conveys information about the current and subsequent stages of the machine after it reads a character $c \in \Gamma$. This initiates certain actions of the read/write head, namely

- l: moving the head exactly one field to the left.
- r: moving the head exactly one field to the right.
- x: overwriting the content of a field with $x \in \Gamma \cup \{\$\}$ without moving the head.

A fundamental question of theoretical computer science concerns the types of functions that are computable using Turing machines. For example, it emerged that functions defined on words (e. g., $f : \Sigma^\star \longrightarrow \Sigma^\star$) are Turing-computable if there is at least one Turing machine that stops after a finite number of steps in the final state. We wish to emphasize that this also holds for other functions (e. g., multivariate functions over several variables).

We conclude this section with an important observation regarding *Turing completeness.* This term is relevant for basic paradigms of programming languages (see Chapter 2). A programming language is deemed Turing-complete if all functions that are computable with this language can be computed by a universal Turing machine. For example, most modern programming languages (from different paradigms), such as `Java`, `C++`, and `Scheme`, are Turing-complete [122].

11.4 Computability

We now turn to a fundamental problem in theoretical computer science: the determination as to whether or not a function is computable [164]. This problem can be discussed intuitively as well as mathematically. We begin with the intuitive discussion, and then provide its mathematical formulation. It is generally accepted that function $f : \mathbb{N} \longrightarrow \mathbb{N}$ is computable if an algorithm to compute f exists. Therefore, assuming an arbitrary $n \in \mathbb{N}$ as input, the algorithm should stop after a finite number of computation steps with output $f(n)$. When discussing this simple model, we did not take into account any considerations regarding a particular processor or memory. Evidently, however, it is necessary to specify such steps to implement an algorithm. In practical terms, this is complex, and can only be accomplished by a general mathematical definition to decide whether a function $f : \mathbb{N} \longrightarrow \mathbb{N}$ is computable.

A related problem is whether any arbitrary problem can be solved using an algorithm, and, if not, whether the algorithm can identify the problem as noncomputable. This is known as the decision problem formulated by Hilbert, which turned out to be invalid [36]. A counter-example is Godel's well-known *incompleteness theorem* [36]. Put simply, it states that no algorithm exists that can verify whether an arbitrary statement over $\mathbb{N}$ is true or false. To explore Gödel's statement in depth, several formulations of the term *algorithm* as a computational procedure have been proposed. A prominent example thereof was proposed by Church, who explored the well-known Lambda calculus, which can be understood as a mathematical programming language (see [122]). It was in this context also that Turing developed the concept of a Turing machine [36, 122] (see Section 11.3). Another contribution by Gödel is an alternative computational procedure based on the definition of complex mathematical functions composed of simple functions. The result of all these developments was that the Church-Turing thesis, which states that all the above-mentioned computational processes (algorithms) are equivalent, was proven.

Furthermore, it has been proven that computability does not depend on a specific programming language (see [122]). In other words, most programming languages are equipotent [122]. For example, suppose that we solve a problem by using an imperative programming language, such as `Fortran` (see Section 2.2). Then, an equivalent algorithm exists that can be implemented using a functional language, such as `Scheme` (see Section 2.3).

A mathematical definition of *computable* can be formulated as follows:

Definition 11.4.1 (Computable function). A function $f : \mathbb{N}^k \longrightarrow \mathbb{N}$ is called *computable* if an algorithm exists that computes $f(n_1, n_2, \ldots, n_k)$. That means $n_1, n_2, \ldots, n_k$ is the input of f such that the algorithm stops after a finite number of computation steps in the case where f is defined for $n_1, n_2, \ldots, n_k$. In the case where f is not defined on $n_1, n_2, \ldots, n_k$, the algorithm does not terminate.

We wish to note that a similar definition can be given for functions defined on words (e. g., $f : \Sigma^\star \longrightarrow \Sigma^\star$, see [36, 164]). Examples of computable functions include the following:
- The functions $f_1 : \mathbb{N}^2 \longrightarrow \mathbb{N}$, $f_1 := a \cdot b$ and $f_2 : \mathbb{N}^2 \longrightarrow \mathbb{N}$, $f_2 := a + b$.
- The (successor) function $f : \mathbb{N} \longrightarrow \mathbb{N}$, $f(n) := n + 1$.
- The recursive function $\text{sum} : \mathbb{N} \longrightarrow \mathbb{N}$ defined by $\text{sum}(n) := n + \text{sum}(n-1)$, $\text{sum}(0) := 0$.

11.5 Complexity of algorithms

Algorithms play a central role not only in mathematics and computer science, but also in machine learning and data science [37]. The term *algorithm* may be understood intuitively as a description of a general method for solving a class of problems. Mathematically speaking, an algorithm is defined by a set of rules that are executed sequentially, some of which may be repeated under certain conditions. Programming languages are excellent tools for implementing algorithms. For example, the class of recursive algorithms has been often used to implement recursive problems. A prominent example is the well-known Ackermann function [122], which can easily be coded using functional programming languages (see Section 2.3). By contrast, iterative algorithms have been used to compute problems efficiently. The imperative implementation (see Section 2.2) of the shortest path problem, proposed by Dijkstra [58], is a standard case study in computer science, which is frequently used to illustrate iterative algorithms. Examples of typical algorithms in mathematics include the GCD-algorithm proposed by Euclid [122] and the Gaussian elimination method for solving linear equation systems [27].

It seems plausible that many algorithms exist to address a particular problem. For example, the square of a real number can be computed using either a functional or an imperative algorithm (see Sections 2.2 and 2.3). However, this raises the question as to what type of algorithm is most suited to solving a given problem.

Listing important properties/questions in the context of algorithm design offers insight into the complexity of the latter problem. Such properties and questions include

- What level of effort is required to implement a particular algorithm?
- How can the algorithm be simplified as far as possible?
- How much memory is required?
- What is the time complexity (i. e., execution time) of an algorithm?
- What is the correctness of the algorithm?
- Does the algorithm terminate?

In attempting to define a reasonable measure for assessing algorithms, time complexity has emerged as crucial. This measure should be rather abstract and general, as an algorithm's execution time depends on several factors, including (i) the style of programming, (ii) the particular programming language used, (iii) processor speed, and (iv) whether a compiler or interpreter is used. It would be unreasonable to define a cost function to judge each algorithm's time complexity separately, as it is not clear what kind of data structure should be used. For example, a list depends on the number of elements, whereas a matrix depends on the number of rows and columns. Hence, it is impossible to estimate the parameters of an algorithm in advance and, consequently, the evaluation of its time complexity is an intricate process.

11.5.1 Bounds

Let n be the input size of an algorithm (i. e., the number of data elements to be processed). The time complexity of an algorithm is determined by the maximal number of steps (e. g., value assignments, arithmetic operations, memory allocations, etc.) in relation to input size required to obtain a specific result.

In the following, we describe how to measure the time complexity of an algorithm asymptotically, and describe several forms thereof. First, we state an upper bound for the time complexity that will be attained in the worst case (O-notation). To begin, we provide a definition of real polynomials, as they play a crucial role in the asymptotic measurement of algorithms' time complexity.

Definition 11.5.1 ([151]). The function $f : \mathbb{R} \longrightarrow \mathbb{R}$, defined by

$$f(x) = a_n x^n + a_{n-1} x^{n-1} + \cdots + a_0, \quad a_n \neq 0,\ a_k \in \mathbb{R},\ k = 0, 1, \ldots, n, \tag{11.8}$$

is a real polynomial of degree n.

By definition, the input variable x and the value of the function $f(x)$ are real numbers. In terms of the coefficients c_k, a polynomial is called real if its coefficients are real. For instance, complex polynomials possess complex-valued coefficients.

To define an asymptotic upper bound for the time complexity of an algorithm, the O-notation is required.

Definition 11.5.2 (O-notation [37]). Let $f, g : \mathbb{N} \longrightarrow \mathbb{R}_+$ be two functions. We define

$$O(g(n)) = \{f(n) \mid \exists c > 0, \exists n_0 > 0, \forall n \geq n_0 :\ f(n) \leq c \cdot g(n)\}. \tag{11.9}$$

Definition 11.5.2 means that $g(n)$ is an asymptotic upper bound of $f(n)$ if a constant $c > 0$ exists and a natural number n_0 such that $f(n)$ is less or equal $c \cdot g(n)$ for $n \geq n_0$.

In contrast to the worst case, described by the O-notation, we now define an asymptotic lower bound that describes the "least" complexity. This is provided by the Ω-notation.

Definition 11.5.3 (Ω-notation [37]). Let $f, g : \mathbb{N} \longrightarrow \mathbb{R}_+$ be two functions. We define

$$\Omega(g(n)) = \{f(n) \mid \exists c > 0, \exists n_0 > 0, \forall n \geq n_0 :\ c \cdot g(n) \leq f(n)\}. \tag{11.10}$$

According to Definition 11.5.3, $g(n)$ is an asymptotic lower bound of $f(n)$ if a constant $c > 0$ exists and a natural number n_0 such that $f(n) \geq c \cdot g(n)$ for $n \geq n_0$.

To simultaneously define upper and lower bounds for the time complexity, the Θ-notation is used.

Definition 11.5.4 (Θ-notation [37]). Let $f, g : \mathbb{N} \longrightarrow \mathbb{R}_+$ be two functions. We define

$$\Theta(g(n)) = \{f(n) \mid \exists c_1, c_2 > 0, \exists n_0 > 0, \forall n \geq n_0 : c_1 \cdot g(n) \leq f(n) \leq c_2 \cdot g(n)\}. \tag{11.11}$$

According to Definition 11.5.4, $g(n)$ is an exact asymptotic bound of $f(n)$ if two constants $c_1, c_2 > 0$ exist, and a natural number n_0 such that $f(n)$ lies in between $c_1 \cdot g(n)$, and $c_2 \cdot g(n)$ if $n \geq n_0$.

11.5.2 Examples

In this section, some examples are given to illustrate the definitions of the asymptotic bounds. In practice, the O-notation is the most important and widely used. Hence, the following examples will focus on it.

To simplify the notation, we denote the number of calculation steps in an algorithm by $f(n)$. Let $f(n) := n^2+3n$. To determine the complexity class $O(n^k), k \in \mathbb{N}$, the constants c and n_0 must be determined. Using Definition 11.5.2, setting $c = 4$ and $g(n) = n^2$, the following inequalities can be verified:

$$n^2 + 3n \leq 4n^2 \quad \text{or} \quad 3n \leq 3n^2. \tag{11.12}$$

This gives $1 \leq n$. That means, with $c = 4$ and $n_0 = 1$, we have

$$n^2 + 3n \leq c \cdot n^2. \tag{11.13}$$

Thus, we obtain $n^2 + 3n \in O(n^2)$.

A second example is the function

$$f(n) := c_5 n^5 + c_4 n^4 + c_3 n^3 + c_2 n^2 + c_1 n + c_0. \tag{11.14}$$

If n goes to infinity, we can disregard the terms $c_4n^4 + c_3n^3 + c_2n^2 + c_1n + c_0$ as well as the constant c_5, and obtain $f(n) \in O(n^5)$. We see that the O-notation always emphasizes the dominating power of the polynomial (here n^5).

To demonstrate the general case, we use the polynomial

$$f(n) = a_k n^k + a_{k-1} n^{k-1} + \cdots + a_1 n + a_0, \quad a_k \neq 0, \tag{11.15}$$

and obtain

$$\begin{aligned} f(n) &= \left|a_k n^k + a_{k-1} n^{k-1} + \cdots + a_1 n + a_0\right| \\ &= n^k \left|a_k + \frac{a_{k-1}}{n} + \frac{a_{k-2}}{n^2} + \cdots + \frac{a_0}{n^k}\right| \\ &\leq n^k \left(|a_k| + \frac{|a_{k-1}|}{n} + \frac{|a_{k-2}|}{n^2} + \cdots + \frac{|a_0|}{n^k}\right) \\ &\leq n^k \left(|a_k| + |a_{k-1}| + |a_{k-2}| + \cdots + |a_0|\right) = cn^k. \end{aligned} \tag{11.16}$$

Inequality (11.16) has been obtained using the triangle inequality [178]. By setting $c := |a_k| + |a_{k-1}| + |a_{k-2}| + \cdots + |a_0|$, inequality (11.16) is satisfied for $n \geq 1$. That means, $f(n) \leq cn^j$ for $j \geq k$ and $n \in \mathbb{N}$. Finally, we obtain $f(n) \in O(n^j)$ for $j \geq k$.

In the final example, we use a simple imperative program (see Section 2.2) to calculate the sum of the first n natural numbers ($\text{sum} = 1 + 2 \cdots + n$). Basically, the pseudocode of this program consists of the initialization step, sum $= 0$, and a for-loop with variable i and body sum $= i + 1$ for $1 \leq i \leq n$. The first value assignment requires constant costs, say, c_1. In each step of the for-loop to increment the value of the variable sum, constant costs c_2 are required. Then we obtain the upper bound for the time complexity

$$f(n) = c_1 + c_2 \cdot n, \tag{11.17}$$

and finally, $f(n) \in O(n)$.

11.5.3 Important properties of the O-notation

In view of the importance of the O-notation for practical use, several of its properties are listed below:

$$c = O(1), \tag{11.18}$$
$$c \cdot O(f(n)) = O(f(n)), \tag{11.19}$$
$$O(f(n)) + O(f(n)) = O(f(n)), \tag{11.20}$$
$$O(\log_b(n)) = O(\log(n)), \tag{11.21}$$
$$O(f(n) + g(n)) = O(\max\{f(n), g(n)\}), \tag{11.22}$$
$$O(f(n)) \cdot O(g(n)) = O(f(n) \cdot g(n)). \tag{11.23}$$

An algorithm with a constant number of steps has time complexity $O(1)$ (see equation (11.18)). The second rule given by equation (11.19) means that constant factors can be neglected. If we execute a program with time complexity $O(f(n))$ sequentially, the final program will have the same complexity (see equation (11.20)). According to equation (11.21), the logarithmic complexity does not depend on the base b. Moreover, the sequential execution of two programs with different time complexities has the complexity of the program with higher time complexity (see equation (11.22)). Finally, the overall complexity of a nested program (for example, two nested loops) is the product of the individual complexities (see equation (11.23)).

11.5.4 Known complexity classes

Finally, we list some examples of algorithm complexity classes:

- $O(1)$ consists of programs with constant time complexity (e. g., value assignments, arithmetic operations, Hashing).
- $O(n)$ consists of programs with linear time complexity (e. g., calculating sums and linear searching procedures).
- $O(n^2)$ consists of programs with quadratic time complexity (e. g., a simple sorting algorithm, such as Bubblesort [37]).
- $O(n^3)$ consists of programs with cubic time complexity (e. g., a simple algorithm to solve the shortest path problem proposed by Dijkstra [58] where, n is the number of vertices in a network).

- $O(n^k)$ generally consists of programs with polynomial time complexity. Obviously, $O(n)$, $O(n^2)$ and $O(n^3)$ are also polynomial.
- $O(\log(n))$ consists of programs with logarithmic time complexity (e. g., binary searching [37]).
- $O(2^n)$ consists of programs with exponential time complexity (e. g., enumeration problems and recursive functions [37]).

Algorithms with complexity $O(1)$ are highly desirable in practice. Logarithmic and linear time complexity are also favorable for practical applications as long as $\log(n) < n$, $n > 1$. Quadratic and cubic time complexity remain sufficient when n is relatively small. Algorithms with complexity $O(2^n)$ can only be used under certain constraints, since 2^n grows significantly compared to n^k. Such algorithms could possibly be used when searching for graph isomorphisms or cycles, whose graphs have bounded vertex degrees, for example (see [130]).

11.6 Summary

At this juncture, it is worth reiterating that, despite the apparent novelty of the term data science, the fields on which it is based have long histories, among them theoretical computer science [61]. The purpose of this chapter has been to show that computability, complexity, and the computer, in the form of a Turing machine, are mathematically defined. This aspect can easily be overlooked in these terms' practical usage.

The salient point is that data scientists should recognize that all these concepts possess mathematical definitions which are neither heuristic nor ad-hoc. As such, they may be revisited if necessary (e. g., to analyze an algorithm's runtime). Our second point is that not every detail about these entities must be known. Given the intellectual complexity of these topics, this is encouraging, because acquiring an in-depth understanding of these is a long-term endeavor. However, even a basic understanding is preferable and helps in improving practical programming and data analysis skills.

12 Linear algebra

One of the most important and widely used subjects of mathematics is linear algebra [27]. For this reason, we begin this part of the book with this topic. Furthermore, linear algebra plays a pivotal role for the mathematical basics of data science.

This chapter opens with a brief introduction to some basic elements of linear algebra, e. g., vectors and matrices, before discussing advanced operations, transformations, and matrix decompositions, including Cholesky factorization, QR factorization, and singular value decomposition [27].

12.1 Vectors and matrices

Vectors and matrices are fundamental objects that are used to study problems in many fields, including mathematics, physics, engineering, and biology (see e. g. [27, 21, 186]).

12.1.1 Vectors

Vectors define quantities, which require both a magnitude, i. e., a length, and a direction to be fully characterized. Examples of vectors in physics are velocity or force. Hence, a vector extends a scalar, which defines a quantity fully described by its magnitude alone. From an algebraic point of view, a vector, in an n-dimensional real space, is defined by an ordered list of n real scalars, $x_1, x_2, \ldots, x_n$ arranged in an array.

Definition 12.1.1. A *vector* is said to be a *row vector* if its associated array is arranged horizontally, i. e.,

$$(x_1, x_2, \ldots, x_n),$$

whereas a vector is called a *column vector* when its array is arranged vertically, i. e.,

$$\begin{pmatrix} x_1 \\ x_2 \\ \vdots \\ x_n \end{pmatrix}.$$

Geometrically, a vector can be regarded as a displacement between two points in space, and it is often denoted using a symbol surmounted by an arrow, e. g., $\overrightarrow{V}$.

https://doi.org/10.1515/9783110796063-012

Definition 12.1.2. Let $\overrightarrow{V} = (x_1, x_2, \dots, x_n)$ be an n-dimensional real vector. Then, the *p-norm* of $\overrightarrow{V}$, denoted $\|\overrightarrow{V}\|_p$, is defined by the following quantity

$$\|\overrightarrow{V}\|_p = \left(\sum_{i=1}^{n} |x_i|^p\right)^{\frac{1}{p}}, \qquad (12.1)$$

where $|x_i|$ denotes the modulus or the absolute value of x_i.

In particular,

1. the 1-norm of the vector $\overrightarrow{V}$ is defined by

$$\|\overrightarrow{V}\|_1 = \sum_{i=1}^{n} |x_i|,$$

2. the 2-norm of the vector $\overrightarrow{V}$ is defined by

$$\|\overrightarrow{V}\|_2 = \left(\sum_{i=1}^{n} |x_i|^2\right)^{\frac{1}{2}},$$

3. when $p = \infty$, the p-norm, also called the maximum norm, is defined by

$$\|\overrightarrow{V}\|_\infty = \max_{i \in 1,\dots,n} |x_i|.$$

Definition 12.1.3. Let E^n denote an n-dimensional space. Let d be a function defined by

$$d : E^n \times E^n \longrightarrow \mathbb{R},$$

such that for any $x, y, z \in E^n$ the following relations hold:

1. $d(x, y) \geq 0$;
2. $d(x, y) = 0 \iff x = y$;
3. $d(x, y) = d(y, x)$;
4. $d(x, z) \leq d(x, y) + d(y, z)$.

Such a function, d, is called a *metric*, and the pair (E^n, d) is called a *metric space*.

When $E^n = \mathbb{R}^n$ and $d(x, y) = (\sum_{i=1}^{n}(x_i - y_i)^2)^{1/2}$, then the pair $(E^n, d) = (\mathbb{R}^n, d)$ is called an n-dimensional *Euclidean space*, also referred to as an n-dimensional *Cartesian space*.

From Definition 12.1.3, it is clear that $\mathbb{R}$, the set of real numbers (or the real line), is a 1-dimensional Euclidean space, whereas $\mathbb{R}^2$, the real plane, is a 2-dimensional Euclidean space.

Remark 12.1.1. The p-norm, with $p = 2$, of a vector in an n-dimensional Euclidean space is referred to as the *Euclidean norm.*

Let $A = \binom{x_A}{y_A}$ and $B = \binom{x_B}{y_B}$ be two points in a 2-dimensional Euclidean space. Then, the vector $\overrightarrow{AB} = \vec{V}$ is the displacement from the point A to the point B, which can be specified in a cartesian coordinates system by

$$\overrightarrow{AB} = \vec{V} = \begin{pmatrix} x_B - x_A \\ y_B - y_A \end{pmatrix}.$$

This is illustrated in Figure 12.1 (a).

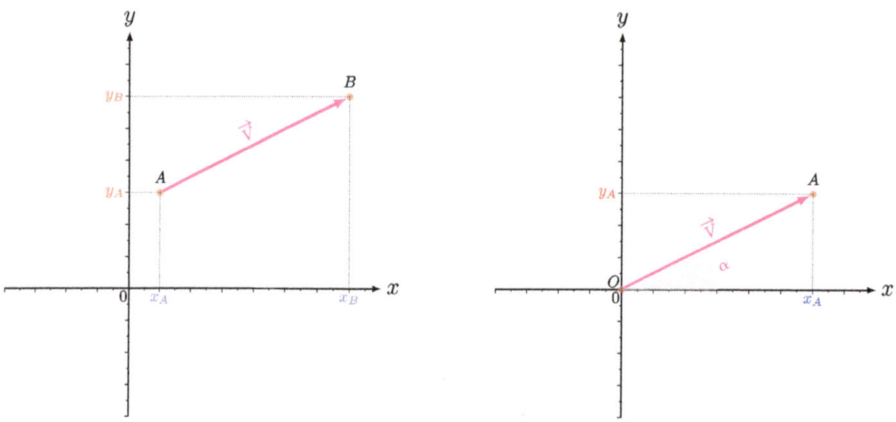

(a) (b)

Figure 12.1: (a) Vector representation in a two-dimensional space. (b) Decomposition of a standard vector in a 2-dimensional space.

Definition 12.1.4. The magnitude of a vector $\overrightarrow{AB}$ is defined by the non-negative scalar given by its *Euclidean norm*, denoted $\|\overrightarrow{AB}\|_2$ or simply $\|\overrightarrow{AB}\|$.

Specifically, the magnitude of a 2-dimensional vector $\overrightarrow{AB}$ is given by

$$\|\overrightarrow{AB}\| = \sqrt{(x_B - x_A)^2 + (y_B - y_A)^2}.$$

In applications, the Euclidean norm is sometimes also referred to as the Euclidean distance.

Using R, the norm of a vector can be computed as illustrated in Listing 12.1.

Listing 12.1: Definition of a vector and computation of its norm

```
#Defining a 3-dimensional row vector from a given list of 3 numbers
listnb <- c(3, 2, -5)
V <- matrix(listnb, nrow=1)
```

```
V
     [,1] [,2] [,3]
[1,]    3    2   -5
#Defining a 3-dimensional column vector from a given list of 3
     numbers
listnb <- c(12, 1, -3)
W<- matrix(listnb, ncol=1)
W
     [,1]
[1,]   12
[2,]    1
[3,]   -3
# Norm of the vector V
NormV<-sqrt(sum(V^2))
NormV
[1] 6.164414
# Norm of the vector W
NormW<-sqrt(sum(W^2))
NormW
[1] 12.40967
```

Definition 12.1.5. Two n-dimensional vectors $\overrightarrow{V}$ and $\overrightarrow{W}$ are said to be parallel if they have the same direction.

Definition 12.1.6. Two n-dimensional vectors $\overrightarrow{V}$ and $\overrightarrow{W}$ are said to be equal if they have the same direction and the same magnitude.

Various transformations and operations can be performed on vectors, and some of the most important will be presented in the following sections.

Example 12.1.1. For supervised learning, k-NN (k nearest neighbors) [96] is a simple yet efficient way to classify data. Suppose that we have a high-dimensional data set with two classes, whose data points represent vectors. Let x be a point that we wish to assign to one of these two classes. To predict the class label of a point x, we calculate the Euclidean distance, introduced above (see Remark 12.1.1), between x and all other points x_i, i. e., $d_i = \|x - x_i\|$. Then, we order these distances d_i in an increasing order. The k-NN classifier now uses the nearest k distances to obtain

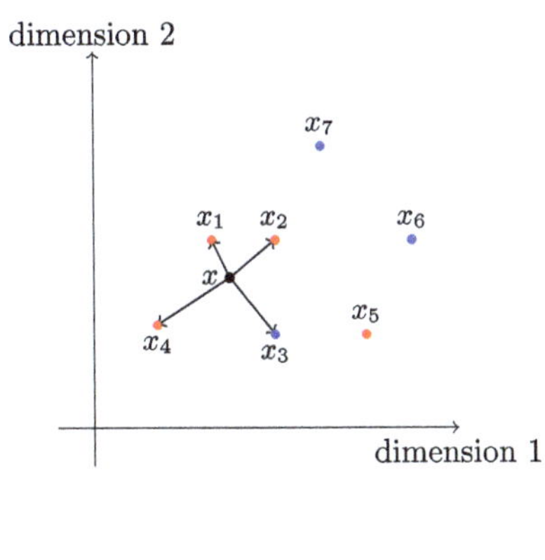

Figure 12.2: An example where the Euclidean distance $\|x - x_i\|$ is used for the classifier k-NN. A point x is assigned the label i based on a majority vote, considering its nearest k neighbors. In this example, $k = 4$.

a majority vote for the prediction of the label for the point x. For instance, in Figure 12.2, a two-dimensional example is shown for $k = 4$. Among the four nearest neighbors of x are three red points and one blue point. This means the predicted class label of x would be "red". In the extreme case $k = 1$, the point x would be assigned to the class with the single nearest neighbor.

The k-NN method is an example of an instance-based learning algorithm. There are many variations of the k-NN approach presented here, e. g., considering weighted voting to overcome the limitations of majority voting in case of ties.

12.1.1.1 Vector translation

Let $\vec{V} = \overrightarrow{AB}$ denote the displacement between two points A and B. The same displacement $\vec{V}$, starting from a point A' to another point B', defines a vector $\overrightarrow{A'B'}$.

The vector $\overrightarrow{A'B'}$ is called a *translation* of the vector $\overrightarrow{AB}$, and the two vectors $\overrightarrow{AB}$ and $\overrightarrow{A'B'}$ are equal, when they have the same direction, and $\|\overrightarrow{AB}\| = \|\vec{V}\| = \|\overrightarrow{A'B'}\|$. Hence, the *translation* of a vector $\overrightarrow{AB}$ is a transformation that maps a pair of points A and B to another pair of points A' and B', such that the following relations hold:

1. $\overrightarrow{AA'} = \overrightarrow{BB'}$;
2. $\overrightarrow{AA'}$ and $\overrightarrow{BB'}$ are parallel.

In a two-dimensional space, the vector $\overrightarrow{AB}$ and its translation $\overrightarrow{A'B'}$ form opposite sides of a parallelogram, as illustrated in Figure 12.3 (a). Thus,

$$A' = \begin{pmatrix} x_{A'} \\ y_{A'} \end{pmatrix} = \begin{pmatrix} x_A + k_x \\ y_A + k_y \end{pmatrix} \quad \text{and} \quad B' = \begin{pmatrix} x_{B'} \\ y_{B'} \end{pmatrix} = \begin{pmatrix} x_B + k_x \\ y_B + k_y \end{pmatrix},$$

where k_x and k_y are scalars.

Definition 12.1.7. A vector $\vec{V} = \overrightarrow{A'B'}$ is called a *standard vector* if its initial point (i. e., the point A') coincides with the origin of the coordinate system. Hence, using vector translation, any given vector can be transformed into a standard vector, as illustrated in Figure 12.3 (a).

12.1.1.2 Vector rotation

A vector *transformation*, which changes the direction of a vector while its initial point remains unchanged, is called a *rotation*. This results in an angle between the original vector and its rotated counterpart, called the *rotation angle*. Let $\vec{V} = (x_A, y_A)$ be a 2-dimensional vector, and $\vec{V}' = (x_{A'}, y_{A'})$ its rotation by an angle θ (see Figure 12.3 (b)). Then, the following properties of the vector rotation should be noted:

$$x_{A'} = x_A \cos(\theta) - y_A \sin(\theta);$$
$$y_{A'} = x_A \sin(\theta) + y_A \cos(\theta);$$
$$\|\vec{V}\| = \|\vec{V}'\|. \quad (12.2)$$

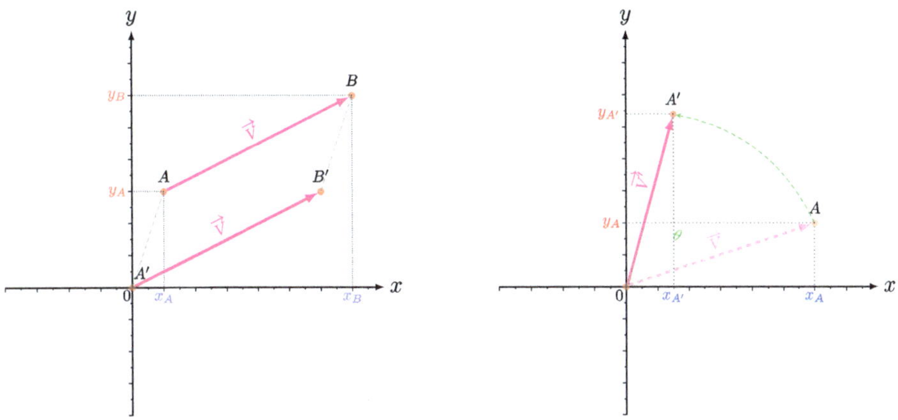

(a) (b)

Figure 12.3: Vector transformation in a 2-dimensional space: (a) Translation of a vector. (b) Rotation of a vector.

Various operations can be carried out on vectors, including the product of a vector by a scalar, the sum, the difference, the scalar or dot product, the cross product, and the mixed product. In the following sections, we will discuss such operations.

12.1.1.3 Vector scaling

Let $\vec{V} = (v_1, v_2, \ldots, v_n)$ be an n-dimensional vector, and let k be a scalar. Then, the product of k with $\vec{V}$, denoted $k \times \vec{V}$, is a vector $\vec{U}$ defined as follows:

$$\vec{U} = (k \times v_1, k \times v_2, \ldots, k \times v_n).$$

Geometrically, the vector $\vec{U}$ is aligned with $\vec{V}$, but k times longer or shorter.

Definition 12.1.8. If $\vec{V}$ is non-null (i. e., not all of its components are zero), then $\vec{V}$ and $\vec{U} = k\vec{V}$ are said to be *parallel* if $k > 0$, and *anti-parallel* if $k < 0$. In the particular case where $k = -1$, then $\vec{V}$ and $\vec{U}$ are said to be opposite vectors (see Figure 12.4 (b) for an illustration).

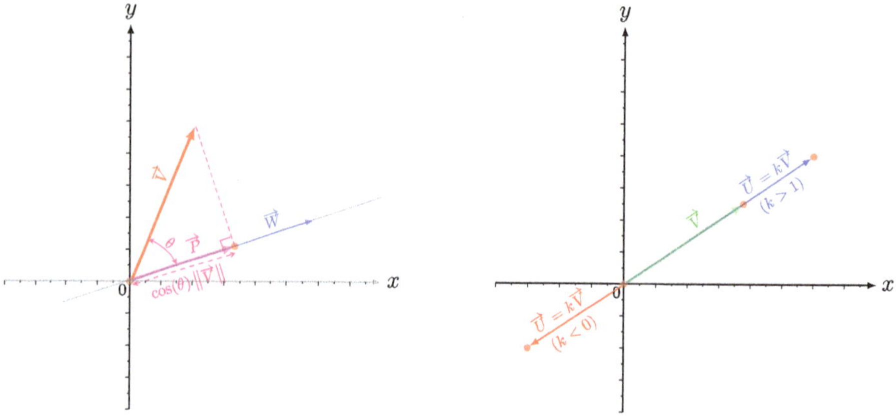

(a) (b)

Figure 12.4: Vector transformation in a 2-dimensional space: (a) Orthogonal projection of a vector. (b) Vector scaling.

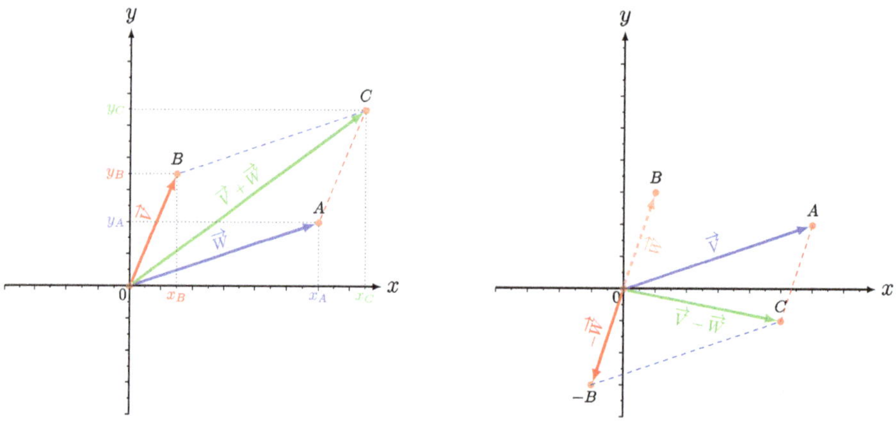

(a) (b)

Figure 12.5: Vector operations in a two-dimensional space: (a) Sum of two vectors. (b) Difference between two vectors.

Definition 12.1.9. For any scalar k, the vectors $\overrightarrow{V}$ and $\overrightarrow{U} = k \times \overrightarrow{V}$ are said to be *collinear.*

12.1.1.4 Vector sum

Let $\overrightarrow{V} = (v_1, v_2, \ldots, v_n)$ and $\overrightarrow{W} = (w_1, w_2, \ldots, w_n)$ be two n-dimensional vectors. Then, the sum of $\overrightarrow{V}$ and $\overrightarrow{W}$, denoted $\overrightarrow{V} + \overrightarrow{W}$, is a vector $\overrightarrow{S}$ defined as follows:

$$\overrightarrow{S} = \overrightarrow{V} + \overrightarrow{W} = (v_1 + w_1, v_2 + w_2, \ldots, v_n + w_n).$$

In a two-dimensional space, the vector sum $\vec{S}$ can be obtained geometrically, as illustrated in Figure 12.5 (a); i. e., we translate the vector $\vec{W}$ until its initial point coincides with the terminal point of $\vec{V}$. Since translation does not change a vector, the translated vector is identical to $\vec{W}$. Then, the vector $\vec{S}$ is given by the displacement from the initial point of $\vec{V}$ to the terminal point of the translation of the translation of $\vec{W}$. Note that the sum of vectors is commutative, i. e.,

$$\vec{V} + \vec{W} = \vec{W} + \vec{V}.$$

This means that if $\vec{V}$ has been translated instead of $\vec{W}$, the result will be the same sum vector $\vec{S}$. This is illustrated in Figure 12.5 (a).

12.1.1.5 Vector difference

Let $\vec{V} = (v_1, v_2, \ldots, v_n)$, $\vec{W} = (w_1, w_2, \ldots, w_n)$ be two n-dimensional vectors. Then, the difference between $\vec{V}$ and $\vec{W}$, denoted $\vec{V} - \vec{W}$, is the a vector $\vec{D}$ defined by the sum of $\vec{V}$ and the opposite of $\vec{W}$, i. e.,

$$\vec{D} = \vec{V} + (-\vec{W}) = (v_1 - w_1, v_2 - w_2, \ldots, v_n - w_n).$$

This is illustrated geometrically in a 2-dimensional space in Figure 12.5 (b). Note that, in contrast with the sum, the difference between two vectors is *not* commutative, i. e., $\vec{V} - \vec{W} \neq \vec{W} - \vec{V}$.

12.1.1.6 Vector decomposition

It is often convenient to decompose a vector $\vec{V}$ into the vector components $\vec{V}_{||}$ and $\vec{V}_{\perp}$, which are respectively parallel and perpendicular to the direction of another vector $\vec{W}$, and such that

$$\vec{V} = \vec{V}_{||} + \vec{V}_{\perp}.$$

In this case, the vector components of $\vec{V}$ are given by

$$\vec{V}_{||} = \frac{\vec{V} \cdot \vec{W}}{\vec{W} \cdot \vec{W}} \vec{W},$$
$$\vec{V}_{\perp} = \vec{V} - \vec{V}_{||}.$$

In a two-dimensional orthonormal space, the standard components of a vector $\vec{V} = \overrightarrow{OA}$, where O denotes the origin of the coordinate system, with respect to the x-axis and the y-axis, are simply the coordinates of the point A, i. e.,

$$\vec{V} = \overrightarrow{OA} = \begin{pmatrix} x_A - x_O \\ y_A - y_O \end{pmatrix} = \begin{pmatrix} x_A - 0 \\ y_A - 0 \end{pmatrix} = \begin{pmatrix} x_A \\ y_A \end{pmatrix}.$$

If α denotes the angle between the vector $\overrightarrow{V}$ and the x-axis, as illustrated in Figure 12.1 (b), then we have the following relationships:

$$\begin{aligned} x_A &= \cos(\alpha) \times \|\overrightarrow{V}\|, \\ y_A &= \sin(\alpha) \times \|\overrightarrow{V}\|, \\ \frac{x_A}{y_A} &= \tan(\alpha). \end{aligned} \tag{12.3}$$

12.1.1.7 Vector projection

The projection of an n-dimensional vector $\overrightarrow{V}$ onto the direction of a vector $\overrightarrow{W}$, in an m-dimensional space, is a *transformation* that maps the terminal point of the vector $\overrightarrow{V}$ to a point in the space associated with the direction of $\overrightarrow{W}$. This results in a vector $\overrightarrow{P}$ that is collinear to $\overrightarrow{W}$.

Definition 12.1.10. Let θ denote the angle between $\overrightarrow{V}$ and $\overrightarrow{W}$. If the magnitude of the vector $\overrightarrow{P}$ is given by

$$\|\overrightarrow{P}\| = \cos(\theta) \times \|\overrightarrow{V}\|,$$

then the projection of $\overrightarrow{V}$ onto the direction of $\overrightarrow{W}$ is said to be *orthogonal*.

Clearly, in a two-dimensional space, as depicted in Figure 12.4 (a), the vector $\overrightarrow{P}$, the orthogonal project of $\overrightarrow{V}$ onto the direction of $\overrightarrow{W}$, is nothing but the vector component of V parallel to W. Thus,

$$\overrightarrow{P} = \begin{pmatrix} x_P \\ y_P \end{pmatrix} = \frac{\overrightarrow{V} \cdot \overrightarrow{W}}{\overrightarrow{W} \cdot \overrightarrow{W}} \begin{pmatrix} x_W \\ y_W \end{pmatrix}.$$

12.1.1.8 Vector reflection

The reflection of an n-dimensional vector $\overrightarrow{V}$ with respect to the direction of a vector $\overrightarrow{W}$, in an m-dimensional space, is a *transformation* that maps the vector $\overrightarrow{V}$ to an n-dimensional vector $\overrightarrow{U}$, such that (see Figure 12.6)

$$\overrightarrow{U} = \overrightarrow{V} - 2\frac{\overrightarrow{V} \cdot \overrightarrow{W}}{\|\overrightarrow{W}\|^2}\overrightarrow{W}.$$

In a two-dimensional orthonormal space, the components of the vector $\overrightarrow{U}$ are given by

$$\overrightarrow{U} = \begin{pmatrix} x_U \\ y_U \end{pmatrix} = \begin{pmatrix} x_V \\ y_V \end{pmatrix} - k \begin{pmatrix} x_W \\ y_W \end{pmatrix}, \quad \text{with } k = 2\frac{\overrightarrow{V} \cdot \overrightarrow{W}}{\|\overrightarrow{W}\|^2}.$$

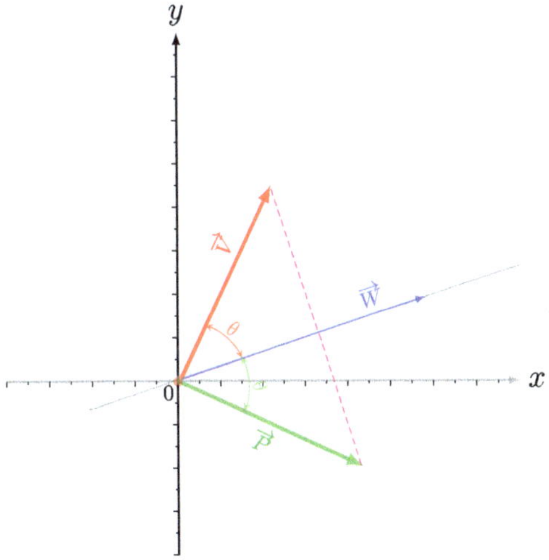

Figure 12.6: Vector reflection in a two-dimensional space.

12.1.1.9 Dot product or scalar product

Let $\overrightarrow{V} = (v_1, v_2, \ldots, v_n)$ and $\overrightarrow{W} = (w_1, w_2, \ldots, w_n)$ be two n-dimensional vectors. The *dot product*, also called the *scalar product*, of $\overrightarrow{V}$ and $\overrightarrow{W}$, denoted $\overrightarrow{V} \cdot \overrightarrow{W}$, is a *scalar* p, defined as follows:

$$p = \overrightarrow{V} \cdot \overrightarrow{W} = v_1 w_1 + v_2 w_2 + \cdots + v_n w_n.$$

Geometrically, the dot product, can be defined through the orthogonal projection of a vector onto another. Let α be the angle between two vectors $\overrightarrow{V}$ and $\overrightarrow{W}$. Then,

$$\overrightarrow{V} \cdot \overrightarrow{W} = \cos(\alpha) \times \|\overrightarrow{V}\| \times \|\overrightarrow{W}\|, \quad \text{with } \cos(\alpha) = \frac{\overrightarrow{V} \cdot \overrightarrow{W}}{\|\overrightarrow{V}\| \times \|\overrightarrow{W}\|}.$$

In Figure 12.4 (a), the norm of the projected vector $\overrightarrow{P}$ can be interpreted as the dot product between the vectors $\overrightarrow{V}$ and $\overrightarrow{W}$.

Definition 12.1.11. When the angle α between two vectors, $\overrightarrow{V}$ and $\overrightarrow{W}$, is $\frac{\pi}{2} + k\pi$, where k is an integer, then the two vectors are said to be *perpendicular* or *orthogonal* to each other, and their dot product is given by

$$\cos\left(\frac{\pi}{2} + k\pi\right) \times \|\overrightarrow{V}\| \times \|\overrightarrow{W}\| = 0 \times \|\overrightarrow{V}\| \times \|\overrightarrow{W}\| = 0.$$

Furthermore, the dot product has the following properties:

1. For any vector $\overrightarrow{V}$: $\overrightarrow{V} \cdot \overrightarrow{V} = \|\overrightarrow{V}\|^2$;
2. For any two vectors $\overrightarrow{V}$ and $\overrightarrow{W}$: $\overrightarrow{V} \cdot \overrightarrow{W} = \overrightarrow{W} \cdot \overrightarrow{V}$;
3. For any two vectors $\overrightarrow{V}$ and $\overrightarrow{W}$: $(\overrightarrow{V} \cdot \overrightarrow{W})^2 \leq (\overrightarrow{V} \cdot \overrightarrow{V})(\overrightarrow{V} \cdot \overrightarrow{V})$. (This is referred to as the Cauchy–Schwarz inequality [27]);

4. For any two vectors $\vec{V}$ and W and a scalar k: $k \times (\vec{V} \cdot \vec{W}) = (k \times \vec{V}) \cdot \vec{W}$;
5. For any three vectors $\vec{U}$, $\vec{V}$, and $\vec{W}$: $(\vec{U} + \vec{V}) \cdot \vec{W} = (\vec{U} \cdot \vec{W}) + (\vec{V} \cdot \vec{W})$.

12.1.1.10 Cross product

The cross product is applicable to vectors in an n-dimensional space, with $n \geq 3$. To illustrate this, let $\vec{V}$ and $\vec{W}$ be two three-dimensional standard vectors defined as follows:

$$\vec{V} = \overrightarrow{OA} = \begin{pmatrix} x_A \\ y_A \\ z_A \end{pmatrix} \quad \text{and} \quad \vec{W} = \overrightarrow{OB} = \begin{pmatrix} x_B \\ y_B \\ z_B \end{pmatrix}.$$

Then, the *cross product* of the vector $\vec{V}$ by the vector $\vec{W}$, denoted $\vec{V} \times \vec{W}$, is a vector $\vec{C}$ perpendicular to both $\vec{V}$ and $\vec{W}$, defined by

$$\vec{C} = \begin{pmatrix} x_C \\ y_C \\ z_C \end{pmatrix} = \begin{pmatrix} y_A \times z_B - y_B \times z_A \\ -x_A \times z_B + xB \times z_A \\ x_A \times y_B - x_B \times y_A \end{pmatrix},$$

or

$$\vec{C} = \|\vec{V}\| \times \|\vec{W}\| \times \sin(\theta) \times \vec{u},$$

where, $\vec{u}$ is the unit vector[1] normal to both $\vec{V}$ and $\vec{W}$, and θ is the angle between $\vec{V}$ and $\vec{W}$.

Thus,

$$\|\vec{C}\| = \|\vec{V}\| \times \|\vec{W}\| \times \sin(\theta) = \mathcal{A},$$

where $\mathcal{A}$ denotes the area of the parallelogram spanned by $\vec{V}$ and $\vec{W}$, as illustrated in Figure 12.7.

The cross product has the following properties:

1. For any vector $\vec{V}$, we have: $\vec{V} \times \vec{V} = 0$;
2. For any two vectors $\vec{V}$ and $\vec{W}$, we have: $\vec{V} \times \vec{W} = -(\vec{W} \times \vec{V})$;
3. For any two vectors $\vec{V}$ and W and a scalar k, we have: $(k \times \vec{V}) \times \vec{W} = \vec{V} \times (k \times \vec{W}) = k \times (\vec{V} \times \vec{W})$;
4. $\vec{V} \times (\vec{U} + \vec{W}) = \vec{V} \times \vec{U} + \vec{V} \times \vec{W}$;
5. $\vec{V} \times (\vec{U} \times \vec{W}) \neq (\vec{V} \times \vec{U}) \times \vec{W}$.

1 Note that the direction of the vector $\vec{u}$ for the cross product $\vec{V} \times \vec{W}$ is determined by the right-hand rule, i. e., it is given by the direction of the right-hand thumb when the other four fingers are rotated from $\vec{V}$ to $\vec{W}$.

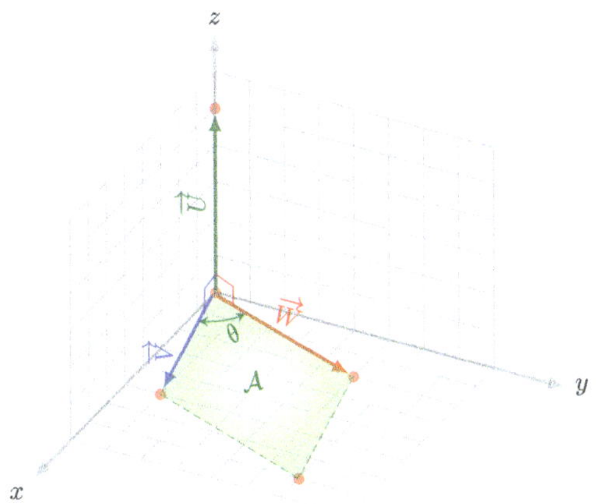

Figure 12.7: Cross product of two vectors in a three-dimensional space.

12.1.1.11 Mixed product

This is an *operation* on vectors, which involves both a cross and a scalar product. To illustrate this, let $\vec{V}$, $\vec{U}$, and $\vec{W}$ denote three three-dimensional vectors. Then, the mixed product between $\vec{V}$, $\vec{U}$, and $\vec{W}$ is a scalar p, defined by

$$\begin{aligned} p &= (\vec{V} \times \vec{U}) \cdot \vec{W} = (\vec{U} \times \vec{W}) \cdot \vec{V} = (\vec{W} \times \vec{V}) \cdot \vec{U} \\ &= \vec{V} \cdot (\vec{U} \times \vec{W}) = \vec{U} \cdot (\vec{W} \times \vec{V}) = \vec{W} \cdot (\vec{V} \times \vec{U}) \\ &= \pm \mathcal{V}, \end{aligned} \tag{12.4}$$

where $\mathcal{V}$ denotes the volume of the parallelepiped spanned by $\vec{V}$, $\vec{U}$, and $\vec{W}$.

In R, the above operations can be carried out using the scripts in Listing 12.2.

Listing 12.2: Vector operations

```
#Defining two 2-dimensional row vectors V and W
V <- matrix(c(2, -5), nrow=1)
V
     [,1] [,2]
[1,]    2   -5
W<- matrix(c(12, 1), nrow=1)
W
     [,1] [,2]
[1,]   12    1
#Rotation of vector V by an angle theta=pi/2
theta<-pi/2
xVp<-V[1,1]*cos(theta) - V[1,2]*sin(theta)
yVp<-V[1,1]*sin(theta) + V[1,2]*cos(theta)
Vprime<- matrix(c(xVp, yVp), nrow=1)
Vprime
     [,1] [,2]
[1,]    5    2
#V and Vprime have the same norm
sqrt(sum(V^2))
[1] 5.385165
sqrt(sum(Vprime^2))
```

```
[1] 5.385165
#Product of a vector by a scalar k
k <- 5
U<-k*V
U
     [,1] [,2]
[1,]   10  -25
#Sum of the vectors V and W: S=V+W
S<-V+W
S
     [,1] [,2]
[1,]   14   -4
#Difference of the vectors V and W: D=V-W
D<-V-W
D
     [,1] [,2]
[1,]  -10   -6
#Dot product of V and W
p<- sum(V*W)
p
[1] 19
#Finding the angle theta between V and W
NormV<-sqrt(sum(V^2))
NormW<-sqrt(sum(W^2))
theta<-acos(p/(NormV*NormW))      # p is the dot product of V and W
theta
[1] 1.273431     # This value of theta is in radian
theta<- theta*180/pi
theta
[1] 72.96223     # This is the value of theta in degree
#Orthogonal projection of V onto the direction of W
P<-(p/sum(W^2))*W     # p is the dot product of V and W
 P
         [,1]      [,2]
[1,] 1.572414 0.1310345
NormP<- sqrt(sum(P^2))
[1] 1.577864
p/NormW    # Norm of the vector P using the dot product of V and W
[1] 1.577864
#Defining two 3-dimensional row vectors V and W
V <- matrix(c(3, 1, 0), nrow=1)
W <- matrix(c(2, 4, 0), nrow=1)
xC<-V[1, 2]*W[1,3]  - W[1,2]*V[1,3]
yC<- -(V[1, 1]*W[1,3]  - W[1,1]*V[1,3])
zC<-xC<-V[1, 1]*W[1,2]  - W[1,1]*V[1,2]
C<-matrix(c(xC, yC, zC), nrow=1)
C
     [,1] [,2] [,3]
[1,]    0    0   10
sum(C*V)
[1] 0   #C and V are orthogonal since their dot product is zero
 sum(C*W)
[1] 0  #C and W are orthogonal since their dot product is zero
#Norm of the vector C
NormC<-sqrt(sum(C^2))
NormC
[1] 10
#Computing the area, A, of the parallelogram spanned by V and W
NormV<-sqrt(sum(V^2))
NormW<-sqrt(sum(W^2))
```

```
p<- sum(V*W)
theta<-acos(p/(NormV*NormW))
A<-NormV*NormW*sin(theta)
A
[1] 10  # A equal the norm of the vector C
```

12.1.2 Vector representations in other coordinates systems

For various problems, the quantities characterized by vectors must be described in different coordinate systems [27]. Depending on the dimension of its space, a vector can be represented in different ways. For instance, in a two-dimensional space, a standard vector $\vec{V} = \overrightarrow{OA}$, where O denotes the origin point, can be specified either by:

1. The pair (x_A, y_A), where x_A and y_A denote the coordinates of the point A, the terminal point of $\vec{V}$, in a two-dimensional Euclidean space. The pair (x_A, y_A) defines the representation of the vector $\vec{V}$ in *cartesian coordinates*.
2. The pair (r, θ), where $r = \|\vec{V}\|$ is the magnitude of $\vec{V}$ and θ is the angle between the vector $\vec{V}$ and a reference axis in a cartesian system, e. g., the x-axis. The pair (ρ, θ) defines the representation of the vector $\vec{V}$ in *polar coordinates*.

The polar coordinates can be recovered from cartesian coordinates, and vice versa. Let $\vec{V} = \overrightarrow{OA} = \binom{x_A}{y_A}$ be a standard vector in a two-dimensional cartesian space, as depicted in Figure 12.8. Then, the polar coordinates of $\vec{V}$ can be obtained as follows:

$$
\begin{aligned}
r &= \sqrt{x_A^2 + y_A^2}, \\
\theta &= \tan^{-1}\left(\frac{y_A}{x_A}\right).
\end{aligned} \tag{12.5}
$$

Conversely, the cartesian coordinates can be recovered as follows:

$$
\begin{aligned}
x_A &= r\cos(\theta), \\
y_A &= r\sin(\theta).
\end{aligned} \tag{12.6}
$$

In R, the above coordinate transformations can be carried out using the commands in Listing 12.3.

Listing 12.3: Coordinate system transformations of a 2-dimensional vector

```
#Defining a 2-dimensional row vector V in a cartesian coordinates
    system
V <- matrix(c(2, -5), nrow=1)
#Coordinates of the vector V in polar coordinates
rV<- sqrt(sum(V^2))
```

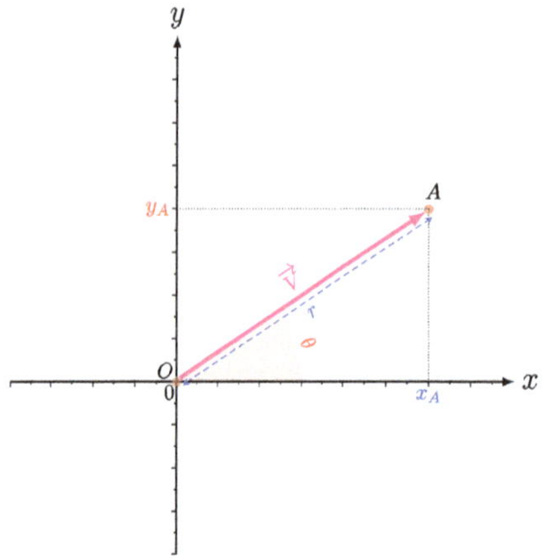

Figure 12.8: Representation of a 2-dimensional vector in a polar coordinates system.

```
thetaV<-acos(V[1,1]/r)*180/pi
rV
[1] 5.385165
thetaV
[1] 68.19859
#Recovering cartesian coordinates
xV<-rV*cos(thetaV*pi/180)
yV<-rV*sin(thetaV*pi/180)
xV
[1] 2
yV
[1] 5
```

In a three-dimensional space, a standard vector $\vec{V} = \overrightarrow{OA}$, where O denotes the origin point, can be specified either by one of the following:

1. The triplet (x_A, y_A, z_A), where x_A, y_A and z_A denote the coordinates of the point A, the terminal point of $\vec{V}$, in a three-dimensional Euclidean space. The triplet (x_A, y_A, z_A) defines the representation of the vector $\vec{V}$ in *cartesian coordinates* (see Figure 12.9 (a) for illustration).
2. The triplet (ρ, θ, z_A), where ρ is the magnitude of the projection of $\vec{V}$ on the x–y plane, θ is the angle between the projection of the vector $\vec{V}$ on the x–y plane and the x-axis, and z_A is the third coordinate of A in a cartesian system. The triplet (ρ, θ, z_A) defines the representation of the vector $\vec{V}$ in *cylindrical coordinates* (see Figure 12.9 (b) for illustration).
3. The triplet (r, θ, φ), where $r = \|\vec{V}\|$ is the magnitude of $\vec{V}$, θ is the angle between the projection of the vector $\vec{V}$ on the x–y plane and the x-axis, and φ is angle between the vector $\vec{V}$ and the x–z plane. The triplet (ρ, θ, φ) defines the representation of the vector $\vec{V}$ in *spherical coordinates* (see Figure 12.9 (c) for illustration).

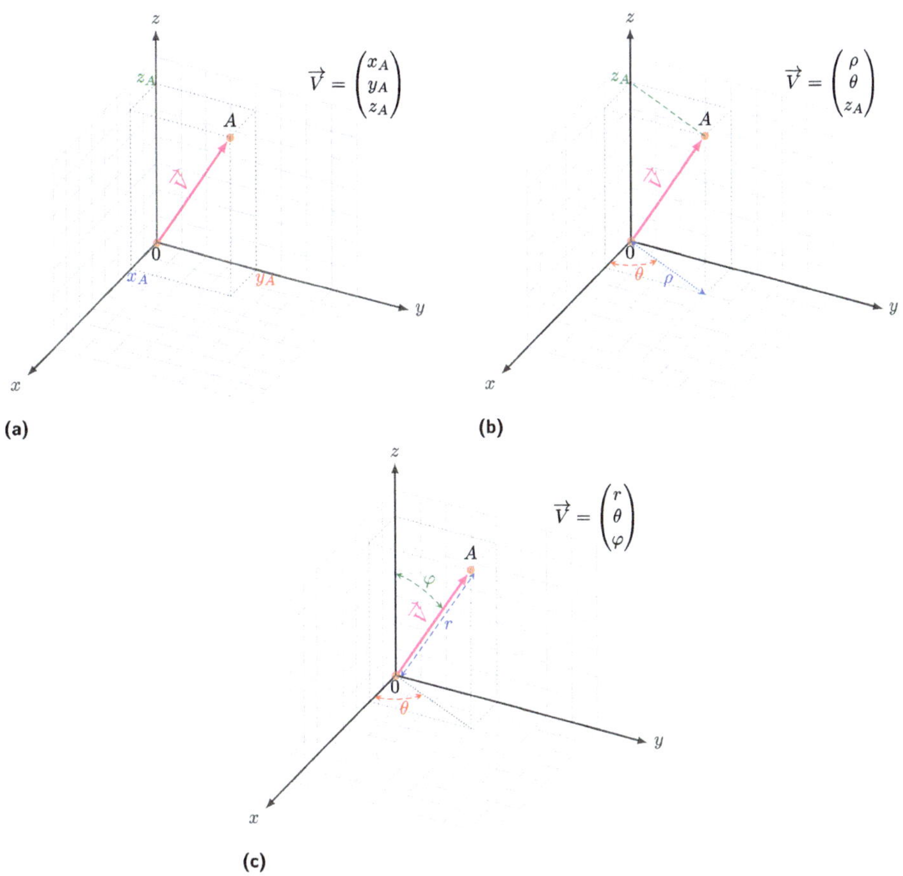

Figure 12.9: Representation of a point in a three-dimensional space in different coordinate systems: (a) cartesian coordinates system; (b) cylindrical coordinates systems; (c) spherical coordinates system.

Mutual relationships exist between cartesian, cylindrical and spherical coordinates. Let

$$\vec{V} = \overrightarrow{OA} = \begin{pmatrix} x_A \\ y_A \\ z_A \end{pmatrix}$$

be a standard vector in a three-dimensional cartesian space. Then we have the following relationships between the different coordinate systems:

1. The cylindrical coordinates of $\overrightarrow{V}$ can be obtained as follows:

$$\begin{aligned}\rho &= \sqrt{x_A^2 + y_A^2},\\ \theta &= \tan^{-1}\left(\frac{y_A}{x_A}\right),\\ z_A &= z_A.\end{aligned} \tag{12.7}$$

   Conversely, the cartesian coordinates can be recovered as follows:

$$\begin{aligned}x_A &= \rho\cos(\theta),\\ y_A &= \rho\sin(\theta),\\ z_A &= z_A.\end{aligned} \tag{12.8}$$

2. The spherical coordinates of $\overrightarrow{V}$ can be obtained as follows:

$$\begin{aligned}r &= \sqrt{x_A^2 + y_A^2 + z_A^2},\\ \theta &= \tan^{-1}\left(\frac{y_A}{x_A}\right),\\ \varphi &= \cos^{-1}\left(\frac{z_A}{r}\right).\end{aligned} \tag{12.9}$$

   Conversely the cartesian coordinates can be recovered as follows:

$$\begin{aligned}x_A &= r\sin(\varphi)\cos(\theta),\\ y_A &= r\sin(\varphi)\sin(\theta),\\ z_A &= r\cos(\varphi).\end{aligned} \tag{12.10}$$

Relationships between cylindrical and spherical coordinates also exist. From cylindrical coordinates, spherical coordinates can be obtained as follows:

$$\begin{aligned}r &= \sqrt{\rho^2 + z_A^2},\\ \theta &= \theta,\\ \varphi &= \tan^{-1}\left(\frac{\rho}{z_A}\right).\end{aligned} \tag{12.11}$$

Conversely, the cylindrical coordinates can be recovered as follows:

$$\begin{aligned}\rho &= \sqrt{r^2 - z_A^2},\\ \theta &= \theta,\\ z_A &= r\cos(\varphi).\end{aligned} \tag{12.12}$$

In R, the above coordinate system transformations can be carried out using the scripts in Listing 12.4.

Listing 12.4: A three-dimensional vector in different coordinate systems

```
#Defining a 3-dimensional row vector W in a cartesian coordinates
    system
W <- matrix(c(3, -2, 7), nrow=1)
#Coordinates of the vector W in cylindrical coordinates
rhoW<-sqrt(W[1,1]^2 + W[1,2]^2)
thetaW<-atan(W[1,2]/W[1,1])*180/pi
zW<-W[1, 3]
rhoW
[1] 3.605551
thetaW
[1] -33.69007
zW
[1] 7
#Recovering cartesian coordinates
xW<-rhoW*cos(thetaW*pi/180)
yW<-rhoW*sin(thetaW*pi/180)
xW
[1] 3
yW
[1] -2
zW
[1] 7
#Vector W in spherical coordinates
rW<- sqrt(sum(W^2))
thetaW<- atan(W[1,2]/W[1,1])*180/pi
phiW<- atan(sqrt(W[1,1]^2 + W[1,2]^2)/W[1,3])*180/pi
rW
[1] 7.874008
thetaW
[1] -33.69007
phiW
[1] 27.25203
#Recovering cartesian coordinates
xW<-rW*sin(phiW*pi/180)*cos(thetaW*pi/180)
yW<-rW*sin(phiW*pi/180)*sin(thetaW*pi/180)
zW<-rW*cos(phiW*pi/180)
xW
[1] 3
yW
[1] -2
zW
[1] 7
#From cylindrical to spherical coordinates
rW<-sqrt(rhoW^2 + zW^2)
phiW<-atan(rhoW/zW)*180/pi
rW
[1] 7.874008
thetaW
[1] -33.69007
phiW
[1] 27.25203
#From spherical to cylindrical coordinates
rhoW<-sqrt(rW^2-zW^2)
zW=rW*cos(phiW*pi/180)
```

```
rhoW
[1] 3.605551
thetaW
[1] -33.69007
zW
[1] 7
```

Example 12.1.2. Classification methods are used extensively in data science [41, 64]. An important classification technique for high-dimensional data is referred to as *support vector machine (SVM)* classification [41, 64] (see also Section 18.5.2).

For high-dimensional data, the problem of interest is to classify the (labeled) data by determining a separating hyperplane. When using linear classifiers, it is necessary to construct a hyperplane for optimal separation of the data points. To this end, it is necessary to determine the distance between a point representing a vector and the hyperplane.

Let $H : \delta_1 \cdot x + \delta_2 \cdot y + \delta_3 \cdot z - a = 0$ be a three-dimensional hyperplane, and let

$$\delta = \begin{pmatrix} \delta_1 \\ \delta_2 \\ \delta_2 \end{pmatrix}$$

be a three-dimensional point with

$$\|\delta\| = \sqrt{(\delta_1)^2 + (\delta_2)^2 + (\delta_3)^2}. \tag{12.13}$$

The distance between δ and H is given by

$$d_{a,H} = \frac{\delta_1 \cdot x + \delta_2 \cdot y + \delta_3 \cdot z - a}{\|\delta\|}. \tag{12.14}$$

A two-dimensional hyperplane is shown in Figure 12.10 to illustrate the SVM concept for a two-class classification problem. The data points represented by rectangles and circles represent the two classes, respectively. Figure 12.10 illustrates a case of a two-class problem, where a linear classifier represented by a hyperplane, can be used to separate the two classes. The optimal hyperplane is the one whose distance from the points representing the support vectors (SV) is maximal.

12.1.2.1 Complex vectors

A complex number is a number of the form $x + iy$, where x and y are real numbers and i is the *imaginary unit,* such that $i = \sqrt{-1}$, see [158]. Specifically, the number x is called the *real* part of the complex number $x + iy$, whereas the part iy is called the *imaginary* part. The set of complex numbers is commonly denoted by $\mathbb{C}$; $\mathbb{R}$ is a

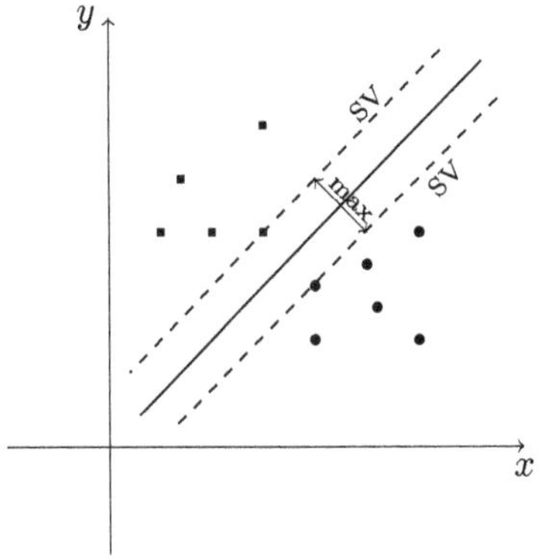

Figure 12.10: Constructing a two-dimensional hyperplane for SVM-classification.

subset of $\mathbb{C}$, since any real number can be viewed as a complex number, for which the imaginary part is zero, i. e. $y = 0$. Any complex number $z = x_z + iy_z$ can be represented by the pair of reals (x_z, y_z); thus, a complex number can be viewed as a particular two-dimensional standard real vector. Let θ_z denote the angle between the vector $z = (x_z, y_z)$ and the x-axis. Then, using the vector decomposition in a two-dimensional space, we have

$$x_z = r_z \cos(\theta_z), \quad y_z = r_z \sin(\theta_z), \quad \text{where } r_z = \sqrt{x_z^2 + y_z^2}. \tag{12.15}$$

The number r_z is called the *modulus* or the *absolute value* of z, whereas θ is called the *argument* of z.

From (12.15), we can deduce the following alternative description of a complex number $z = x_z + iy_z$:

$$\begin{aligned} z &= x_z + iy_z \\ &= r_z \cos(\theta_z) + ir_z \sin(\theta_z) \\ &= r_z\big[\cos(\theta_z) + i\sin(\theta_z)\big] = r_z e^{i\theta_z}. \end{aligned} \tag{12.16}$$

This representation of a complex number is referred to as the *Euler formula* [158].

A complex number $z = x_z + iy_z$ can be represented either by the pair (x_z, y_z) or the pair (r_z, θ_z), as illustrated in Figure 12.11.

Let $z = x_z + iy_z$, and let $w = x_w + iy_w$ be two complex numbers and n an integer. Then, the following elementary operations can be performed on these complex numbers [158]:

- *Complex conjugate:* The complex number $\bar{z} = x_z - iy_z$ is called the *complex conjugate* of z.
- *Power of a complex number:* $z^n = r_z^n[\cos(n\theta) + i\sin(n\theta)]$.
- *Complex addition:* $z + w = (x_z + iy_z) + (x_w + iy_w) = (x_z + x_w) + i(y_z + y_w)$.
- *Complex subtraction:* $z - w = (x_z + iy_z) - (x_w + iy_w) = (x_z - x_w) + i(y_z - y_w)$.

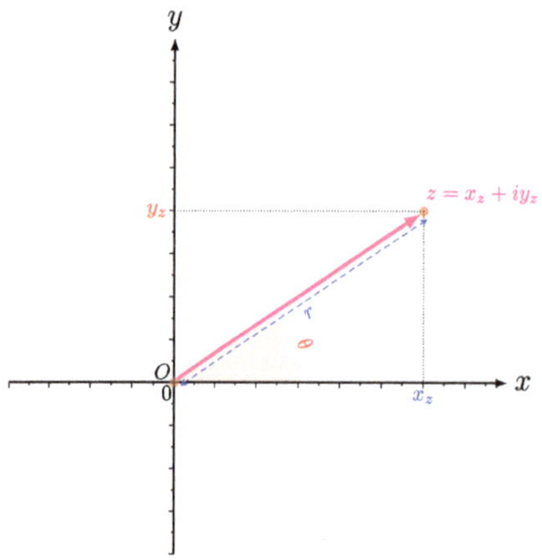

Figure 12.11: Vector representation of a complex number.

- *Complex multiplication:* $z \times w = (x_z + iy_z) \times (x_w + iy_w) = (x_z x_w - y_z y_w) + i(x_z y_w + y_z x_w)$.
- *Complex division:* $\frac{z}{w} = \frac{x_z + iy_z}{x_w + iy_w} = \frac{(x_z x_w + y_z y_w) + i(y_z x_w - x_z y_w)}{x_w^2 + y_w^2}$.
- *Complex exponentiation:* $z^w = (x_z + iy_z)^{x_w + y_w} = (x_z^2 + y_z^2)^{\frac{x_w + iy_w}{2}} e^{ir_z(x_z + iy_z)}$, where r_z is the complex modulus of z.

In R, the above basic operations on complex numbers can be performed using the script in Listing 12.5.

Listing 12.5: Basic operations on complex numbers

```
#Defining tow complex numbers z and w
z<- -3+ 8i
z
[1] -3+8i
w<- -5 - 2i
w
[1] -5-2i
#the imaginary number i is the square root of -1
sqrt(as.complex(-1))  #as.complex enables R to recognize -1 as a
    complex number
[1] 0+1i
#Complex conjugate of z and w
zbar<- Conj(z)
zbar
[1] -3-8i
wbar<- Conj(w)
wbar
[1] -5+2i
#Getting the real part of the complex number z
Re(z)
[1] -3
#Getting the imaginary part of the complex number z
Im(z)
```

```
[1] 8
#Modulus of the complex number z
rz<-Mod(z)
rz
[1] 8.544004
#Argument of the complex number z in degree
thetaz<-Arg(z)*180/pi
thetaz
[1] 110.556
#Power of a complex number
n<-3
zn<-z^n
zn
[1] 549-296i
rz^n*(cos(n*thetaz*pi/180) + 1i*sin(n*thetaz*pi/180))
[1] 549-296i  # This is equivalent to zn
#Sum of the complex numbers z and w
s<-z+w
s
[1] -8+6i
#Difference of the complex numbers z and w
d<-z-w
d
[1] 2+10i
#Product of the complex numbers z and w:
p<-z*w
p
[1] 31-34i
#Division of the complex numbers z and w
q<-z/w
q
[1] -0.034483-1.586207i
#Exponentiation t=z^w
t<-z^w
t
[1] 0.000205779-0.001021052i
```

An n-dimensional complex vector is a vector of the form $\overrightarrow{V} = (x_1, x_2, \ldots, x_n)$, whose components $x_1, x_2, \ldots, x_n$ can be complex numbers. The concept of vector operations and vector transformations, previously introduced in relation to real vectors, can be generalized to complex vectors using the elementary operations on complex numbers.

12.1.3 Matrices

In the two foregoing sections, we have presented some basic concepts of vector analysis. In this section, we will discuss a generalization of vectors also known as matrices.

Let m and n be two positive integers. We call A an $m \times n$ real matrix if it consists of an ordered set of m vectors in an n-dimensional space. In other words, A is defined by a set of $m \times n$ scalars $a_{ij} \in \mathbb{R}$, with $i = 1, \ldots, m$ and $j = 1, \ldots, n$, represented in the following rectangular array

$$A = \begin{pmatrix} a_{11} & a_{12} & \cdots & a_{1n} \\ a_{21} & a_{22} & \cdots & a_{2n} \\ \vdots & \vdots & \ddots & \vdots \\ a_{m1} & a_{m2} & \cdots & a_{mn} \end{pmatrix}. \qquad (12.17)$$

The matrix A, defined by (12.17), has m rows and n columns. For any entry a_{ij}, with $i = 1, \dots, m$ and $j = 1, \dots, n$, of the matrix A, the index i is called the row index, whereas the index j is the column index. The set of entries $(a_{i1}, a_{i2}, \dots, a_{in})$ is called the ith row of A, and the set $(a_{1j}, a_{2j}, \dots, a_{mj})$ is the jth column of A. When $n = m$, A is called a *squared matrix*, and the set of entries $(a_{11}, a_{22}, \dots, a_{nn})$ is called its *main diagonal*.

In the case $m = 1$ and $n > 1$, the matrix A is reduced to one row, and it is called a *row vector*; likewise, when $m > 1$ and $n = 1$, the matrix A is reduced to a single column, and it is called a *column vector*. In the case $m = n = 1$, the matrix A is reduced to a single value, i. e., a real scalar. An $m \times n$ matrix A can be viewed as a list of m n-dimensional row vectors or a list of n m-dimensional column vectors. If the entries a_{ij} are complex numbers, then A is called a complex matrix.

The R programming environment provides a wide range of functions for matrix manipulation and matrix operations. Several of these are illustrated in the three listings below.

Listing 12.6: Defining a matrix

```
#Defining a matrix from a given dimension (m, n)
listnb <- c(3, 2, -5, 12, 1, -3, 2, -13, 5, -1, 4, 10)
A<- matrix(listnb, nrow=3, ncol=4, byrow=TRUE)
 A
          [,1] [,2] [,3] [,4]
[1,]       3    2   -5   12
[2,]       1   -3    2  -13
[3,]       5   -1    4   10
#Getting the dimension of a matrix
dim(A)
[1] 3 4
#Defining a diagonal matrix given a vector of its diagonal entries
diagonal<-c(3, 2, 12)
diag(diagonal)
[,1] [,2] [,3]
[1,]       3    0    0
[2,]       0    2    0
[3,]       0    0   12
#Defining an m by m identity matrix
diag(1, 3)
          [,1] [,2] [,3]
[1,]       1    0    0
[2,]       0    1    0
[3,]       0    0    1
#Defining an m by n matrix of the same element
```

```
array(1, dim=c(3, 4))
     [,1] [,2] [,3] [,4]
[1,]    1    1    1    1
[2,]    1    1    1    1
[3,]    1    1    1    1
```

Listing 12.7: Searching elements in a matrix

```
#Accessing a component of a matrix at the position (i, j)
A[2, 3 ]
[1]  2
#Accessing the components of the ith row of a matrix i
A[2,  ]
[1]   1 -3  2 -13
#Accessing the components of the jth column of a matrix
A[,3]
[1] -5  2  4
#Finding the minimum entry in a matrix
min(A)
[1] -13
#Accessing the position the minimum entry of a matrix
which(A == min(A), arr.ind = TRUE)
     row col
[1,]   2   4
#Finding the maximum entry in a matrix
max(A)
[1]  12
# Accessing the position of the maximum entry of a matrix
which(A == max(A), arr.ind = TRUE)
      row col
[1,]   1   4
#Accessing the positions of some specific entries of a matrix
which(A == 10, arr.ind = TRUE)
     row col
[1,]   3   4
#Finding the positions in a matrix satisfying a given criterion,
    e.\,g. greater than 3
indices <- which(A > 3, arr.ind = TRUE)
indices
     row col
[1,]   3   1
[2,]   3   3
[3,]   1   4
[4,]   3   4
A[indices]
[1]  5  4 12 10
```

Listing 12.8: Extracting and binding submatrices

```
#Extracting a submatrix of a matrix
SubA1<-A[1:2,1:2]
SubA1
     [,1] [,2]
[1,]    3    2
[2,]    1   -3
```

```
SubA2<-A[,2:3]
SubA2
     [,1] [,2]
[1,]    2   -5
[2,]   -3    2
[3,]   -1    4
SubA3<-A[,1]
SubA3
[1] 3 1 5
#Binding matrices, with the same number of rows, by columns
cbind(SubA2, SubA3)
             SubA3
[1,]  2 -5     3
[2,] -3  2     1
[3,] -1  4     5
#Binding matrices, with the same number of columns, by rows
> rbind(SubA2, SubA1)
     [,1] [,2]
[1,]    2   -5
[2,]   -3    2
[3,]   -1    4
[4,]    3    2
[5,]    1   -3
```

Example 12.1.3. In this example, we demonstrate the utility of computing powers of adjacency matrices of networks, see Definition 16.2.2 in Section 16.2.1. They can be used to determine the number of walks with a certain length from v_i to v_j; v_i to v_j are two vertices $\in V$, and $G = (V, E)$ is a connected network. The application of Definition 16.2.2 in Section 16.2.1 to the graph shown in Figure 12.12 yields the following matrix:

$$A(G) = \begin{bmatrix} 0 & 1 & 1 & 0 & 0 \\ 1 & 0 & 0 & 0 & 0 \\ 1 & 0 & 0 & 1 & 1 \\ 0 & 0 & 1 & 0 & 0 \\ 0 & 0 & 0 & 0 & 0 \end{bmatrix}. \tag{12.18}$$

If we square this matrix, we obtain

$$A^2(G) = \begin{bmatrix} 2 & 0 & 0 & 1 & 1 \\ 0 & 1 & 1 & 0 & 0 \\ 0 & 1 & 2 & 0 & 0 \\ 1 & 0 & 0 & 1 & 1 \\ 0 & 0 & 0 & 0 & 0 \end{bmatrix}. \tag{12.19}$$

The power of the adjacency matrix (12.18) (here 2) gives the length of the walk. The entry a_{ij} of $A^2(G)$ gives the number of walks of length 2 from v_i to v_j. For instance, $a_{11} = 2$ means there exist two walks of length 2 from vertex 1 to vertex 1. Moreover, a_{14} means there exists only one walk of length 2 from vertex 1 to vertex 4. These numbers can be understood by inspection of the network, G, shown in Figure 12.12.

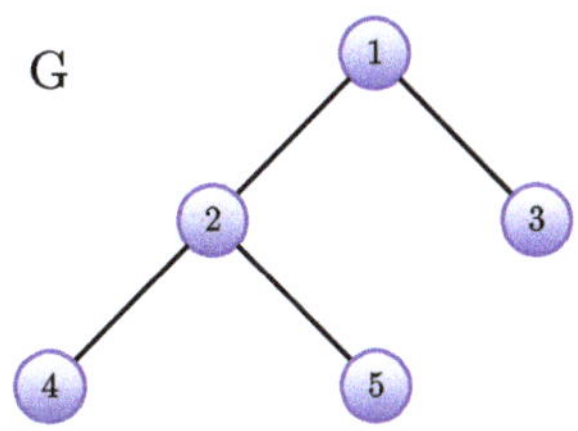

Figure 12.12: Walks in an example graph G for $A^2(G)$.

12.2 Operations with matrices

Let A be an $m \times n$ matrix. Then, A^T, the transpose of A, is the matrix obtained by interchanging the rows and columns of A. Consequently, A^T is an $n \times m$ matrix. A matrix A is called symmetric if $A = A^T$. The transposition may be regarded as a particular rotation of a matrix. Using R, the transposition of a matrix A can be performed as follows:

Listing 12.9: Matrix manipulation

```
#Transposing a matrix
t(A)
      [,1] [,2] [,3]
[1,]     3    1    5
[2,]     2   -3   -1
[3,]    -5    2    4
[4,]    12  -13   10
#Flipping a matrix
apply(A, 1, rev)
      [,1] [,2] [,3]
[1,]    12  -13   10
[2,]    -5    2    4
[3,]     2   -3   -1
[4,]     3    1    5
apply(A, 2, rev)
      [,1] [,2] [,3] [,4]
[1,]     5   -1    4   10
[2,]     1   -3    2  -13
[3,]     3    2   -5   12
```

Let A and B be two $m \times n$ real matrices. Some mathematical operations, which require the matrices to have the same dimensions (i. e., having the same number of rows and the same number of columns) include:

- *Matrix addition*: The sum of the matrices A and B is an $m \times n$ real matrix, C, whose entries are $c_{ij} = a_{ij} + b_{ij}$ for $i = 1, \ldots, m, j = 1, \ldots, n$. In R, this operation is carried out using the command `C <- A+B`.

- *Matrix subtraction*: The difference $A - B$ is an $m \times n$ real matrix, C, whose entries are $c_{ij} = a_{ij} - b_{ij}$ for $i = 1, \ldots, m, j = 1, \ldots, n$. In R, this operation is carried out using the command `C <- A-B`.
- *Matrix element-wise multiplication*: The element-wise product of the matrices A and B is an $m \times n$ real matrix, C, whose entries are $c_{ij} = a_{ij} \times b_{ij}$ for $i = 1, \ldots, m$ and $j = 1, \ldots, n$. In R, this operation is performed using the command `C <- A*B`.
- *Matrix comparison:* The matrix A is equal to B if $a_{ij} = b_{ij}$ for $i = 1, \ldots, m, j = 1, \ldots, n$.

Listing 12.10: Operations with matrices of the same dimension

```
listnb<-c(3, 2, -5, 12, 1, -3, 2, -13, 5, -1, 4, 10)
A <- matrix(listnb, nrow=3, ncol=4, byrow=TRUE)
A
     [,1] [,2] [,3] [,4]
[1,]    3    2   -5   12
[2,]    1   -3    2  -13
[3,]    5   -1    4   10
listnb<-c(1, -3, 5, 0, 2, 9, 1, 5, 7, 3, -2, 6)
B <- matrix(listnb, nrow=3, ncol=4, byrow=TRUE)
B
     [,1] [,2] [,3] [,4]
[1,]    1   -3    5    0
[2,]    2    9    1    5
[3,]    7    3   -2    6
#Sum of two matrices
A+B
     [,1] [,2] [,3] [,4]
[1,]    4   -1    0   12
[2,]    3    6    3   -8
[3,]   12    2    2   16
#Difference between two matrices
A-B
     [,1] [,2] [,3] [,4]
[1,]    2    5  -10   12
[2,]   -1  -12    1  -18
[3,]   -2   -4    6    4
#Element wise product of two matrices
A*B
     [,1] [,2] [,3] [,4]
[1,]    3   -6  -25    0
[2,]    2  -27    2  -65
[3,]   35   -3   -8   60
#Comparing two matrices
all.equal(A, A)
[1] TRUE
all.equal(A, B)
[1] "Mean relative difference: 1.262295"
```

An important operation on matrices is matrix multiplication. Let A and B be two matrices; the matrix multiplication, $A \times B$, requires the number of columns of the matrix A to be equal to the number of rows of the matrix B, i. e., if A is an $m \times n$ real matrix, then B must be an $n \times l$ real matrix. The result of this operation is an

$m \times l$ real matrix, C, whose entries c_{ik} for $i = 1, \ldots, m, k = 1, \ldots, l$, are obtained as follows:

$$c_{ik} = \sum_{j=1}^{1} a_{ij} \times b_{jk}. \tag{12.20}$$

When $m = 1$, then, the result is a product between a row vector and a matrix.

Note that, even if both products $A \times B$ and $B \times A$ are defined, i. e., if $l = m$, $A \times B$ generally differs from $B \times A$.

Definition 12.2.1. Let A be an $n \times n$ matrix, and let 0_n denote the n-dimensional null vector.

- A is said to be *positive definite* if and only if $x^T Ax > 0$, for all $x \in \mathbb{R}^n$, $x \neq 0_n$.
- A is said to be *positive semidefinite* if and only if $x^T Ax \geq 0$, for all $x \in \mathbb{R}^n$.
- A is said to be *negative definite* if and only if $x^T Ax < 0$, for all $x \in \mathbb{R}^n$, $x \neq 0_n$.
- A is said to be *negative semidefinite* if and only if $x^T Ax \leq 0$, for all $x \in \mathbb{R}^n$.
- A is said to be *indefinite* if and only if there exist x and $y \in \mathbb{R}^n$ such that $x^T Ax > 0$ and $y^T Ay < 0$.

Using R, matrix multiplications can be carried out as follows:

Listing 12.11: Matrix multiplications

```
listnb <- c(3, 2, -5,  1, -3, 2,  5, -1, 4)
A <- matrix(listnb, nrow=3, ncol=3, byrow=TRUE)
A
     [,1] [,2] [,3]
[1,]    3    2   -5
[2,]    1   -3    2
[3,]    5   -1    4
listnb <- c(1, -3, 5, 0, 2, 9, 1, 5, 7, 3, -2, 6)
B <- matrix(listnb, nrow=3, ncol=4, byrow=TRUE)
B
       [,1] [,2] [,3] [,4]
[1,]     1   -3    5    0
[2,]     2    9    1    5
[3,]     7    3   -2    6
Vector <- matrix(c( 5, 3, 5), nrow=1, ncol=3, byrow=TRUE)
Vector
     [,1] [,2] [,3]
[1,]    5    3    5
#Product of two matrices
A%*%B
       [,1] [,2] [,3] [,4]
[1,]   -28   -6   27  -20
[2,]     9  -24   -2   -3
[3,]    31  -12   16   19
#Product of a vector and a matrix
V%*%A
    [,1] [,2] [,3]
#Product of a scalar and a matrix
5*A
```

```
     [,1] [,2] [,3]
[1,]   15   10  -25
[2,]    5  -15   10
[3,]   25   -5   20
```

12.3 Special matrices

Special matrices are characterized by their patterns, which can be used to define matrix classes. Examples of such special matrices include [27]:

- *Diagonal matrix:* A matrix A is called diagonal, if and only if its entries $a_{ij} = 0$ for all $i \neq j$.
- *Identity matrix:* If the nonzero entries of a diagonal matrix are all equal to unity, then the matrix is called an *identity* matrix, and it is often denoted I.
- *Upper trapezoidal matrix:* An $m \times n$ matrix, A, is said to be upper trapezoidal if and only if its entries $a_{ij} = 0$ for all $i > j$. If $m = n$, i. e., A is a square matrix, then an upper trapezoidal matrix is referred to as an *upper triangular matrix.*
- *Lower trapezoidal matrix:* An $m \times n$ matrix, A, is said to be lower trapezoidal if and only if its entries, a_{ij}, for all $j > i$ are zeros. If $m = n$, i. e., A is a squared matrix, then a lower trapezoidal matrix is referred to as a *lower triangular matrix.*
- *Tridiagonal matrix:* A matrix, A, is said to be tridiagonal if and only if its entries $a_{ij} = 0$ for all i, j such that $|i - j| > 1$.
- *Orthogonal matrix:* A matrix, A, is said to be orthogonal if and only if $A^T A = I$.
- *Symmetric matrix:* A matrix, A, is said to be symmetric if and only if $A^T = A$.
- *Skew-symmetric matrix:* A matrix, A, is said to be skew-symmetric if and only if $A^T = -A$.
- *Sparse matrix:* A matrix is called sparse if it has relatively few nonzero entries. The sparsity of an $n \times m$ matrix, generally expressed in %, is given by

  $$\frac{r}{nm}\%, \quad \text{where } r \text{ is the number of nonzero entries in } A.$$

  Diagonal and tridiagonal matrices are typical examples of sparse matrices.

Definition 12.3.1. Let A be an $n \times n$ squared matrix, and let I_n be the $n \times n$ identity matrix. If there exists an $n \times n$ matrix B such that

$$AB = I_n = BA, \tag{12.21}$$

then B is called the *inverse* of A. If a squared matrix, A, has an inverse, then A is called an *invertible* or *nonsingular matrix*; otherwise, A is called a *singular matrix.*

The inverse of the identity matrix is the identity matrix, whereas the inverse of a lower (respectively, upper) triangular matrix is also a lower (respectively, upper) triangular matrix.

Note that for a matrix to be invertible, it must be a squared matrix.

Using R, the inverse of a squared matrix, A, can be computed as follows:

Listing 12.12: Inverse of a matrix

```
A <- matrix(c(3, 2, -5, 1, -3, 2, 5, -1, 4), nrow=3, ncol=3,
    byrow=TRUE)
A
     [,1] [,2] [,3]
[1,]    3    2   -5
[2,]    1   -3    2
[3,]    5   -1    4
#Computing the inverse of the nonsingular matrix
B=solve(A)
B
            [,1]        [,2]  [,3]
[1,]  0.11363636  0.03409091 0.125
[2,] -0.06818182 -0.42045455 0.125
[3,] -0.15909091 -0.14772727 0.125
B%*%A
             [,1] [,2]          [,3]
[1,] 1.000000e+00    0  0.000000e+00
[2,] 0.000000e+00    1 -1.110223e-16
[3,] 1.110223e-16    0  1.000000e+00
```

12.4 Trace and determinant of a matrix

Let A be an $n \times n$ real matrix. The *trace* of A, denoted $\operatorname{tr}(A)$, is the sum of the diagonal entries of A, that is,

$$\operatorname{tr}(A) = \sum_{i=1}^{n} a_{ii}.$$

The *determinant* of A, denoted $\det(A)$, can be computed using the following recursive relation [27]:

$$\det(A) = \begin{cases} a_{11}, & \text{if } n = 1, \\ \sum_{i=1}^{n} (-1)^{i+j} a_{ij} \det(M_{ij}), & \text{if } n > 1, \end{cases}$$

where, M_{ij} is the $(n-1) \times (n-1)$ matrix obtained by removing the ith row and the jth column of A.

Let A and B be two $n \times n$ matrices and k a real scalar. Some useful properties of the determinant for A and B include the following:

1. $\det(AB) = \det(A)\det(B)$;

2. $\det(A^T) = \det(A)$;
3. $\det(kA) = k^n \det(A)$;
4. $\det(A) \neq 0$ if and only if A is nonsingular.

Remark 12.4.1. If an $n \times n$ matrix, A, is a diagonal, upper triangular, or lower triangular matrix, then

$$\det(A) = \prod_{i=1}^{n} a_{ii},$$

i. e., the determinant of a triangular matrix is the product of the diagonal entries. Therefore, the most practical means of computing a determinant of a matrix is to decompose it into a product of lower and upper triangular matrices.

Using R, the trace and the determinant of a matrix are computed as follows:

Listing 12.13: Trace and determinant of a matrix

```
A <- matrix(c(3, 2, -5,  1, -3,  2, 5, -1, 4), nrow=3, ncol=3,
     byrow=TRUE)
A
     [,1] [,2] [,3]
[1,]    3    2   -5
[2,]    1   -3    2
[3,]    5   -1    4
#Computing the trace of the matrix A
sum(diag(A))
[1] 4
#Computing the determinant of the matrix A
det(A)
[1] -88
```

12.5 Subspaces, dimension, and rank of a matrix

The dimension and rank of a matrix are essential properties for solving systems of linear equations.

Definition 12.5.1. Consider m vectors $\{A_i, i = 1, 2, \ldots, m\}$, whereas $A_i \in \mathbb{R}^n$. If the only set of scalars λ_i for which

$$\sum_{i=1}^{m} \lambda_i A_i = 0_n$$

is $\lambda_1 = \lambda_2 = \ldots = \lambda_m = 0$, then the vectors A_i, $i = 1, 2, \ldots, m$ are said to be linearly independent.

Otherwise, the vectors are said to be linearly dependent.

Definition 12.5.2. A *subspace* of $\mathbb{R}^n$ is a nonempty subset of $\mathbb{R}^n$, which is also a vector space.

Definition 12.5.3. The set of all linear combinations of a set of m vectors $\{A_i, i = 1, 2, \ldots, m\}$ in $\mathbb{R}^n$ is a subspace called the *span* of $\{A_i, i = 1, 2, \ldots, m\}$, and defined as follows:

$$\text{span}\{A_i, i = 1, 2, \ldots, m\} = \{V \in \mathbb{R}^n\}, \quad \text{such that}$$

$$V = \sum_{i=1}^{m} \lambda_i A_i \quad \text{with } \lambda_i \in \mathbb{R}\ \forall\, i = 1, \ldots, m.$$

If the vectors $\{A_i, i = 1, 2, \ldots, m\}$ are linearly independent, then any vector $V \in \text{span}\{A_i, i = 1, 2, \ldots, m\}$ is a unique linear combination of the vectors $\{A_i, i = 1, 2, \ldots, m\}$.

Definition 12.5.4. A linearly independent set of vectors, which spans a subspace S is called a *basis* of S.

All the bases of a subspace S have the same number of components, and this number is called the *dimension* of S, denoted $\dim(S)$.

Two key subspaces are associated with any $m \times n$ matrix A, i. e., $A \in \mathbb{R}^{m\times n}$:

1. the subspace

$$\text{im}(A) = \{b \in \mathbb{R}^m : b = Ax \text{ for some } x \in \mathbb{R}^n\},$$

referred to as the *range* or the *image* of A; and

2. the subspace

$$\ker(A) = \{x \in \mathbb{R}^n : Ax = 0\},$$

called the *null space* or the *kernel* of A.

If the matrix, A, is defined by a set of n vectors $\{A_i, i = 1, 2, \ldots, n\}$, where $A_i \in \mathbb{R}^m$, then

$$\text{im}(A) = \text{span}\{A_i, i = 1, 2, \ldots, n\}.$$

Definition 12.5.5. The rank of a matrix, A, denoted $\text{rank}(A)$, is the maximum number of linearly independent rows or columns of the matrix A, and it is defined as follows:

$$\text{rank}(A) = \dim(\text{im}(A)).$$

Let A be an $m \times n$ real matrix. Then, the following properties should be noted:

- If $m = n$, then

1. if $\text{rank}(A) = n$, then A is said to have a *full rank*;
2. A is a nonsingular matrix if and only if it has a full rank, i. e., $\text{rank}(A) = n$;

- If $m \leq n$, then A has a full rank if the rows of A are linearly independent.

Let A be an $m \times n$ real matrix and B an $n \times p$ real matrix, then the following relationships hold;

- $\text{rank}(A^T A) = \text{rank}(AA^T) = \text{rank}(A) = \text{rank}(A^T)$;
- $\text{rank}(AB) \leq \min(\text{rank}(A), \text{rank}(B))$;
- If $\text{rank}(A) = n$, then $\text{rank}(AB) = \text{rank}(A)$;
- $\text{rank}(A) + \text{rank}(B) - n \leq \text{rank}(AB)$ (this is known as the Sylvester's rank inequality).

Definition 12.5.6. Let A be an $m \times n$ real matrix, i. e., $A \in \mathbb{R}^{m\times n}$, and $u \in \mathbb{R}^m$ and $v \in \mathbb{R}^n$. Then, the matrix $B \in \mathbb{R}^{m\times n}$ such that

$$B = A + uv^T \tag{12.22}$$

is called the *rank-1 modification* of A.

Let $A \in \mathbb{R}^{n\times n}$, and $U, V \in \mathbb{R}^{n\times p}$ such that

1. A is nonsingular, and
2. $(I_n V^T A^{-1} U)$, where I_n denotes the $n \times n$ identity matrix, is nonsingular.

Then,

$$\left(A + UV^T\right)^{-1} = A^{-1} - A^{-1}U\left(I_n + V^T A^{-1} U\right)^{-1} V^T A^{-1}. \tag{12.23}$$

The above equation (12.23) is referred to as the *Sherman–Morrison–Woodbury formula.*

If $p = 1$, then the above matrices U and V reduce to two vectors $u, v \in \mathbb{R}^n$. Then, the *Sherman–Morrison–Woodbury formula* simplifies to

$$\left(A + uv^T\right)^{-1} = A^{-1} - \frac{A^{-1}uv^T A^{-1}}{1 + v^T A^{-1} u}. \tag{12.24}$$

Since $B = A + uv^T$, due to (12.22), then if the inverse of A is known, the *Sherman–Morrison–Woodbury formula* provides the easiest way to compute the inverse of the matrix B, the *rank-1 change* of A. Thus,

$$B^{-1} = \left(I_n - \frac{1}{1 + v^T(A^{-1}u)}(A^{-1}u)v^T\right)A^{-1}.$$

Using R, the rank of a matrix can be determined as follows:

Listing 12.14: Trace and determinant of a matrix

```
library(Matrix)
listnb<-c(1, 0, 0, 0, -1, 1, 0, 0, 2, 0, 1, 0, 0, 1, -1, -1)
A<-matrix(listnb, nrow=4, ncol=4, byrow=TRUE)
A
     [,1] [,2] [,3] [,4]
[1,]    1    0    0    0
[2,]   -1    1    0    0
[3,]    2    0    1    0
[4,]    0    1   -1   -1
#Determining the rank of the matrix A
 rankMatrix(A)
[1] 4
attr(,"method")
[1] "tolNorm2"
attr(,"useGrad")
[1] FALSE
attr(,"tol")
[1] 8.881784e-16
#Determining the inverse of the matrix A
invA<-solve(A) #Since A is a lower triangular matrix then it is
    easy to invert
#Computing a matrix B=A+u transpose(v)
u<-matrix(c(1, -2, -1, 0), nrow=4)
v<-matrix(c(0, 0, 0, -1), nrow=4)
B<-A+u%*%t(v)
B
     [,1] [,2] [,3] [,4]
[1,]    1    0    0   -1
[2,]   -1    1    0    2
[3,]    2    0    1    1
[4,]    0    1   -1   -1
invB<-(diag(4) - as.numeric(1/(1+t(v)%*%(invA%*%u)))*(invA%*%u)%*%
    t(v))%*%invA
invB
[,1] [,2] [,3] [,4]
[1,]   -2   -1    1    1
[2,]    4    2   -1   -1
[3,]    7    3   -2   -3
[4,]   -3   -1    1    1
#This is identical to the costly inverse of B obtained using the
    function solve()
solve(B)
     [,1] [,2] [,3] [,4]
[1,]   -2   -1    1    1
[2,]    4    2   -1   -1
[3,]    7    3   -2   -3
[4,]   -3   -1    1    1
```

12.6 Eigenvalues and eigenvectors of a matrix

In this section, we introduce the eigenvalues of a matrix as zeros of a graph polynomial. Eigenvalues have various applications in many scientific disciplines. For instance, eigenvalues are used extensively in mathematical chemistry [90, 186] and computer science [28]. Let A be an $n \times n$ matrix. The eigenvalues of A, denoted $\lambda_i(A)$, $i = 1, 2, \dots, n$ or $\lambda = \{\lambda_i,\ i = 1, 2, \dots, n\}$, are the n zeros of the polynomial in λ of degree n defined by $\det(A - \lambda I)$, i. e., the eigenvalues are solutions to the following equation: [27]

$$\det(A - \lambda I) = 0.$$

The polynomial $\det(A - \lambda I)$ is called the *characteristic polynomial.*

If A is a real matrix, then the eigenvalues of A are either real or pairs of complex conjugates. If A is a symmetric matrix, then all its eigenvalues are real.

The following properties hold for eigenvalues:

1. $\det(A) = \prod_{i=1}^{n} \lambda_i(A)$
2. $\operatorname{tr}(A) = \sum_{i=1}^{n} a_{ii} = \sum_{i=1}^{n} \lambda_i(A)$

A squared matrix, A, is called nonsingular if and only if all its eigenvalues are nonzero.

Definition 12.6.1. The *spectral radius* of a squared matrix A, denoted $\rho(A)$, is given by

$$\rho(A) = \max_{i=1,2,\dots,n} |\lambda_i(A)|.$$

Definition 12.6.2. A non-null vector x, such that

$$Ax = \lambda_i(A)x, \tag{12.25}$$

is called the *right eigenvector* associated with the *eigenvalue* $\lambda_i(A)$.

For each eigenvalue $\lambda_i(A)$, its right eigenvector x is found by solving the system $(A - \lambda_i(A)I)x = 0$.

Let A be an $n \times n$ real matrix. The following properties hold:

- If A is diagonal, upper triangular or lower triangular, then its eigenvalues are given by its diagonal entries, i. e.,

$$\lambda_i(A) = a_{ii}, \quad \text{for } i = 1, 2, \dots, n.$$

- If A is orthogonal, then $|\lambda_i(A)| = 1$ for all $i = 1, 2, \dots, n$.
- If A is symmetric, then there exists an orthogonal matrix $Q \in \mathbb{R}^{n\times n}$ such that

$$Q^T AQ = D,$$

where D is an $n\times n$ diagonal matrix, whose diagonal entries are $\lambda_1(A), \lambda_2(A), \dots, \lambda_n(A)$.

If A is nonsingular, i. e., $\lambda_i(A) \neq 0$ for $i = 1, \dots, n$, then

$$\lambda_i(A^{-1}) = \frac{1}{\lambda_i(A)}, \quad \text{for } i = 1, \dots, n.$$

Eigenvalues can be used to determine the definiteness of symmetric matrices. Let A be an $n \times n$ symmetric real matrix and $\lambda_i(A)$, $i = 1, 2, \dots, n$ its eigenvalues. Then we have the following relationships:
- A is said to be *positive definite* if and only if $\lambda_i(A) > 0$ for all $i = 1, \dots, n$.
- A is said to be *positive semidefinite* if and only if $\lambda_i(A) \geq 0$ for all $i = 1, \dots, n$.
- A is said to be *negative definite* if and only if $\lambda_i(A) < 0$ for all $i = 1, \dots, n$.
- A is said to be *negative semidefinite* if and only if $\lambda_i(A) \leq 0$ for all $i = 1, \dots, n$.
- A is said to be *indefinite* if and only if $\lambda_i(A) > 0$ for some i and $\lambda_j(A) < 0$ for some j.

Remark 12.6.1. If a nonsingular $n \times n$ symmetric matrix, A, is *positive semi-definite* (respectively *negative semidefinite*), then A is *positive definite* (respectively *negative definite*).

Using R, the eigenvalues for a matrix, A, and their associated eigenvectors, as well as the spectral radius of the matrix A, can be computed as follows:

Listing 12.15: Eigenvalues and Eigenvectors of a matrix

```
A <- matrix(c(7, 0, -3,  -9, -2,  3, 18, 0, -8), nrow=3, ncol=3,
     byrow=TRUE)
A
      [,1] [,2] [,3]
[1,]     7    0   -3
[2,]    -9   -2    3
[3,]    18    0   -8
#Computing eigenvalues and eigenvectors of the matrix A
Eigv<-eigen(A)
Eigv
$values  #Eigenvalues
[1] -2 -2  1
$vectors  # Eigenvectors
      [,1]      [,2]      [,3]
[1,]     0 0.3162278  0.4082483
[2,]     1 0.0000000 -0.4082483
[3,]     0 0.9486833  0.8164966
#Getting the spectral radius of the matrix A
rho<-max(abs(Eigv$values))
rho
[1] 2
```

12.7 Matrix norms

The concept of a vector norm discussed earlier can be generalized to a matrix [134, 86].

Definition 12.7.1. A *matrix norm*, denoted by $\|\cdot\|$, is a scalar function defined from $\mathbb{R}^{m\times n}$ to $\mathbb{R}$, such that
1. $\|A\| \geq 0$ for all $A \in \mathbb{R}^{m\times n}$;
2. $\|A\| = 0 \Longleftrightarrow A = 0_{m\times n}$, where $0_{m\times n}$ denotes an $m \times n$ null matrix;
3. $\|A + B\| \leq \|A\| + \|B\|$ for all $A,\ B \in \mathbb{R}^{m\times n}$;
4. $\|kA\| = |k| \times \|A\|$, for all $k \in \mathbb{R}$ and $A \in \mathbb{R}^{m\times n}$.

Furthermore, if

$$\|AB\| \leq \|A\| \times \|B\|, \quad \text{for all } A \in \mathbb{R}^{m\times n} \quad \text{and} \quad B \in \mathbb{R}^{n\times q},$$

then the matrix norm is said to be *consistent.*

Definition 12.7.2. Let $A \in \mathbb{R}^{m\times n}$ and $x \in \mathbb{R}^n$. Then, the *subordinate* matrix p-norm of A, denoted $\|A\|_p$, is defined in terms of vector norms as follows:

$$\|A\|_p = \max_{x\neq 0_n} \frac{\|Ax\|_p}{\|x\|_p}.$$

In particular,
1. the subordinate matrix 1-norm of A is defined by

$$\|A\|_1 = \max_{x\neq 0_n} \frac{\|Ax\|_1}{\|x\|_1} = \max_{j=1,2,\dots,n} \sum_{i=1}^{m} |a_{ij}|.$$

2. the subordinate matrix 2-norm of A is defined by

$$\|A\|_2 = \max_{x\neq 0_n} \frac{\|Ax\|_2}{\|x\|_2};$$

if $m = n$, then

$$\|A\|_2 = \rho(A) = \max_{i=1,2,\dots,n} \left|\lambda_i(A)\right|,$$

where $\rho(A)$ denotes the spectral radius of A.
3. in the case where $p = \infty$, the subordinate matrix ∞-norm of A is defined by

$$\|A\|_\infty = \max_{x\neq 0_n} \frac{\|Ax\|_\infty}{\|x\|_\infty} = \max_{i=1,2,\dots,m} \sum_{j=1}^{n} |a_{ij}|.$$

Furthermore, if $m = n$, we have

$$\|A\|_2 \leq \sqrt{\|A\|_1 \times \|A\|_\infty} \leq \sqrt{n} \times \|A\|_2.$$

Remark 12.7.1. The subordinate matrix p-norm is consistent and, for any $A \in \mathbb{R}^{m\times n}$ and $x \in \mathbb{R}^n$,

$$\|Ax\|_p = \|Ax\|_p \|x\|_p.$$

Definition 12.7.3. The *Frobenius norm* of a matrix A is defined by

$$\|Ax\|_F = \left(\sum_{i=1}^{m}\sum_{j=1}^{n} |a_{ij}|^2\right)^{\frac{1}{2}} = \operatorname{tr}(AA^T).$$

Listing 12.16: Matrix norms

```
#The package "Matrix" is required here
require(Matrix)
```

12.8 Matrix factorization

Matrix factorization is an essential tool for solving systems of linear equations [27]. The most commonly used factorization methods are the *LU factorization* for a *squared* matrix, and the *QR factorization* for a *rectangular* matrix, i. e., squared or not.

12.8.1 LU factorization

Let $A \in \mathbb{R}^{n\times n}$. The LU factorization of A consists of the decomposition of A into a product of a unit lower triangular matrix L and an upper triangular matrix U, that is,

$$A = LU,$$

where

$$L = \begin{bmatrix} 1 & 0 & 0 & \cdots & 0 \\ l_{21} & 1 & 0 & \cdots & 0 \\ \vdots & \vdots & \vdots & \ddots & \vdots \\ l_{n1} & l_{n2} & l_{n3} & \cdots & 1 \end{bmatrix} \quad \text{and} \quad U = \begin{bmatrix} u_{11} & u_{12} & u_{13} & \cdots & u_{1n} \\ 0 & u_{22} & u_{23} & \cdots & u_{2n} \\ \vdots & \vdots & \vdots & \ddots & \vdots \\ 0 & 0 & 0 & \cdots & u_{nn} \end{bmatrix}.$$

Therefore, the determinants of L and U are $\det(L) = 1$ and $\det(U) = \prod_{i=1}^{n} u_{ii}$, respectively. Consequently,

$$\det(A) = \det(LU) = \det(L) \times \det(U) = \prod_{i=1}^{n} u_{ii}.$$

However, when a principal submatrix of A is singular, then a permutation, i. e., the reordering of the columns of A, is required. If A is nonsingular, then there exists a permutation matrix $P \in \mathbb{R}^{n\times n}$ such that

$$PA = LU. \tag{12.26}$$

An equivalent formulation of the LU factorization (12.26) is

$$PA = LD\hat{U},$$

where $D \in \mathbb{R}^{n\times n}$ is a diagonal matrix, whose diagonal entries are u_{ii} and $\hat{U} \in \mathbb{R}^{n\times n}$ is a unit upper triangular matrix; i. e., $U = D\hat{U}$.

Computing the LU factorization of A is formally equivalent to solving the following nonlinear system of n^2 equations where the unknowns are the $n^2 + n$ coefficients of the triangular matrices L and U:

$$a_{ij} = \sum_{k=1}^{\min(i,j)} l_{ik} u_{kj}.$$

Using R, the LU factorization of a matrix, A, is performed using the command *expand(lu(A))*, which outputs three matrices L, U, and P. The matrices L and U are the lower and upper triangular matrices we are looking for, whereas the matrix P contains all the row permutation operations that have been carried out on the original matrix A for the purpose of obtaining L and U. Therefore, the product LU gives a row-permuted version of A, whereas the product PLU enables the recovery of the original matrix A.

Listing 12.17: LU Factorization

```
#The package "Matrix" is required here
require(Matrix)
A <- matrix(-c(3, 2, -5,  1, -3,  2, 5, -1, 4), nrow=3, ncol=3,
    byrow=TRUE)
A
     [,1] [,2] [,3]
[1,]    3    2   -5
[2,]    1   -3    2
[3,]    5   -1    4
#Getting the unit lower triangular matrix L
L<-expand(lu(A))$L
L
```

```
3 x 3 Matrix of class "dtrMatrix" (unitriangular)
     [,1]        [,2]        [,3]
[1,] 1.0000000           .          .
[2,] 0.2000000  1.0000000           .
[3,] 0.6000000 -0.9285714  1.0000000
#Getting the upper triangular matrix U
U<-expand(lu(A))$U
U
3 x 3 Matrix of class "dtrMatrix"
     [,1]       [,2]       [,3]
[1,] 5.000000 -1.000000  4.000000
[2,]        . -2.800000  1.200000
[3,]        .         . -6.285714
#Getting the permutation matrix P
P<-expand(lu(A))$P
P
3 x 3 sparse Matrix of class "pMatrix"
[1,] . . |
[2,] . | .
[3,] | . .
#Getting a row-permuted version of the matrix A
L%*%U
3 x 3 Matrix of class "dgeMatrix"
     [,1] [,2] [,3]
[1,]    5   -1    4
[2,]    1   -3    2
[3,]    3    2   -5
#Getting the original matrix A
P%*%L%*%U
3 x 3 Matrix of class "dgeMatrix"
     [,1] [,2] [,3]
[1,]    3    2   -5
[2,]    1   -3    2
[3,]    5   -1    4
```

Let A be an $n \times n$ symmetric matrix. If A has an LU factorization, then there exists a unit lower triangular matrix $L \in \mathbb{R}^{n \times n}$, and a diagonal matrix $D \in \mathbb{R}^{n \times n}$ such that

$$A = LDL^T. \tag{12.27}$$

If a principal submatrix of A is singular, then a permutation, i. e., a reordering of both rows and columns of A is required, and this results in the following factorization:

$$PAP^T = LDL^T, \tag{12.28}$$

where $P \in \mathbb{R}^{n \times n}$ is a permutation matrix.

12.8.2 Cholesky factorization

If an $n \times n$ real matrix, A, is positive definite, then there exists a unit lower triangular matrix $L \in \mathbb{R}^{n \times n}$ and a diagonal matrix $D \in \mathbb{R}^{n \times n}$ with $d_{ii} > 0$ for $i = 1, 2, \ldots, n$

such that

$$A = LDL^T = \tilde{L}\tilde{L}^T, \tag{12.29}$$

where $\tilde{L} = LD^{\frac{1}{2}}$, with $D^{\frac{1}{2}}$ a diagonal matrix, whose diagonal entries are $\sqrt{d_{ii}}$ for $i = 1, 2, \ldots, n$. The factorization (12.29) is referred to as the *Cholesky factorization*.

An illustration of Cholesky factorization, using R, is provided in Listing 12.18.

Listing 12.18: Cholesky factorization

```
#The package "Matrix" is required here
require(Matrix)
A <- matrix(c(1, 1, 1,  1, 2,  3, 1, 3, 6), nrow=3, ncol=3,
     byrow=TRUE)
A    #Note that A needs to be a squared symmetric matrix
      [,1] [,2] [,3]
[1,]     1    1    1
[2,]     1    2    3
[3,]     1    3    6
LtildeT<-chol(A)
LtildeT #This is the matrix LtildeT, the transpose of Ltilde
     [,1] [,2] [,3]
[1,]    1    1    1
[2,]    0    1    2
[3,]    0    0    1
#The original matrix A can be recovered as follows
t(LtildeT)%*%LtildeT
     [,1] [,2] [,3]
[1,]    1    1    1
[2,]    1    2    3
[3,]    1    3    6
```

12.8.3 QR factorization

Let $A \in \mathbb{R}^{m\times n}$. Then,

1. if $m = n$, and A is nonsingular, then there exits an orthogonal matrix $Q \in \mathbb{R}^{n\times n}$ and a nonsingular upper triangular matrix R such that the QR factorization of A is defined by

$$A = QR \Longleftrightarrow Q^T A = R,$$

since Q is orthogonal, i. e., $Q^T Q = I_n$;

2. if $m > n$ and $\operatorname{rank}(A) = n$, then there exists an orthogonal matrix $Q \in \mathbb{R}^{m\times m}$ and a nonsingular upper triangular matrix $R \in \mathbb{R}^{n\times n}$ such that the QR factorization of A is defined by

$$A = Q\begin{bmatrix} R \\ 0_{m-n,n}\end{bmatrix} \Longleftrightarrow Q^T A = \begin{bmatrix} R \\ 0_{m-n,n}\end{bmatrix}, \tag{12.30}$$

since Q is orthogonal, i. e., $Q^TQ = I_m$. Here, $0_{m-n,n}$ denotes the $(m-n) \times n$ matrix of zeros.

When $\operatorname{rank}(A) < n$, i. e., a principal submatrix of A is singular, then a permutation, i. e., the reordering, of the columns of A, is introduced, and the QR factorization of A is defined by

$$Q^TAP = Q\begin{bmatrix} R \\ 0_{m-n,n} \end{bmatrix},$$

where $P \in \mathbb{R}^{n\times n}$ is a permutation matrix for reordering the columns of A.

Let $V \in \mathbb{R}^{m\times n}$ and $W \in \mathbb{R}^{m\times(m-n)}$ denote the n first columns and $(m-n)$ last columns of the orthogonal matrix $Q \in \mathbb{R}^{m\times m}$, respectively; that is, $Q = [V, W]$. Then, the submatrices V and W are also orthogonal. Indeed,

$$\begin{aligned} Q^TQ &= \begin{bmatrix} V^T \\ W^T \end{bmatrix} \begin{bmatrix} V & W \end{bmatrix} \\ &= \begin{bmatrix} V^TV & V^TW \\ W^TV & W^TW \end{bmatrix}. \end{aligned}$$

Since Q is orthogonal, then $Q^TQ = I_m = \left[\begin{smallmatrix} I_n & 0 \\ 0 & I_{m-n} \end{smallmatrix}\right]$, and therefore

$$\begin{bmatrix} V^TV & Y^TY \\ W^TV & W^TW \end{bmatrix} = \begin{bmatrix} I_n & 0 \\ 0 & I_{m-n} \end{bmatrix},$$

i. e., $V^TV = I_n$, $W^TW = I_m$ $V^TW = 0_{n,m-n}$ and $W^TV = 0_{m-n,n}$ (that is, V and W are orthogonal). Substituting Q with $\begin{bmatrix} V & W \end{bmatrix}$ in (12.30) gives

$$Q^TA = \begin{bmatrix} R \\ 0_{m-n,n} \end{bmatrix} \Longleftrightarrow \begin{bmatrix} V^T \\ W^T \end{bmatrix} A = \begin{bmatrix} R \\ 0_{m-n,n} \end{bmatrix},$$

and therefore

$$V^TA = R \Longleftrightarrow A = VR, \tag{12.31}$$

$$W^TA = 0_{m-n,n}. \tag{12.32}$$

Equations (12.31) and (12.32) yield several important results, which link the QR factorization of a matrix, A, to its subspaces $\operatorname{im}(A)$ (i. e., the range of A) and $\ker(A)$ (i. e. the kernel or the null space of A). In particular,

1. since V is an orthogonal matrix, then, thanks to (12.31), the columns of V form an orthogonal basis for the subspace $\operatorname{im}(A)$, that is, A is uniquely determined by the linear combination of the column of V through $A = VR$. Conse-

quently, the matrix VV^T provides an *orthogonal projection* onto the subspace $\text{im}(A)$.

2. also, since W is an orthogonal matrix, then, thanks to (12.32), the columns of W form an orthogonal basis for the subspace $\ker(A)$, and the matrix WW^T provides an *orthogonal projection* on to the subspace $\ker(A)$.

Listing 12.19: QR Factorization

```
#The package "Matrix" is required here
require(Matrix)
A<- matrix(c(1, -1, 4,  1, 4,  -2, 1, 4, 2, 1, -1, 0), nrow=4,
    byrow=TRUE)
[,1] [,2] [,3]
[1,]    1   -1    4
[2,]    1    4   -2
[3,]    1    4    2
[4,]    1   -1    0
QRfact<-qr(A)
#Getting the rank of the matrix A
QRfact$rank
#Getting the orthogonal matrix Q
Q<-qr.Q(QRfact)
Q
     [,1] [,2] [,3]
[1,] -0.5  0.5 -0.5
[2,] -0.5 -0.5  0.5
[3,] -0.5 -0.5 -0.5
[4,] -0.5  0.5  0.5
#Getting the upper triangular matrix R
R<-qr.R(QRfact)
R
     [,1] [,2] [,3]
[1,]   -2   -3   -2
[2,]    0   -5    2
[3,]    0    0   -4
#If no permutations have been performed, then the original matrix A
    can be recovered exactly as via Q%*%R, otherwise this product
    will yield an A with some permuted columns
Q%*%R
     [,1] [,2] [,3]
[1,]    1   -1    4
[2,]    1    4   -2
[3,]    1    4    2
[4,]    1   -1    0
```

12.8.4 Singular value decomposition

The *singular value decomposition* (SVD) is another type of matrix factorization that generalizes the eigendecomposition of a square normal matrix to any matrix. It is a popular methods because it has widespread applications for recommender systems and the determination of a pseudoinverse. Let $A \in \mathbb{R}^{m \times n}$. Then,

- if $m \geq n$, then the SVD of A is given by

$$A = U \begin{bmatrix} D \\ 0_{m-n,n} \end{bmatrix} V^T,$$

where $U \in \mathbb{R}^{m\times m}$ and $V \in \mathbb{R}^{n\times n}$ are orthogonal matrices, i. e., $U^TU = I_m$ and $V^TV = I_n$, and $D \in \mathbb{R}^{n\times n}$ is a diagonal matrix whose diagonal entries, d_{ii} or simply denoted d_i for $i = 1, 2, \ldots, n$, are ordered in descending order, that is,

$$d_1 \geq d_2 \geq \ldots \geq 0.$$

- if $n > m$, then the SVD of A is given by

$$A = U \begin{bmatrix} D & 0_{m,n-m} \end{bmatrix},$$

where $D \in \mathbb{R}^{m\times m}$ is a diagonal matrix, whose diagonal entries $d_{ii} = d_i$ for $i = 1, 2, \ldots, m$, are rearranged in descending order.

Definition 12.8.1. The *singular values* of a matrix $A \in \mathbb{R}^{m\times n}$, denoted $\sigma_i(A)$, are given by the diagonal entries of the matrix D, that is,

$$\sigma_i(A) = d_i, \quad \text{for } i = 1, 2, \ldots, p,$$

where $p = \min(m, n)$.

The columns of U are called the left singular vectors, whereas the columns of V are called the right singular vectors.

The following relationships should be noted:

- The singular values of a matrix $A \in \mathbb{R}^{m\times n}$ are given by

$$\sigma_i(A) = \sqrt{\lambda_i(A^TA)} \quad \text{for } i = 1, 2, \ldots, p,$$

where $p = \min(m, n)$ and $\lambda_i(A^TA)$, $i = 1, 2, \ldots, p$, are the nonzero eigenvalues of the matrix A^TA, rearranged in descending order.

- Let r denote the rank of a matrix $A \in \mathbb{R}^{m\times n}$, then

$$\sigma_1(A) \geq \cdots \geq \sigma_r(A) > \sigma_{r+1} = \sigma_{r+2} = \cdots = \sigma_{\max(m,n)} = 0;$$

that is, the rank of the matrix is the number of its nonzero singular values. However, due to rounding errors, this approach to determine the rank is not straightforward in practice, as it is unclear how small the singular value should be to be considered as zero.

Furthermore, if A has a full rank, i. e., $r = \min(m, n)$, then the *condition number* of A, denoted $\kappa(A)$, is given by

$$\kappa(A) = \frac{\sigma_1(A)}{\sigma_r(A)}.$$

Listing 12.20: Singular Value Decomposition

```
#The package "Matrix" is required here
require(Matrix)
A<- matrix(c(1, -1, 4,  1, 4,  -2, 1, 4, 2, 1, -1, 0), nrow=4,
    byrow=TRUE)
[,1] [,2] [,3]
[1,]    1   -1    4
[2,]    1    4   -2
[3,]    1    4    2
[4,]    1   -1    0
SVDA<-svd(A)
#Getting the matrix U
U<-SVDA$u
U
           [,1]         [,2]       [,3]
[1,] -0.3132791  0.771564156 -0.2377918
[2,]  0.7480871 -0.146888948 -0.4108397
[3,]  0.5693222  0.618934107  0.2068642
[4,] -0.1345142  0.005741101 -0.8554957
#Getting the matrix V
V<-SVDA$v
V
           [,1]      [,2]       [,3]
[1,]  0.1448567 0.2543877 -0.9561922
[2,]  0.9523837 0.2261920  0.2044564
[3,] -0.2682942 0.9402787  0.2095093
#Getting the diagonal matrix D
D<-diag(SVDA$d)
  [,1]     [,2]     [,3]
[1,] 6.003285 0.000000 0.000000
[2,] 0.000000 4.911206 0.000000
[3,] 0.000000 0.000000 1.356697
#Getting the singular values of A
singv<-SVDA$d
singv
[1] 6.003285 4.911206 1.356697
#The original matrix A can be recovered as follows:
round(U%*%D%*%t(V))
  [,1] [,2] [,3]
[1,]    1   -1    4
[2,]    1    4   -2
[3,]    1    4    2
[4,]    1   -1    0
```

12.9 Systems of linear equations

A system of m linear equations in n unknowns consists of a set of algebraic relationships of the form

$$\sum_{j=1}^{n} a_{ij}x_j = b_i, \quad i = 1,\dots,m, \tag{12.33}$$

where x_j are the unknowns, whereas a_{ij}, the coefficients of the system, and b_i, the entries of the right-hand side, are assumed to be known constants.

The system (12.33) can be rewritten in the following matrix form:

$$Ax = b, \tag{12.34}$$

where A is an $m \times n$ matrix with entries a_{ij}, $i = 1,\dots,m$, $j = 1,\dots,n$, b is a column vector of size m with entries b_i, $i = 1,\dots,m$ and x is a column vector of size n with entries x_j, $j = 1,\dots,n$.

Theoretically, the system (12.34) has a solution if and only if $b \in \operatorname{im}(A)$. If, in addition, $\ker(A) = \{0\}$, then the solution is unique. When a solution exists for the system (12.34), then it is given by Cramer's method, as follows:

$$x = \frac{\det(M_j)}{\det(A)}, \tag{12.35}$$

where M_j is the matrix obtained by substituting the jth column of A with the right-hand side term b.

However, when the size of the matrix A is large, Cramer's method is not sustainable, and computing the solution, x, requires several efficient numerical methods. More often, the efficiency with which these methods work depends on the patterns or structure of the matrix A. Depending on the form of the matrix A, the systems of the form (12.34) can be categorized as follows:

1. *Triangular linear systems:* If $A \in \mathbb{R}^{n\times n}$ is either a nonsingular lower or an upper triangular matrix, then the system (12.34) can be solved efficiently.
   For instance, if A is a nonsingular lower triangular matrix, i. e., $A = L \in \mathbb{R}^{n\times n}$, then the solution to the system (12.34) can be readily obtained using the following method, known as *forward substitution*:

$$x_1 = \frac{b_1}{l_{11}}, \tag{12.36}$$

$$x_i = \frac{(b_i - \sum_{j=1}^{i-1} l_{ij}x_j)}{l_{ii}} \quad \text{for } i = 2,3,\dots,n. \tag{12.37}$$

If $A = L$ is a unit lower triangular matrix, then $l_{ii} = 1$ for all $i = 1, 2, \ldots, n$. Therefore, the denominators in (12.36) and (12.37) simplify.
However, if A is a nonsingular upper triangular matrix, i. e., $A = U \in \mathbb{R}^{n\times n}$, then the solution to the system (12.34) can easily be obtained using the following method, known as *backward substitution*:

$$x_n = \frac{b_n}{u_{nn}}, \tag{12.38}$$

$$x_i = \frac{(b_i - \sum_{j=i+1}^{n} u_{ij}x_j)}{u_{ii}} \quad \text{for } i = n-1, n-2, \ldots, 1. \tag{12.39}$$

2. *Well-determined linear systems:* If $A \in \mathbb{R}^{n\times n}$, then the system (12.34) has n linear equations in n variables, and a such system is said to be *well-determined.* If A is nonsingular, then the solution to the system is given by

$$x = A^{-1}b.$$

Since factorization methods, such as LU factorization, are efficient ways to calculate the inverse of a squared matrix, they can be purposely used here. Let L be a unit lower triangular matrix, U an upper triangular matrix, and P a permutation matrix such that $PA = LU$. Then $A = P^{-1}LU$, and the system (12.34) can be rewritten as follows

$$P^{-1}LUx = b \Longleftrightarrow LUx = Pb, \tag{12.40}$$

where the right-hand side term Pb is a permutation of b, i. e., the reordering of the entries of b.
The system (12.40) can be solved in two stages, as follows: First, solve for y the system $Ly = Pb$ using forward substitution, and then use the obtained values of y to solve for x the system $Ux = y$.
Furthermore, if A is symmetric, then it is more convenient to use the LDL^T factorization (12.27)–(12.28) to solve the system (12.34). If A is symmetric positive definite, then the Cholesky factorization (12.29), i. e., $A = \tilde{L}\tilde{L}^T$, is likely to be the most efficient method to solve the system (12.34).
3. *Over-determined linear systems:* If $A \in \mathbb{R}^{m\times n}$ with $m > n$, then the system (12.34) has more equations than variables, and such a system is said to be *over-determined.* When $b \in \operatorname{im}(A)$, then the system (12.34) has a solution, and so does

$$A^TAx = A^Tb.$$

If A is a full rank matrix, that is $\operatorname{rank}(A) = n$, then the matrix A^TA is nonsingular and therefore invertible. Thence,

$$x = (A^TA)^{-1}A^Tb.$$

The matrix $A^+ = (A^T A)^{-1} A^T$ is referred to as the *pseudoinverse* of A or the *Moore–Penrose generalized inverse* of A. Note that when A is a squared matrix, that is, $m = n$, then $A^+ = A^{-1}$.

If $b \notin \text{im}(A)$, then the system (12.34) has no solution.

4. *Under-determined linear systems:* If $A \in \mathbb{R}^{m\times n}$ with $m < n$, then the system (12.34) has fewer equations than variables, and such a system is said to be *under-determined.* If the equations in (12.34) are consistent, then the system has an infinite number of solutions. If A is a full rank matrix, that is, $\text{rank}(A) = m$, then the matrix AA^T is a nonsingular matrix. Thus, one of the solutions to the system (12.34) is given by

$$\bar{x} = A^T \left(AA^T\right)^{-1} b.$$

Consider the following linear system:

$$\begin{cases} 3x & + & 2y & - & 5z & = & 12 \\ x & - & 3y & + & 2z & = & -13 \\ 5x & - & y & + & 4z & = & 10 \end{cases} \tag{12.41}$$

Thus,

$$A = \begin{pmatrix} 3 & 2 & -5 \\ 1 & -3 & 2 \\ 5 & -1 & 4 \end{pmatrix} \quad \text{and} \quad b = \begin{pmatrix} 12 \\ -13 \\ 10 \end{pmatrix}.$$

Using R, the linear system (12.41) can be solved as follows:

Listing 12.21: Solving a well-determined linear system

```
A <- matrix(c(3, 2, -5,  1, -3,  2, 5, -1, 4), nrow=3, ncol=3,
       byrow=TRUE)
A
       [,1] [,2] [,3]
[1,]     3    2   -5
[2,]     1   -3    2
[3,]     5   -1    4
b <- matrix(c(12, -13, 10), nrow=3, ncol=1, byrow=TRUE)
b
      [,1]
[1,]   12
[2,]  -13
[3,]   10
#Solving the system Ax=b
x<-solve(A,b)
> x
         [,1]
[1,] 2.170455
[2,] 5.897727
[3,] 1.261364
```

12.10 Exercises

1. Let $\vec{U} = \begin{pmatrix}-1, & -2, & 4\end{pmatrix}$, and let $\vec{V} = \begin{pmatrix}2, & 3, & 5\end{pmatrix}$ be two 3-dimensional vectors:
   (a) Compute the Euclidean norms of $\vec{U}$ and $\vec{V}$.
   (b) Compute the dot product of $\vec{U}$ and $\vec{V}$.
   (c) Compute the orthogonal projection of $\vec{U}$ onto the direction of $\vec{V}$.
   (d) Compute the reflection of $\vec{V}$ with respect to the direction of $\vec{U}$.
   (e) Compute the cross product of $\vec{U}$ and $\vec{V}$.
   (f) Compute the components of $\vec{U}$ and $\vec{V}$ in cylindrical and spherical coordinates.
2. Let $z = 5 + 2i$ and $w = 7 + 4i$ be two complex numbers.
   (a) Compute the conjugates of z and w, the sum of z and w, and difference $z - w$.
   (b) Compute the product $z \times w$ and the divisions $\frac{z}{w}$ and $\frac{w}{z}$.
3. Let

$$A = \begin{pmatrix} 1 & 3 & 0 \\ 2 & -2 & 1 \\ -4 & 1 & -1 \end{pmatrix} \quad \text{and} \quad B = \begin{pmatrix} 7 & 2 & 1 \\ 0 & 3 & -1 \\ -3 & 4 & -2 \end{pmatrix}$$

   be two 3 by 3 matrices, and let $V = \begin{pmatrix}17, & 9, & 6\end{pmatrix}$.
   (a) Compute the sum of A and B.
   (b) Compute the difference $B - A$.
   (c) Compute the transpose and the inverse matrices of A and B.
   (d) Compute the following matrix products: $A \times B$, $V \times A$ and $V \times B$.
   (e) Compute the trace and determinant of A and B.
   (f) Find the rank of A and B.
   (g) Compute the eigenvalues and eigenvectors of A and B.
   (h) Compute the spectral radius of A and B.
   (i) Compute the subordinate matrices 1-norm of A and B.
   (j) Compute the subordinate matrices 2-norm of A and B.
   (k) Compute the subordinate matrices ∞-norm of A and B.
   (l) Compute the Frobenius norm of A and B.
   (m) Compute the LU, Cholesky and QR factorization of A and B.
4. Use the appropriate R functions to solve the following linear systems:

$$\begin{cases} 2x & & & + & 3z & = & 3 \\ 4x & - & 3y & + & 7z & = & 5 \\ 8x & - & 9y & + & 15z & = & 10 \end{cases}$$

$$\begin{cases} 2x & - & y & + & z & = & 8 \\ x & + & 2y & + & 3z & = & 9 \\ 3x & & & - & z & = & 3 \end{cases}.$$

13 Analysis

Similar to linear algebra, also analysis [158] is omnipresent in nearly all applications of mathematics. In general, analysis deals with examining convergence, limits of functions, differentiation, integration as well as metrics. In this chapter, we provide an introduction to these topics and demonstrate how to conduct a numerical analysis using R.

13.1 Introduction

Differentiation and integration are fundamental mathematical concepts, having a wide range of applications in many areas of science, particularly in physics, chemistry, and engineering [158]. Both concepts are intimately connected, as integration is the inverse process of differentiation, and vice versa. These concepts are especially important for descriptive models, e. g., providing information about the position of an object in space and time (physics) or the temporal evolution of the price of a stock (finance). Such models require the precise definition of the *functional*, describing the system of interest, and related mathematical objects defining the dynamics of the system.

13.2 Limiting values

The concept of limiting values forms the basis of many areas in mathematics [158]. For instance, limiting values are important for investigating the values of functions. For a given function, $f(x)$, we can distinguish two types of limiting values:

- If x goes to $\pm\infty$
- If x goes to a finite value x_0

Before we begin investigating limiting values, we introduce a class of functions, namely, real sequences. For limiting values of complex sequences or functions, we refer to the reader to [158].

Definition 13.2.1. A real sequence is a function $a_n : \mathbb{N} \longrightarrow \mathbb{R}$.

We also write $(a_n)_{n\in\mathbb{N}} = (a_1, a_2, a_3, \ldots, a_n, \ldots)$. Typical examples of sequences include:

$$(a_n)_{n\in\mathbb{N}} = \left(\frac{1}{2}, \frac{1}{4}, \frac{1}{6}, \ldots\right), \tag{13.1}$$

$$(b_n)_{n\in\mathbb{N}} = (1^3, 2^3, 3^3 \ldots). \tag{13.2}$$

https://doi.org/10.1515/9783110796063-013

From the above sequences, it can be observed that a_n and b_n have the closed forms: $a_n = \frac{1}{2n}$ and $b_n = n^3$, respectively. Now, we are ready to define the limiting value of a real sequence.

Definition 13.2.2. A number l is called the limiting value or limes of a given real sequence $(a_n)_{n\in\mathbb{N}}$, if for all $\varepsilon > 0$ exists $N_0(\varepsilon)$ such that $|a_n - l| < \varepsilon$, for all $n > N_0(\varepsilon)$. In this case, the sequence, $(a_n)_{n\in\mathbb{N}}$, is said to converge to l, and the following shorthand notation is used to summarize the previous statement: $\lim_{n\longrightarrow\infty} a_n = l$.

Example 13.2.1. Let us consider the sequence $a_n = 1 - \frac{1}{n}$. We want to show that $(a_n)_{n\in\mathbb{N}}$ converges to 1. By setting $l = 1$ in Definition 13.2.2, we obtain

$$|a_n - 1| = \left|\left(1 - \frac{1}{n}\right) - 1\right| = \left|\frac{1}{n}\right| = \frac{1}{n} < \varepsilon. \tag{13.3}$$

Thus, we find $n > \frac{1}{\varepsilon} =: N_0(\varepsilon)$. In summary, for all $\varepsilon > 0$, there exists a number $N_0(\varepsilon) := \frac{1}{\varepsilon}$ such that $|a_n - 1| < \varepsilon$ for all $n > N_0(\varepsilon) := \frac{1}{\varepsilon}$. For example, if we set $\varepsilon = \frac{1}{10}$, then $n \geq 11$. This means that for all elements of the given sequence $a_n = 1 - \frac{1}{n}$, starting from $n = 11$, $|a_n - 1| < \frac{1}{10}$ holds.

In Figure 13.1, we visualize the concept introduced in Definition 13.2.2.

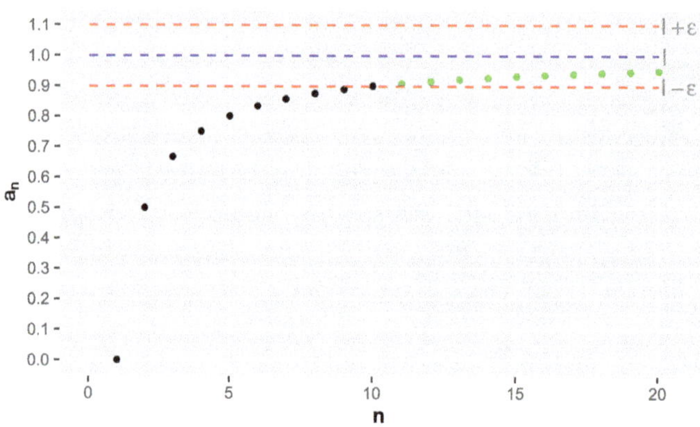

Figure 13.1: Elements of the sequence $a_n = 1 - \frac{1}{n}$ are shown as points. The elements that lie in the ε-strip are indicated by green points.

Before we give some examples of basic limiting values of sequences, we provide the following proposition, which is necessary for the calculations that follow [158].

Proposition 13.2.1. *Let $(a_n)_{n\in\mathbb{N}}$ and $(b_n)_{n\in\mathbb{N}}$ be two convergent sequences with $\lim_{n\longrightarrow\infty} a_n = a$ and $\lim_{n\longrightarrow\infty} b_n = b$. Then, the following relationships hold:*

$$\lim_{n\to\infty}(a_n + b_n) = \lim_{n\to\infty} a_n + \lim_{n\to\infty} b_n = a + b, \tag{13.4}$$

$$\lim_{n\to\infty}(a_n \cdot b_n) = \lim_{n\to\infty} a_n \cdot \lim_{n\to\infty} b_n = a \cdot b, \tag{13.5}$$

$$\lim_{n\to\infty} \frac{a_n}{b_n} = \frac{\lim_{n\to\infty} a_n}{\lim_{n\to\infty} b_n} = \frac{a}{b}. \tag{13.6}$$

Example 13.2.2. Let us examine the convergence of the following two sequences:

$$a_n = \frac{3n+1}{n+5}, \tag{13.7}$$

$$b_n = (-1)^n. \tag{13.8}$$

For a_n, we have

$$\lim_{n\to\infty} \frac{3n+1}{n+5} = \lim_{n\to\infty} \frac{n(3+\frac{1}{n})}{n(1+\frac{5}{n})} = \frac{\lim_{n\to\infty}(3+\frac{1}{n})}{\lim_{n\to\infty}(1+\frac{5}{n})}$$
$$= \frac{3+\lim_{n\to\infty}(\frac{1}{n})}{1+\lim_{n\to\infty}(\frac{5}{n})} = \frac{3+0}{1+0} = 3. \tag{13.9}$$

Note that the sequences $\lim_{n\to\infty}(\frac{1}{n})$ and $\lim_{n\to\infty}(\frac{5}{n})$ converge to 0. By examining the values of b_n, we observe that its values alternate, i. e., they always flip between -1 and 1. According to Definition 13.2.2, the sequence b_n is not convergent and, hence, does not have a limiting value.

In the following, we generalize the concept of limiting values of sequences to functions.

Definition 13.2.3. Let $f(x)$ be a real function and x_n a sequence that belongs to the domain of $f(x)$. If all sequences of the values $f(x_n)$ converge to l, then l is called the limiting value for $x \to \pm\infty$, and we write $\lim_{x\to\pm\infty} = l$.

For a general function, $f : X \to Y$, we call the set X domain and Y the co-domain of function f.

Example 13.2.3. Let us determine the limiting value of the function $f(x) = \frac{2x-1}{x}$ for large and positive x. This means, we examine $\lim_{x\to\infty} \frac{2x-1}{x}$ and find

$$\lim_{x\to\infty} \frac{2x-1}{x} = \lim_{x\to\infty}\left(2 - \frac{1}{x}\right) = 2 - \lim_{x\to\infty}\left(\frac{1}{x}\right) = 2. \tag{13.10}$$

Here, we used Proposition 13.2.1 for functions as it can be formulated accordingly (see [158]).

The limiting value of $f(x) = \frac{2x-1}{x}$ for large x can be seen in Figure 13.2.

We conclude this section by stating the definition for the convergence of a function, $f(x)$, if x tends to a finite value x_0.

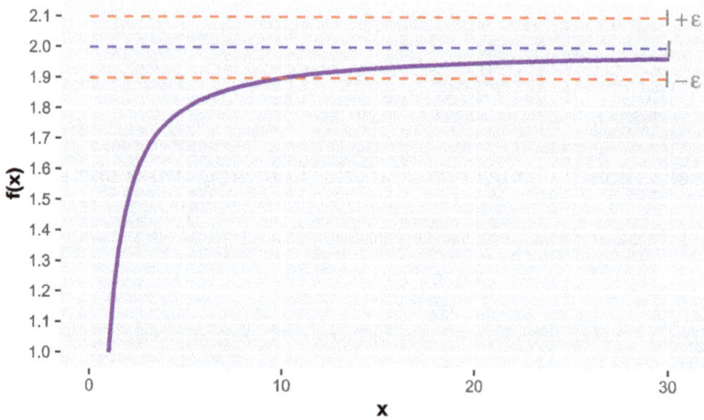

Figure 13.2: Limiting value for $f(x) = \frac{2x-1}{x}$ with $l = 2$.

Definition 13.2.4. Let $f(x)$ be a real function defined in a neighborhood of x_0. If for all sequences x_n in the domain of $f(x)$ with $x_n \to x_0$, $x_n \neq x_0$ the equation $\lim_{n\to\infty} f(x_n) = l$ holds, we call l the limiting value of $f(x)$ at x_0. Symbolically, we write $\lim_{x\to x_0} f(x) = l$.

Example 13.2.4. Let us calculate the limiting value of $\lim_{x\to -2} \frac{2x^3-8x}{x+2}$. Note that the function $f(x) = \frac{2x^3-8x}{x+2}$ is not defined at $x = -2$. However, if we factorize $2x^3 - 8x$, we obtain $2x^3 - 8x = 2x(x+2)(x-2)$. Hence, we obtain

$$\lim_{x\to -2} \frac{2x^3 - 8x}{x+2} = \lim_{x\to -2} \frac{2x(x+2)(x-2)}{x+2} = \lim_{x\to -2} 2x(x-2) = 16. \tag{13.11}$$

The following sections will utilize the concepts introduced here to define differentiation and integration.

13.3 Differentiation

Let $f : \mathbb{R} \longrightarrow \mathbb{R}$ be a given continuous function. Then, f is called differentiable at the point x_0 if the following limit exists:

$$\lim_{h\longrightarrow 0} \frac{f(x_0 + h) - f(x_0)}{h}. \tag{13.12}$$

If f is differentiable at the point x_0, the derivative of f denoted $\frac{\mathrm{d}f(x)}{\mathrm{d}x}$ or $f'(x)$ is finite at x_0, and can be approximated by

$$f'(x_0) = \frac{\mathrm{d}f(x_0)}{\mathrm{d}x} \approx \frac{f(x_0 + h) - f(x_h)}{h}, \quad \text{for } h \longrightarrow 0. \tag{13.13}$$

Therefore, the derivative of a function f at a point x_0 can be viewed as the slope of the tangent line of $f(x)$ at the point x_0, as illustrated geometrically in Figure 13.3. The tangent line in Figure 13.3 (left) corresponds to the limit of the displacement of the secant line in Figure 13.3 (left) when h tends to zero, i. e., when $x_0 + h$ is getting closer to x_0. The intermediate dashed lines correspond to the different positions of the secant line as h decreases to 0. Figure 13.3 (right) shows the tangent line when $h \approx 0$, i. e., $x_0 \approx x_0 + h$, which corresponds approximately to equation (13.13).

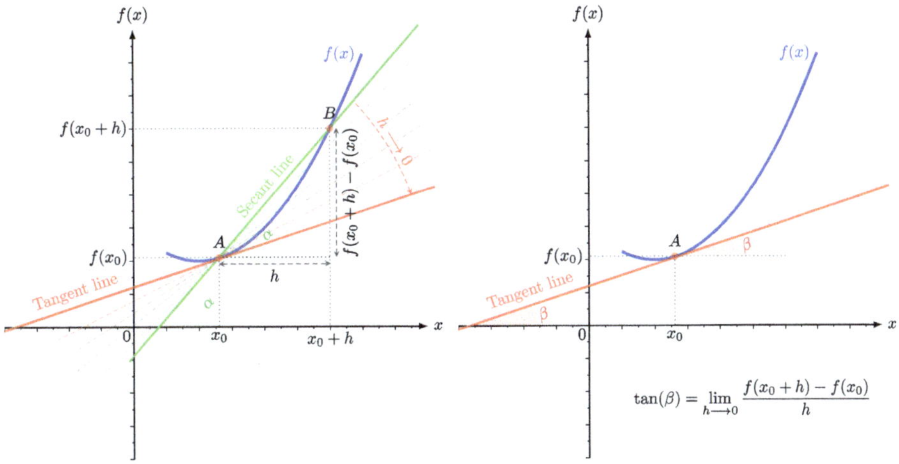

Figure 13.3: Geometric interpretation of the derivative.

The above approximation can be extended to multivariate real functions as follows: Let f be a scalar valued multivariable real function, i. e., $f : \mathbb{R}^n \longrightarrow \mathbb{R}$. Then, the first-order partial derivative of f at a point $x = (x_1, x_2, \ldots, x_n)$ with respect to the variable x_i, generally denoted $\frac{\partial f(x)}{\partial x_i}$ or $\partial_{x_i} f(x)$, is defined as follows:

$$\frac{\partial f(x)}{\partial x_i} = \lim_{h \longrightarrow 0} \frac{f(x_1, x_2, \ldots, x_i + h, \ldots, x_n) - f(x_1, x_2, \ldots, x_i, \ldots, x_n)}{h}. \tag{13.14}$$

Definition 13.3.1. The differential of f is given by

$$df = \frac{\partial f}{\partial x_1} dx_1 + \frac{\partial f}{\partial x_2} dx_2 + \cdots + \frac{\partial f}{\partial x_i} dx_i + \cdots + \frac{\partial f}{\partial x_n} dx_n.$$

Definition 13.3.2. The gradient of a function f, denoted ∇f, is defined, in Cartesian coordinates, as follows:

$$\nabla f = \frac{\partial f}{\partial x_1} e_1 + \frac{\partial f}{\partial x_2} e_2 + \cdots + \frac{\partial f}{\partial x_i} e_i + \cdots + \frac{\partial f}{\partial x_n} e_n,$$

where the e_k, $k = 1, \dots, n$, are the orthogonal unit vectors pointing in the coordinate directions. Thus, in $(\mathbb{R}^n, \|\cdot\|_2)$, where $\|x\|_2 = \sqrt{\langle x, x\rangle}$ is the Euclidian norm, the gradient of f can be rewritten as follows:

$$\nabla f = df^T = \left(\frac{\partial f}{\partial x_1}, \frac{\partial f}{\partial x_2}, \dots, \frac{\partial f}{\partial x_n}\right)^T.$$

When f is a function of a single variable, i. e., $n = 1$, then $\nabla f = f'$.

The orthogonal unit vectors e_i are explicitly given by

$$e_i = \begin{pmatrix} 0 \\ 0 \\ \vdots \\ 0 \\ 1 \\ 0 \\ \vdots \\ 0 \end{pmatrix} \tag{13.15}$$

with a 1 at the ith component and zeros otherwise.

Definition 13.3.3. The Hessian of f, denoted $\nabla^2 f$, is an $n \times n$ matrix of second-order partial derivatives of f, if these exist, organized as follows:

$$\nabla^2 f = \begin{bmatrix} \frac{\partial^2 f}{\partial x_1 \partial x_1} & \frac{\partial^2 f}{\partial x_1 \partial x_2} & \cdots & \frac{\partial^2 f}{\partial x_1 \partial x_n} \\ \frac{\partial^2 f}{\partial x_2 \partial x_1} & \frac{\partial^2 f}{\partial x_2 \partial x_2} & \cdots & \frac{\partial^2 f}{\partial x_2 \partial x_n} \\ \vdots & \vdots & \ddots & \vdots \\ \frac{\partial^2 f}{\partial x_n \partial x_1} & \frac{\partial^2 f}{\partial x_n \partial x_2} & \cdots & \frac{\partial^2 f}{\partial x_n \partial x_n} \end{bmatrix}.$$

Thus, the Hessian matrix describes the local curvature of the function f.

Example 13.3.1. Let $f : \mathbb{R}^3 \mapsto \mathbb{R}$ defined by $f(x) = f(x_1, x_2, x_3) = x_1^3 + x_2^2 + \log(x_3)$. Then,

$$\nabla f(x) = \begin{pmatrix} 3x_1^2, & 2x_2, & \frac{1}{x_3} \end{pmatrix}^T,$$

and

$$\nabla^2 f(x) = \begin{pmatrix} 6x_1 & 0 & 0 \\ 0 & 2 & 0 \\ 0 & 0 & -\frac{1}{x_3^2} \end{pmatrix}.$$

At the point $\bar{x} = (1, 1/2, 1)$, we have $\nabla f(\bar{x}) = (3, 1, 1)$ and

$$\nabla^2 f(\bar{x}) = \begin{pmatrix} 6 & 0 & 0 \\ 0 & 2 & 0 \\ 0 & 0 & -1 \end{pmatrix}.$$

Definition 13.3.4. Let f be a multivalued function, i. e., $f : \mathbb{R}^n \longrightarrow \mathbb{R}^m$. Then, the Jacobian of f, denoted J_f, is an $m \times n$ matrix of the first-order partial derivatives, if they exist, of the m real-valued component functions $(f_1, f_2, \dots, f_m)$ of f, organized as follows:

$$J_f = \begin{bmatrix} \frac{\partial f_1}{\partial x_1} & \frac{\partial f_1}{\partial x_2} & \cdots & \frac{\partial f_1}{\partial x_n} \\ \frac{\partial f_2}{\partial x_1} & \frac{\partial f_2}{\partial x_2} & \cdots & \frac{\partial f_2}{\partial x_n} \\ \vdots & \vdots & \ddots & \vdots \\ \frac{\partial f_m}{\partial x_1} & \frac{\partial f_m}{\partial x_2} & \cdots & \frac{\partial f_m}{\partial x_n} \end{bmatrix}.$$

The Jacobian generalizes the gradient of a scalar-valued function of several variables to m real-valued component functions. Therefore, the Jacobian for a scalar-valued multivariable function, i. e., when $m = 1$, is the gradient.

Example 13.3.2. Let $f : \mathbb{R}^3 \mapsto \mathbb{R}^2$ defined by

$$f(x) = f(x_1, x_2, x_3) = \left(\begin{smallmatrix} f_1(x_1,x_2,x_3) \\ f_2(x_1,x_2,x_3) \end{smallmatrix}\right) = \left(\begin{smallmatrix} x_1 x_2^2 \\ x_3^2 + 2x_1 x_2 \end{smallmatrix}\right).$$

Then,

$$J_f(x) = \begin{bmatrix} x_2^2 & 2x_1x_2 & 0 \\ 2x_2 & 2x_1 & 2x_3 \end{bmatrix}.$$

At the point $\bar{x} = (1, 1/2, 1)$, we have

$$J_f(\bar{x}) = \begin{bmatrix} 1/4 & 1 & 0 \\ 1 & 2 & 2 \end{bmatrix}.$$

Using R, the gradient of a function f at a point x is computed using the command `grad(f, x)`. Since the gradient of a function of a single variable is nothing but the first derivative of the function, then the same command is used to compute the derivative of a function of one variable at a given point. By contrast, the Hessian and the Jacobian of a function f at a point x are computed using the command `hessian(f, x)` and `jacobian(f, x)`, respectively.

For example, the gradient, the Hessian, and the Jacobian of the following function $f(x, y, z) = x^2y + \sin(z)$ at the point $(x = 2, y = 2, z = 5)$ can be computed using R as follows:

Listing 13.1: Numerical differentiation

```
#The package "numDeriv" is required here
library(numDeriv)
f <- function(x){x[1]^2*x[2]+ sin(x[3])}
#Computing the gradient of f at the point (2, 2, 5)
grad(f, c(2,2,5))
[1] 8.0000000 4.0000000 0.2836622
#Computing the Hessian of f at the point (2, 2, 5)
hessian(f, c(2,2,5))
              [,1]          [,2]          [,3]
[1,]  4.000000e+00  4.000000e+00 -1.800931e-16
[2,]  4.000000e+00  1.684171e-13 -3.068900e-17
[3,] -1.800931e-16 -3.068900e-17  9.589243e-01
#Computing the Jacobian of f at the point (2, 2, 5)
jacobian(f, c(2,2,5))
     [,1] [,2]      [,3]
[1,]    8    4 0.2836622
```

Let us consider the following example, from economics, for determining extreme values of economic functions [182] (see also Example 13.8.1). In this example, the economic functions of interest are real polynomials [135].

Example 13.3.3. Let

$$C(x) = \frac{1}{3}x^3 - \frac{3}{2}x^2 + 7 \tag{13.16}$$

be an economic cost function [182] describing the costs depending on a quantity unit x. To find the minima of $C(x)$, we use its derivative, i. e.,

$$C'(x) = x^2 - 3x. \tag{13.17}$$

By solving

$$C'(x) = x^2 - 3x = 0, \tag{13.18}$$

we find $x = 0$, and $x = 3$. To check whether $x = 3$ corresponds to a minimum or maximum, we determine

$$C''(x) = 2x - 3. \tag{13.19}$$

This yields $C''(3) = 3 > 0$. Hence, we found a minimum of $C(x)$ at $x = 3$. This can also be observed, graphically, in Figure 13.4.

In the following section, we provide some formal definitions of extrema of a function.

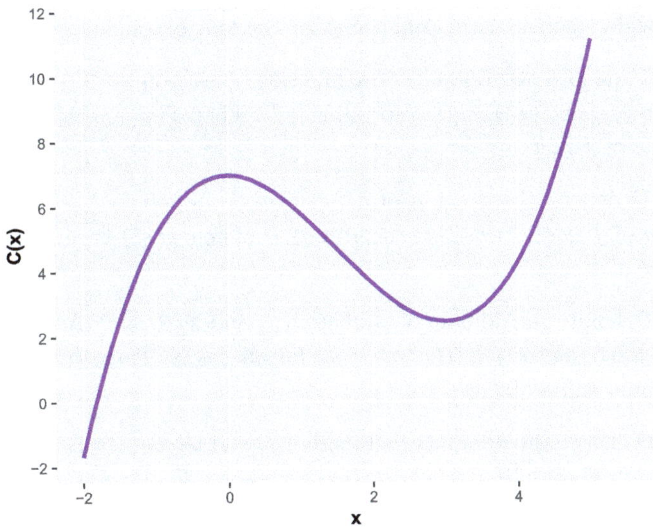

Figure 13.4: An example of an economic cost function $C(x)$ with its minimum located at $x = 3$.

13.4 Extrema of a function

The extrema of a function refer to the largest (i. e., maximum) and smallest (i. e., minimum) values of a function, either on its entire domain (global or absolute extrema) or within a given range (local extrema). Therefore, we can distinguish four types of extrema: *global maxima*, *global minima*, *local maxima*, and *local minima*. These are illustrated in Figure 13.5.

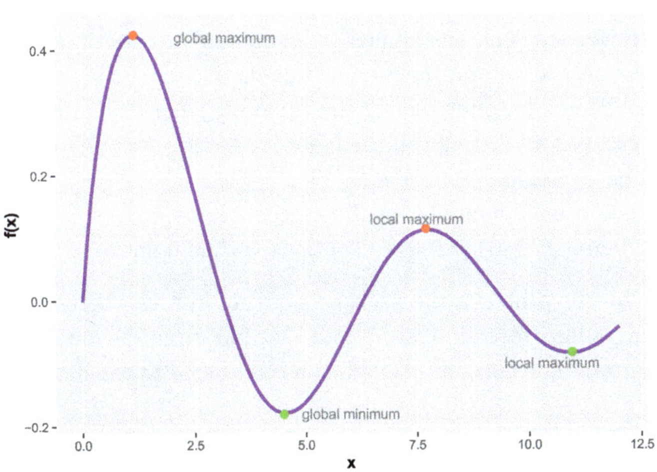

Figure 13.5: The four different types of extrema of a function.

In the following, we provide mathematical definitions for the four extrema:

Definition 13.4.1. Let $\mathcal{D}$ denote the domain of a function f. A point $x^* \in \mathcal{D}$ is called a *global maximum* of f if $f(x^*) \geq f(x)$ for all $x \in \mathcal{D}$. Then $f(x^*)$ is referred to as the maximum value of f in $\mathcal{D}$.

Definition 13.4.2. Let $\mathcal{D}$ denote the domain of a function f. A point $x^* \in \mathcal{D}$ is called a *global minimum* of f if $f(x^*) \leq f(x)$ for all $x \in \mathcal{D}$. Then $f(x^*)$ is referred to as the minimum value of f in $\mathcal{D}$.

Definition 13.4.3. Let $\mathcal{D}$ denote the domain of a function f, and let $\mathcal{I} \subset \mathcal{D}$. A point $x^* \in \mathcal{I}$ is called a *local maximum* of f if $f(x^*) \geq f(x)$ for all $x \in \mathcal{I}$. Then $f(x^*)$ is referred to as the maximum value of f in $\mathcal{I}$.

Definition 13.4.4. Let $\mathcal{D}$ denote the domain of a function f, and let $\mathcal{I} \subset \mathcal{D}$. A point $x^* \in \mathcal{I}$ is called a *local minimum* of f if $f(x^*) \leq f(x)$ for all $x \in \mathcal{I}$. Then $f(x^*)$ is referred to as the minimum value of f in $\mathcal{I}$.

To characterize extrema of continuous functions, we invoke the well-known Weierstrass extreme value theorem.

Theorem 13.4.1 (Weierstrass extreme value theorem). *Let $\mathcal{D}$ denote the domain of a function f, and let $\mathcal{I} = [a,b] \subset \mathcal{D}$. If f is continuous on $\mathcal{I}$, then f achieves both its maximum value, denoted M, and its minimum value, denoted m. In other words, there exist x_M^* and x_m^* in $\mathcal{I}$ such that*
- $f(x_M^*) = M$ *and* $f(x_m^*) = m$,
- $m \leq f(x) \leq M$.

We want to emphasize that extrema of functions possess horizontal tangents. These extrema can be calculated using basic calculus. Suppose that we have a real and a continuous function on a domain $\mathcal{D}$. The points $x \in \mathcal{D}$, satisfying the equation $f'(x) = 0$, are candidates for extrema (maximum or minimum). In Section 13.3, we explained that the first derivative of a function at a point x corresponds to the slope of the tangent at x. Therefore, after solving the equation $f'(x) = 0$ and after calculating $f''(x)$, it is necessary to distinguish the following cases:
- $f''(x_0) > 0 \Longrightarrow f(x)$ has a minimum at $x_0 \in \mathcal{D}$
- $f''(x_0) < 0 \Longrightarrow f(x)$ has a maximum at $x_0 \in \mathcal{D}$
- $f'(x_0) = 0$, $f''(x_0) = 0$ and $f'''(x_0) \neq 0 \Longrightarrow f(x)$ has a saddle point at $x_0 \in \mathcal{D}$

For a numerical solution to this problem, the package `ggpmisc` in `R` can be used to find extrema of a function, as illustrated in Listing 13.2. The plot from the output of the script is shown in Figure 13.6, where the colored dots correspond to the different extrema of the function

$$f(x) = 23.279 - 29.3598 \exp(-0.00093393x) \sin(0.00917552x + 20.515),$$

for $x \in [0, 1500]$.

Listing 13.2: Finding extrema of a function (see Figure 13.6)

```
#Finding Extrema
library(ggpmisc)
set.seed(10)
x <- 1:1500
f <- function(x) {
  23.279 - 29.3598*exp(-0.00093393*x)*sin(0.00917552*x + 20.515)
}
fx = f(x)
# Finding maxima of f(x)
x[ggpmisc:::find_peaks(fx)]
fx[ggpmisc:::find_peaks(fx)]
# Finding minima of f(x)
x[ggpmisc:::find_peaks(-fx)]
fx[ggpmisc:::find_peaks(-fx)]
# Plotting f(x) and its extrema
ggplot(data = data.frame(x, fx), aes(x = x, y = fx)) + geom_line() +
  scale_x_continuous('x') +
  scale_y_continuous('f(x)') +
  stat_peaks(col = "red") +
  stat_valleys(col = "blue")
```

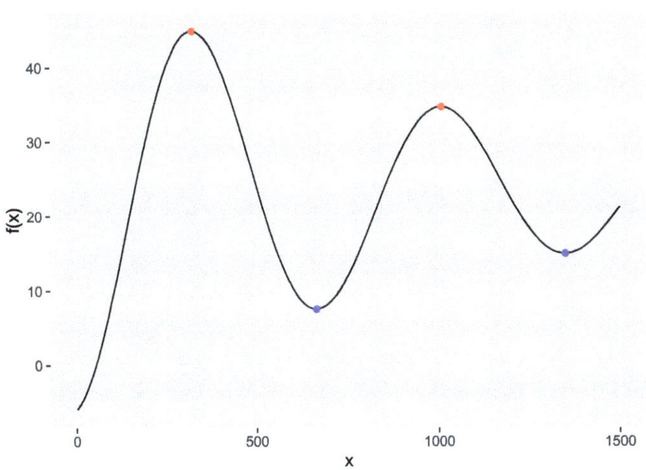

Figure 13.6: Finding extrema of a function using R, see Listing 13.2.

13.5 Taylor series expansion

A Taylor series expansion is an expression that approximates a smooth function $f(x)$ in the neighborhood of a certain point $x = x_0$. In simple terms, this approximation breaks the nonlinearity of a function down into its polynomial components. This yields a function that is more linear than $f(x)$. The simplest, yet most frequently used approximation, is the linearization of a function. Taylor series expansions have many applications in mathematics, physics, and engineering. For instance, they are used to approximate solutions to differential equations, which are otherwise difficult to solve.

Definition 13.5.1. A one-dimensional *Taylor series expansion* of an infinitely differentiable function $f(x)$, at a point $x = x_0$, is given by

$$\begin{aligned} f(x) &= \sum_{n=0}^{\infty} \frac{f^{(n)}(x_0)}{n!}(x-x_0)^n \\ &= f(x_0) + \frac{f'(x_0)}{1!}(x-x_0) + \frac{f''(x_0)}{2!}(x-x_0)^2 + \frac{f^{(3)}(x_0)}{3!}(x-x_0)^3 + \cdots \end{aligned}$$

where $f^{(n)}$ denotes the nth derivative of f.

If $x_0 = 0$, then the expansion may also be called a Maclaurin series.

Below, we provide examples of Taylor series expansions for some common functions, at a point $x = x_0$:

$$\begin{aligned} \exp(x) &= \exp(x_0)\left[1 + (x-x_0) + \frac{1}{2}(x-x_0)^2 + \frac{1}{6}(x-x_0)^3 + \cdots\right] \\ \ln(x) &= \ln(x_0) + \frac{x-x_0}{x_0} - \frac{(x-x_0)^2}{2x_0^2} + \frac{(x-x_0)^3}{3x_0^3} - \cdots \\ \cos(x) &= \cos(x_0) - \sin(x_0)(x-x_0) - \frac{1}{2}\cos(x_0)(x-x_0)^2 + \frac{1}{6}\sin(x_0)(x-x_0)^3 + \cdots \\ \sin(x) &= \sin(x_0) + \cos(x_0)(x-x_0) - \frac{1}{2}\sin(x_0)(x-x_0)^2 - \frac{1}{6}\cos(x_0)(x-x_0)^3 + \cdots \end{aligned}$$

The accuracy of a Taylor series expansion depends on both the function to be approximated, the point at which the approximation is made, and the number of terms used in the approximation, as illustrated in Figure 13.7 and Figure 13.8.

Several packages in `R` can be used to obtain the Taylor series expansion of a function. For instance, the library `Ryacas` can be used to obtain the expression of the Taylor series expansion of a function, which can then be evaluated. The library `pracma`, on the other hand, provides an approximation of the function at a given point using its corresponding Taylor series expansion. The scripts below illustrate the usage of these two packages.

Listing 13.3: Taylor Series Expression with Ryacas

```
library(Ryacas)
yacas("texp := Taylor(x,0,5) Exp(x)")
expression(x + x^2/2 + x^3/6 + x^4/24 + x^5/120 + 1)
yacas("texp := Taylor(x,0,5) Cos(x)")
expression(1 - x^2/2 + x^4/24)
yacas("texp := Taylor(x,0,5) Sin(x)")
expression(x - x^3/6 + x^5/120)
```

Listing 13.4: Taylor Series Approximation with pracma, see Figure 13.7

```
# Taylor Series Expansion Using pracma
library(pracma)
library(ggplot2)

fx <- function(x) {
  e <- exp(1)
  return(e^x)
}
fxts <- taylor(fx, 0, 5)

x <- seq(-1.0, 1.0, length.out=100)
fxval <- fx(x)
fxapprox <- polyval(fxts, x)

pdata <- data.frame(x, fxval, fxapprox)
ggplot(data = pdata, aes(x = x))+
  geom_line(aes(y = fxval, colour = "blue"), size = 1) +
  geom_line(aes(y = fxapprox, colour = "red"))+
  labs(y= "f(x)") +
  scale_color_discrete(name = " ", labels = c("f(x)=exp(x)",
      "Taylor  series approximation of f(x)"))+
  theme(legend.position="top")
```

Figure 13.7, produced using Listing 13.4, shows the graph of the function $f(x) = \exp(x)$ alongside its corresponding Taylor approximation of order $n = 5$, for $x \in [-1, 1]$. It is clear that this Taylor series approximation of the function $f(x)$ is quite accurate for $x \in [-1, 1]$, since the graphs of the both functions match in this interval.

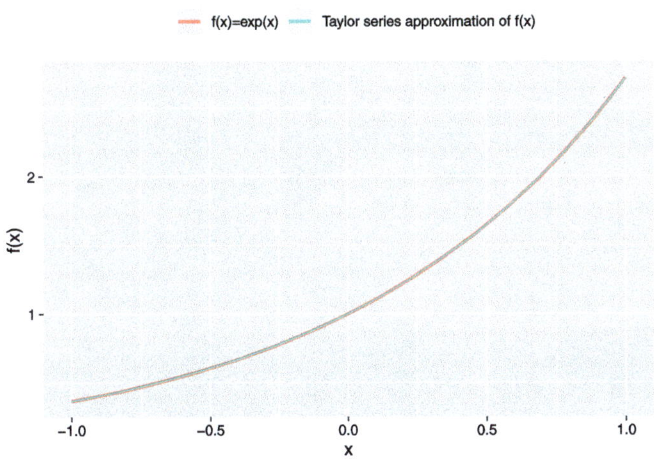

Figure 13.7: Taylor series approximation of the function $f(x) = \exp(x)$. The approximation order is $n = 5$.

On the other hand, Figure 13.8, produced using Listing 13.5, shows the graph of the function $f(x) = \frac{1}{1-x}$ alongside its corresponding Taylor approximation of order $n = 5$, for $x \in [-1, 1]$. The Taylor series approximation of the function $f(x)$ is accurate on most of the interval $x \in [-1, 1]$, except nearby 1, where the function $f(x)$ and its Taylor approximation diverge. In fact, when x tends to 1, $f(x)$ tends to ∞, and the corresponding Taylor series approximation cannot keep pace with the growth of the function $f(x)$.

Listing 13.5: Taylor Series Approximation (see Figure 13.8)

```
# Taylor Series Expansion Using pracma
library(pracma)
library(ggplot2)

fx <- function(x) (1/(1-x))
fxts <- taylor(fx, 0, 5)

x <- seq(-1.0, 1.0, length.out=100)
fxval <- fx(x)
fxapprox <- polyval(fxts, x)

pdata <- data.frame(x, fxval, fxapprox)
ggplot(data = pdata, aes(x = x))+
  geom_line(aes(y = fxval, colour = "blue"), size = 1) +
  geom_line(aes(y = fxapprox, colour = "red"))+
  labs(y= "f(x)") +
  scale_color_discrete(name = " ", labels = c("f(x)=exp(x)",
      "Taylor series approximation of f(x)"))+
  theme(legend.position="top")
```

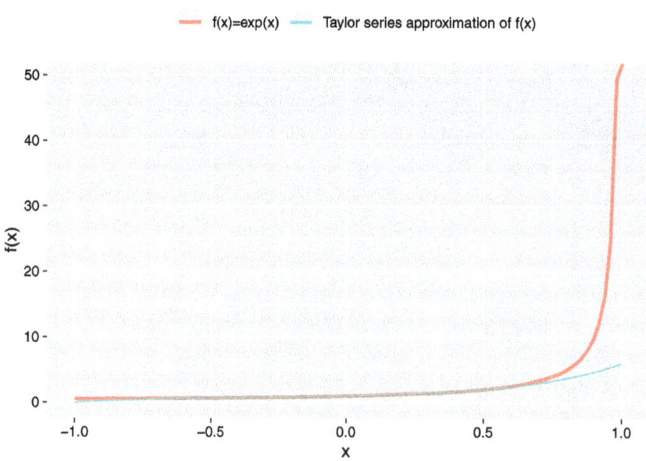

Figure 13.8: Taylor series approximation of the function $f(x) = \frac{1}{1-x}$. The approximation order is $n = 5$.

13.6 Integrals

The integral of a function $f(x)$ over the interval $[a,b]$, denoted $\int_a^b f(x)\mathrm{d}x$, is given by the area between the graph of $f(x)$ and the line $f(x)=0$, where $a \leq x \leq b$.

Definition 13.6.1 (Definite integral). The definite integral of a function $f(x)$ from a to b is denoted

$$\int_a^b f(x)\mathrm{d}x.$$

Definition 13.6.2 (Indefinite integral). The indefinite integral of a function $f(x)$ is a function $F(x)$ such that its derivative is $f(x)$, i. e., $F'(x) = f(x)$, and it is denoted

$$\int f(x)\mathrm{d}x = F(x) + C.$$

The function F is also referred to as the *antiderivative* of f, whereas C is the called the integration constant.

Theorem 13.6.1 (Uniqueness Theorem). *If two functions, F and G, are antiderivatives of a function f on an interval I, then there exists a constant C such that*

$$F(x) = G(x) + C.$$

This result justifies the integration constant C for the indefinite integral.

Theorem 13.6.2 (First fundamental theorem of calculus). *Let f be a bounded function on the interval $[a,b]$ and continuous on (a,b). Then, the function*

$$F(x) = \int_a^x f(z)\,dz, \quad a \leq x \leq b,$$

has a derivative at each point in (a,b) and

$$F'(x) = f(x), \quad a < x < b.$$

Theorem 13.6.3 (Second fundamental theorem of calculus). *Let f be a bounded function on the interval $[a,b]$ and continuous on (a,b). Let F be a continuous function on $[a,b]$ such that $F'(x) = f(x)$ on (a,b). Then,*

$$\int_a^b f(x)\,dx = F(b) - F(a).$$

The results from the above theorems demonstrate that the differentiation is simply the inverse of integration.

13.6.1 Properties of definite integrals

The following properties are useful for evaluating integrals.

1. Order of integration: $\int_a^b f(x)\mathrm{d}x = -\int_b^a f(x)\mathrm{d}x$.
2. Zero width interval: $\int_a^a f(x)\mathrm{d}x = 0$.
3. Constant multiple: $\int_a^b kf(x)\mathrm{d}x = k\int_a^b f(x)\mathrm{d}x$.
4. Sum and difference: $\int_a^b (f(x) \pm g(x))\mathrm{d}x = \int_a^b f(x)\mathrm{d}x \pm \int_a^b g(x)\mathrm{d}x$.
5. Additivity: $\int_a^b f(x)\mathrm{d}x + \int_b^c f(x)\mathrm{d}x = \int_a^c f(x)\mathrm{d}x$.

13.6.2 Numerical integration

The antiderivative, $F(x)$, is not always easy to obtain analytically. Therefore, the integral is often approximated numerically. The numerical estimation is generally carried out as follows: The interval $[a, b]$ is subdivided into $n \in \mathbb{N}$ subintervals. Let $\Delta x_i = x_{i+1} - x_i$ denote the length of the ith subinterval, $i = 1, 2, 3 \ldots, n$, and let $\tilde{x}_i$ be a value in the subinterval $[x_i, x_{i+1}]$. Then,

$$\int_a^b f(x)\mathrm{d}x \approx \sum_{i=1}^{n} f(\tilde{x}_i)\Delta x_i. \tag{13.20}$$

The last term in equation (13.20) is known as the *Riemann sum*. When n tends to ∞, then Δx_i tends to 0, for all $i = 1, 2, 3 \ldots, n$, and, consequently, the Riemann sum tends toward the real value of the integral of $f(x)$ over the interval $[a, b]$, as illustrated in Figure 13.9.

Using R, a one-dimensional integral over a finite or infinite interval is computed using the command `integrate(f, lowerLimit, upperLimit)`, where `f` is the function to be integrated, `lowerLimit` and `upperLimit` are the lower and upper limits of the integral, respectively.

The integral $\int_{-\infty}^{+\infty} \frac{1}{\sqrt{2\pi}} e^{-\frac{(x-5)^2}{2}} dx$ can be computed as follows:

Listing 13.6: One-dimensional numerical integration

```
f <- function(x) {1/sqrt(2*pi)*exp(-(x-5)^2/2)}
#Computing the integral of f
integrate(f, lower = -Inf, upper = Inf)
1 with absolute error < 2e-06
#This means that the numerical estimation of the integral is 1 with
    an absolute error less than 2e-6
```

Using R, an n-fold integral over a finite or infinite interval is computed using the command `adaptIntegrate(f, lowerLimit, upperLimit)`.

The integral $\int_0^3 \int_1^5 \int_{-2}^{-1} \frac{5}{2} \sin(x) \cos(yz)\, dx\, dy\, dz$ can be computed as follows:

Listing 13.7: Example of n-dimensional numerical integration

```
#The package "cubature" is required here
library(cubature)
#Let us pose "x[1]=x",   "x[2]=y", "x[3]=z"
f<-function(x){5/2*sin(x[1])*cos(x[2]*x[3])}
#Lower limits of the integral
lb <- c(0,1,-2)
#Upper limits of the integral
ub <- c(3,5,-1)
adaptIntegrate(f,lowerLimit=lb,upperLimit=ub)
$integral
[1] -2.740785     #Numerical estimation of the  integral
$error
[1] 2.732541e-05  #Relative error of the numerical estimation
```

13.7 Polynomial interpolation

In many applications, results of experimental measurements are available in the form of discrete data sets. However, efficient exploitation of these data requires their synthetic representation by means of elementary (continuous) functions. Such an approximation, also termed *data fitting*, is the process of finding a function, generally a polynomial, whose graph will pass through a given set of data points.

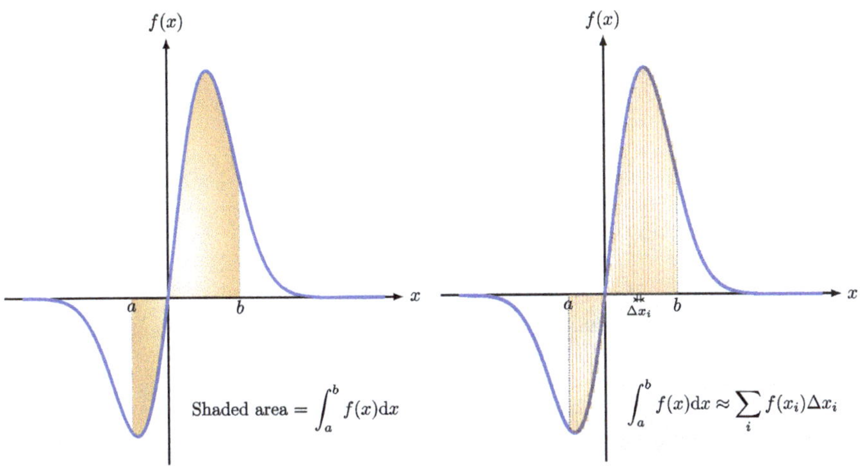

Figure 13.9: Geometric interpretation of the integral. Left: Exact form of an integral. Right: Numerical approximation.

Let (x_i, y_i), $i = 0, \dots, m$ be $m+1$, given pairs of data. Then, the problem of interest is to find a polynomial function of degree n, $P_n(x)$, such that $P_n(x_i) = y_i$ for $i = 0, \dots, m$, i. e.,

$$P_n(x_i) = a_n x_i^n + a_{n-1} x_i^{n-1} + \cdots + a_1 x_i + a_0 = y_i, \quad i = 0, \dots, m. \tag{13.21}$$

Note that this approach was developed by Lagrange, and the resulting interpolation polynomial is referred to as the Lagrange polynomial [99, 131]. When $n = 1$ and $n = 2$, the process is called a linear interpolation and quadratic interpolation, respectively.

Let us consider the following data points:

x_i	1	2	3	4	5	6	7	8	9	10
y_i	−1.05	0.25	1.08	−0.02	−0.27	0.79	−1.02	−0.17	0.97	2.06

Using R, the Lagrange polynomial interpolation for the above pairs of data points (x, y) can be carried out using Listing 13.8. In Figure 13.10 (left), which is an output of Listing 13.8, the interpolation points are shown as dots, whereas the corresponding Lagrange polynomial is represented by the solid line.

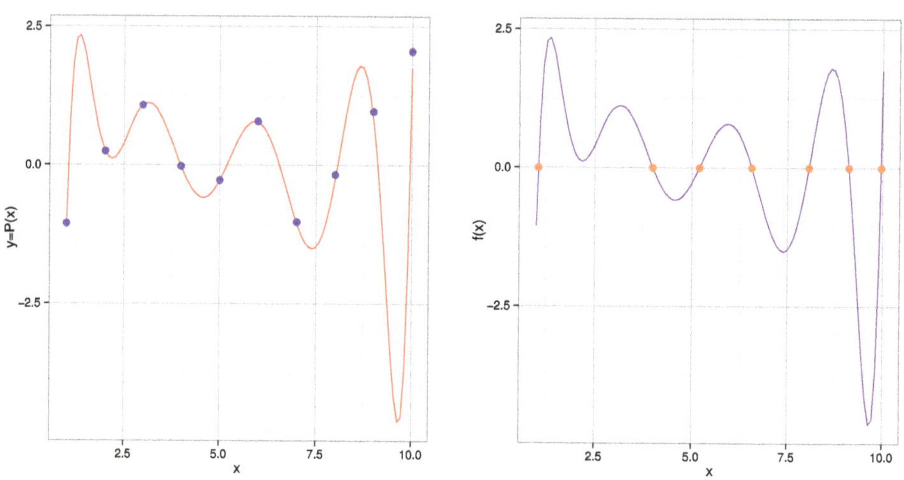

Figure 13.10: Left: Polynomial interpolation of the data points in blue. Right: Roots of the interpolation polynomial.

Listing 13.8: Polynomial interpolation, see Figure 13.10

```
#The packages "polynom" and "ggplot2" are required here
library(polynom)
library(ggplot2)
x <- 1:10
```

```
y <- c(-1.05, 0.25, 1.08, -0.02, -0.27, 0.79, -1.02,-0.17, 0.97,
    2.06 )
poly.calc(x, y)
-229 + 641.943*x - 728.7627*x^2 + 445.0133*x^3 - 162.3738*x^4 +
    36.9856*x^5 - 5.29601*x^6 + 0.4626149*x^7 - 0.02249529*x^8 +
    0.0004662423*x^9
#Plotting the interpolation polynomial and the data
Px<-function(x)
{
-229 + 641.943*x - 728.7627*x^2 + 445.0133*x^3 - 162.3738*x^4 +
    36.9856*x^5 - 5.29601*x^6 + 0.4626149*x^7 -
0.02249529*x^8 + 0.0004662423*x^9
}
xy<-data.frame(x, y)
ggplot(data.frame(x=c(1, 10)), aes(x))+ stat_function(fun=Px,
    colour="red") + geom_point(data=xy, aes(x, y),colour = "blue",
    size=3)+
scale_x_continuous('x') + scale_y_continuous('y=P(x)') +
    theme(legend.position = "none") + theme_bw()
```

13.8 Root finding methods

One of the fundamental problems in applied mathematics concerns the identification of roots of complex and real functions [135]. Given a function f, a root of f is a value of x such that $f(x) = 0$. In this case, x is also called a zero of f. In cases where f is considered to be an algebraic polynomial with real or complex-valued coefficients, established results are available to determine the roots analytically by closed expressions. Let

$$f(x) = a_n x^n + a_{n-1} x^{n-1} + \cdots + a_1 x + a_0 \tag{13.22}$$

be a real polynomial, i. e., its coefficients are real numbers, and n is the degree of this polynomial.

Then we write $\deg(f(x)) = n$.

If $n = 2$,

$$f(x) = a_2 x^2 + a_1 x + a_0 = 0 \tag{13.23}$$

yields the following (see [135] for more detail):

$$x_{1,2} = \frac{-a_1 \pm \sqrt{a_1^2 - 4a_2 a_0}}{2a_2}. \tag{13.24}$$

For $n = 3$,

$$f(x) = a_3 x^3 + a_2 x^2 + a_1 x + a_0 = 0, \tag{13.25}$$

leads to the formulas due to Cardano [135]. For some special cases where $n = 4$, analytical expressions are also known. In general, the well-known theorem due to

Abel and Ruffini [184] states that general polynomials with $\deg(f(x)) \geq 5$ are not solvable by radicals. Radicals are n^{th} root expressions that depend on the polynomial coefficients. Another classical theorem proves the existence of a zero of a continuous function.

Theorem 13.8.1 (Intermediate value theorem). *Let $f : \mathbb{R} \longrightarrow \mathbb{R}$ be a continuous function, and let a and $b \in \mathbb{R}$ with $a < b$ and such that $f(a)$ and $f(b)$ are nonzero and of opposite signs. Then, there exists x^* with $a < x^* < b$ such that $f(x^*) = 0$.*

Using R, the root(s) of a function, within a specified interval, can be obtained via the package `rootSolve`.

Let us consider the following function:

$$f(x) = a_0 + a_1 x + a_2 x^2 + a_3 x^3 + a_4 x^4 + a_5 x^5 + a_6 x^6 + a_7 x^7 + a_8 * x^8 + a_9 x^9, \quad (13.26)$$

where $a_0 = -229$, $a_1 = 641.943$, $a_2 = -728.7627$, $a_3 = 445.0133$, $a_4 = -162.3738$, $a_5 = 36.9856$, $a_6 = -5.29601$, $a_7 = 0.4626149$, $a_8 = -0.02249529$, $a_9 = 0.0004662423$.

Using the function `uniroot.all` from the package `rootSolve`, the root(s) of the function (13.26) within the interval $[1, 10]$ can be obtained using Listing 13.9. In Figure 13.10 (right), which is an output of Listing 13.9, the function $f(x)$ is represented by the solid line, whereas its corresponding roots in the interval $[0, 10]$ are shown as dots. Obviously, all the roots lie on the horizontal line $f(x) = 0$.

Listing 13.9: Finding root(s) of a function, see Figure 13.10

```
#The packages "rootSolve" and "ggplot2" are required here
library(rootSolve)
library(ggplot2)
fx <- function (x)
{
-229 + 641.943*x - 728.7627*x^2 + 445.0133*x^3 - 162.3738*x^4 +
    36.9856*x^5 - 5.29601*x^6 + 0.4626149*x^7 - 0.02249529*x^8 +
    0.0004662423*x^9
}
#Getting the roots of the function f, if they exist
roots <- uniroot.all(fx, c(1, 10))
roots
[1] 1.045204  3.987667  5.189483  6.551222  8.061845  9.112360
    9.959951
#The values of f evaluated at the roots rounds to zero
froots<-round(fx(roots))
froots
[1]  0 0 0 0 0 0 0
#Plotting the function f and its roots in the interval [1, 10]
rootsdata<-data.frame(roots, froots)
ggplot(data.frame(x=c(1, 10)), aes(x)) + stat_function(fun=fx,
    colour="purple") + geom_point(data=rootsdata, aes(roots,
    froots), colour="sienna1", size=3) + scale_x_continuous('x') +
    scale_y_continuous('f(x)') + theme(legend.position = "none") +
    theme_bw()
```

Example 13.8.1. In economics, for example, root-finding methods and basic derivatives find frequent application [182]. For instance, these are used to explore *profit* and *revenue* functions (see [182]). Generally, the revenue function $R(x)$ and the profit function $P(x)$ are defined by

$$R(x) = px, \tag{13.27}$$

and

$$P(x) = R(x) - C(x), \tag{13.28}$$

respectively [182]. Here, x is a unit of quantity, p is the sales price per unit of quantity, and $C(x)$ is a cost function. The unit of quantity x is the variable and p is a parameter, i. e., a fixed number. Suppose that we have a specific profit function defined by

$$P(x) = -\frac{1}{10}x^2 + 50x - 480. \tag{13.29}$$

This profit function $P(x)$ is shown in Figure 13.11, and to find its maximum, we need to find the zeros of its derivative:

$$P'(x) = -\frac{2}{10}x + 50 = 0. \tag{13.30}$$

From this, we find $x = 250$. Using this value, we obtain the maximizing unit of quantity for $P(x)$, i. e., $P(250) = 5770$. To find the so-called break-even points, it is necessary to identify the zeros of $P(x)$, i. e.,

$$P(x) = -\frac{1}{10}x^2 + 50x - 480 = 0. \tag{13.31}$$

Between the two zeros of $P(x)$, we make a profit. Outside this interval, we make a loss. Therefore,

$$x^2 - 500x + 4800 = 0 \tag{13.32}$$

yields to

$$x_{1,2} = \frac{500}{2} \pm \sqrt{\left(\frac{500}{2}\right)^2 - 4800}. \tag{13.33}$$

Specifically, $x_1 = 480.02$, and $x_2 = 9.79$. This means that the profit interval of $P(x)$ corresponds to $[9.79, 480.02]$. Graphically, this is also evident in Figure 13.11.

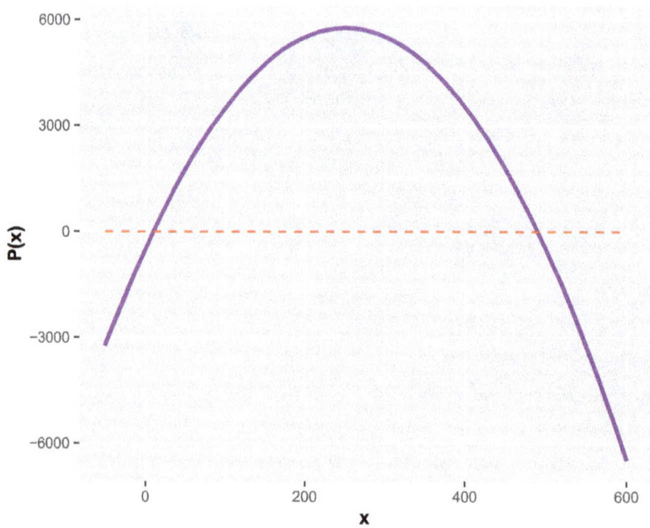

Figure 13.11: An example of a profit function. The profit interval of the profit function is its positive part between the zeros 9.79 and 480.02.

When the zeros of polynomials cannot be calculated explicitly, techniques for estimating bounds are required. For example, various bounds have been proven for real zeros (positive and negative), as well as for complex zeros [155, 50, 135]. For the latter case, bounds for the moduli of a given polynomial are sought. Zero bounds have proven useful in cases where the degree of a given polynomial is large and, therefore, numerical techniques may fail.

The following well-known theorems are attributed to Cauchy [155]:

Theorem 13.8.2. *Let*

$$f(z) = a_n z^n + a_{n-1} z^{n-1} + \cdots + a_0, \quad a_n \neq 0,\, a_k \in \mathbb{C},\, k = 0, 1, \ldots, n, \tag{13.34}$$

be a complex polynomial. All the zeros of $f(z)$ lie in the closed disk $|z| \leq \rho$. Here, ρ is the positive root of another equation, namely

$$|a_0| + |a_1|z + \cdots + |a_{n-1}|z^{n-1} - |a_n|z^n = 0. \tag{13.35}$$

Theorem 13.8.3. *Let $f(z)$ be a complex polynomial given by equation* (13.34). *All the zeros of $f(z)$ lie in the closed disk*

$$|z| \leq 1 + \max_{0 \leq j \leq n-1} \left| \frac{a_j}{a_n} \right|. \tag{13.36}$$

Below, we provide some examples, which illustrate the results from these two theorems.

Example 13.8.2. Let $f(z) := z^3 + 4z^2 + 1000z + 99$ be a polynomial, whose real and complex zeros are as follows:

$$z_1 = -0.099\,, \tag{13.37}$$
$$z_2 = -1.950 - 31.556i\,, \tag{13.38}$$
$$z_3 = -1.950 + 31.556i\,, \tag{13.39}$$
$$|z_1| = 0.099, \tag{13.40}$$
$$|z_2| = |z_3| = 31.616. \tag{13.41}$$

Using Theorem 13.8.2 and Theorem 13.8.3 gives the bounds $\rho = 33.78$ and 1001, respectively. Considering that the largest modulus of $f(z)$ is $\max(z_i) = 31.616$, Theorem 13.8.2 gives a good result. The bound given by Theorem 13.8.3 is useless for $f(z)$. This example demonstrates the complexity of the problem of determining zero bounds efficiently (see [155, 50, 135]).

13.9 Further reading

One of the best, most thorough and yet very readable introduction to analysis, at the time of writing, is [78]. Another excellent, but more practical textbook is [148]. Unfortunately, both books are only available in German or Russian.

13.10 Exercises

1. Evaluate the gradient, the Hessian, and the Jacobian matrix of the following functions using R:

   $f(x, y) = y\cos(x^2) + \sqrt{xy^2}$ at the point $(x = \pi, y = 5)$
   $g(x, y, z) = e^{\sin(x*y)} + z * y\cos(x * y) + x^2 * y^3 + \sqrt{z}$ at the point $(x = 5, y = 3, z = 21)$

2. Use R to find the extremum of the function $f(x) = 3x^x$, and determine whether it is a minimum or a maximum.
3. Use R to find the global extrema of the function $g(y) = y^3 - 6y^2 - 15y + 100$ in the interval $[-3, 6]$.
4. Use R to find the points, where the function $f(x) = 2y^3 - 3y^2$ achieves its global minimum and global maximum and the corresponding extreme values.
5. Use R to find the global maximum and minimum of the function $f(x) = 2x^2 - 4x + 6$ in the interval $[-3, 6]$. Calculate the difference between the maximal and minimal values of $f(x)$.

6. Use R to find the extrema of the function $f(y) = y^{\frac{2}{3}}(y+1)^2$ on the interval $[-1, 1]$.
   Find the critical numbers of the function f.
7. Use R to find the Taylor series expansion of the function $f(x) = \ln(1+x)$. Plot the graph of the function f and the corresponding Taylor series approximation for $x \in [-1; 1]$.
8. Evaluate the following integral using R:

$$I_1 = \int_{-\pi}^{\pi} \frac{\sin^3 x}{\cos^2 x + 1}.$$

9. Use R to find the polynomial interpolation of the following pairs of data points:

x_i	1	2	3	4	5	6	7	8	9	10
y_i	−2.05	0.75	1.8	−0.02	−0.75	1.71	−2.12	−0.25	1.70	3.55

10. Find the real roots of the following functions using R:

$$f(x) = 2x - 1$$
$$g(x) = 23x^2 - 3x - 1$$
$$h(x) = 23x^8 - 3x^7 + x^4 - x^2 - 20$$

14 Differential equations

Differential equations can be seen as applications of the methods from analysis, discussed in the previous chapter. The general aim of differential equations is to describe the dynamical behavior of functions [78]. This dynamical behavior is the result of an equation that contains derivatives of a function. In this chapter, we introduce ordinary differential equations and partial differential equations [3]. We discuss the general properties of such equations and demonstrate specific solution techniques for selected differential equations, including the heat equation and the wave equation. Due to the descriptive nature of differential equations, physical laws as well as biological and economical models are often formulated with such models.

14.1 Ordinary differential equations (ODE)

Problems from many fields, such as physics, biology, engineering, and economics can be modeled using ordinary differential equations (ODEs) or systems of ODEs [78, 3]. A general formulation of a first-order ODE problem is given by

$$\frac{dy(t)}{dt} = y'(t) = f\big(y(t), t, k\big), \tag{14.1}$$

where t is the independent variable, $y : \mathbb{R} \longrightarrow \mathbb{R}^n$ is called the state vector, $f : \mathbb{R}^{n+1} \longrightarrow \mathbb{R}^n$ is referred to as the vector-valued function, which controls how y changes over t, and k is a vector of parameters. When $n = 1$, the problem is called a single scalar ODE.

By itself, the ODE problem (14.1) does not provide a unique solution function $y(t)$. If, in addition to equation (14.1), the initial state at $t = t_0$, $y(t_0)$, is known, then the problem is called an *initial value* ODE problem. On the other hand, if some conditions are specified at the extremes ("boundaries") of the independent variable t, e. g., $y(t_0) = C_1$ and $y(t_{\max}) = C_2$ with C_1 and C_2 given, then the problem is called a *boundary value* ODE problem.

14.1.1 Initial value ODE problems

Initial value ODE problems govern the evolution of a system from its initial state $y(t_0) = C$ at t_0 onward, and we are seeking a function $y(t)$, which describes the state of the system as a function of t. Thus, a general formulation of a first-order initial value ODE problem can be written as follows:

$$\frac{dy(t)}{dt} = y'(t) = f\big(y(t), t, k\big) \quad \text{for } t > t_0, \tag{14.2}$$

$$y(t_0) = C, \tag{14.3}$$

where C is given.

https://doi.org/10.1515/9783110796063-014

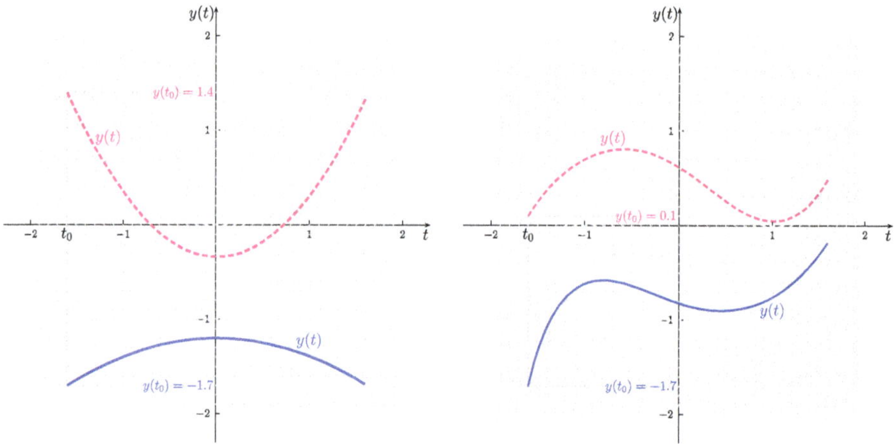

Figure 14.1: Examples of initial value ODE problems. Left: Solutions of the ODE $y'(t) = \frac{2t}{1+t^2}(y(t)+1)$. Right: Solutions of the ODE $y'(t) = (y(t))^2 + t^2 - 1$.

Some examples of initial value ODE problems, depicted in Figure 14.1, illustrate the evolution of the ODE's solution, depending on its initial condition.

Equation (14.2) may represent a system of ODEs, where

$$y(t) = \big(y_1(t), \dots, y_n(t)\big)^T \quad \text{and} \quad f\big(y(t), t, k\big) = \big(f_1\big(y(t), t, k\big), \dots, f_n\big(y(t), t, k\big)\big),$$

and each entry of $f(y(t), t, k)$ can be a nonlinear function of all the entries of y.

The system (14.2) is called *linear* if the function $f(y(t), t, k)$ can be written as follows:

$$f\big(y(t), t, k\big) = G(t, k)y + h(t, k), \tag{14.4}$$

where $G(t, k) \in \mathbb{R}^{n\times n}$, and $h(t, k) \in \mathbb{R}^n$.

If $G(t.k)$ is constant and $h(t, k) \equiv 0$, then the system (14.4) is called *homogeneous*. The solution to the homogeneous system, $y'(t) = Gy(t)$ with data $y(t_0) = C$, is given by $y(t) = Ce^{G(t-t_0)}$.

An ODE's order is determined by the highest-order derivative of the solution function $y(t)$ appearing in the ODEs or the systems of ODEs. Higher-order ODEs or systems of ODEs can be transformed into equivalent first-order system of ODEs.

Let

$$y^{(n)} = f\big(t, y, y', y'', \dots, y^{(n-1)}\big) \tag{14.5}$$

be an ODE of order n. Then, by making the following substitutions:

$$y_1(t) = y(t), \quad y_2(t) = y', \quad \dots, \quad y_n(t) = y^{(n-1)}(t), \tag{14.6}$$

Equation (14.5) can be rewritten in the form of a system of n first-order ODEs as follows:

$$\begin{aligned}
y_1'(t) &= y_2(t),\\
y_2'(t) &= y_3(t),\\
y_3'(t) &= y_4(t),\\
&\vdots\\
y_n'(t) &= f\big(t, y_1(t), y_2(t), \ldots, y_n(t)\big).
\end{aligned}$$

Analytical solutions to ODEs consist of closed-form formulas, which can be evaluated at any point t. However, the derivation of such closed-form formulas is generally nontrivial. Thus, numerical methods are generally used to approximate values of the solution function at a discrete set of points. Since higher-order ODEs can be reduced to a system of first-order ODEs, most numerical methods for solving ODEs are designed to solve first-order ODEs.

In `R`, numerical methods for solving ODE problems are implemented within the package **`deSolve`**, and the function *ode()* from the package **`deSolve`** is dedicated to solving initial value ODE problems. Further details about solving differential equations using `R` can be found in [177] and [176].

Let us use the function *ode()* to solve the following ODE problem:

$$y' = kty \tag{14.7}$$

with the initial condition $y(0) = 10$, and where $k = 1/5$.

In `R`, this problem can be solved using Listing 14.1. Figure 14.2 (left), which is an output of Listing 14.1, shows the evolution of the solution $y(t)$ to the problem (14.7), for $t \in [0, 4]$.

Listing 14.1: Solving an ODE, see Figure 14.2 (left)

```
#The packages "deSolve" and "ggplot2" are required here
library(deSolve)
library(ggplot2)
#Defining the parameter in the ODE
k<-1/5
#Defining the initial condition of the ODE
InitialState<-c(y=10)
#Specifying the ODE to be solved
EqODE<-function(t, y, parms) list(k*t*y)
#Defining the time limits and steps
t <- seq(0, 4, by = 0.05)
#Solving the ODE
SolODE <- ode(y = InitialState, times = t, func = EqODE, parms =
    NULL)
#Snapshot of the solution
head(SolODE)
        time          y
```

```
[1,] 0.00 10.00000
[2,] 0.05 10.00250
[3,] 0.10 10.01001
#Plotting the solution of the ODE
dSolODE<-data.frame(SolODE)
ggplot(dSolODE, aes(time, y)) + geom_line(color="firebrick4") +
    xlab("t")
```

Let us consider the following system of ODEs:

$$\frac{dy_1}{dt} = k_1 y_2 y_3, \tag{14.8}$$

$$\frac{dy_2}{dt} = k_2 y_1 y_3, \tag{14.9}$$

$$\frac{dy_3}{dt} = k_3 y_1 y_2, \tag{14.10}$$

with the initial conditions $y_1(0) = -1$, $y_2(0) = 0$, $y_3 = 1$, and where k_1, k_2 and k_3 are parameters, with values of 1, -1, and $-1/2$, respectively.

The system (14.8)–(14.10), known as the Euler equations, can be solved in R using Listing 14.2. Figure 14.2 (center), which is an output of Listing 14.2, shows the evolution of the solution $(y_1(t), y_2(t), y_3(t))$ to the problem (14.8)–(14.10), for $t \in [0, 15]$.

Listing 14.2: Solving Euler equations, see Figure 14.2 (center)

```
#The packages "deSolve" and "ggplot2" are required here
library(deSolve)
library(ggplot2)
#Defining parameters in the ODEs
Parameters<-c(k1=1, k2=-1, k3=-1/2)
#Defining initial conditions of the ODE
InitialState<-c(y1=0, y2=1, y3=1)
#Specifying the system of ODEs to be solved
EulerODEs <- function(t, InitialState, Parameters)
{
  with(as.list(c(InitialState, Parameters)),{
    dy1<-k1*y2*y3
    dy2<-k2*y1*y3
    dy3<-k3*y1*y2
    list(c(dy1, dy2, dy3))
  })
}
#Defining the time limits and steps
t <- seq(0, 15, by = 0.05)
#Solving the system of ODEs
SolEulerODEs <- ode(y = InitialState, times = t, func = EulerODEs,
    parms = Parameters)
#Snapshot of the solution
head(SolEulerODEs)
 time         y1        y2        y3
[1,] 0.00 0.00000000 1.0000000 1.0000000
[2,] 0.05 0.04996781 0.9987509 0.9993756
[3,] 0.10 0.09975152 0.9950130 0.9975097
```

```
#Plotting the solution of the system of ODEs
dSolEulerODEs  <- data.frame(SolEulerODEs)
ggplot(dSolEulerODEs, aes(t)) + geom_line(aes(y=y1, colour="y1")) +
    geom_line(aes(y=y2, colour="y2")) + geom_line(aes(y=y3,
    colour="y3")) + scale_colour_manual(" ",
    breaks=c("y1","y2","y3"), labels=c(expression(y[1]),
    expression(y[2]), expression(y[3]) ),
    values=c("firebrick3","seagreen3","slateblue1")) + ylab("y") +
    xlab("t")
```

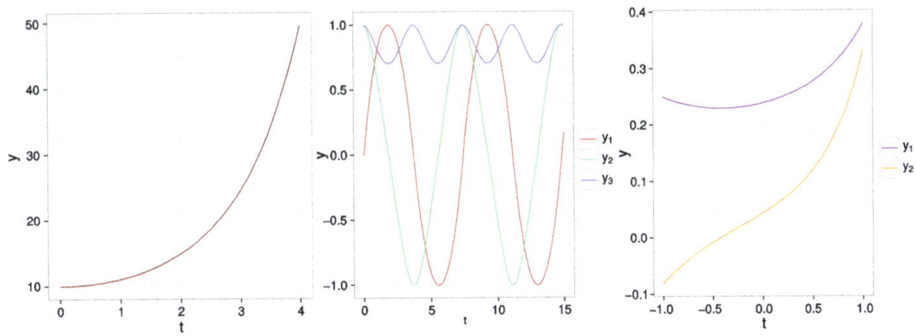

Figure 14.2: Left: Numerical solution of the ODE (14.7) with the initial condition $y(0) = 10$ and the parameter $k = 1/5$. Center: Numerical solution of the Euler equations (14.8)–(14.10) with initial conditions $y_1(0) = 1$, $y_2(0) = y_3(0) = 1$. Right: Numerical solution of BV ODEs system (14.13) with the boundary conditions $y(-1) = 1/4$, $y(1) = 1/3$.

14.1.1.1 Boundary Value ODE problems

A very simplistic formulation of a boundary value ODE problem can be written as follows:

$$\frac{dy(t)}{dt} = y'(t) = f\big(y(t), t, k\big) \quad \text{for } t > t_0, \tag{14.11}$$

$$y(t_0) = C_1, \quad y(t_{\max}) = C_2, \tag{14.12}$$

where C_1 and C_2 are given constants or functions.

In R, the function *bvpshoot()* from the package `deSolve` is dedicated to solving boundary value ODE problems.

Let us use the function *bvpshoot()* to solve the following boundary value ODE problem:

$$y''(t) - 2y^2(t) - 4ty(t)y'(t) \quad \text{with } y(-1) = 1/4, \;\; y(1) = 1/3. \tag{14.13}$$

Since the problem (14.13) is a second-order ODE problem, it is necessary to write its equivalent first-order ODE system. Using the substitution (14.6), the second-order

ODE (14.13) can be rewritten in the following form:

$$y_1'(t) = y_2(t), \tag{14.14}$$

$$y_2'(t) = 2y_1^2(t) + 4ty_1(t)y_2(t), \tag{14.15}$$

with the boundary conditions $y_1(-1) = 1/4$, and $y_2(1) = 1/3$.

Then, the problem (14.14)–(14.15) can be solved in R using Listing 14.3. Figure 14.2 (right), which is an output of Listing 14.3, shows the evolution of the solution $(y_1(t), y_2(t))$ to the problem (14.14)–(14.15), for $t \in [-1, 1]$.

Listing 14.3: Solving a system of Boundary Value ODE, see Figure 14.2 (right)

```
#The packages "deSolve" and "bvpSolve" are required here
library(rootSolve)
library(bvpSolve)
#Specifying the BV ODEs to be solved
SystBVODEs <- function(t,y,k)
{ list(c(
  y[2],
  k*y[1]*y[1] +2*k*t*y[1]*y[2]
))
}
#Defining the boundary values
yb1<-c(1/4,NA)
yb2<-c(NA, 1/3)
#Defining the time limits and steps
t <- seq(-1, 8, by = 0.05)
#Solving the BV ODEs
SolBVODEs<-bvptwp(yini=yb1, yend=yb2, x=t, parms=2, func=SystBVODEs)
#Snapshot of the solution
         x         1           2
[1,] -1.00 0.2500000 -0.08075594
[2,] -0.99 0.2492027 -0.07871783
[3,] -0.98 0.2484255 -0.07671780
#Changing the names of the columns of SolBVODEs
colnames(SolBVODEs)[1] <- "t"
colnames(SolBVODEs)[2] <- "y1"
colnames(SolBVODEs)[3] <- "y2"
dSolBVODEs <- data.frame(SolBVODEs)
ggplot(dSolBVODEs, aes(t)) + geom_line(aes(y=y1, colour="y1")) +
    geom_line(aes(y=y2, colour="y2")) + scale_colour_manual(" ",
    breaks=c("y1","y2"), labels=c(expression(y[1]),
    expression(y[2])), values=c("darkmagenta","orange2")) +
    ylab("y") + xlab("t") + theme_bw()
```

14.2 Partial differential equations (PDE)

Partial differential equations (PDEs) arise in many fields of engineering and science. In general, most physical processes are governed by PDEs [102]. In many cases, simplifying approximations are made to reduce the governing PDEs to ODEs or even to algebraic equations. However, because of the ever-increasing requirement for more accurate modeling of physical processes, engineers and scientists are increasingly required to solve the actual PDEs that govern the physical problem being investigated. A PDE is an equation stating a relationship between a function of two or more independent variables, and the partial derivatives of this function with respect to these independent variables. For most problems in engineering and science, the independent variables are either space (x, y, z) or space and time (x, y, z, t). The dependent variable, i. e., the function f, depends on the physical problem being modeled.

14.2.1 First-order PDE

A general formulation of a first-order PDE with m independent variables can be written as follows:

$$F\big(x, u(x), \nabla u(x)\big) = 0, \tag{14.16}$$

where $x \in \mathbb{R}^m$, $u(x) = u(x_1, x_2, \dots, x_m)$ is the unknown function, and F is a given function.

A first-order PDE, with two independent variables, $x, y \in \mathbb{R}$ and the dependent variable $u(x, y)$, is called a first-order quasilinear PDE if it can be written in the following form:

$$f\big(x, y, u(x, y)\big)\frac{\partial}{\partial x}u(x, y) + g\big(x, y, u(x, y)\big)\frac{\partial}{\partial y}u(x, y) = h\big(x, y, u(x, y)\big), \tag{14.17}$$

where f, g, and h are given functions.

The equation (14.17) is said to be

- linear, if the functions f, g, and h are independent of the unknown u;
- nonlinear, if the functions f, g, and h depend further on the derivatives of the unknown u.

14.2.2 Second-order PDE

The general formulation of a linear second-order PDE, in two independent variables x, y and the dependent variable $u(x, y)$, can be written as follows:

$$A\frac{\partial^2 u}{\partial x^2} + B\frac{\partial^2 u}{\partial x \partial y} + C\frac{\partial^2 u}{\partial y^2} + D\frac{\partial u}{\partial x} + E\frac{\partial u}{\partial y} + Fu + G = 0, \tag{14.18}$$

where A, B, C, D, F are functions of x, y.

If $G = 0$, the equation (14.18) is said to be homogeneous, and it is nonhomogeneous if $G \neq 0$.

The PDE (14.18) can be classified according to the values assumed by A, B, and C at a given point (x, y). The PDE (14.18) is called

- an elliptic PDE, if $B^2 - 4AC < 0$,
- a parabolic PDE, if $B^{-}4AC = 0$,
- a hyperbolic PDE, if $B^2 - 4AC > 0$.

14.2.3 Boundary and initial conditions

There are three types of boundary conditions for PDEs. Let R denote a domain and ∂R its boundary. Furthermore, let n and s denote the coordinates normal (outward) and along the boundary ∂R, respectively, and let f, g be some functions on the boundary ∂R. Then, the three boundary conditions, for PDEs, are:

- Dirichlet conditions, when $u = f$ on the boundary ∂R,
- Neumann conditions, when $\frac{\partial u}{\partial n} = f$ or $\frac{\partial u}{\partial s} = g$ on the boundary ∂R,
- Mixed (Robin) conditions, when $\frac{\partial u}{\partial n} + ku = f$, $k > 0$ on the boundary ∂R.

Dirichlet conditions can only be applied if the solution is known on the boundary and if the function f is analytic. These are frequently used for the flow (velocity) into a domain. Neumann conditions occur more frequently [102].

14.2.4 Well-posed PDE problems

A mathematical PDE problem is considered well-posed, in the sense of Hadamard, if

- the solution exists,
- the solution is unique,
- the solution depends continuously on the auxiliary data (e. g., boundary and initial conditions).

Parabolic PDE

In this section, we will illustrate the solution to the heat equation, which is a prototype parabolic PDE. The heat equation, in a one-dimensional space with zero production and consumption, can be written as follows:

$$\frac{\partial u(x,t)}{\partial t} - D\frac{\partial^2 u(x,t)}{\partial x^2}, \quad x \in (a,b). \tag{14.19}$$

Let us use R to solve the equation (14.19) with $a = 0$, $b = 1$, i. e., $x \in [0, 1]$, and the following boundary and initial conditions:

$$u(x,0) = \cos\left(\frac{\pi}{2}x\right), \quad u(0,t) = \sin(t), \quad u(1,t) = 0. \tag{14.20}$$

The heat equation (14.19)–(14.20) can be solved using Listing 14.4. The corresponding solution, $u(x,t)$, is depicted in Figure 14.3 for color levels (left) and a contour plot (right).

Listing 14.4: Solving the Heat Equation, see Figure 14.3

```
#The package "ReacTran" is required here
library(ReacTran)
#Mesh setup
GridPts <- 100
xgrid <- setup.grid.1D(x.up = 0, x.down = 1, N = GridPts)
x <- xgrid$x.mid
#Defining the time limits and steps
Timesteps <- seq(from = 0, to = 15, by = 0.03)
#Definition of the coefficient D
Dconst<-0.02
#Specifying the PDE to be solved
HeatEq <- function (t, u, parms) {
tran <- tran.1D(C = u, C.up = sin(t),  C.down = 0, D = Dconst, dx =
    xgrid)
list(du = tran$dC, flux.up = tran$flux.up, flux.down =
    tran$flux.down)
}
#Initial condition
InitialCond <- cos(pi*x/2)
#Solving the PDE
SolHEq <-ode.1D(y = InitialCond, times = Timesteps, func = HeatEq,
    parms = NULL, dimens = GridPts)
#Graphs of the solution
image(SolHEq, grid = x, mfrow = NULL, xlab = "t", ylab = "x",
    legend = TRUE, main = "u(x, t)")
#Graphs of the solution with contour plot
image(SolHEq, grid = x, mfrow = NULL, xlab = "t", ylab = "x",
    add.contour = TRUE, main = "u(x, t)")
```

Hyperbolic PDE

A prototype of hyperbolic PDEs is the wave equation, defined as follows:

$$\frac{\partial^2 u}{\partial t^2} = \nabla \cdot \left(c^2 \nabla u\right). \tag{14.21}$$

Let us consider the following wave equation in a two-dimensional space:

$$\frac{\partial^2 u(t,x,y)}{\partial t^2} = \gamma_1 \frac{\partial^2 u(t,x,y)}{\partial x^2} + \gamma_2 \frac{\partial^2 u(t,x,y)}{\partial y^2}, \quad x \in (a,b), \; y \in (c,d). \tag{14.22}$$

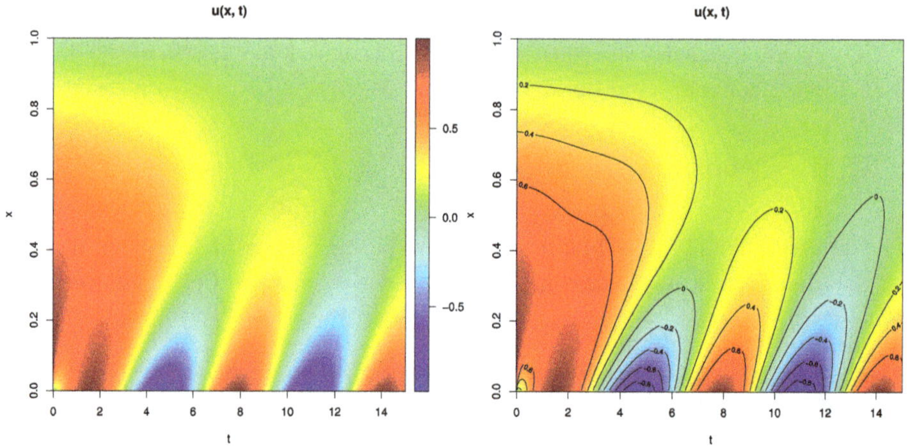

Figure 14.3: Solution to the heat equation in equation (14.19) with the boundary and initial conditions provided in equation (14.20).

We use R to solve Equation (14.22) with $a = c = -4$, $b = d = -4$, $\gamma_1 = \gamma_2 = 1$, and the following boundary and initial conditions:

$$
\begin{aligned}
u(t, x = -4, y) = u(t, x = 4, y) = u(t, x, y = -4) = u(t, x, y = 4) = 0,\\
\frac{\partial}{\partial t} u(t = 0, x, y) = 0,\\
u(t = 0, x, y) = e^{-(x^2+y^2)}.
\end{aligned}
\tag{14.23}
$$

The wave equation (14.22)–(14.23) can be solved using Listing 14.5. The corresponding solution, $u(t, x, y)$, is depicted in Figure 14.4, for $t = 0$, $t = 1$, $t = 2$ and $t = 3$, respectively.

Listing 14.5: Solving the Wave Equation, see Figure 14.4

```
#The packages "ReacTran" is required here
library(ReacTran)
#Mesh setup
Nx <- 100
Ny <- 100
xgrid <- setup.grid.1D (x.up = -4, x.down = 4, N = Nx)
ygrid <- setup.grid.1D (x.up = -4, x.down = 4, N = Ny)
x <- xgrid$x.mid
y <- ygrid$x.mid
#Defining the time limits and steps
t <- 0:3
#Specifying the PDE to be solved
WaveEq2D<-function(t, C, params) {
  u <- matrix(nrow = Nx, ncol = Ny, data = C[1 : (Nx*Ny)])
  v <- matrix(nrow = Nx, ncol = Ny, data = C[(Nx*Ny+1) : (2*Nx*Ny)])
  dv <- tran.2D (C = u, C.x.up = 0, C.x.down = 0, D.x = 1, D.y = 1,
      C.y.up = 0, C.y.down = 0, dx = xgrid, dy = ygrid)$dC
  list(c(v, dv))
}
```

```
#Initial condition
peak <- function (x, y, x0, y0) exp(-((x-x0)^2 + (y-y0)^2))
uinitial <- outer(x, y, FUN = function(x, y) peak(x, y, 0,0))
vinitial <- rep(0, Nx*Ny)
#Solving the PDE
SolWEq <- ode.2D (y = c(uinitial, vinitial), times = t, parms =
    NULL, func = WaveEq2D, names = c("u", "v"), dimens = c(Nx, Ny),
    method = "ode45")
#Plotting the solution
mr <- par(mar = c(0, 0, 1, 0))
image(SolWEq, main = paste("t =", t), which = "u", grid = list(x =
    x, y = y), method = "persp", border = NA, box = FALSE,
    legend=TRUE, shade = 0.5, theta = 30, phi = 60, mfrow = c(2,
    2), ask = FALSE)
```

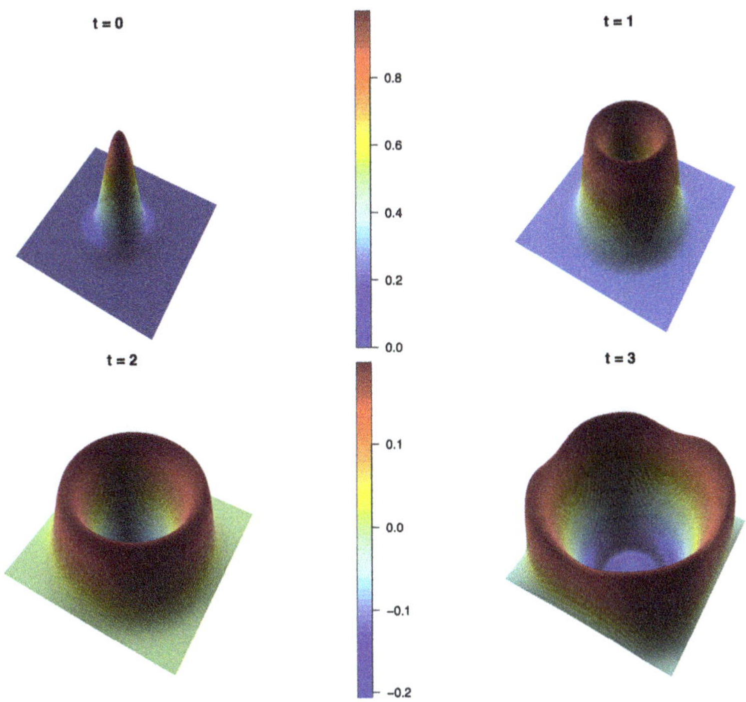

Figure 14.4: Solution to the wave equation in equation (14.22) with the boundary and initial conditions provided in equation (14.23).

Elliptic PDE

A prototype of elliptic PDEs is the Poisson's equation. Let us use R to solve the following Poisson's equation in a two-dimensional space:

$$\gamma_1 \frac{\partial^2 u(x,y)}{\partial x^2} + \gamma_2 \frac{\partial^2 u(x,y)}{\partial y^2} = x^2 + y^2, \quad x \in (a,b), \quad y \in (c,d), \tag{14.24}$$

with $a = c = 0$, $b = d = 2$, $\gamma_1 = \gamma_2 = 1$ and the following boundary and initial conditions:

$$\begin{aligned} u(x=0,y) &= \sin(y), \quad u(x=2,y) = 1, \\ u(x,y=0) &= \cos(x), \quad u(x,y=2) = 1. \end{aligned} \tag{14.25}$$

The Poisson's equation (14.24)–(14.25) can be solved using Listing 14.6. The corresponding solution, $u(x,y)$, is depicted in Figure 14.5 for color levels (left) and a contour plot (right).

Listing 14.6: Solving the Poisson's Equation, see Figure 14.5

```
#The package "ReacTran" is required here
library(ReacTran)
#Mesh setup
Nx <- 100
Ny <- 100
xgrid <- setup.grid.1D (x.up = 0, x.down = 2, N = Nx)
ygrid <- setup.grid.1D (x.up = 0, x.down = 2, N = Ny)
x   <- xgrid$x.mid
y   <- ygrid$x.mid
#Specifying the PDE to be solved
PoissonEq <- function(t, U, parms) {
  u <- matrix(nrow = Nx, ncol = Ny, data = U)
  du <- tran.2D(C = u, C.x.up = sin(y), C.x.down = 1, C.y.up =
       cos(x), C.y.down = 1, D.x=1, D.y=1,
  dx = xgrid, dy = ygrid)$dC+x^2+y^2
  list(du)
}
# Solving the PDE
SolPEq <- steady.2D(y = runif(Nx*Ny), func = PoissonEq, parms =
    NULL, nspec = 1, dimens = c(Nx, Ny), lrw = 1e7)
#Plotting the graph of the solution with legend
image(SolPEq, grid = list(x, y), main = "u(x,y)", legend = TRUE)
#Plotting the graph the solution with contour plot
image(SolPEq, grid = list(x, y), main = "u(x,y)", add.contour =
    TRUE)
```

14.3 Exercises

Use R to solve the following differential equations:

1. Solve the heat equation (14.19) with $a = 0$, $b = 1$, i.e., $x \in [0,1]$, and the following boundary and initial conditions:
   (a) $u(x,0) = 6\sin(\frac{\pi x}{2})$, $u(0,t) = \cos(t)$, $u(1,t) = 0$.
   (b) $u(x,0) = 12\sin(\frac{9\pi x}{5}) - 7\sin(\frac{4\pi x}{3})$, $u(0,t) = \cos(\pi t)$, $u(1,t) = 0$.
2. Solve the wave equation (14.22) with $a = c = -4$, $b = d = 4$, $\gamma_1 = \gamma_2 = 1$, and the following boundary and initial conditions:

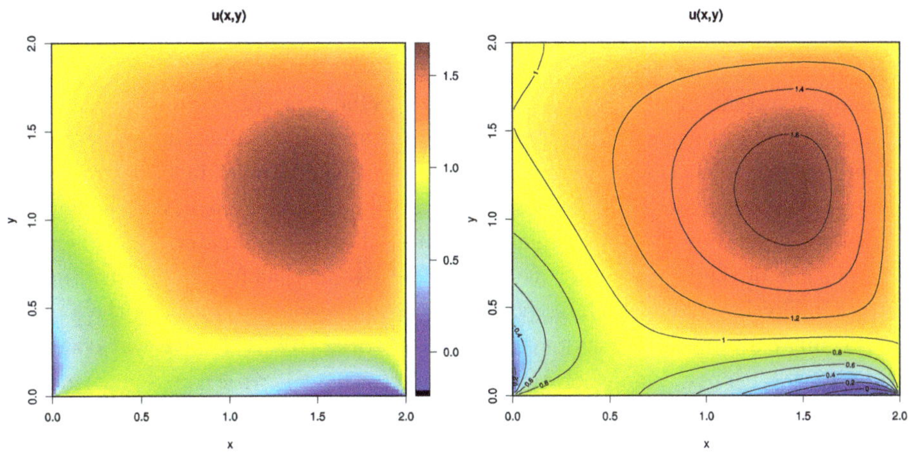

Figure 14.5: Solution to the Poisson's equation in equation (14.24) with the boundary and initial conditions provided in equation (14.25).

(a)

$$u(t,x=-4,y)=u(t,x=4,y)=u(t,x,y=-4)=u(t,x,y=4)=0,$$
$$\frac{\partial}{\partial t}u(t=0,x,y)=0,$$
$$u(t=0,x,y)=e^{-(2x^3+3y^2)}.$$

(b)

$$u(t,x=-4,y)=u(t,x=4,y)=u(t,x,y=-4)=u(t,x,y=4)=0,$$
$$\frac{\partial}{\partial t}u(t=0,x,y)=0,$$
$$u(t=0,x,y)=e^{-(5x^2+7y^3)}.$$

3. Solve the Poisson's equation (14.24) with $a=c=-0$, $b=d=2$, $\gamma_1=\gamma_2=1$, and the following boundary and initial conditions:

(a)

$$u(x=0,y)=\cos(y);\quad u(x=2,y)=1,$$
$$u(x,y=0)=\sin(x);\quad u(x,y=2)=1.$$

(b)

$$u(x=0,y)=\cos(y)\sin(y);\quad u(x=2,y)=1,$$
$$u(x,y=0)=\sin(x)\cos(x);\quad u(x,y=2)=1.$$

15 Dynamical systems

Dynamical systems [179] may be regarded as specific types of the differential equations discussed in the previous chapter. Generally speaking, a dynamical system is a model in which a function describes the time evolution of a point in space. This evolution can be continuous or discrete, and it can be linear or nonlinear. In this chapter, we discuss general dynamical systems and define their key characteristics. Then, we discuss some of the most important dynamical systems that find widespread applications in physics, chemistry, biology, economics and medicine, including the logistic map, cellular automata or random Boolean networks [108, 181]. We will conclude this chapter with case studies of dynamical system models with complex attractors [165].

15.1 Introduction

The theory of dynamical systems can be viewed as the most natural way of describing the behavior of an integrated system over time [109, 56]. In other words, a dynamical system can be cast as the process by which a sequence of states is generated on the basis of certain dynamical laws. Generally, this behavior is described through a system of differential equations describing the rate of change of each variable as a function of the current values of the other variables influencing the one under consideration. Thus, the system states form a continuous sequence, which can be formulated as follows. Let $x = (x_1, x_2, \dots, x_n)$ be a point in $\mathbb{C}^n$ that defines a curve through time, i. e.,

$$x = x(t) = \big(x_1(t), x_2(t), \dots, x_n(t)\big), \quad -\infty < t < \infty.$$

Suppose that the laws, which describe the rate and direction of the change of $x(t)$, are known and defined by the following equations:

$$\frac{x(t)}{dt} = f\big(x(t)\big), \quad t \in \mathbb{R},\ x \in \mathbb{C}^n,\ x(t_0) = x_0, \tag{15.1}$$

where $f(\cdot) = (f_1(x), \dots, f_n(x))^T$ is a differentiable vector function.

However, when those states form a discrete sequence, a discrete time formulation of the systems (15.1) can be written as follows:

$$x(k+1) = f\big(x(k)\big), \quad k \in \mathbb{Z},\ x(k) \in \mathbb{C}^n\ \forall\, k,\ x(0) = x_0. \tag{15.2}$$

Definition 15.1.1. A sequence, $x(t)$, is called a dynamical system if it satisfies the set of ordinary differential equations (15.1) (respectively (15.2)) for a given time interval $[t_0, t]$.

https://doi.org/10.1515/9783110796063-015

Definition 15.1.2. A curve $\mathcal{C} = \{x(t)\}$, which satisfies the equations (15.1) (respectively (15.2)), is called the orbit of the dynamical system $x(t)$.

Definition 15.1.3. A point $x^* \in \mathbb{C}^n$ is said to be a fixed point, also called a critical point, or a stationary point, if it satisfies $f(x^*) = 0$.

Definition 15.1.4. A critical point x^* is said to be stable if every orbit, originating near x^*, remains near x^*, i. e., $\forall\, \varepsilon > 0$, $\exists\, \xi > 0$ such that

$$\|x(0) - x^*\| < \xi \Longrightarrow \|x(t) - x^*\| \leq \varepsilon, \quad \forall\, t > 0.$$

A critical point x^* is said to be asymptotically stable if every orbit, originating sufficiently near x^*, converges to x^* when $t \longrightarrow +\infty$, i. e., if for some $\varepsilon > 0$, $\|x(0) - x^*\| < \xi$, then $\|x(t) - x^*\| \longrightarrow 0$ as $t \longrightarrow +\infty$.

Definition 15.1.5. A point $\bar{x} \in \mathbb{C}^n$ is said to be a periodic point for a dynamical system $x(t)$ if $\exists\, k \in \mathbb{N}$ such that $f^k(\bar{x}) = \bar{x}$ and $f^j(\bar{x}) \neq \bar{x}$ for $j = 1, \ldots, k-1$. The integer k is called the period of the point $\bar{x}$.

Definition 15.1.6. An attractor is a minimal set of points $A \subset \mathbb{C}^n$ such that every orbit originating within its neighborhood converges asymptotically towards the set A. A stable fixed point is an attractor known as a map sink. A dynamical system may have more than one attractor. The set of states that lead to an attractor is called the basin of the attractor.

Depending on the form of the functions f_i and the initial conditions x_0, in (15.1) (respectively (15.2)), the evolution of a dynamical system can lead to one of the following regimes:

1. *steady state:* In such a regime, in response to any change in the initial condition, the dynamical system restores itself and resumes its original course again, leading to the formation of relatively stable patterns; thus, the system is wholly or largely insensitive to the alteration of its initial conditions.
2. *periodic:* In this regime, in response to any change in the initial condition, the trajectory of the system will eventually stabilize and alternate periodically between relatively stable patterns.
3. *chaotic:* In such a regime, in response to any change in the initial condition, the dynamical system generates a totally different orbit, i. e., any small perturbations can lead to different trajectories. Hence, the system is highly sensitive to the alteration of its initial conditions.

In the subsequent sections, we will illustrate the use of R to simulate and visualize some basic dynamical systems, including population growth models, cellular automata, Boolean networks, and other "abstract" dynamical systems, such as strange attractors and fractal geometries. These dynamical systems are well known for their sensitivity to initial conditions, which is the defining feature of chaotic systems.

15.2 Population growth models

Population growth models are among the simplest dynamical system models used to describe the evolution of a population in a specified environment.

15.2.1 Exponential population growth model

The exponential growth model describes the evolution of a population or the concentration (number of organisms per area unit) of an organism living in an environment, whose resources and conditions allow them to grow indefinitely. Supposing that the growth rate of the organism is r, then the evolution of the population number of organisms $x(t)$ over time is governed by the following equation:

$$\frac{dx}{dt} = rx. \tag{15.3}$$

If r is constant, then the solution of (15.3) is given by

$$x(t) = x(0)e^{rt}. \tag{15.4}$$

The solution (15.4) can be plotted in R using Listing 15.1, and the corresponding output, which shows the evolution of the population for $x(0) = 2$, $r = 0.03$ and $t \in [0, 100]$, is depicted in Figure 15.1 (left).

Listing 15.1: Exponential growth model, see Figure 15.1 (left)

```
library(ggplot2)
ExpoGrowth <- function(t, r, x0)
{
  x0*exp(r*t)
}
x<-ExpoGrowth(t = 0:100, r = 0.03, x0 = 2)
#Plotting the solution
t<-0:100
datatx<-data.frame(cbind(t, x))
ggplot(datatx, aes(t, x)) + geom_line(color="orangered2") +
     xlab("Time (t)") + ylab("Population (x)") +theme_bw()
```

15.2.2 Logistic population growth model

In contrast with the exponential growth model, the logistic population model assumes that the availability of resources restricts the population growth. Let K be the "carrying capacity" of the living environment of the population, i. e., the population number or the concentration (number of organisms per area unit) such that

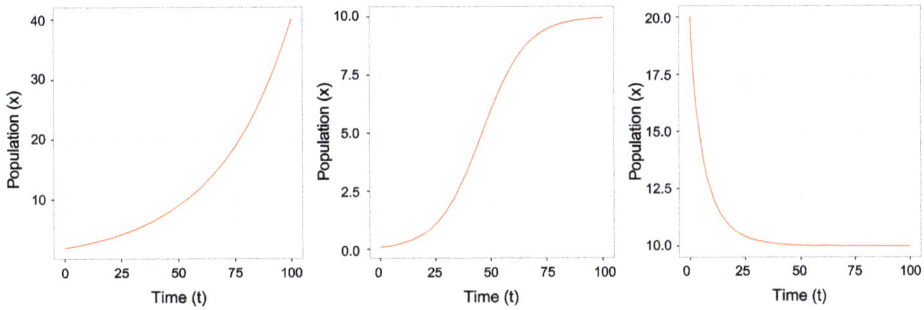

Figure 15.1: Left: Exponential population growth for $r = 0.03$ and $x_0 = 2$. Center: Logistic population growth model for $r = 0.1$, $x_0 = 0.1 < K = 10$. Right: Logistic population growth model for $r = 0.1$, $x_0 = 20 > K = 10$.

the growth rate of the organism population is zero. In this situation, a larger population results in fewer resources, and this leads to a smaller growth rate. Hence, the growth rate is no longer constant. When the growth rate is assumed to be a linearly decreasing function of x of the form

$$r\left(1 - \frac{x(t)}{K}\right),$$

with positive K and r, we obtain the following logistic equation

$$\frac{dx}{dt} = rx\left(1 - \frac{x}{K}\right), \tag{15.5}$$

where the expression $\frac{dx}{dt}$ represents the growth rate of the organism's population over time.

The growth rate $\frac{dx}{dt}$ is zero if $x = 0$, or $x + K$. Thus, the solution to the equation (15.5) is given by

$$x(t) = \frac{Kx(0)e^{rt}}{K + x(0)(e^{rt} - 1)}. \tag{15.6}$$

The solution (15.6) can be plotted in R using Listing 15.2. The corresponding output, which shows the evolution of the population over the time interval $[0, 100]$, is depicted in Figure 15.1 (center) for $x(0) = 0.1$, $r = 0.1$, $K = 10$, and in Figure 15.1 (right) for $x(0) = 20$, $r = 0.1$, $K = 10$.

Listing 15.2: Logistic growth model, see Figure 15.1 (center)

```
library(ggplot2)
LogGrowth <- function(t, r, x0, K)
{
  K *x0*exp(r * t) / (K + x0 * (exp(r * t) - 1))
}
```

```
x<-LogGrowth(t = 0:100, r = 0.1, K = 10, x0 = 0.1)
#Plotting the solution
t<-0:100
datatx<-data.frame(cbind(t, x))
ggplot(datatx, aes(t, x)) + geom_line(color="orangered2") +
    xlab("Time (t)") + ylab("Population (x)") +theme_bw()
```

15.2.3 Logistic map

The logistic map is a variant of the logistic population growth model (15.5) with nonoverlapping generations. Let y_n denote the population number of the current generation and y_{n+1} denote the population number of the next generation. When the growth rate is assumed to be a linearly decreasing function of y_n, then we get the following logistic equation:

$$y_{n+1} = ry_n\left(1 - \frac{y_n}{K}\right). \tag{15.7}$$

Substituting y_n for Kx_n and y_{n+1} for Kx_{n+1} in Equation (15.7) gives the following recurrence relationship, also known as the logistic map:

$$x_{n+1} = rx_n(1 - x_n), \tag{15.8}$$

where, x_{n+1} denotes the population size of the next generation, whereas x_n is the population size of the current generation; and r is a positive constant denoting the growth rate of the population between generations.

The graph x_n versus x_{n+1} is called the cobweb graph of the logistic map.

For any initial condition, over time, the population x_n will settle into one of the following types of behavior:

1. *fixed*, i. e., the population approaches a stable value
2. *periodic*, i. e., the population alternates between two or more fixed values
3. *chaotic*, i. e., the population will eventually visit any neighborhood in a subinterval of $(0, 1)$.

15.2.3.1 Stable and unstable fixed points

When $0 \leq r \leq 4$, the map

$$x \mapsto f(x) = rx(1 - x) \tag{15.9}$$

defines a dynamical system on the interval $[0, 1]$.

The point $x = 0$ is a trivial fixed point of the dynamical system defined by (15.9). Furthermore, when $r \leq 1$, we have $f(x) < x$ for all $x \in (0, 1)$; thus, the system converges to the fixed point $x = 0$. However, when $r > 1$, the graph of the function $f(x)$ is a parabola achieving its maximum at $x = 1/2$ and $f(0) = f(1) = 0$.

The intersection between the graph of f and the straight line of equation $y = x$ defines a point S, whose abscissa, x^*, satisfies $x^* = rx^*(1 - x^*)$.

Hence, the point $x^* = \frac{r-1}{r}$ is another fixed point of the system.

When $1 < r < 3$, the point x^* is asymptotically stable, i. e., for any x in the neighborhood of x^*, the sequence generated by the map (15.9)—the orbit of x—remains close to or converges to x^*. In R, such a dynamics of the system can be illustrated using the scripts provided in Listing 15.3 and Listing 15.4.

Figure 15.2 (left), produced using Listing 15.4, shows the cobweb graph of the logistic map for $r = 2.5$, which corresponds to a stable fixed point. When $r = 3$ the logistic map has an asymptotically stable fixed point, and the corresponding cobweb graph and the graph of the population dynamics are depicted in Figure 15.2 (center) (produced using Listing 15.4) and Figure 15.2 (right) (produced using Listing 15.3), respectively.

Listing 15.3: Logistic map model, see Figure 15.2 (right)

```
LogisticMap<-function(r, x0, N)
{
  x<-array(dim=N)
  x[1]<-x0
  for(i in 2:N)
    x[i]<- r*x[i-1]*(1-x[i-1])
  t<-seq(1,N)
  x<-cbind(t,x)
  return(x)
}
#Plotting the population dynamics over time
datatx1<-LogisticMap(r=3, x0=0.2, N=100)
datatx2<-LogisticMap(r=2.5, x0=0.2, N=100)
plot(datatx1[,1], datatx1[,2], xaxt="n", yaxt="n", type="l",
     xlab="Time",ylab="Population", col = "orangered", lwd=0.35)
lines(datatx2[,1], datatx2[,2], col="purple4", lwd=0.35)
legend("bottomright", legend=c("r=3","r=2.5"),
       col=c("orangered","purple4"), lwd=c(1,1), cex=1, inset = .02)
```

Listing 15.4: Cobweb of the logistic map, see Figure 15.2 (left & center)

```
Cobweb<-function(r, x0, N)
{
  xn<-seq(0,1,length.out=N)
  xn1<-r*xn*(1-xn)
  plot(xn,xn1, xaxt="n", yaxt="n", type='l', xlab=expression(x[n]),
       ylab=expression(x[n+1]), col="orangered", lwd=0.8)
  lines(x=c(0,1), y=c(0,1), col="orangered",lwd=0.8)

  xn<-x0
  xn1<-r*x0*(1-x0)

  for (i in 1:N)
  {
```

```
        s<-r*xn1*(1 - xn1)
        lines(x=c(xn, xn), y=c(xn, xn1), col="purple4", lwd=0.08)
        lines(x=c(xn, xn1), y=c(xn1, xn1), col="purple4", lwd=0.08)
        lines(x=c(xn1, xn1), y=c(xn1, s), col="purple4", lwd=0.08)
        lines(x=c(xn1, s), y=c(s, s), col="purple4", lwd=0.2)
        xn<-xn1
        xn1<-s
    }
}
#Plotting the cobweb graphs
Cobweb(r=3, x0=0.2,N=100)
```

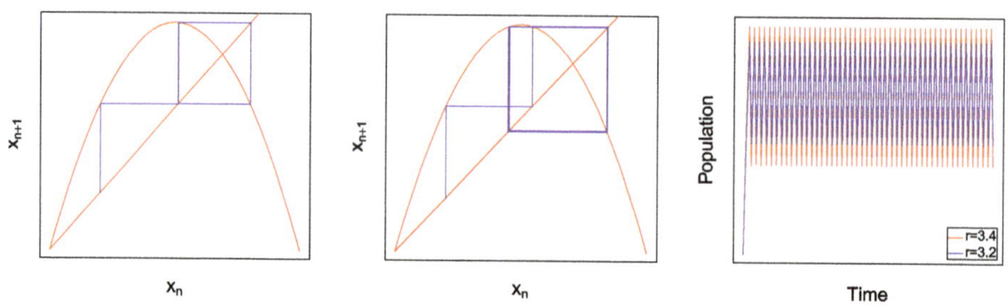

Figure 15.2: Left: Cobweb graph of a stable fixed point for $r = 2.5$. Center: Cobweb graph of an asymptotically stable fixed point for $r = 3$; Right: Population number dynamics over time.

15.2.3.2 Periodic fixed points: bifurcation

Due to its discrete nature, regulation of the growth rate in the logistic map (15.8) operates with a one period delay, leading to overshooting of the dynamical system. Beyond the value $r = 3$, the dynamical system (15.8) is no longer asymptotically stable, but exhibits some periodic behavior. The parameter value $r = 3$ is known as a bifurcation point. This behavior can be illustrated, in R, using Listing 15.5.

Figure 15.3 (left) and Figure 15.3 (center), produced using Listing 15.4, show the cobweb graphs of the logistic map for $r = 3.2$ and $r = 3.4$, which both correspond

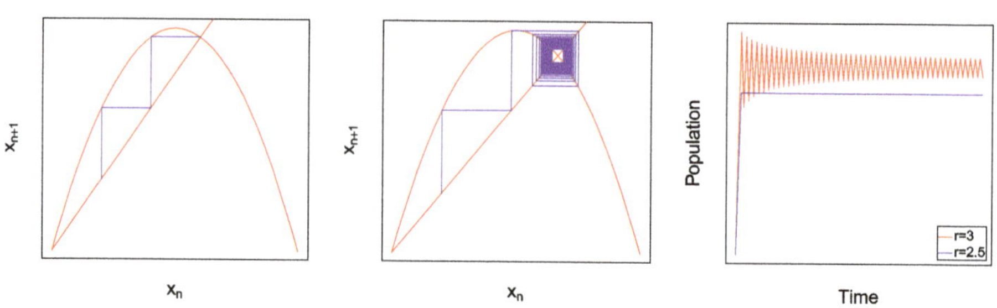

Figure 15.3: Left: Cobweb graph of periodic fixed points for $r = 3.2$. Center: Cobweb graph of periodic fixed points for $r = 3.4$; Right: Dynamics of the population number over time.

to periodic fixed points. Figure 15.3 (right), produced using Listing 15.3, illustrates the dynamics of the populations over time for both cases.

15.2.3.3 Chaotic motion

For larger values of r in the logistic map (15.8), further bifurcations occur, and the number of periodic points explodes. For instance, for $r \geq 3$, the structure of the orbits of the dynamical system becomes complex and, hence, chaotic behavior ensues. Such behavior can be illustrated in R, using the scripts provided in Listing 15.3 and Listing 15.4.

Figure 15.4 (left) and Figure 15.4 (center), produced using Listing 15.4, show the cobweb graphs of the logistic map for $r = 3.8$ and $r = 3.9$, which both correspond to chaotic motions. Figure 15.4 (right), produced using Listing 15.3, illustrates the dynamics of the populations over time for both cases, where the chaotic evolution of the populations can be clearly observed.

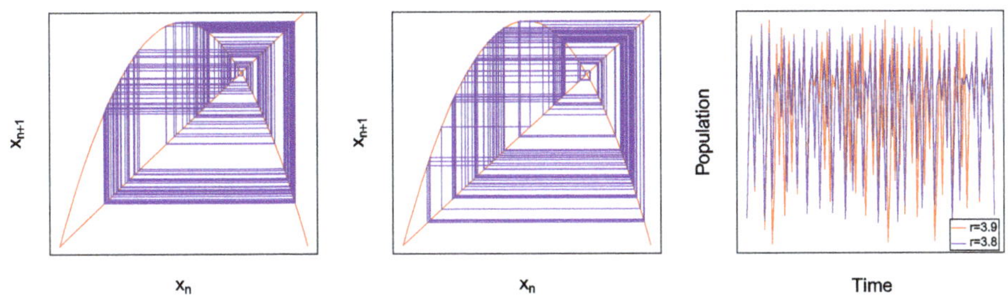

Figure 15.4: Left: Cobweb graph of a chaotic motion for $r = 3.8$. Center: Cobweb graph of a chaotic motion for $r = 3.9$; Right: Dynamics of the population number over time.

Figure 15.5 (left), (center), and (right), produced using Listing 15.5, illustrates the bifurcation phenomenon, which can be visualized through the graph of the growth rate, r, versus the population size, x. Such a graph is also known as the bifurcation diagram of a logistic map model. Figure 15.5 (left) depicts the bifurcation diagram for $0 \leq r \leq 4$, whereas Figure 15.5 (center) and Figure 15.5 (right) show the zoom corresponding to the ranges $3 \leq r \leq 4$ and $3.52 \leq r \leq 3.92$, respectively.

Listing 15.5: Bifurcation of the logistic map, see Figure 15.5

```
fxn<-function(x,r)
  fxr<-r*x*(1-x)

bifurcation <-function(x0,N,rmin,rmax,MaxIter,fxn)
{
  xmat <-array(dim=c(N,MaxIter))
  rvect = seq(rmin,rmax,length.out=N)
  for (i in 1:N)
  {
```

```
      r <- rvect[i]
      for (j in 1:MaxIter)
      {
        if (j == 1)
        {
          xn = x0
          for (k in 1:400)
          {
            xn1 = fxn(xn,r)
            xn = xn1
          }
        }
        xn1 = fxn(xn,r)
        xmat[i,j] = xn1
        xn = xn1
      }
    }
    return(xmat)
  }
x0<-0.2; rmin<-3; rmax<-4; N<-500; MaxIter<-1000;
Matx<-bifurcation(x0,N, rmin, rmax, MaxIter, fxn)
Lab.palette <- colorRampPalette(c("firebrick","red","orange"),
    space = "Lab")
matplot(Matx,pch = "17", col =Lab.palette(256), cex=0.035, axes=F,
    ann=F)
```

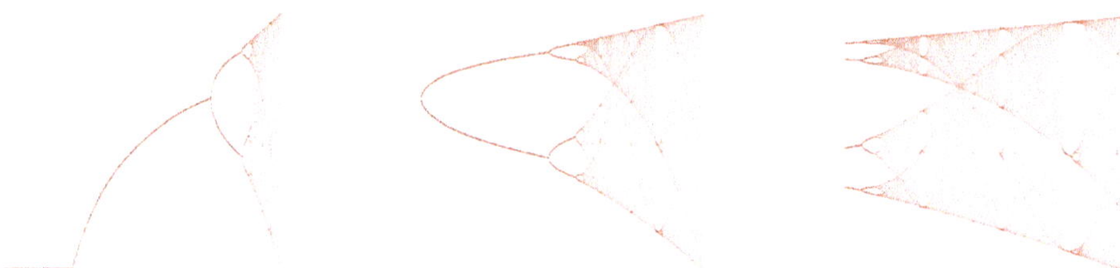

Figure 15.5: Bifurcation diagram for the logistic map model—growth rate r versus population size x: Left $0 \leq r \leq 4$. Center: zoom for $3 \leq r \leq 4$. Right: zoom for $3.52 \leq r \leq 3.92$.

15.3 The Lotka–Volterra or predator–prey system

The Lotka–Volterra equations, also known as the predator–prey system, are among the earliest dynamical system models in mathematical ecology, and were derived independently by Vito Volterra [193], and Alfred Lotka [120]. The model involves two species: the first (the prey), whose population number or concentration at time t is $x_1(t)$ and the second (the predator), which feeds on the preys, and whose population number or concentration at time t is $x_2(t)$. Furthermore, the model is based on the following assumptions about the environment, as well as the evolution of the populations of the two species:

1. The prey population has an unlimited food supply, and it grows exponentially in the absence of interaction with the predator species.

2. The rate of predation upon the prey species is proportional to the rate at which the predator species and the prey meet.

The model describes the evolution of the population numbers x_1 and x_2 over time through the following relationships:

$$\frac{dx_1}{dt} = x_1(\alpha - \beta x_2),$$
$$\frac{dx_2}{dt} = -x_2(\gamma - \delta x_1), \tag{15.10}$$

where, $\frac{dx_1}{dt}$ and $\frac{dx_2}{dt}$ denote the growth rates of the two populations over time; α is the growth rate of the prey population in the absence of interaction with the predator species; β is the death rate of the prey species caused by the predator species; γ is the death (or emigration) rate of the predator species in the absence of interaction with the prey species; and δ is the growth rate of the predator population.

The predator–prey model (15.10) is a system of ODEs. Thus, it can be solved using the function *ode()* in R. When the parameters α, β, γ, and δ are set to 0.2, 0.002, 0.1, and 0.001, respectively, the system (15.10) can be solved in R, using the scripts provided in Listing 15.6 and Listing 15.7.

The corresponding outputs are shown in Figure 15.6, where the solution in the phase plane (x_1, x_2) for $x_2(0) = 25$, the evolution of the population of the species over time for $x_2(0) = 25$, and the solution in the phase plane (x_1, x_2) for $10 \leq x_1(0) \leq 150$ are depicted in Figure 15.6 (left), Figure 15.6 (center), and Figure 15.6 (right), respectively.

Listing 15.6: Lotka-Volterra model, see Figure 15.6

```
library(deSolve)
# Building the model
LotVolt <- function(t, state, parameters)
{
  with(as.list(c(state)),
    {
    dx1 <- 0.2*x1 - 0.002*x1*x2
    dx2 <- -0.1*x2 + 0.001*x1*x2
    list(c(dx1, dx2))
    })
}
# Initial condition
xinitial <-c(x1=100,x2=25)
# Time steps
t <- seq(0, 100, 0.02)
# Solving the model
sol <- ode(y = xinitial, times = t, func = LotVolt, parms = 0)
#Snapshot of the solution
head(sol)
time        x1       x2
[1,] 0.00 100.0000 25.00000
[2,] 0.02 100.3005 25.00008
```

```
# Plotting the solution in the phase plane
plot(sol[ , 2], sol[ ,3], xaxt="n", yaxt="n", col="purple4",
    type="l", xlab = "Prey population", ylab = "Predator
    population", lwd=0.35)
#Plot population evolution over time
plot(sol[,1],  sol[ , 2], xaxt="n", yaxt="n", type="l",
    xlab="Time",ylab="Population", col = "seagreen3", lwd=0.35)
lines(sol[,1], sol[ , 3], col="orangered3", lwd=0.35)
legend("topright", legend=c("Prey","Predator"),
    col=c("seagreen3","orangered3"), lwd=c(1,1), cex=1, inset = .02)
```

Listing 15.7: Lotka-Volterra model for various initial prey populations

```
library(deSolve)
#Plotting solution of Lotka-Volterra model
# for various initial prey populations
x<-10
sol <- ode(y = c(x1=x, x2=25 ), times = t, func = LotVolt, parms =
    0)

plot(sol[ , 2], sol[ ,3], xaxt ="n", yaxt="n", col="red", type="l",
    xlab = "Prey population",  ylab = "Predator population",
    lwd=0.35)

while (x< 150)
{
  x<-x+7
  sol <- ode(y =c(x1=x, x2=25 ), times = t, func = LotVolt, parms =
      0)
  lines(sol[,2], sol[ , 3], col=x, lwd=0.35)
}
```

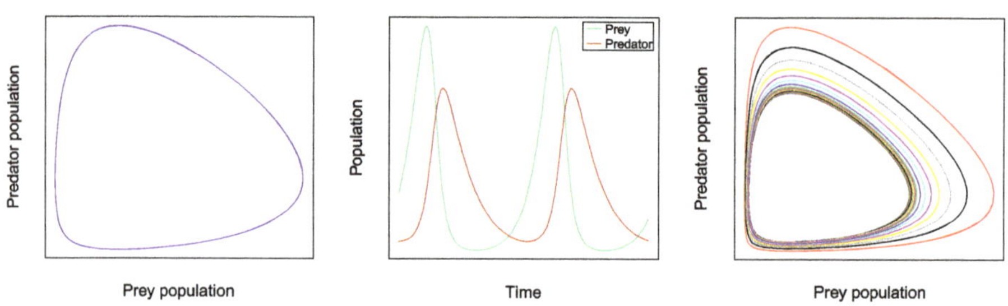

Figure 15.6: Solutions of the system (15.10) with $\alpha = 0.2$, $\beta = 0.002$, $\gamma = 0.1$, $\delta = 0.001$, and the initial conditions $x_1(0) = 100$. Left: Solution in the phase plane (x_1, x_2) for $x_2(0) = 25$. Center: evolution of the population of the species over time for $x_2(0) = 25$. Right: solution in the phase plane (x_1, x_2) for $10 \leq x_1(0) \leq 150$.

15.4 Cellular automata

A cellular automaton (CA) is a model used to describe the behaviors and the physics of discrete dynamical systems [194, 62, 206, 205]. A CA is characterized by the following features:
- An n-dimensional grid of cells;
- Each cell has a state, which represents its current status;
- Each cell has a neighborhood, which consists of the cell itself and all its immediate surroundings.

The most elementary and yet interesting cellular automaton consists of a one-dimensional grid of cells, where the set of states for the cells is 0 or 1, and the neighborhood of a cell is the cell itself, as well as its immediate successor and predecessor, as illustrated below:

A one-dimensional CA	0	1	1	0	1	0	0	0	0	1

At each time point, the state of each cell of the grid is updated according to a specified rule, so that the new state of a given cell depends on the state of its neighborhood, namely the current state of the cell under consideration and its adjacent cells, as illustrated below:

A cell (in red) and its neighborhood	000	001	010	011	100	101	110	111
Rule for updating the cell in red	1	0	0	0	1	1	0	1

The cells at the boundaries do not have two neighbors, and thus require special treatments. These cells are called the boundary conditions, and they can be handled in different ways:
- The cells can be kept with their initial condition, i. e., they will not be updated at all during the simulation process.
- The cells can be updated in a periodic way, i. e., the first cell on the left is a neighbor of the last cell on the right, and vice versa.
- The cells can be updated using a desired rule.

Depending on the rule specified for updating the cell and the initial conditions, the evolution of elementary cellular automata can lead to the following system states:
- *Steady state:* The system will remain in its initial configuration, i. e., the initial spatiotemporal pattern can be a final configuration of the system elements.
- *Periodic cycle:* The system will alternate between coherent periodic stable patterns.
- *Self-organization:* The system will always converge towards a coherent stable pattern.
- *Chaos:* The system will exhibit some chaotic patterns.

For a finite number of cells N, the number of possible configurations for the system is also finite and is given by 2^N. Hence, at a certain time point, all configurations will be visited, and the CA will enter a periodic cycle by repeating itself indefinitely. Such a cycle corresponds to an attractor of the system for the given initial conditions. When a cellular automaton models an orderly system, then the corresponding attractor is generally small, i. e., it has a cycle with a small period.

Using the R Listing 15.8, we illustrate some spatiotemporal evolutions of an elementary cellular automaton using both deterministic and random initial conditions, whereby the cells at the boundaries are kept to their initial conditions during the simulation process.

Figure 15.7 shows the spatiotemporal patterns of an elementary cellular automaton with a simple deterministic initial condition, i. e., all the cells are set to 0, except the middle one, which is set to 1. Complex localized stable structures (using Rule 182), self-organization (using Rule 210) and chaotic patterns (using Rule 89) are depicted in Figure 15.7 (left), Figure 15.7 (center), and Figure 15.7 (right), respectively.

Figure 15.8 shows spatiotemporal patterns of an elementary cellular automaton with a random initial condition, i. e., the states of the cells are allocated randomly. Complex localized stable structures (using Rule 182), self-organization (using Rule 210) and chaotic patterns (using Rule 89) are depicted in Figure 15.8 (left), Figure 15.8 (center), and Figure 15.8 (right), respectively.

Listing 15.8: Implementation of an elementary cellular automaton

```
library(HapEstXXR)

# This function returns the cell update for a given rule number
RuleCA<-function(l, m, r, RuleNb)
{
  RuleBin=dec2bin(RuleNb, npos=8)
  InvRuleBin=rev(RuleBin)
  n=paste(c(l,m,r), collapse="")
  index=strtoi(n, 2)
  newval=InvRuleBin[index+1]
  return(newval)
}

CA<-function(InitialCd, MaxIter, RuleNb)
{ Ncells<-length(InitialCd)
  cellMat<-array(0, dim=c(MaxIter, Ncells))
  for (i in 1:Ncells)
    cellMat[1,i]<-InitialCd[i]

  for (i in 2:MaxIter)
  {
    for (j in 2:(Ncells-1))
    {
      l=cellMat[i-1,j-1]
      m=cellMat[i-1,j]
      r=cellMat[i-1,j+1]
```

```
            cellMat[i,j]=RuleCA(l,m,r, RuleNb)
        }
    }

    cellMat<-apply(cellMat, 1, rev)
    return(cellMat)
}

#Visualizing the spatio-temporal patterns
Ncell=500
MaxIter=500
RuleNb=182

#Deterministic initial condition
InitialCd<-array(0, dim=Ncell)
ind<-round(dim(InitialCd)/2)
InitialCd[ind]<-1
xy<-CelAuto(InitialCd, MaxIter, RuleNb)
Lab.palette <- colorRampPalette(c("oldlace","lightsalmon1"), space =
     "Lab")
image(xy, col=Lab.palette(256),  frame.plot=FALSE, xaxt='n',
    yaxt='n', xlab="Cells", ylab="Time")

#Random initial condition
InitialCd<-replicate(Ncell,sample(0:1,1))
xy<-CelAuto(InitialCd, MaxIter, RuleNb)
image(xy, col=Lab.palette(256),  frame.plot=FALSE, xaxt='n',
    yaxt='n', xlab="Cells", ylab="Time")
```

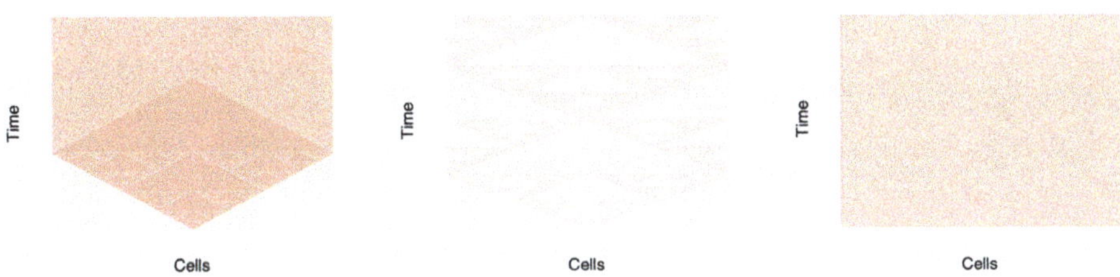

Figure 15.7: Spatiotemporal patterns of an elementary cellular automaton with a simple deterministic initial condition, i. e., all the cells are set to 0 except the middle, one which is set to 1. Left: complex localized stable structures (Rule 182). Center: self-organization (Rule 210). Right: chaotic patterns (Rule 89).

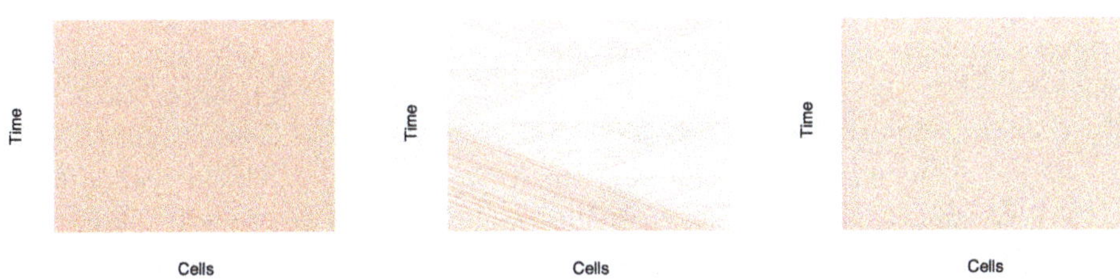

Figure 15.8: Spatiotemporal patterns of an elementary cellular automaton with a random initial condition, i. e., the states of the cells are allocated randomly. Left: complex localized stable structures (Rule 182). Center: self-organization (Rule 210). Right: chaotic patterns (Rule 89).

15.5 Random Boolean networks

Random Boolean networks (RBNs) were first introduced in the late 1960s to model the genetic regulation in biological cells [109], and since then have been widely used as a mathematical approach for modeling complex adaptive and nonlinear biological systems. A Random Boolean network is usually represented as a directed graph, defined by a pair $(\mathcal{X}, \mathcal{F})$, where $\mathcal{X} = \{x_1, \ldots, , x_N\}$ is a finite set of nodes, and $\mathcal{F} = f_1, \ldots, f_N$ is a corresponding set of Boolean functions, called *transition* or *regulation functions*. Let $x_i(t)$ represent the state of the node x_i at time t, which takes the value of either 1 (on) or 0 (off). Then, the vector $x(t) = (x_1(t), \ldots, x_N(t))$ represents the state of all the nodes in $\mathcal{X}$, at the time step t. The total number of possible states for each time step is 2^N. The state of a node x_i at the next time step $t+1$ is determined by $x_i(t+1) = f_i(x_j(t), \ldots, x_k(t))$, where $\{x_j, \ldots, x_k\}$ is the set of the immediate predecessors (or input nodes) of x_i. If all the N nodes have the same number of input nodes, K, then the RBN is referred to as an NK network, and K is also called the number of connections of the network. Like most dynamical systems, RBNs also enjoy three main regimes which, for an NK network, are correlated with the number of connections K [109]. In particular,

- if $K < 2$ the evolution of the RBN leads to stable (ordered) dynamics,
- if $K = 2$ the evolution of the RBN leads to periodic (critical) dynamics,
- if $K \geq 3$ the evolution of the RBN leads to a chaotic regime.

RBNs can be viewed as a generalization of cellular automata, in the sense that, in Boolean networks,

- a cell neighborhood is not necessarily restricted to its immediate adjacent cells,
- the size of the neighborhood of a cell and the position of the cells within the neighborhood are not necessarily the same for every cell of the grid,
- the state transition rules are not necessarily identical or unique for every cell of the grid,
- the updating process of the cells is not necessarily synchronous.

The updating process of the nodes in a Boolean network can be synchronous or asynchronous, deterministic or nondeterministic. According to the specified update process, Boolean networks can be cast in different categories [85], including the following:

1. *Classical random Boolean networks* (CRBNs): In RBNs of this type, at each discrete time step, all the nodes in the network are updated synchronously in a deterministic manner, i. e., the nodes are updated at time $t + 1$, taking into account the state of the network at time t.
2. *Asynchronous random Boolean networks* (ARBNs): In RBNs of this type, at each time step, a single node is chosen at random and updated, and thus the update process is asynchronous and nondeterministic.

3. *Deterministic asynchronous random Boolean networks* (DARBNs): For this class of Boolean networks, each node is labeled with two integers $u, v \in \mathbb{N}$ $(u < v)$. Let m denote the number of time steps from the beginning of the simulation to the current time. Then, the only nodes to be updated during the current time step are those such that $u = (m \mod v)$. If several nodes have to be updated at the same time step, then the changes, made in the network by updating one node, are taken into account during the updating process of the next node. Hence, the update process is asynchronous and deterministic.
4. *Generalized asynchronous random Boolean networks* (GARBNs): For this class of Boolean networks, at each time step, a random number of nodes are selected and updated synchronously; i. e., if several nodes have to be updated at the same time step, then the changes, made in the node-states by updating one node, are not taken into account during the updating process of the next node. Thus, the update process is semi-synchronous and nondeterministic.
5. *Deterministic generalized asynchronous random Boolean networks* (DGARBNs): This type of Boolean networks is similar to the DARBN, except that, in this case, if several nodes have to be updated at the same time step, the changes, made in the node-states by updating one node, are not taken into account during the updating process of the next node. Thus, the update process is semi-synchronous and deterministic.

In the context of genomics, a gene regulatory network (GRN) can be modeled as a Boolean network, where the status of a given gene (active/expressed or inactive/not expressed) is represented as a Boolean variable, whereas the interactions/dependencies between genes are described through the transition functions, and the input nodes for a gene x_i consist of genes regulating x_i. Let us consider the following simple GRN with three genes A, B, C, i. e., $\mathcal{X} = \{x_1, x_2, x_3\}$, where $A = x_1$, $B = x_2$, and $C = x_3$ and $\mathcal{F} = \{f_1, f_2, f_2\}$ with

$$\begin{cases} f_1 = f_1(x_1, x_3) = x_1 \vee x_3, \\ f_2 = f_2(x_1, x_3) = x_1 \wedge x_3, \\ f_3 = f_3(x_1, x_2) = \neg x_1 \vee x_2, \end{cases}$$

where $\vee$, $\wedge$, and $\neg$ are the logical disjunction (OR), conjunction (AND), and negation (NOT), respectively.

At a given time point t, the state-vector is $x(t) = (x_1(t), x_2(t), x_3(t))$ and the state evolution at the time point $t + 1$ is given by

$$\begin{cases} x_1(t+1) = f_1(x_1(t), x_3(t)) = x_1(t) \vee x_3(t), \\ x_2(t+1) = f_2(x_1(t), x_3(t)) = x_1(t) \wedge x_3(t), \\ x_3(t+1) = f_3(x_1(t), x_2(t)) = \neg x_1(t) \vee x_2(t). \end{cases} \tag{15.11}$$

The corresponding truth table, i. e., the nodes-state at time $t+1$ for any given configuration of the state vector x at time t, is as follows:

$x(t) = (x_1(t), x_2(t), x_3(t))$	000	001	010	011	100	101	110	111
$x(t+1) = (x_1(t+1), x_2(t+1), x_3(t+1))$	001	101	001	101	100	110	101	111

An RBN with N nodes can be represented by an N by N matrix, known as the adjacency matrix, for which the value of the component (i, j) is 1 if there is an edge from node i to node j, and 0 otherwise. If we substitute the nodes x_1, x_2, x_3 with their associated gene labels A, B, and C, respectively, then the corresponding adjacency matrix is written as follows:

	A	B	C
A	1	1	1
B	0	0	1
C	1	1	0

To draw the corresponding network using the package **igraph** in R, we can save the adjacency matrix as a csv (comma separated values) or a text file and then load the file in R. The corresponding text or csv file, which we will call here "ExampleBN1.txt", will be in the following format:

```
Nodes, A, B, C
A, 1, 1, 1
B, 0, 0, 1
C, 1, 1, 0
```

Listing 15.9: Visualization of a Random Boolean Network

```
#Load the graph package (install if needed)
library(igraph)
library(BoolNet)

#Load the adjacency matrix in the file "ExampleBN1.txt"
adjMat=read.csv(file.choose(), header=TRUE, row.names=1,
    check.names=FALSE)

#Converting the data to matrix
Mat=as.matrix(adjMat)

#Converting the data matrix into an graph object
BNet=graph.adjacency(Mat, mode="directed", weighted=TRUE, diag=TRUE)

#Visualization of the Boolean network
plot(BNet, layout=layout.fruchterman.reingold,
    vertex.label.color="purple", edge.color="firebrick3",
    vertex.color="oldlace", vertex.label.cex=1.5,
```

```
    vertex.frame.color="seashell1", edge.arrow.size=0.7,
    edge.curved=TRUE)
```

Using the R package Boolnet [140], we can also draw a given Boolean network, generate an RBN and analyze it, e. g., find the associated attractors and plot them. However, the dependency relations of the network must be written into a text file using an appropriate format. For instance, the dependency relations (15.11) can be written in a textual format as follows:

```
targets, factors
A, A | C
B, A & C
C, ! A | B
```

Here, the symbols |, & and ! respectively denote the logical disjunction (OR), conjunction (AND) and negation (NOT). Let us call the corresponding text file "ExampleBN1p.txt", and this must be in the current working R directory.

Figure 15.9, produced using Listing 15.10, shows the visualization and analysis of the Boolean network represented in the text file "ExampleBN1p.txt". The network graph, the state transition graph as well as attractor basins, and the state transition table when the initial state is (010) i. e., ($A = 0, B = 1, C = 0$), are depicted in Figure 15.9 (top), Figure 15.9 (bottom left) and Figure 15.9 (bottom right), respectively.

Listing 15.10: Visualization and analysis of a Boolean network – Example 1

```
#Load the graph package (install if needed)
library(igraph)
library(BoolNet)

#Load the network data in the file "ExampleBN1p.txt"
BNet1<-loadNetwork("ExampleBN1p.txt")

#Plotting the network
plotNetworkWiring(BNet1, edge.color="firebrick3",
    vertex.label.cex=1.5, vertex.color="oldlace",
    edge.arrow.size=0.7, vertex.frame.color="purple",
    vertex.label.color="purple", edge.curved=TRUE)

#Identification of attractors
AttractorsBNet1 <- getAttractors(BNet1)

#Visualizing state transitions and all attractor basins
plotStateGraph(AttractorsBNet1, layout=layout.fruchterman.reingold,
    vertex.size=4, edge.arrow.size=0.7, vertex.label.cex=1,
    vertex.frame.color="seashell1",
    colorSet=c("slateblue3","seagreen3", "firebrick3"),
    edge.curved=TRUE,  drawLabels=TRUE)

#Visualizing state transition graph to an attractor for a given
    initial state
```

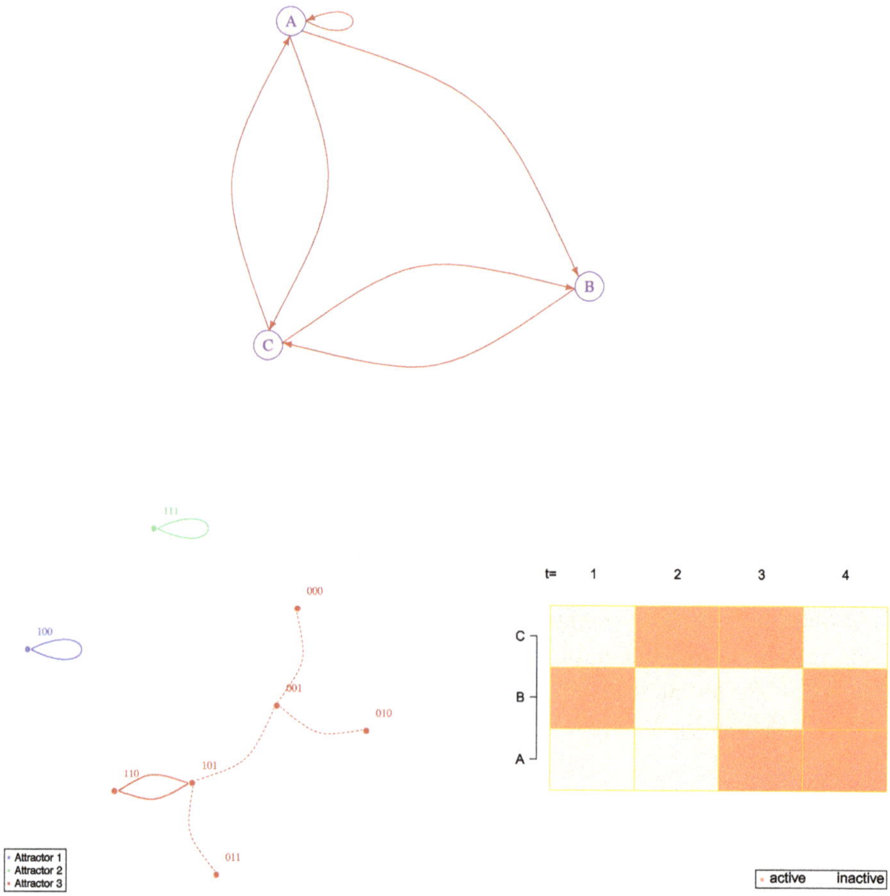

Figure 15.9: Visualization and analysis of a Boolean network—Example 1. Top: network graph. Bottom left: state transition graph and attractor basins. Bottom right: state transition table when the initial state is (010), i. e., $(A = 0, B = 1, C = 0)$.

```
plotSequence(network=BNet1, startState=c(0,1,0),
     includeAttractorStates="all", mode="graph", drawLabels=TRUE,
     vertex.size=7, edge.arrow.size=0.7, vertex.label.cex=1,
     vertex.frame.color=c("moccasin"),
     vertex.label.color="firebrick4",edge.color="slateblue",
     vertex.color="oldlace")

#Visualizing state transition table to an attractor for a given
     initial state
InitialState<-c(0,1,0) # A=0, B=0, C=0
plotSequence(network=Data, startState=InitialState,
     includeAttractorStates="all", mode="table",
     onColor="lightsalmon",offColor="oldlace", drawLegend=TRUE)
```

Figure 15.10, produced using Listing 15.11, shows the visualization and analysis of an RBN generated within the listing. The network graph, the state transition graph, as well as attractor basins, and the state transition table when the initial state is (11111111) are depicted in Figure 15.10 (top), Figure 15.10 (bottom left), and Figure 15.10 (bottom right), respectively.

Listing 15.11: Visualization and analysis of a Boolean network—Example 2

```
#Load the graph package (install if needed)
library(igraph)
library(BoolNet)

#Generating a random Boolean network with 10 nodes and each with 3
    degrees
BNet2<-generateRandomNKNetwork(n=10, k=3)

#Plotting the network
plotNetworkWiring(BNet2,edge.color="firebrick3", vertex.size=18,
    vertex.color="oldlace", edge.arrow.size=0.7,
    vertex.frame.color="purple")

#Identification of attractors
AttractorsBNet2 <- getAttractors(BNet2)

#Visualizing state transitions and all attractor basins
plotStateGraph(AttractorsBNet2, layout=layout.fruchterman.reingold,
    vertex.size=4, edge.arrow.size=0.7, vertex.label.cex=1,
    vertex.frame.color=c("seashell1"),
    colorSet=c("slateblue3","seagreen3", "firebrick3"))

#Visualizing state transition table to an attractor for a given
    initial state
InitialState<-rep(1,8) # i.e. all the 8 nodes are set to 1
plotSequence(network=BNet2, startState=InitialState,
    includeAttractorStates="all", mode="table",
    onColor="lightsalmon",offColor="oldlace", plotFixed=FALSE)
```

Figure 15.11, produced using Listing 15.12, shows spatiotemporal patterns of RBNs with $N = 1000$. Critical dynamics (for $K = 2$) and chaotic patterns (for $K = 7$) are shown in Figure 15.11 (left) and Figure 15.11 (right), respectively.

Listing 15.12: Visualizing different regimes of RNBs

```
library(igraph)
library(BoolNet)
N=1000
#Generating a random Boolean network with N=500 and k=2
RBNK2 <-generateRandomNKNetwork(n=N, k=2)
#Generating a random Boolean network with N=500 and k=7
RBNK7 <-generateRandomNKNetwork(n=N, k=7)

Tmax=200
STransK2=array(dim=c(Tmax, N))
STransK7=array(dim=c(Tmax, N))
```

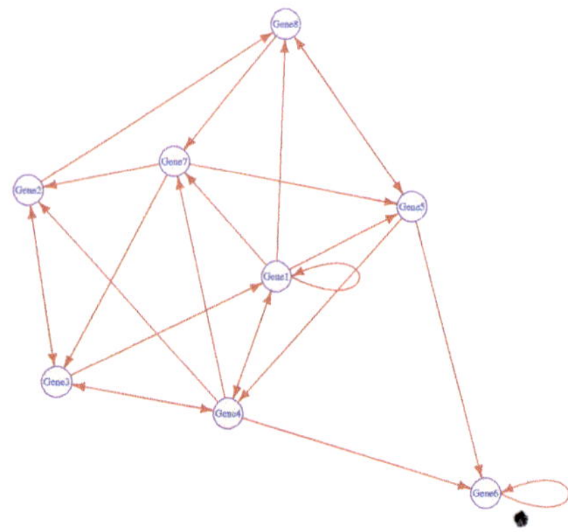

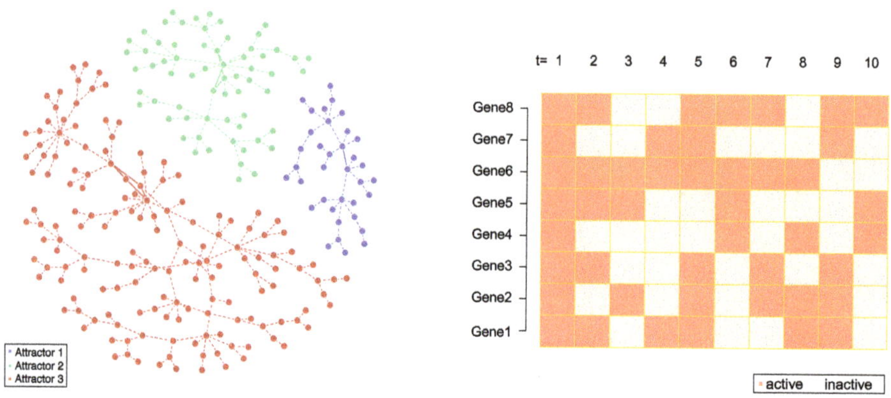

Figure 15.10: Visualization and analysis of a Boolean network—Example 2. Top: network graph. Bottom left: state transition graph and attractor basins. Bottom right: state transition table when the initial state is (11111111).

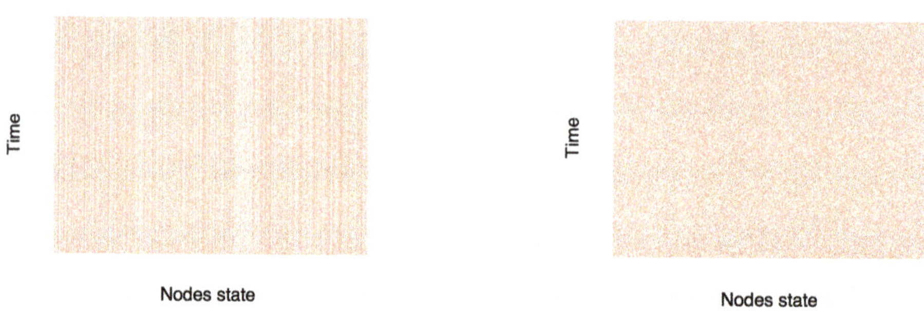

Figure 15.11: Spatiotemporal patterns of RBNs with $N = 1000$. Left: critical dynamics $(K = 2)$. Right: chaotic patterns $(K = 7)$.

```
#Generating random initial states
InitialState<-replicate(N,sample(0:1,1))
STransK2[1,]<-InitialState
STransK&[1,]<-InitialState

#Simulation of state transitions of the networks
for (i in 2:Tmax)
{
  STransK2[i,]<-stateTransition(RBNK2, STransK2[i-1,])
  STransK7[i,]<-stateTransition(RBNK7, STransK7[i-1,])
}

#Flipping the state-transition matrices
STransK2<-apply(STransK2, 1, rev)
STransK7<-apply(STransK7, 1, rev)

#Visualizing state transition table for a given initial state
Lab.palette <- colorRampPalette(c("oldlace","lightsalmon1"), space =
     "Lab")
image(STransK2, col=Lab.palette(256),  frame.plot=FALSE, xaxt='n',
     yaxt='n', xlab="Nodes state", ylab="Time")
image(STransK7, col=Lab.palette(256),  frame.plot=FALSE, xaxt='n',
     yaxt='n', xlab="Nodes state", ylab="Time")
```

15.6 Case studies of dynamical system models with complex attractors

In this section, we will provide implementations, in R, for some exemplary dynamical system models, which are known for their complex attractors.

15.6.1 The Lorenz attractor

The Lorenz attractor is a seminal dynamical system model due to Lorenz Edward [119], a meteorologist who was interested in modeling weather and the motion of air as it heats up. The state variable in the system, $x(t)$, is in $\mathbb{R}^3$, i.e., $x(t) = (x_1(t), x_2(t), x_3(t))$, and the system is written as:

$$\begin{aligned}\frac{dx_1}{dt} &= a(x_2 - x_1),\\ \frac{dx_2}{dt} &= rx_1 - x_2 - x_1x_3,\\ \frac{dx_3}{dt} &= x_1x_2 - bx_3,\end{aligned} \tag{15.12}$$

where, a, r, and b are constants.

The chaotic behavior of the Lorenz system (15.12) is often termed the Lorenz butterfly. In R, the Lorenz attractor can be simulated using Listing 15.13.

Figure 15.12, produced using Listing 15.13, shows some visualizations of the Lorenz attractor for $a = 10$, $r = 28$, $b = 8/3$, $(x_0, y_0, z_0) = (0.01, 0.01, 0.01)$, $dt = 0.02$ after 10^6 iterations. Representations of the attractor in the plane (x, y), in the space (x, y, z) and in the plane (x, z) are given in Figure 15.12 (left), Figure 15.12 (center), and Figure 15.12 (right), respectively.

Listing 15.13: Lorenz attractor, see Figure 15.12

```
library(scatterplot3d)
lorenz<-function(a, b, r, x0, y0, z0, MaxIter, dt)
{
  x<-array(dim=MaxIter); y<-array(dim=MaxIter);
      z<-array(dim=MaxIter)
  x[1]<-x0; y[1]<-y0; z[1]<-z0
  for(i in 2:MaxIter)
  {
    x[i]=x[i-1]+(-a*x[i-1]+a*y[i-1])*dt
    y[i]=y[i-1]+(-x[i-1]*z[i-1]+r*x[i-1]-y[i-1])*dt
    z[i]=z[i-1]+(x[i-1]*y[i-1]-b*z[i-1])*dt
  }
  xyz<-cbind(x, y, z)
  return(xyz)
}

a<-10; r<-28; b<- 8/3; x0<-0.01; y0<-0.01
z0<-0.01; MaxIter<-1e6; dt<-0.002

xyz<-lorenz(a, b, r, x0, y0, z0, MaxIter,dt)
scatterplot3d(xyz, highlight.3d=TRUE, xlab=expression(x[n]),
    ylab=expression(y[n]),zlab=expression(z[n]), col.axis="purple",
    angle=55, col.grid="skyblue", scale.y=0.7, pch=17,
    cex.symbols=0.03, lty.axis=3, lty.grid=3, col.lab="white")

Lab.palette <- colorRampPalette(c("firebrick", "red", "orange"),
    space = "Lab")
plot(xyz[,1], xyz[,2], pch=17, cex=.035, col=Lab.palette(256),
    axes=F, ann=F)
plot(xyz[,1], xyz[,3], pch=17, cex=.035, col=Lab.palette(256),
    axes=F, ann=F)
```

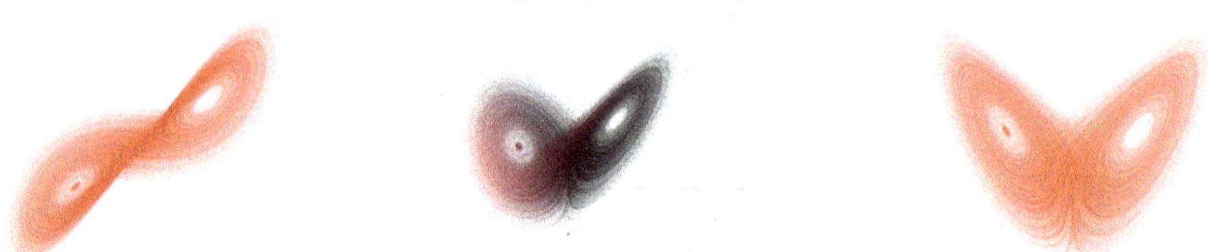

Figure 15.12: Lorenz attractor for $a = 10$, $r = 28$, $b = 8/3$, $(x_0, y_0, z_0) = (0.01, 0.01, 0.01)$, $dt = 0.02$ after 10^6 iterations: Left in the plane (x, y). Center in the space (x, y, z). Right in the plane (x, z).

15.6.2 Clifford attractor

The Clifford attractor is defined by the following recurrence equations:

$$\begin{cases} x_{n+1} = \sin(ay_n) + c\cos(ax_n), \\ y_{n+1} = \sin(bx_n) + d\cos(by_n), \end{cases} \tag{15.13}$$

where, a, b, c, and d are the parameters of the attractor.

In R, the system (15.13) can be solved using Listing 15.14.

Figure 15.13 shows some visualizations of the Clifford's attractor for different values of the parameters and initial conditions: Figure 15.13 (left) displays the output of Listing 15.14 when $a = -1.4$, $b = 1.6$, $c = 1$, $d = 0.3$, $(x_0, y_0,) = (\pi/2, \pi/2)$ after 1.5×10^6 iterations; Figure 15.13 (center) shows the output of Listing 15.14 when $a = -1.4$, $b = 1.6$, $c = 1$, $d = 0.7$, $(x_0, y_0,) = (\pi/2, \pi/2)$ after 1.5×10^6 iterations; Figure 15.13 (right) shows output of Listing 15.14 when $a = -1.4$, $b = 1.6$, $c = 1$, $d = 0. - 1$, $(x_0, y_0,) = (\pi/2, \pi/2)$ after 2×10^6 iterations.

Listing 15.14: Clifford attractor, see Figure 15.13

```
clifford<-function(a,b,c,d,x0, y0,MaxIter){
  x<-array(dim=MaxIter); y<-array(dim=MaxIter)
  x[1]<-x0; y[1]<-y0
  for (k in 2:MaxIter)
  {
    x[k]<-sin(a*y[k-1])+c*cos(a*x[k-1])
    y[k]<-sin(b*x[k-1])+d*cos(b*y[k-1])
  }
  xy<-cbind(x,y)
  return(xy)
}

a<--1.4; b<-1.6; c<-1; d<-0.3
x0<-pi/2; y0<-pi/2; MaxIter<-1.5e6
xy<-clifford(a,b,c,d,x0, y0, MaxIter)
plot(xy[,1], xy[,2], pch=17, cex=.02, col="gold", axes=F, ann=F)
```

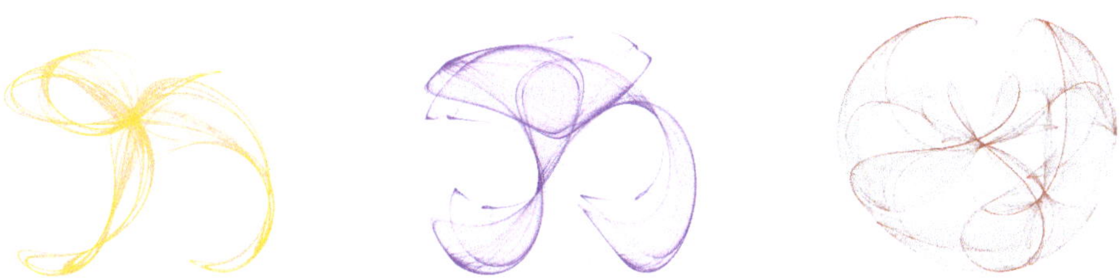

Figure 15.13: Clifford attractor. Left: $a = -1.4$, $b = 1.6$, $c = 1$, $d = 0.3$, $(x_0, y_0,) = (\pi/2, \pi/2)$ after 1.5×10^6 iterations. Center: $a = -1.4$, $b = 1.6$, $c = 1$, $d = 0.7$, $(x_0, y_0,) = (\pi/2, \pi/2)$ after 1.5×10^6 iterations. Right: $a = -1.4$, $b = 1.6$, $c = 1$, $d = 0. - 1$, $(x_0, y_0,) = (\pi/2, \pi/2)$ after 2×10^6 iterations.

15.6.3 Ikeda attractor

The Ikeda attractor is a dynamical system model that is used to describe a mapping in the complex plane, corresponding to the plane-wave interactivity in an optical ring laser. Its discrete-time version is defined by the following complex map:

$$z_{n+1} = a + bz_n e^{i\frac{k-p}{1+\|z_n\|^2}}, \tag{15.14}$$

where, $z_k = x_k + iy_k$.

The resulting orbit of the map (15.14) is generally visualized by plotting z in the real-imaginary plane (x, y), also called the phase-plot. In R, the orbit of the Ikeda attractor can be obtained using Listing 15.15. Figure 15.14 (left), produced using Listing 15.15, shows a representation of the Ikeda's attractor in the plane (x, y).

Listing 15.15: Ikeda attractor, see Figure 15.14

```
ikeda<-function(a,b,p,k,MaxIter)
{
  x<-array(dim=MaxIter); y<-array(dim=MaxIter);
      z<-array(dim=MaxIter)
  z[1]<-0; x[1]<-0; y[1]<-0
  for (i in 2:MaxIter)
  {
    z[i]<- a +b*z[i-1]*exp(1i*k -1i*p/(1+abs(z[i-1]^2)))
    x[i]<-Re(z[i])
    y[i]<-Im(z[i])
  }
  xy<-cbind(x,y)
  return(xy)
}

a<-0.85; b<-0.9; k<-0.4; p<-7.7; MaxIter<-5e5
xy<-ikeda(a,b,p,k,MaxIter)
plot(xy[,1], xy[,2], pch=17, cex=.015, col="violetred", axes=F,
     ann=F)
```

15.6.4 The Peter de Jong attractor

The Peter de Jong attractor is a well-known strange attractor, and its time-discrete version is defined by the following system:

$$\begin{aligned} x_{n+1} &= \sin(ay_n) - \cos(bx_n), \\ y_{n+1} &= \sin(cx_n) - \cos(dy_n), \end{aligned} \tag{15.15}$$

where, a, b, c, and d are the parameters of the attractor.

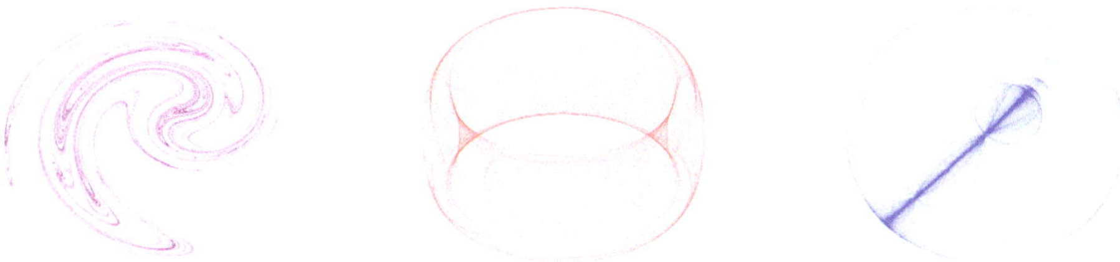

Figure 15.14: Left: Ikeda attractor for $a = 0.85$, $b = 0.9$, $k = 0.4$, $p = 7.7$, $z_0 = 0$ after 1.5×10^6 iterations. Center: de Jong attractor (15.16) for $a = 1.4$, $b = 1.56$, $c = 1.4$, $d = -6.56$, $(x_0, y_0,) = (0, 0)$ after 1.5×10^6 iterations. Right: de Jong attractor (15.15) for $a = 2.01$, $b = -2$, $c = 2$, $d = -2$, $(x_0, y_0,) = (0, 0)$ after 1.5×10^6 iterations.

A variant of Peter de Jong attractor is given by

$$\begin{aligned} x_{n+1} &= d\sin(ax_n) - \sin(by_n), \\ y_{n+1} &= c\cos(ax_n) + \cos(by_n). \end{aligned} \tag{15.16}$$

In R, the orbit of Peter de Jong attractor can be obtained using Listing 15.16. Figure 15.14 (center), produced using Listing 15.16, shows a representation of the de Jong attractor (15.16), in the plane (x, y), for $a = 1.4$, $b = 1.56$, $c = 1.4$, $d = -6.56$, $(x_0, y_0,) = (0, 0)$ after 1.5×10^6 iterations. Figure 15.14 (right), produced also using Listing 15.16, shows a representation of the de Jong attractor (15.15) for $a = 2.01$, $b = -2$, $c = 2$, $d = -2$, $(x_0, y_0,) = (0, 0)$ after 1.5×10^6 iterations.

Listing 15.16: de Jong attractor, see Figure 15.14

```
deJong1<-function(a,b,c,d,x0, y0,MaxIter)
{
  x<-array(dim=MaxIter);   y<-array(dim=MaxIter)
  x[1]<-x0; y[1]<-y0
  for (k in 2:MaxIter)
  {
    x[k]<-sin(a*y[k-1])- cos(b*x[k-1])
    y[k]<-sin(c*x[k-1])- cos(d*y[k-1])
  }
  xy<-cbind(x,y)
  return(xy)
}

deJong2<-function(a,b,c,d,x0, y0,MaxIter)
{
  x<-array(dim=MaxIter); y<-array(dim=MaxIter)
  x[1]<-x0; y[1]<-y0
  for (k in 2:MaxIter)
  {
    x[k]<-d*sin(a*x[k-1])- sin(b*y[k-1])
    y[k]<-c*cos(a*x[k-1])+ cos(b*y[k-1])
  }
  xy<-cbind(x,y)
  return(xy)
}
```

```
a<- 1.4; b<- -2.3; c<-2.4; d<- - 2.1; x0<-0; y0<-0; MaxIter<-1.5e6
xy<-deJong1(a,b,c,d,x0, y0, MaxIter)
plot(xy[,1], xy[,2], pch=17, cex=.015, col="royalblue1", axes=F,
     ann=F)

a<- 1.4; b<-1.56; c<-1.40; d<- - 6.56; x0<-0; y0<-0; MaxIter<-1.5e6
xy<-deJong2(a,b,c,d,x0, y0, MaxIter)
plot(xy[,1], xy[,2], pch=17, cex=.02, col="gold", axes=F, ann=F)
```

15.6.5 Rössler attractor

The Rössler attractor [157] is a dynamical system that has some applications in the field of electrical engineering [113]. It is defined by the following equations:

$$\begin{cases} \frac{dx}{dt} = -y - z, \\ \frac{dy}{dt} = x + ay, \\ \frac{dz}{dt} = b + z(x - c), \end{cases} \tag{15.17}$$

where, a, b, and c are the parameters of the attractor. This attractor is known to have some chaotic behavior for certain values of the parameters.

In R, the system (15.17) can be solved and its results visualized using Listing 15.17. Figure 15.15, produced using Listing 15.17, shows some visualizations of the Rössler attractor for different values of its parameters and initial conditions. Figure 15.15 (left) shows the output of Listing 15.17 when $a = 0.5$, $b = 2$, $c = 4$, $(x_0, y_0, z_0) = (0.3, 0.4, 0.5)$, $dt = 0.03$ after 2×10^6 iterations. Figure 15.15 (center) shows the output of Listing 15.17 when $a = 0.5$, $b = 2$, $c = 4$, $(x_0, y_0, z_0) = (0.03, 0.04, 0.04)$, $dt = 0.03$. After 2×10^6 iterations. Figure 15.15 (right) shows the output of Listing 15.17 when $a = 0.2$, $b = 0.2$, $c = 5.7$, $(x_0, y_0, z_0) = (0.03, 0.04, 0.04)$, $dt = 0.08$. After 2×10^6 iterations.

Listing 15.17: Rössler attractor, see Figure 15.15

```
library(scatterplot3d)
rossler<-function(a,b,c,x0,y0,z0,MaxIter,dt)
{
  x<-array(dim=MaxIter); y<-array(dim=MaxIter);
      z<-array(dim=MaxIter)
  x[1]<-x0; y[1]<-y0; z[1]<-z0
  for (i in 2:MaxIter)
  {
    x[i]<-x[i-1]-dt*(y[i-1]+z[i-1])
    y[i]<-y[i-1]+dt*(x[i-1]+a*y[i-1])
    z[i]<-z[i-1]+dt*(b+z[i-1]*(x[i-1]-c))
  }
  xyz<-cbind(x,y,z)
  return(xyz)
}
```

```
a<-0.5; b<-2; c<-4; x0<-0.3; y0<-0.4;
z0<-0.5; dt<-0.03; MaxIter<-2e6
xyz<-rossler(a,b,c,x0,y0,z0,MaxIter,dt)
scatterplot3d(xyz, highlight.3d=TRUE, xlab=expression(x[n]),
    ylab=expression(y[n]),zlab=expression(z[n]), col.axis="purple",
    angle=55, col.grid="skyblue", scale.y=0.7, pch=17,
    cex.symbols=0.02, lty.axis=3, lty.grid=3, col.lab="white")
```

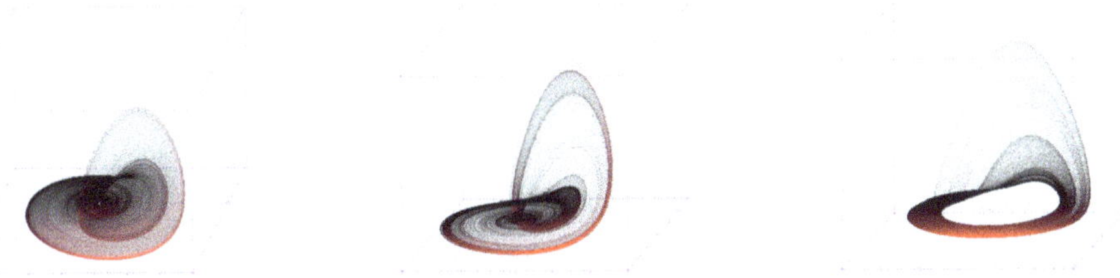

Figure 15.15: Rössler's attractor. Left: $a = 0.5$, $b = 2$, $c = 4$, $(x_0, y_0, z_0) = (0.3, 0.4, 0.5)$, $dt = 0.03$ after 2×10^6 iterations. Center: $a = 0.5$, $b = 2$, $c = 4$, $(x_0, y_0, z_0) = (0.03, 0.04, 0.04)$, $dt = 0.03$. After 2×10^6 iterations. Right: $a = 0.2$, $b = 0.2$, $c = 5.7$, $(x_0, y_0, z_0) = (0.03, 0.04, 0.04)$, $dt = 0.08$. After 2×10^6 iterations.

15.7 Fractals

There exist various definitions of the word "fractal", and the simplest of these is the one suggested by Benoit Mandelbrot [125], who refers to a "fractal" as an object, which possesses self-similarity. In this section, we will provide examples of implementations for some classical fractal objects, using R.

15.7.1 The Sierpińsky carpet and triangle

The Sierpińsky carpet and triangle are geometry fractals named after Wacław Sierpińsky, who introduced them in the early nineteenth century [172]. The Sierpińsky carpet can be constructed using the following iterative steps:
Step 1: Set $x_0 = 0$, $n = 1$, and choose the number of iterations N.
Step 2: If $n \leq N$, then the following applies:

- Set

$$x_n = \begin{pmatrix} x_{n-1} & x_{n-1} & x_{n-1} \\ x_{n-1} & I_{n-1} & x_{n-1} \\ x_{n-1} & x_{n-1} & x_{n-1} \end{pmatrix},$$

  where, I_{n-1} is a 3^{n-1} by 3^{n-1} matrix of unity elements.
- Set $n = n + 1$ and go to Step 2.

Otherwise, go to Step 3.

Step 3: Plot the points in the final matrix x_N.

The construction and visualization of the Sierpińsky carpet can be carried out, in R, using Listing 15.18. Figure 15.16 (left), which is an output of Listing 15.18, shows the visualization of the Sierpińsky carpet after six iterations.

Listing 15.18: The Sierpińsky carpet, see Figure 15.16 (left)

```
sierpinskycarpet<-function(MaxIter)
{
  x<-0
  for (i in 1:MaxIter)
  {
    xi<- array(1, dim=c(3^(i-1),3^(i-1) ))
    c1<-cbind(x,x,x)
    c2<-cbind(x,xi,x)
    x<-rbind(c1,c2,c1)
  }
  return(x)
}
MaxIter<-6
xn<-sierpinskycarpet(MaxIter)
Lab.palette <- colorRampPalette(c("burlywood","seashell1"), space =
    "Lab")
image(xn, col=Lab.palette(256), axes=F)
```

The Sierpińsky triangle can be constructed using the following iterative steps:

Step 1: Select three points (vertices of the triangle) in a two-dimensional plane. Let us call them x_a, x_b, x_c;

Plot the points x_a, x_b, x_c;

Choose the number of iterations N;

Step 2: Select an initial point x_0. Set $n = 1$;

Step 3: If $n \leq N$ then do the following:

- Select one of the three vertices $\{x_a, x_b, x_c\}$ at random, and let us call this point p_n;
- Calculate the point $x_n = \frac{(x_{n-1}+p_n-)}{2}$, and plot x_n;
- Set $n = n + 1$ and go to Step 3;

Otherwise go to Step 4;

Step 4: Plot the points of the sequence $x_0, x_1, \ldots, x_N$.

In R, the construction and the visualization of the Sierpińsky triangle can be achieved using Listing 15.19. Figure 15.16 (center), which is an output of Listing 15.19, shows the visualization of the Sierpińsky triangle after 5e+5 iterations.

Listing 15.19: The Sierpińsky triangle, see Figure 15.16 (center)

```
sierpinskytriangle<-function(MaxIter)
```

```
{
  x<-array(0,dim=MaxIter);   y<-x
  for (i in 2:MaxIter)
  {
    c=sample(1:3,1)
    if (c==1)
    {
      x[i]<-0.5*x[i-1]
      y[i]<-0.5*y[i-1]
    }
    if (c==2)
    {
      x[i]<-0.5*x[i-1]+.25
      y[i]<-0.5*y[i-1]+sqrt(3)/4
    }
    if (c==3)
    {
      x[i]<-0.5*x[i-1]+.5
      y[i]<-0.5*y[i-1]
    }
  }
  xy<-cbind(x,y)
  return(xy)
}
MaxIter<-0.5e6
xy<-sierpinskytriangle(MaxIter)
plot(xy[,1], xy[,2], pch=17, cex=.04, col="firebrick", axes=F,
     ann=F)
```

15.7.2 The Barnsley fern

Named after the mathematician who introduced it, the Barnsley fern [11] is a fractal, which can be constructed using the following iterative process:

Step 1: Set $a = (0, 0.85, 0.2, -0.15)$, $b = (0, 0.04, -0.26, 0.28)$, $c = (0, -0.04, 0.23, 0.26)$, $d = (0.16, 0.85, 0.22, 0.24)$, $e = (0, 0, 0, 0)$, $f = (0, 1.6, 1.6, 0.44)$;
Chose the number of iterations N.

Step 2: Set $x_0 = 0$, $y_0 = 0$, and $n = 1$;

Step 3: If $n \leq N$, then do the following:

- Select at random a value $r \in (0, 1)$,
- If $r < 0.01$ then set $j = 1$ and go to Step 4,
- If $0.01 < r < 0.86$ the set $j = 2$ and go to Step 4,
- If $0.86 < r < 0.93$ the set $j = 3$ and go to Step 4,
- If $0.93 < r$ the set $j = 4$ and go to Step 4,

Step 4: Set $x_n = a_j \times x_{n-1} + b_j \times y_{n-1} + e_j$, $y_n = c_j \times x_{n-1} + d_j \times y_{n-1} + f_j$, where, a_j, b_j, c_j, d_j, e_j, f_j denote the ith component of the vectors a, b, c, d, e and f, respectively.
Set $n = n + 1$ and go to Step 3;

Step 5: Plot the points of the sequence $(x_0, y0), (x_1, y_1), \ldots, (x_N, y_N)$.

In R, the construction and the visualization of the Barnsley fern can be achieved using Listing 15.20. Figure 15.16 (right), which is an output of Listing 15.20, shows the visualization of the Barnsley fern after 1e+6 iterations.

Listing 15.20: The Barnsley fern, see Figure 15.16 (right)

```
barnsleyfern<-function(MaxIt)
{
        a<-c(0, 0.85, 0.2, -0.15); b<-c(0, 0.04, -0.26, 0.28)
        c<-c(0, -0.04, 0.23, 0.26); d<-c(0.16, 0.85, 0.22, 0.24)
        e<-c(0, 0, 0, 0); f<-c(0, 1.6, 1.6, 0.44)
        x<-array(0,dim=MaxIt); y<-x
        x[1]<-0; y[1]<-0
        for (i in 1:MaxIt)
        {
                r<-sample(0:1000,1)/1000
                if (r<0.01)
                        j=1
                if ((r>0.01)&(r<0.86))
                        j=2
                if ((r>0.86)&(r<0.93))
                        j=3
                if (r>0.93)
                        j=4

                x[i+1]=a[j]*x[i]+b[j]*y[i]+e[j];
                y[i+1]=c[j]*x[i]+d[j]*y[i]+f[j];
        }
        xy<-cbind(x,y)
        return(xy)
}
MaxIt<-1e6
xy<-barnsleyfern(MaxIt)
Lab.palette <- colorRampPalette(c("firebrick","red","orange"),
    space = "Lab")
plot(xy[,1], xy[,2], pch=17, cex=.09, col=Lab.palette(256),
    axes=F, ann=F)
```

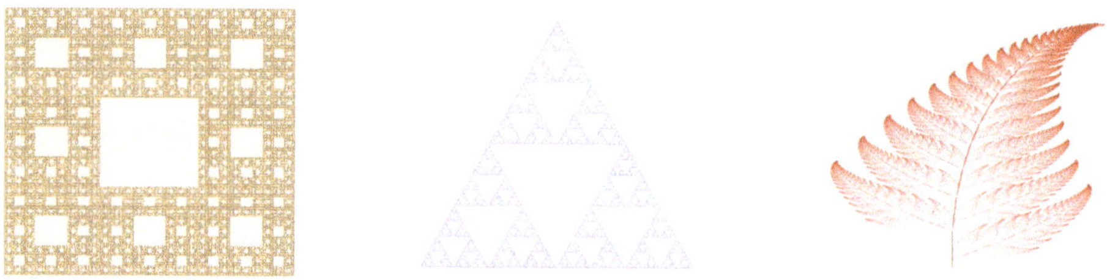

Figure 15.16: Left: The Sierpińsky carpet. Center: The Sierpińsky triangle. Right: The Barnsley fern.

15.7.3 Julia sets

Let z_n be a sequence defined by the following recurrence relationship:

$$z_{n+1} = z_n^m + c \tag{15.18}$$

with c and $z_0 \in \mathbb{C}$ and $m \in \mathbb{N}$.

For a given value of c, the associated Julia set [103] is defined by the boundary between the set of z_0 values that have bounded orbits, and those which do not. For instance, when $m = 2$, for any $c \in \mathbb{C}$ the recurrence relationship $z^2 + c$ defines a quadratic Julia set.

In R, the construction and the visualization of the Julia set can be done using Listing 15.21 and Listing 15.22. Figures 15.17, 15.18, 15.19, which have all been produced using Listing 15.21, illustrate the evolution of the quadratic Julia set according to the value of the complex parameter c.

Listing 15.21: Julia sets

```
fzn<-function(z, c, n)
{
  fz<-z^n+c
  return(fz)
}

JuliaSet<-function(n, c, Nx, Ny, MaxIter)
{
  Matz<-array(0, dim=c(Nx,Ny,2)); MatzColor<-array(0,
      dim=c(Nx,Ny,3))
  scalexy<-5/4; xmin <- -scalexy*4/3; xmax <- scalexy*4/3
  ymin <- -scalexy; ymax <- scalexy;
  for (k in 1:MaxIter)
  {
    for (j in 1:Ny)
    {
      y <- ymin + j*(ymax - ymin)/(Ny - 1)
      for (i in 1:Nx)
      {
        x <- xmin + i*(xmax - xmin)/(Nx - 1)
        if (k==1)
          z<- complex(real=x,imaginary=y)
        else
          z<- complex(real=Matz[i,j,1], imaginary=Matz[i,j,2])

        z<-fzn(z, c, n)
        Matz[i,j,1]=Re(z);
        Matz[i,j,2]=Im(z);
        #Examples of coloring patterns
        scalecolor<-20;
        MatzColor[i,j,1] <- abs(cos(scalecolor*abs(z)));
        MatzColor[i,j,2] <- abs(cos(scalecolor*Arg(z)));
        MatzColor[i,j,3] <- abs(cos(scalecolor*sqrt(abs(z))));
      }
    }
  }
```

```
    return(MatzColor)
}
```

Listing 15.22: Plotting some Julia sets

```
#Plotting Julia sets
c<--0.67319+1i*0.34442; n=2;
MaxIter<-50; Nx<- 800; Ny<- 600
zn<-JuliaSet(n, c, Nx, Ny, MaxIter)
#Plots with various colouring patterns
rgb.palette <- colorRampPalette(c("lightslateblue", "slateblue4",
    "oldlace"), space = "rgb")
image(zn[ , ,1 ], col=rgb.palette(256), axes=F)
rgb.palette <- colorRampPalette(c("skyblue1", "slateblue4",
    "oldlace"), space = "rgb")
image(zn[ , ,2 ], col=rgb.palette(256), axes=F)
rgb.palette <- colorRampPalette(c("turquoise1", "slateblue4",
    "oldlace"),space = "rgb")
image(zn[ , ,3 ], col=rgb.palette(256), axes=F)
```

Figure 15.17: Quadratic Julia sets. Left: $c = 0.7$; Center: $c = -0.074543 + 0.11301i$; Right: $c = 0.770978 + 0.08545i$.

Figure 15.18: Quadratic Julia sets. Left: $c = 0.7$. Center: $c = -0.74543 + 0.11301i$. Right: $c = 0.770978 + 0.08545i$.

15.7.4 Mandelbrot set

The Mandelbrot set [125] is the set of all $c \in \mathbb{C}$, such that the sequence z_n defined by the recurrence relationship (15.19) is bounded.

$$\begin{cases} z_0 = 0, \\ z_{n+1} = z_n^m + c, \; m \in \mathbb{N}. \end{cases} \tag{15.19}$$

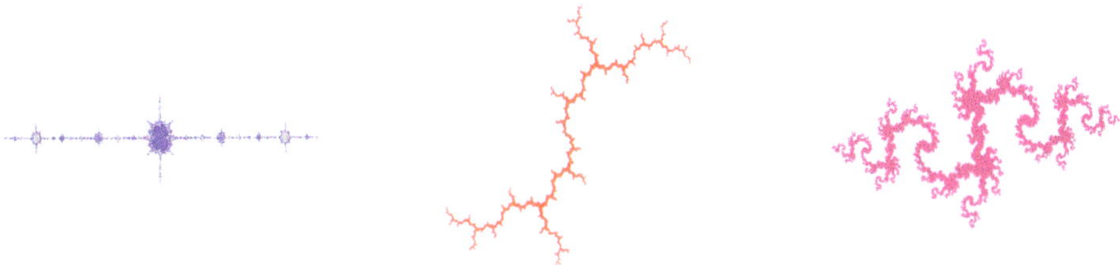

Figure 15.19: Quadratic Julia sets. Left: $c = -1.75$. Center: $c = -i$. Right: $c = -0.835 - 0.2321i$.

Formally, the Mandelbrot set can be defined as follows:

$$\mathcal{M} = \left\{c \in \mathbb{C} : z_0 = 0 \text{ and } |z_n| \nrightarrow \infty, \text{ as } n \longrightarrow \infty\right\}. \tag{15.20}$$

The Mandelbrot system (15.19) can be reformulated in $\mathbb{R}^2$ by substituting $z_n = x_n + iy_n$ and $c = a + ib$ with their real and imaginary parts, respectively. For instance, when $m = 2$, the system (15.19) is called the quadratic Mandelbrot set, and it can be reformulated in $\mathbb{R}^2$ as follows:

$$\begin{cases} x_0 = y_0 = 0, \\ x_{n+1} = x_n^2 - y_n^2 + a, \\ y_{n+1} = 2x_n y_n + b. \end{cases} \tag{15.21}$$

In R, the construction and the visualization of the quadratic Mandelbrot set can be done using the scripts in Listing 15.23 and Listing 15.24. The graphs in Figure 15.20, produced using Listing 15.23 and Listing 15.24, illustrate some visualization of the quadratic Mandelbrot set depending on the values of its parameters.

Listing 15.23: Mandelbrot sets

```
fz2<-function(z, c)
{
  fz<-z^2+c
  return(fz)
}
fz3<-function(z, c)
{
  fz<-z^3- z + c-2/3/sqrt(3)
  return(fz)
}
fzcos<-function(z, c)
{
  fz<-c*cos(z)/sqrt(0.8)
  return(fz)
}

MandelbrotSet<-function(fz, Nx, Ny, MaxIter, scalexy)
{
  Matz<-array(0, dim=c(Nx,Ny,2))
```

```
  MatzColor<-array(0, dim=c(Nx,Ny,2))
  xmin = -scalexy*4 - 0.5; xmax = scalexy*4 - 0.5
  ymin = -scalexy*3; ymax = scalexy*3

  for (k in 1:MaxIter)
  {
    for (j in 1:Ny)
    {
      y <- ymin + j*(ymax - ymin)/(Ny - 1)
      for (i in 1:Nx)
      {
        x <- xmin + i*(xmax - xmin)/(Nx - 1)
        if (k==1)
          z<- complex(real=x,imaginary=y)
        else
          z<- complex(real=Matz[i,j,1], imaginary=Matz[i,j,2])

        scalecolor<-20;
        MatzColor[i,j,1] <- abs(cos(scalecolor*abs(z+1/sqrt(3))));
        MatzColor[i,j,2] <- abs(cos(scalecolor*sqrt(abs(z))));
        z0<- complex(real=x,imaginary=y)
        z<-fz(z, z0)
        Matz[i,j,1]=Re(z);
        Matz[i,j,2]=Im(z);
      }
    }
  }
  return(MatzColor)
}
```

Listing 15.24: Plotting some Mandelbrot sets

```
#Plotting Mandelbrot sets
Nx<-800; Ny<-600;
zn<-MandelbrotSet(fz2, Nx, Ny, MaxIter=26, scalexy=0.38)
rgb.palette <- colorRampPalette(c("red1", "orangered4", "oldlace"),
    space = "rgb")
image(zn[ , ,2], col=rgb.palette(256),  axes=F)

zn<-MandelbrotSet(fz3, Nx, Ny, MaxIter=23, scalexy=0.38)
rgb.palette <- colorRampPalette(c("lightslateblue", "slateblue4",
    "oldlace"), space = "rgb")
image(zn[ , ,1], col=rgb.palette(256),  axes=F)

zn<-MandelbrotSet(fzcos, Nx, Ny, MaxIter=6, scalexy=1.5)
rgb.palette <- colorRampPalette(c("oldlace", "turquoise"), space =
    "rgb")
image(zn[ , , 2], col=rgb.palette(256),  axes=F)
```

15.8 Exercises

1. Consider the following dynamical system:

$$x_{n+1} = x_n^2 \quad \text{for } n = 0, 1, 2, 3, \ldots$$

Figure 15.20: Left: $z_{n+1} = z_n^2 + c$. Center: $z_{n+1} = c * \cos(z_n)/\sqrt{(0.8)}$. Right: $z_{n+1} = z_n^3 - z_n + c - (2/3)/\sqrt{(3)}$.

Use R to simulate the dynamics of x_n using the initial conditions $x_0 = 1$ and $x_0 = 3$, for $n = 1, \ldots, 500$.
Plot the corresponding cobweb graph, as well as the graph of the evolution of x_n, over time.

2. Consider the following dynamical system:

$$z_{t+1} - z_t = z_t(1 - z_t) \quad \text{for} \quad t = 0, 1, 2, 3, \ldots$$

Use R to simulate the dynamics of x_n using the initial conditions $z_0 = 0.2$ and $z_0 = 5$ for $n = 1, \ldots, 500$.
Plot the corresponding cobweb graph, as well as the graph of the evolution of x_n, over time.

3. Let x_n be the number of fish in generation n in a lake. The evolution of the fish population can be modeled using the following model:

$$x_{n+1} = 8x_n e^{-x_n}.$$

Use R to simulate the dynamics of the fish population using the initial conditions $x_0 = 1$ and $x_0 = \log(8)$ for $n = 1, \ldots, 500$.
Plot the corresponding cobweb graph, as well as the graph of the dynamics of the population number, over time.

4. Consider the following predator–prey model x and y:

$$\begin{aligned} \frac{dx}{dt} &= Ax - Bxy, \\ \frac{dy}{dt} &= -Cy + Dxy. \end{aligned} \tag{15.22}$$

Use R to solve the system (15.22) using the following initial conditions and values of the parameters for $t \in [0, 200]$:
(a) $x(0) = 81$, $y(0) = 18$, $A = 1.5$, $B = 1.1$, $C = 2.9$, $D = 1.2$;
(b) $x(0) = 150$, $y(0) = 81$, $A = 5$, $B = 3.1$, $C = 1.9$, $D = 2.1$.
Plot the corresponding solutions in the phase plane (x, y), and the evolution of the population of both species over time.

5. Use `R` to plot, in 3D, the following Lorenz system (15.12) using the parameters $a = 15$, $r = 32$, $b = 3$, and the following initial conditions: $x_1(0) = 0.03$, $x_2(0) = 0.03$, $x_3(0) = 0.03$; $x_1(0) = 0.5$, $x_2(0) = 0.21$, $x_3(0) = 0.55$.

16 Graph theory and network analysis

This chapter provides a mathematical introduction to networks and graphs. To facilitate this introduction, we will focus on basic definitions and highlight basic properties of defining components of networks. In addition to quantify network measures for complex networks, e. g., distance- and degree-based measures, we survey also some important graph algorithms, including breadth-first search and depth-first search. Furthermore, we discuss different classes of networks and graphs that find widespread applications in biology, economics, and the social sciences [23, 10, 53].

16.1 Introduction

A network $G = (V, E)$ consists of nodes $v \in V$ and edges $e \in E$, see [94]. Often, an undirected network is called a *graph,* but in this chapter we will not distinguish between a network and a graph and use both terms interchangeably. In Figure 16.1, we show some examples for undirected and directed networks. The networks shown on the left-hand side are called *undirected networks*, whereas those on the right-hand side are called *directed networks* since each edge has a direction pointing from one node to another. Furthermore, all four networks, depicted in Figure 16.1, are connected [94], i. e., none of them has isolated vertices. For example, removing the edge between the nodes from an undirected network with only two vertices, leaves merely two isolated nodes.

Weighted networks are obtained by assigning weights to each edge. Figure 16.2 depicts two weighted, undirected networks (left) and two weighted, directed networks (right). A weight between two vertices, w_{AB}, is usually a real number. The range of these weights depends on the application context. For example, w_{AB} could be a positive real number indicating the distance between two cities, or two goods in a warehouse [156].

From the examples above, it becomes clear that there exist a lot of different graphs with a given number of vertices. We call two graphs *isomorphic* if they have the same structure, but they might look differently [94].

In general, graphs or networks can be analyzed by using quantitative and qualitative methods [52]. For instance, a quantitative method to analyze graphs is a graph measure to quantify structural information [52]. In this chapter, we focus on quantitative techniques and in Section 16.3 we present important examples thereof.

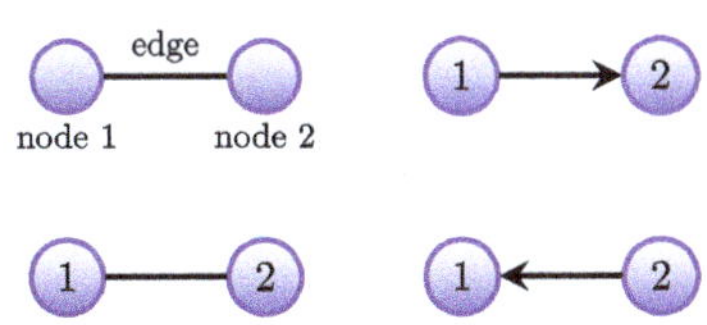

Figure 16.1: Two undirected (left) and two directed (right) networks with two nodes.

https://doi.org/10.1515/9783110796063-016

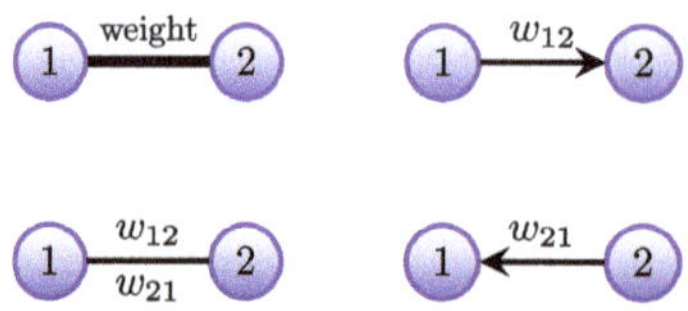

Figure 16.2: Weighted undirected and directed graphs with two vertices.

16.2 Basic types of networks

In the previous section, we discussed the basic units of which networks are made of. In this section, we construct larger networks, which can consist of many vertices and edges. In Section 16.1, we just discussed the graphical visualization of networks without providing a formal characterization thereof. In the following, we will provide such a formal characterization because it is crucial for studying and visualizing graphs.

16.2.1 Undirected networks

To define a network formally, we specify its set of vertices or nodes, V, and its set of edges, E. That means, any vertex $i \in V$ is a node of the network. Similarly, any element $E_{ij} \in E$ is an edge of the network, which means that the vertices i and j are connected with each other. Figure 16.3 shows an example of a network with $V = \{1, 2, 3, 4, 5\}$ and $E = \{E_{12}, E_{23}, E_{34}, E_{14}, E_{35}\}$. For example, node $3 \in V$ and edge E_{34} are *part* of the network shown by Figure 16.3. From Figure 16.3, we further see that node 3 is connected with node 4, but also, node 4 is connected with node 3. For this reason, we call such an edge *undirected.* In fact, the graph shown by Figure 16.3 is an *undirected network.* It is evident that in an undirected network the symbol E_{ij} has the same meaning as E_{ji}, because the order of the nodes in this network is not important.

Definition 16.2.1. An undirected network $G = (V, E)$ is defined by a vertex set V and an edge set $E \subseteq \binom{V}{2}$.

$E \subseteq \binom{V}{2}$ means that all edges of G belong to the set of subsets of vertices with 2 elements. The size of G is the cardinality of the node set V, and is often denoted by $|V|$. The notation $|E|$ stands for the number of edges in the network. From Figure 16.3, we see that this network has 5 vertices ($|V| = 5$) and 5 edges ($|E| = 5$).

In oder to encode a network by utilizing a mathematical representation, we use a matrix representation. The *adjacency matrix* A is a squared matrix with $|V|$ number of rows and $|V|$ number of columns. The matrix elements A_{ij}, of the adjacency matrix provide the connectivity of a network.

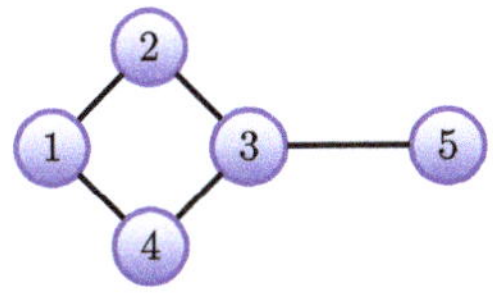

Figure 16.3: An undirected network.

Definition 16.2.2. The adjacency matrix A for an undirected network G is defined by

$$A_{ij} = \begin{cases} 1 & \text{if } i \text{ is connected with } j \text{ in } G, \\ 0 & \text{otherwise,} \end{cases} \tag{16.1}$$

for $i, j \in V$.

As an example, let us consider the graph in Figure 16.3. The corresponding adjacency matrix is

$$A = \begin{pmatrix} 0 & 1 & 0 & 1 & 0 \\ 1 & 0 & 1 & 0 & 0 \\ 0 & 1 & 0 & 1 & 1 \\ 1 & 0 & 1 & 0 & 0 \\ 0 & 0 & 1 & 0 & 0 \end{pmatrix}. \tag{16.2}$$

Since this network is undirected, its adjacency matrix is symmetric, that means $A_{ij} = A_{ji}$ holds for all i and j.

16.2.2 Geometric visualization of networks

From the previous discussions, we see that the graphical visualization of a network is not determined by its definition. This is illustrated in Figure 16.4, where we show the same network as in Figure 16.3, but with different *positions* of the vertices. When comparing their adjacency matrix (16.2), one can see that these networks are identical. In general, a network represents a *topological object* instead of a *geometrical* one. This means that we can arbitrarily deform the network visually as long as V and E remain changed as shown in Figure 16.4. Therefore, the formal definition of a given network does not include any geometric information about coordinates, where the vertices are positioned in a plane as well as features, such as edge length and bendiness. In order to highlight this issue, we included to the right figure of Figure 16.4 a Cartesian coordinate system when drawing the graph. The good news is as long as we do not require a visualization of a network the topological information about it is sufficient to conduct any analysis possible.

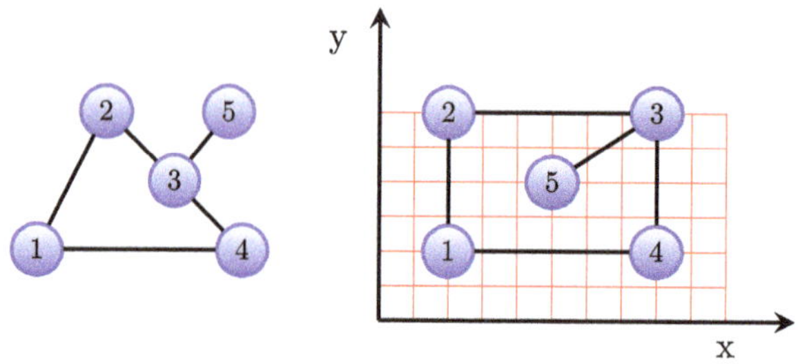

Figure 16.4: Two different visualizations of the network depicted in Figure 16.3.

In contrast, from Figure 16.3 and Figure 16.4, we can see that the visualization of a network is not unique and for a specific visualization often additional information is utilized. This information could either be motivated by certain structural aspects of the network we are trying to visualize, e. g., properties of vertices or edges (see Section 16.3.1) or even from domain specific information (e. g., from biology or economy). An important consequence of the “arbitrariness” of a network visualization is that there is no formal mapping from G to its visualization.

16.2.3 Directed and weighted networks

We will start this section with some basic definitions for directed networks.

Definition 16.2.3. A directed network, $G = (V, E)$, is defined by a vertex set V and an edge set $E \subseteq V \times V$.

$E \subseteq V \times V$ means that all directed edges of G are subsets of all possible combinations of directed edges. The expression $V \times V$ is a cartesian product and the corresponding result is a set of directed edges. If $u, v \in V$, then we write (u, v) to express that there exists a directed edge from u to v.

The definition of the adjacency matrix of a directed graph is very similar to the definition of an undirected graph.

Definition 16.2.4. The components of an adjacency matrix, A, for a directed network, G, are defined by

$$A_{ij} = \begin{cases} 1 & \text{if there is a connection from } i \text{ to } j \text{ in } G \\ 0 & \text{otherwise} \end{cases} \tag{16.3}$$

for $i, j \in V$.

In contrast with equation (16.1), here, we choose the start vertex (i) and the end vertex (j) of a directed edge. Figure 16.5 presents a directed network with the following adjacency matrix:

$$A = \begin{pmatrix} 0 & 0 & 0 & 0 & 0 \\ 1 & 0 & 1 & 0 & 0 \\ 0 & 0 & 0 & 1 & 1 \\ 1 & 0 & 0 & 0 & 0 \\ 0 & 0 & 0 & 0 & 0 \end{pmatrix}. \tag{16.4}$$

Here, we can see that $A^t \neq A$. Therefore, the transpose of the adjacency matrix, A, of a directed graph is not always equal to A.

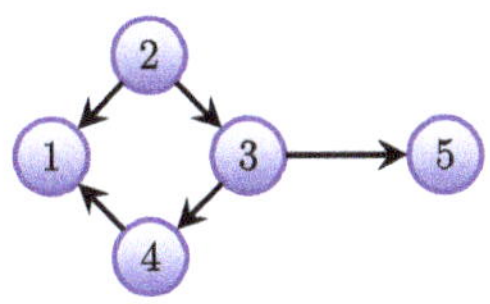

Figure 16.5: A directed network.

For example, the edge set of the directed network, depicted in Figure 16.5, is $E = \{(2,1),(2,3),(4,1),(3,4),(3,5)\}$.

Now, we define a weighted, directed network.

Definition 16.2.5. The components of an adjacency matrix, W, for a directed network, G, are defined by

$$W_{ij} = \begin{cases} w_{ij} & \text{if there is a connection from } i \text{ to } j \text{ in } G, \\ 0 & \text{otherwise,} \end{cases} \tag{16.5}$$

for $i, j \in V$.

In equation (16.5), $w_{ij} \in \mathbb{R}$ denotes the weight associated with an edge from vertex i to vertex j.

Figure 16.6 depicted the weighted direct network with the following adjacency matrix:

$$W = \begin{pmatrix} 0 & 0 & 0 & 0 & 0 \\ 2 & 0 & 1 & 0 & 0 \\ 0 & 0 & 0 & 3 & 3 \\ 1 & 0 & 0 & 0 & 0 \\ 0 & 0 & 0 & 0 & 0 \end{pmatrix}. \tag{16.6}$$

From the adjacency matrix W, we can identify the following (real) weights: $w_{21} = 2$, $w_{23} = 1$, $w_{34} = 3$, $w_{35} = 3$, $w_{41} = 1$.

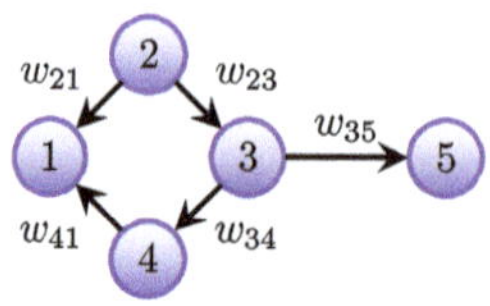

Figure 16.6: Example of a weighted and directed network.

16.2.4 Walks, paths, and distances in networks

We start this section with some basic definitions.

Definition 16.2.6. A walk w of length μ in a network is a sequence of μ edges, which are not necessarily different. We write $w = v_1v_2, v_2v_3, \ldots, v_{\mu-1}v_\mu$. We also call the walk w closed if $v_1 = v_\mu$.

Definition 16.2.7. A path P is a special walk, where all the edges and all the vertices are different.

In a directed graph, the close path is also called a cycle.

Let us illustrate these definitions by way of the network examples depicted in Figure 16.7. If we consider the upper graph on the left hand side, we see that 12, 23, 34 is an undirected path, as all vertices and edges are different. This path has a length of 3. On the other hand, in the upper graph of the right hand side, 12, 23, 32 is a walk of length 3. By considering the same graph, we also find that 14, 43, 34, 41 is a closed walk, as it starts and ends in vertex 1. This closed walk has a length of 4.

Now, let us consider the lower graph on the left hand side of Figure 16.7. In this graph, 12, 23, 34 is a directed path of length 3 as the underlying graph is directed.

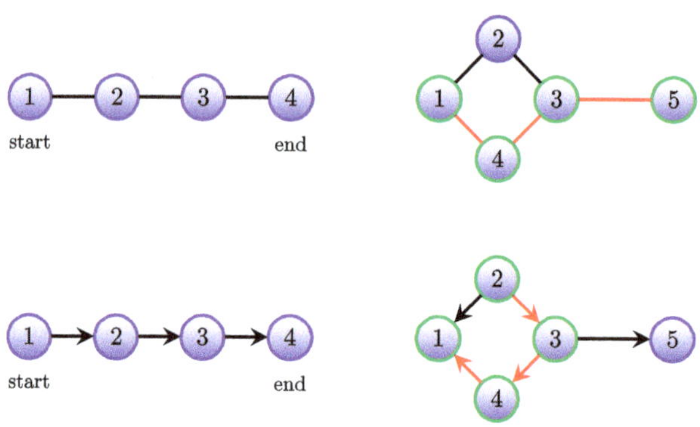

Figure 16.7: Undirected and directed path.

In the lower graph below on the right hand side, the path 23, 34, 41 has a length 3, but does not represent a cycle, as its start and end vertices are not the same.

Now, we define the term *distance* between vertices in a network.

Definition 16.2.8. A shortest path is the minimum path connecting two vertices.

Also, we define the topological distance between two vertices in a network.

Definition 16.2.9. The number of edges in the shortest path connecting the vertices u and v is the topological distance $d(u,v)$.

Again, we consider the upper graph on the right hand side of Figure 16.7. For instance, the path 12, 23, 34, for going from vertex 1 to vertex 4 has length 3 and is obviously not the shortest one. Calculating the shortest path yields $d(1,4) = 1$.

16.3 Quantitative network measures

Many quantitative network measures, also called network scores or indices, have been developed to characterize structural properties of networks, see, e. g., [19, 67, 43]. These measures have often been used for characterizing network classes discussed in section (16.5), or to identify distinct network patterns, such as linear and cyclic subgraphs. In the following, we discuss the most important measures to characterize networks structurally. In case no remark is made, we always assume that the networks are undirected.

In general, we distinguish between global and local graph measures. A global measure maps the entire network to a real number. A local measure maps a component of the graph, e. g., a vertex, an edge, or a subgraph to a real number. The design of these measures depends on the application domain.

16.3.1 Degree and degree distribution

Definition 16.3.1. Let $G = (V, E)$ be a network. The degree k_i of the vertex v_i is the number of edges, which are incident with the vertex v_i.

In order to characterize complex networks by their degree distributions [23, 128], we utilize the following definition:

Definition 16.3.2. Let $G = (V, E)$ be a network. We define the degree distribution as follows:

$$P(k) := \frac{\delta_k}{N}, \tag{16.7}$$

where $|V| := N$ and δ_k denotes the number of vertices in the network, G, of degree k.

It is clear that equation (16.7) represents the proportion of vertices in G possessing degree k.

Degree-based statistics have been used in various application areas in computer science. For example, it has been known that the vertex degrees of many real-world networks, such as www-graphs and social networks [2, 23, 24], are not Poisson distributed. However, the following power law always holds:

$$P(k) \sim k^{-\gamma}, \quad \gamma > 1. \tag{16.8}$$

16.3.2 Clustering coefficient

The clustering coefficient, C_i, is a local measure [198] defined, for a particular vertex v_i, as follows:

$$C_i = \frac{2e_i}{n_i(n_i - 1)} = \frac{e_i}{t_i}. \tag{16.9}$$

Here, n_i is the number of neighbors of vertex i, and e_i is the number of adjacent pairs between all neighbors of v_i. Because $0 \leq e_i \leq t_i$, C_i is the probability that two neighbors of node i are themselves connected with each other. Figure 16.8 depicts an example of graph as well as the calculation of the corresponding local clustering coefficient.

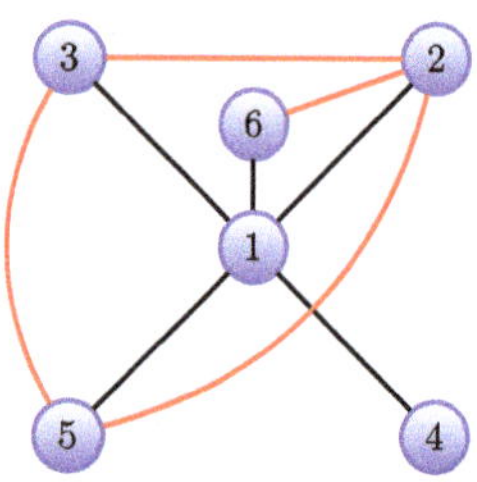

$$e_1 = 4$$
$$n_1 = 5$$
$$t_1 = 10$$
$$C_1 = \tfrac{e_1}{t_1} = \tfrac{4}{10}$$

Figure 16.8: Local clustering coefficient.

16.3.3 Path-based measures

Path- and distance-based measures have been proven useful, especially when characterizing networks [64, 104]. For example, the average path length and the diameter of a network have been used to characterize classes of biological and technical networks, see [64, 104, 196]. An important finding is that the average path lengths and diameters of certain biological networks are rather small compared to the size of a network, see [115, 128, 143].

In the following, we briefly survey important path and distance-based network measures, see [29, 31, 93, 94, 174]. Starting from a network $G = (V, E)$, we define the distance matrix as follows:

Definition 16.3.3. The distance matrix is defined by

$$\left(d(v_i, v_j)\right)_{v_i, v_j \in V}, \tag{16.10}$$

where $d(v_i, v_j)$ is the topological distance between v_i and v_j.

Similarly, the mean or characteristic distance of a network, $G = (V, E)$, can be defined as follows:

Definition 16.3.4.

$$\bar{d}(G) := \frac{1}{\binom{N}{2}} \sum_{1 \leq i < j \leq N} d(v_i, v_j). \tag{16.11}$$

We also define other well-known distance-based graph measures [94] that have been used extensively in various disciplines [57, 197].

Definition 16.3.5. Let $G = (V, E)$ be a network. The eccentricity of a vertex $v \in V$ is defined by

$$\sigma(v) = \max_{u \in V} d(u, v). \tag{16.12}$$

Definition 16.3.6. Let $G = (V, E)$ be a network. The diameter of the network, G, is defined by

$$\rho(G) = \max_{v \in V} \sigma(v). \tag{16.13}$$

Definition 16.3.7. Let $G = (V, E)$ be a network. The radius of the network, G, is defined by

$$r(G) = \min_{v \in V} \sigma(v). \tag{16.14}$$

16.3.4 Centrality measures

These graph measures have been investigated extensively by social scientists for analyzing the communication within groups of people [80, 81, 197]. For instance, it could be interesting to know how *important* or *distinct* vertices, e. g., representing persons, in social networks are [197]. In the context of social networks, *importance* can be seen as *centrality*. Following this idea, numerous centrality measures [92, 197] have been developed to determine whether vertices, e. g., representing persons, may act distinctly with respect to the communication ability in these networks. In this section, we briefly review the most important centrality measures, see [80, 81, 197].

Definition 16.3.8. Let $G = (V, E)$ be a network. The so-called degree centrality of a vertex $v \in V$ is defined by

$$C_D(v) = k_v, \tag{16.15}$$

where k_v denotes the degree of the vertex v.

When analyzing directed networks, the degree centrality can be defined straightforwardly by utilizing the definition of the in-degree and out-degree [94]. Now, let us define the well-known *betweenness centrality* measure [80, 81, 159, 197].

Definition 16.3.9. Let $G = (V, E)$ be a network. The betweenness centrality is defined by

$$C_B(v_k) = \sum_{v_i, v_j \in V, v_i \neq v_j} \frac{\sigma_{v_i v_j}(v_k)}{\sigma_{v_i v_j}}, \tag{16.16}$$

where, $\sigma_{v_i v_j}$ stands for the number of shortest paths from v_i to v_j, and $\sigma_{v_i v_j}(v_k)$ for the number of shortest paths from v_i to v_j that include v_k.

In fact, the quantity

$$\frac{\sigma_{v_i v_j}(v_k)}{\sigma_{v_i v_j}} \tag{16.17}$$

can be seen as the probability that v_k lies on a shortest path connecting v_i with v_j.

A further well-known measure of centrality is called *closeness centrality.*

Definition 16.3.10. Let $G = (V, E)$ be a network. The closeness centrality is defined by

$$C_C(v_k) = \frac{1}{\sum_{i=1}^{N} d(v_k, v_i)}, \tag{16.18}$$

where $d(v_k, v_i)$ is the number of edges on a shortest path between v_k and v_i.

When there exist more than one shortest paths connecting v_k with v_i, $d(v_k, v_i)$ remains unchanged.

The measure $C_C(v_k)$ has often been used to determine how close is a vertex to other vertices in a given network [197].

16.4 Graph algorithms

In this section, we discuss some important graph algorithms. Graph algorithms are frequently used for search problems on graphs. In general, search problems on a graph require to find/visit certain distinct vertices. An example thereof is to find all vertices of an input graph, which manifest a tree-like hierarchy in a graph by selecting an arbitrary root vertex in the input graph. The two most prominent examples of graph algorithms for performing graph-based searches are the breadth-first and depth-first algorithms, see [38].

16.4.1 Breadth-first search

Breadth-first search (BFS) is a well-known and simple graph algorithm [38]. The underlying principle of this algorithm relates to discovering all reachable vertices and touching all edges systematically, starting from a given vertex s. After selecting s, all neighbors of s are discovered, and so forth. Here, discovering vertices in a graph involves determining the topological distance (see Definition 16.2.9) between s and all other reachable vertices.

Starting with a graph $G = (V, E)$, the algorithm BFS uses colors in order to symbolize the state of the vertices as follows:

- white: the unseen vertices are white; initially, all vertices are white;
- grey: the vertex is seen, but it needs to be determined whether it has white neighbors;
- black: the vertex is processed, i. e., this vertex and all of its neighbors were seen.

Figure 16.9 shows an example by using a stack approach, where the colors are omitted. The first graph in Figure 16.9 is the input graph. The start vertex is vertex 2. The two stacks on the left hand side in each situation show the vertices, which have already been visited along with their parents. For instance, we see that after four steps of the algorithm (the fifth graph in the first row of Figure 16.9), we have discovered 3 vertices, whose topological distance equals 1. Also, we see in the fifth graph in the first row of Figure 16.9 that the vertices 1, 4, and 5 have been visited together with their parent relations. Finally, all vertices have been visited in the last graph in Figure 16.10 and, hence, BFS ends.

16.4.2 Depth-first search

Depth-first search (DFS) is another graph algorithm for searching graphs [38]. Suppose we start at a certain vertex. In case a vertex we visit has a still unexplored neighbor, we visit this neighbor and pursue going *in the depth* to find another unexplored neighbor, if it exists. We continue recursively with this procedure, until we cannot go into the depth. Then, we perform backtracking to find an edge, which go into the depth.

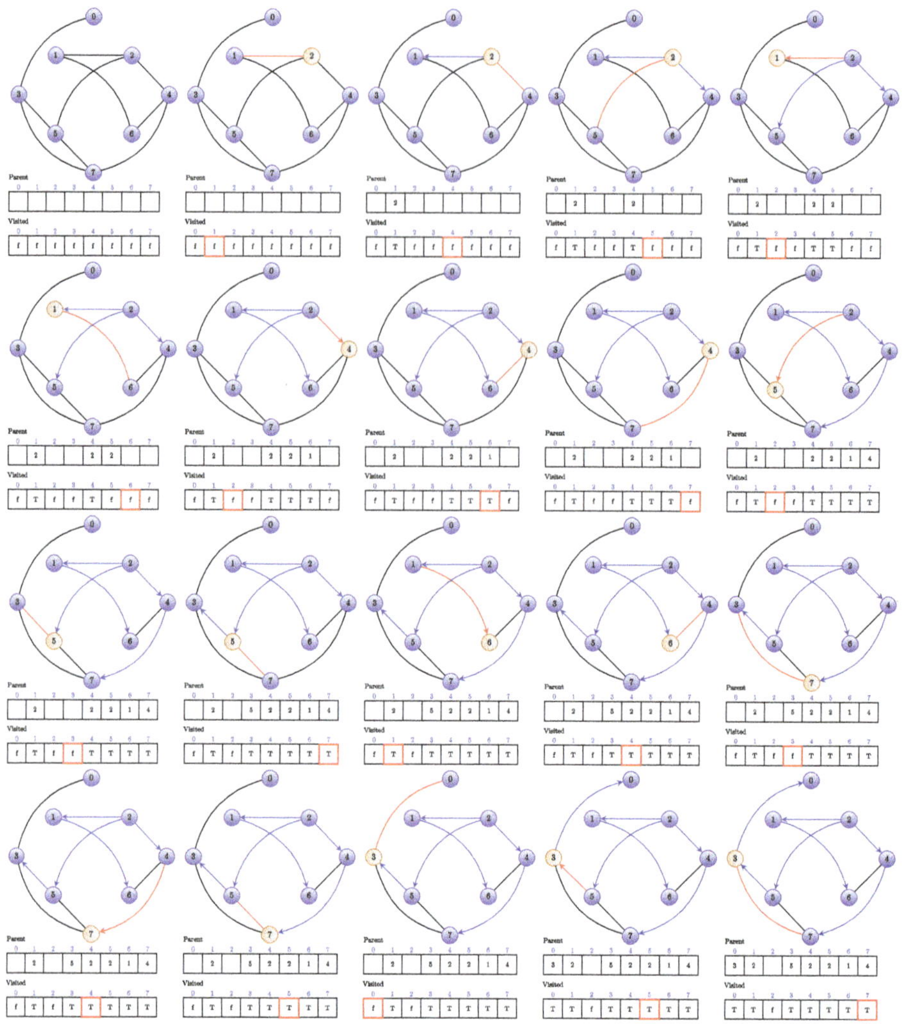

Figure 16.9: The first graph is the input graph to run BFS. The start vertex is vertex 2. The steps are shown together with a stack showing the visited and parent vertices.

We explain the basic steps as follows: To start, we highlight all vertices as not found (white). The basic strategy of DFS is as follows:

- Highlight the actual vertex v as found (grey)
- Whereas there exists an edge $\{u, v\}$ with a not found successor u:
  - Perform the search recursively from u. That is
  - Explore $\{u, w\}$ and visit w. Explore from w in the depth until it ends
  - Highlight u as finished (black)
  - Perform backtracking from u to v
- Highlight v as finished (black)

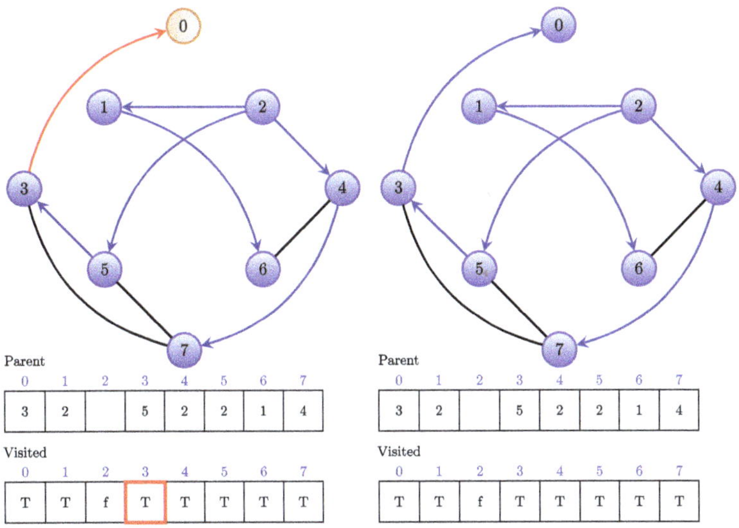

Figure 16.10: The last two graphs when running BFS on the input graph shown in Figure 16.9.

Finally, we obtain all vertices, starting from the start vertex. Figure 16.11 shows an input graph to run DFS. Then, Figure 16.11 shows the steps to explore the vertices in the depth, starting from vertex 0. Figure 16.12 shows the last five graphs before DFS ends.

16.4.3 Shortest paths

Determining the shortest paths in networks has been a long-standing problem in graph theory [58, 38]. For instance, finding the flight with the earliest arrival time in a given aviation network [117] requires the determination of all shortest paths. Other examples for the application of shortest paths are graph optimization problems, e. g., for transportation networks of production processes [156].

A classical algorithm for determining the shortest paths within networks is due to Dijkstra [58]. It is interesting to note that many problems in algorithmic graph theory, e. g., determining minimum spanning trees (see Section 16.4.4) and breadth first search also utilize Dijkstra's method, see [38].

Dijkstra's method can be described as follows. Given a network $G = (V, E)$ and a starting vertex $v \in V$ the algorithms finds the shortest paths to all other vertices in G. In this case, Dijkstra's algorithm [58] generates a so-called shortest path tree containing all the vertices that lie on the shortest path.

We describe the basic steps of the algorithm of Dijkstra in order to determine the shortest paths starting from a given vertex to all other vertices in G. Here, we assume that the input graph has vertex labels and real edge labels [58, 38]:

Figure 16.11: The first graph is the input graph to run DFS. The start vertex is vertex 0. The steps are shown together with a stack showing the visited and parent vertices.

- We create the set of shortest path trees (SPTS), containing the vertices that are in a shortest path tree. These vertices have the property that they have minimum distance from the starting vertex. Before starting, it holds SPTS $= \emptyset$.
- We assign initial distance values ∞ in the input graph. Also, we set the distance value for the starting vertex equal to zero.
- Whereas the vertex set of SPTS does not contain all vertices of the input graph, the following apply:
  - Select a vertex $v \in V$ that is not contained in the vertex set of SPTS with minimum distance

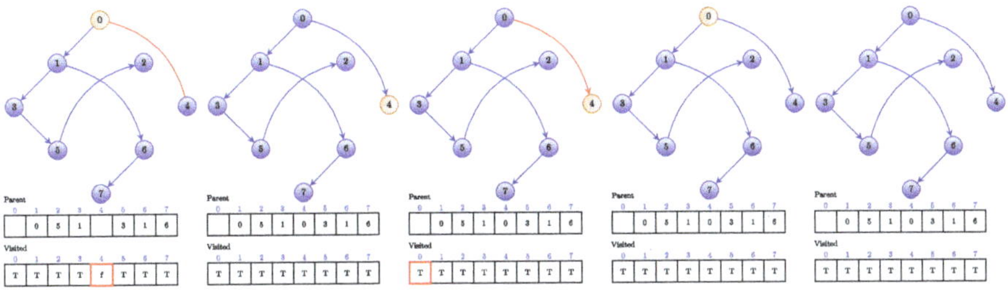

Figure 16.12: The last five graphs when running DFS on the input graph shown in Figure 16.11.

- We put $v \in V$ into the vertex set of SPTS
- We update the distance value of all vertices that are adjacent with $v \in V$. In order to update the distances, we iterate among all adjacent vertices. For all the adjacent vertices $u \in V$ with $v \in V$ we perform the following: If the sum of the assigned distance value of the vertex v (from the starting vertex) and the weight of the edge $\{v, u\}$ is less than the distance value of u, update the distance value of u.

Now we demonstrate the application of this algorithm for an example. The input graph in A is given in Figure 16.13. Because the vertex set of SPTS is initially empty, and we choose vertex 1 as start node. The initial distance values can be seen in Figure 16.13 (B). We perform some steps to see how the set of shortest paths is emerging; see Figure 16.14. The vertices highlighted in red are the ones in the shortest path tree. The graph shown in Figure 16.14 in situation D is the final shortest path tree consisting all vertices of the input graph in Figure 16.13. That means, the set of shortest path trees gives all shortest paths from vertex 1 to all other vertices.

As a remark, we would like to note that the graph shown in Figure 16.13 is a weighted, undirected graph (see Section 16.2.3). So, using the algorithm of Dijkstra [58] makes sense for edge-weighted graphs, as the shortest path between two vertices of a graph depends on these weights. Interestingly, the shortest path problem becomes more simple if we consider unweighted networks. If all edges in a network are unweighted, we may set all edge weights to 1. Then, Dijkstra's algorithm reduces to the search of the topological distances between vertices, see Definition 16.2.9.

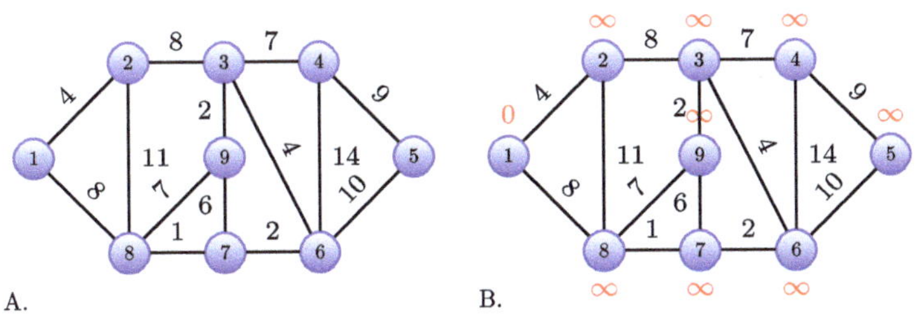

Figure 16.13: (A) The input graph. (B) The graph with initial vertex weights.

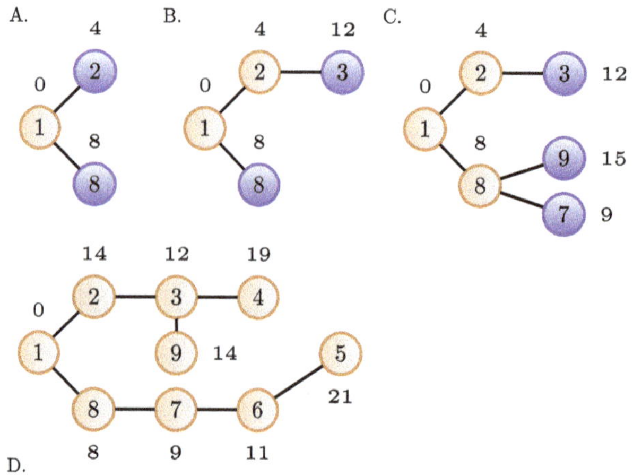

Figure 16.14: Steps when running Dijkstra's algorithm for the graph in (A) shown in Figure 16.13.

Let us consider the graph A in Figure 16.15. In case we determine all shortest paths from vertex 1 to vertex 4, we see that there exist more than one shortest path between these two vertices. We find the shortest paths 1-3-4 and 1-2-4. So, the shortest path problem does not possess a unique solution. The same holds when considering the shortest paths between vertex 1 and vertex 5. The calculations yield the two shortest paths 1-3-4-5 and 1-2-4-5.

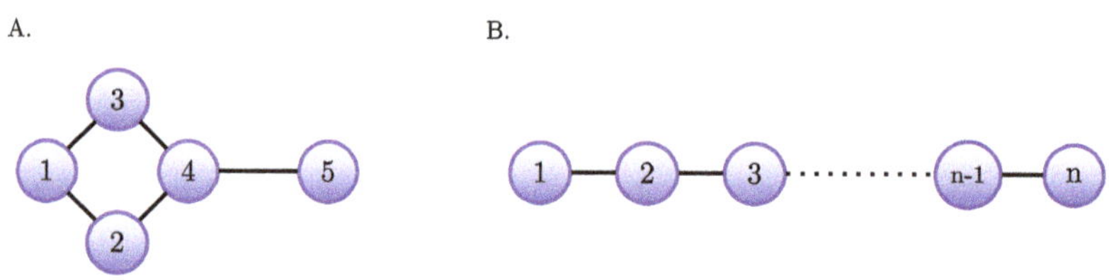

Figure 16.15: Calculating shortest paths in unweighted networks.

Another example when calculating shortest paths in unweighted networks gives the graph in B shown by Figure 16.15. The shown graph P_n is referred to as the *path graph* [186] with n vertices. We observe that there exist $n-1$ pairs of vertices with $d(u,v) = 1$, $n-2$ pairs of vertices with $d(u,v) = 2$, and so forth. Finally, we see that there exists only $n-(n-1) = 1$ pair with $d(u,v) = n-1$. Here, $d(u,v) = n-1$ is just the diameter of P_n.

In Listing 16.1, we shown an example how shortest paths can be found by using R. For this example, we use a small-world network with $n = 25$ nodes. The command *distances()* gives only the length of paths, whereas the command *shortest_paths()* provides one shortest path. In contrast, *all_shortest_paths()* returns all shortest paths.

Listing 16.1: Finding shortest paths with the Dijkstra's method

```
library(igraph)
n <- 25
g <- watts.strogatz.game(dim=1, size=n, nei=3, p=0.10)

distances(g, 1, to=V(g), algorithm="dijkstra") # only the length
shortest_paths(g, from=5, to=23) # gives one shortest path
all_shortest_paths(g, from=5, to=23) # gives all shortest path
```

16.4.4 Minimum spanning tree

In Section 16.5, we will provide Definition 16.5.1, formally introducing what a tree is. Informally, it is an acyclic and connected graph [94]. In this section, we discuss *spanning trees* and the *minimum spanning tree problem* [15, 38].

Suppose, we start with an undirected input graph $G = (V_G, E_G)$. A spanning tree $T = (V_T, E_T)$ of G is a tree, where $V_T = V_G$. In this case, we say that the tree T spans G, as the vertex set of the two graphs are the same and every edge of T belongs to G.

Figure 16.16 shows an input graph G with a possible spanning tree T. It is obvious, by definition, that there often exists more than one spanning tree of a given graph G. The problem of determining spanning trees gets more complex if we consider weighted networks. In case we start with an edge-labeled graph, one could determine the so-called minimum spanning tree [38]. This can be achieved by adding up the costs of all edge weights and, finally, searching for the tree with minimum cost among all existing spanning trees. Again, the minimum spanning tree for a given network is not unique. For instance, well-known algorithms to determine the minimum spanning tree are due to Prim and Kruskal, see, e. g., [38]. We emphasize that the application of those methods may result in different minimum spanning trees. Here, we just demonstrate Kruskal's algorithm [38] representing a greedy approach. Let $G = (V, E)$ be a connected graph with real edge weights. The main steps are the following:

– We arrange the edges according to their weights in ascending order

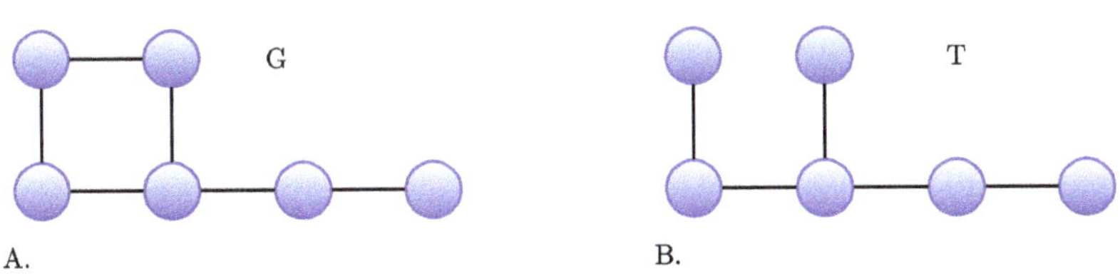

Figure 16.16: The graph G and a spanning tree T.

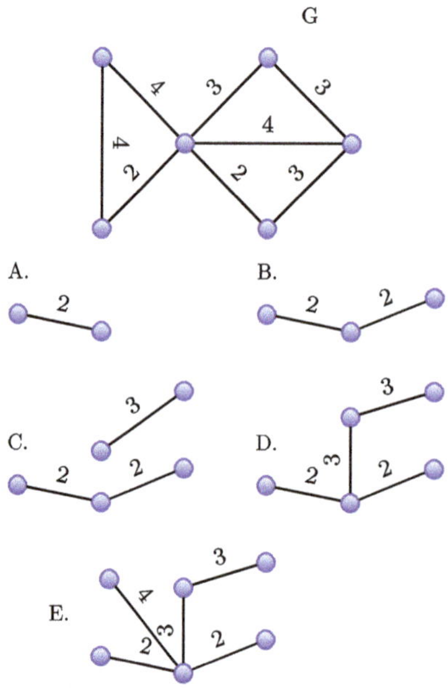

Figure 16.17: The input graph G and some subgraphs to achieve a minimum spanning tree in E.

- We add edges to the resulting minimum spanning tree as follows: we start with the smallest weight and end with the largest weight by consecutively adding edges according to their weight costs
- We only add the described edges if the process does not create a cycle

Figure 16.17 shows the sequence of steps when applying Kruskal's algorithm to the shown input graph G. We choose any subgraph with the smallest weight as depicted in situation A. In B, we choose the next smallest edge, and so on. We repeat this procedure according to the algorithmic steps above until it does not create a cycle. Note, intermediate trees can be disconnected (see C). One possible minimum spanning tree is shown in situation E. Differences between the algorithms due to Kruskal and Prim are explained in, e. g., [38].

In Listing 16.2, we shown an example how the minimum spanning tree can be found by using R. For this example, we use a small-world network with $n = 25$ nodes. The command *mst()* gives the underlying minimal spanning tree.

Listing 16.2: Minimum spanning tree

```
library(igraph)
n <- 25
g <- watts.strogatz.game(dim=1, size=n, nei=3, p=0.10)
mst(g)
```

16.5 Network models and graph classes

In this section, we introduce important network models and classes, which have been used in many disciplines [94, 25]. All of these models are characterized by specific structural properties.

16.5.1 Trees

We start with the formal definition of a tree [94], already briefly introduced in Section 16.4.4.

Definition 16.5.1. A *tree* is a graph $G = (V, E)$ that is connected and acyclic. A graph is acyclic if it does not contain any cycle.

In fact, there exist several characterizations for trees which are equivalent [100].

Theorem 16.5.1. *Let* $G = (V, E)$ *be a graph, and let* $|V| := N$. *The following assertions are equivalent:*

1. $G = (V, E)$ *is a tree.*
2. *Each two vertices of* G *are connected by a unique path.*
3. G *is connected, but for each edge* $e \in E$, $G \backslash \{e\}$ *is disconnected.*
4. G *is connected and has exactly* $N - 1$ *edges.*
5. G *is cycle free and has exactly* $N - 1$ *edges.*

Special types of trees are rooted trees [94]. Rooted trees often appear in graph algorithms, e. g., when performing a search or sorting [38].

Definition 16.5.2. A rooted tree is a tree containing one designated root vertex. There is a unique path from the root vertex to all other vertices in the tree, and all other vertices are directed away from the root.

Figure 16.18 presents a rooted tree, in which the root is at the very top of a tree, whereas all other vertices are placed on some lower levels. The tree in Figure 16.18 is an unordered tree, that means, the order of the vertices is arbitrary. For instance, the order of the green and orange vertex can be swapped.

Classes of rooted trees include ordered and binary-rooted trees [94].

Definition 16.5.3. An ordered tree is a rooted tree assigning a fixed order to the children of each vertex.

Definition 16.5.4. A binary tree is an ordered tree, where each vertex has exactly two children.

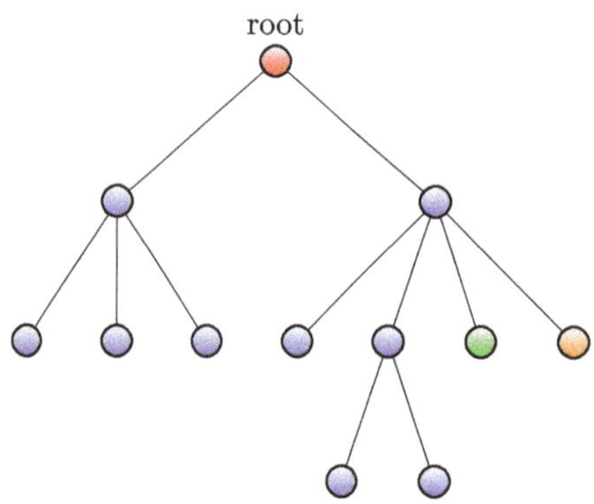

Figure 16.18: A rooted tree with its designated root vertex.

16.5.2 Generalized trees

Undirected and directed rooted trees can be generalized by so-called *generalized trees* [132, 51]. A generalized tree is also hierarchical like an ordinary rooted tree, but its edge set allows a richer connectivity among the vertices. Figure 16.19 shows an undirected generalized tree with four levels, including the root level.

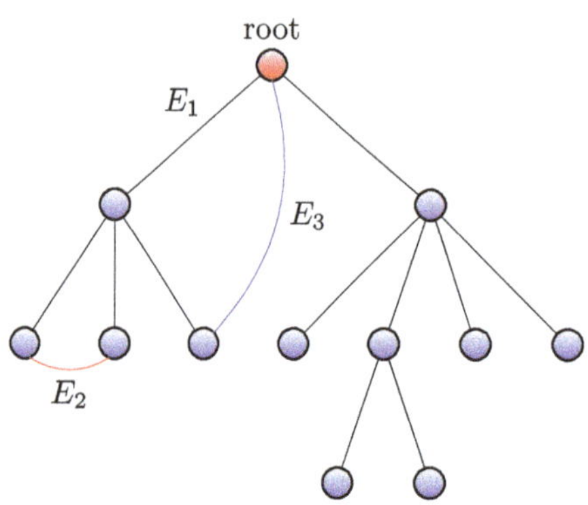

Figure 16.19: A generalized tree.

We now give a formal definition of an undirected generalized tree [63].

Definition 16.5.5. A generalized tree GT is defined by a vertex set V, an edge set E, a level set L, and a multilevel function $\mathcal{L}$. The edge set E will be defined in Definition 16.5.7. The vertex and edge set define the connectivity and the level set and the multilevel function induces a hierarchy between the nodes of GT. The index $r \in V$ indicates the root.

The multilevel function is defined as follows [63].

Definition 16.5.6. The function $\mathcal{L} : V \setminus \{r\} \to L$ is called a multilevel function.

The multilevel function $\mathcal{L}$ assigns to all nodes, except r, an element $l \in L$, which corresponds to the level they possess.

Definition 16.5.7. A generalized tree as defined by Definition 16.5.5 has three edges types [63]:
- Edges with $|\mathcal{L}(m) - \mathcal{L}(n)| = 1$ are called kernel edges (E_1).
- Edges with $|\mathcal{L}(m) - \mathcal{L}(n)| = 0$ are called cross edges (E_2).
- Edges with $|\mathcal{L}(m) - \mathcal{L}(n)| > 1$ are called up edges (E_3).

Note that for an ordinary rooted tree as defined by Definition 16.5.2, we always obtain $|\mathcal{L}(m) - \mathcal{L}(n)| = 1$ for all pairs (m, n). From the above given definitions and the visualization in Figure 16.19, it is clear that a generalized tree is a tree-like graph with a hierarchy, and may contain cycles.

16.5.3 Random networks

Random networks have also been studied in many fields, including computer science and network physics [183]. This class of networks are based on the seminal work of Erdös and Rényi, see [76, 77].

By definition, a random graph with N vertices can be obtained by connecting every pair of vertices with probability p. Then, the expected number of edges for an undirected random graph is given by

$$E(n) = p\frac{N(N-1)}{2}. \tag{16.19}$$

In what follows, we survey important properties of random networks [59]. For instance, the degree distribution of a vertex v_i follows a binomial distribution,

$$P(k_i = k) = \binom{N-1}{k} p^k (1-p)^{N-1-k}, \tag{16.20}$$

since the maximum degree of the vertex v_i is at most $N - 1$; in fact, the probability that the vertex has k edges equals $p^k(1-p)^{N-1-k}$ and there exist $\binom{N-1}{k}$ possibilities to choose k edges from $N - 1$ vertices.

Considering the limit $N \to \infty$, Equation (16.20) yields

$$P(k_i = k) \sim \frac{z^k \exp(-z)}{k!}. \tag{16.21}$$

We emphasize that $z = p(N - 1)$ is the expected number of edges for a vertex. This implies that if N goes to infinity, the degree distribution of a vertex in a random network can be approximated by the Poisson distribution. For this reason, random networks are often referred to as *Poisson random networks* [142].

In addition, one can demonstrate that the degree distribution of the whole random network also follows approximatively the following Poisson distribution:

$$P(X_k = r) \sim \frac{z^r \exp(-z)}{r!}. \tag{16.22}$$

This means that there exist $X_k = r$ vertices in the network that possess degree k [4].

As an application, we recall the already introduced clustering coefficient C_i, for a vertex v_i, represented by equation (16.9). In general, this quantity has been defined as the ratio $|E_i|$ of existing connections among its k_i nearest neighbors divided by the total number of possible connections. This consideration yields the following:

$$C_i = \frac{2|E_i|}{k_i(k_i - 1)}. \tag{16.23}$$

Therefore, C_i is the probability that two neighbors of v_i are connected with each other in a random graph, and $C_i = p$. This can be approximated by

$$C_i \sim \frac{z}{N}, \tag{16.24}$$

as the average degree of a vertex equals $z = p(N - 1) \sim pN$.

The two examples of random networks shown in Figure 16.20 can be generated using the following R code:

Listing 16.3: Generating random networks, see Figure 16.20

```
#Left graph
n <- 50
pc <- 0.01
la <- layout.circle(g)
g <- erdos.renyi.game(n, pc, type="gnp", directed = FALSE,
loops = FALSE)
plot(g, layout = la, vertex.color = "blue", vertex.size = 4,
     vertex.label = "")

#Right graph
n <- 50
pc <- 0.1
la <- layout.circle(g)
g <- erdos.renyi.game(n, pc, type="gnp", directed = FALSE,
loops = FALSE)
plot(g, layout = la, vertex.color = "blue", vertex.size = 4,
vertex.label = "")
```

16.5.4 Small-world networks

Small-world networks were introduced by Watts and Strogatz [198]. These networks possess two interesting structural properties. Watts and Strogatz [198] found that

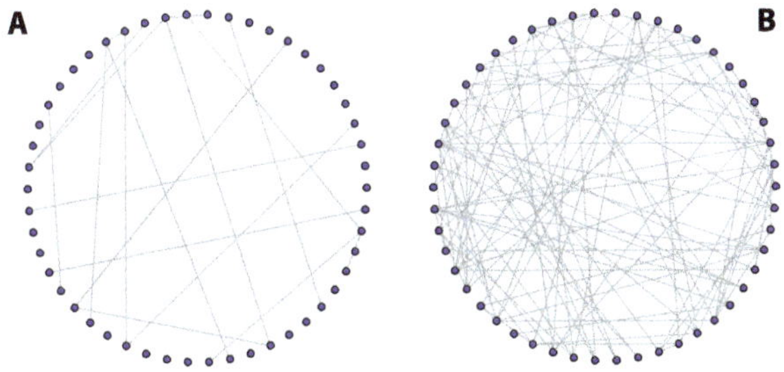

Figure 16.20: Random networks with $p = 0.01$ (left) and $p = 0.1$ (right).

small-world networks have a high clustering coefficient and also a short (average) distance among vertices. Small-world networks have been explored in several disciplines, such as network science, network biology, and web mining [190, 195, 203].

In the following, we present a procedure developed by Watts and Strogatz [198] in order to generate small-world networks.

- To start, all vertices of the graph are arranged on a ring and connect each vertex with its $k/2$ nearest neighbors. Figure 16.21 (left) shows an example using $k = 4$. For each vertex, the connection to its next neighbor (1st neighbor) is highlighted in blue and the connection to its second next neighbor (2nd neighbor) in red.
- Second, start with an arbitrary vertex i and rewire its connection to its nearest neighbor on, e. g., the right side with probability p_{rw} to any other vertex j in the network. Then, choose the next vertex in the ring in a clockwise direction and repeat this procedure.
- Third, after all first-neighbor connections have been checked, repeat this procedure for the second and all higher-order neighbors, if present, successively.

This algorithm guarantees that each connection occurring in the network is chosen exactly once and rewired with probability p_{rw}. Hence, the rewiring probability, p_{rw}, controls the disorder of the resulting network topology. For $p_{rw} = 0$, the regular topology is conserved, whereas $p_{rw} = 1$ results in a random network. Intermediate values $0 < p_{rw} < 1$ give a topological structure that is between these two extremes.

Figure 16.21 (right) shows an example of a small-world network generated with the following R code:

Listing 16.4: Generating the right random network in Figure 16.21

```
# Right
n <- 50
g <- watts.strogatz.game(dim=1, size=n, nei=2, p=0.10)
la <- layout.circle(g)
plot(g, layout = la, vertex.color = "blue", vertex.size = 4,
vertex.label="")
```

The generation of a small-world network by using the Watts–Strogatz algorithm consists of two main parts:

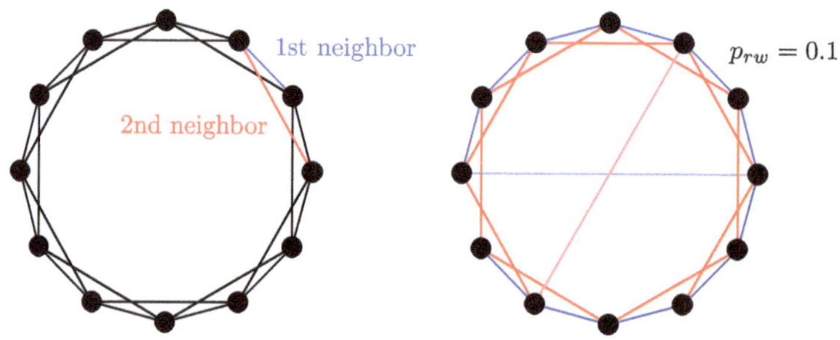

Figure 16.21: Small-world networks with $p_{rw} = 0.0$ (left) and $p_{rw} = 0.10$ (right). The two rewired edges are shown in light blue and red.

- First, the adjacency matrix is initialized in a way that only the nearest $k/2$ neighbor vertices are connected. The order of the vertices is arbitrarily induced by the labeling of the vertices from 1 to N. This allows identifying, e. g., $i + f$ as the fth neighbor of vertex i with $f \in \mathbb{N}$. For instance, $f = 1$ corresponds to the next neighbor of i. The module function is used to ensure that the neighbor indices f remain in the range of $\{1, \ldots, N\}$. Due to this fact the vertices can be seen as organized on a ring. We would like to emphasize that for the algorithm to work, the number of neighbors k needs to be an even number.
- Second, each connection in the network is tested once if it should be rewired with probability p_{rw}. To do this, a random number, c, between 0 and 1 is uniformly sampled and tested in an if-clause. Then, if $c \leq p_{rw}$, a connection between vertex i and $i + f$ is rewired. In this case, we need first to remove the old connection between these vertices and then draw a random integer, d, from $\{1, \ldots, N\} \setminus \{i\}$ to select a new vertex to connect with i. We would like to note that in order to avoid a self-connection of vertex i, we need to remove the index i from the set $\{1, \ldots, N\}$.

16.5.5 Scale-free networks

Neither random nor small-world network have a property frequently observed in real world networks, namely a scale-free behavior of the degrees [4],

$$P(k) \sim k^{-\gamma}. \tag{16.25}$$

To explain this common feature Barabási and Albert introduced a model [8], now known as Barabási–Albert (BA) or *preferential attachment* model [142]. This model results in so called *scale-free* networks, which have a degree distribution following a power law [8]. A major difference between the *preferential attachment* model and the other algorithms, described above, for generating random or small-world networks is that the BA model does not assume a fixed number of vertices, N, and then rewires them iteratively with a fixed probability, but in this model N grows. Each newly added vertex is connected with a certain probability (which is not constant) to other vertices already present in the network. The attachment probability defined by

$$p_i = \frac{k_i}{\sum_j k_j} \tag{16.26}$$

is proportional to the degree k_j of these vertices, explaining the name of the model. This way, each new vertex is added to $e \in \mathbb{N}$ existing vertices in the network.

Figure 16.22 presents two examples of random networks generated using the following R code:

Listing 16.5: Generating random networks, see Figure 16.22

```
# Left
n <- 200
g <- barabasi.game(n, m = 1, directed = FALSE)
la <-  layout.fruchterman.reingold(g)
plot(g, layout = la, vertex.color = "blue", vertex.size = 4,
     vertex.label = "")

# Right
n <- 1000
g <- barabasi.game(n, m = 1, directed = FALSE)
la <- layout.fruchterman.reingold(g)
plot(g, layout = la, vertex.color = "blue", vertex.size = 4,
vertex.label = "")
```

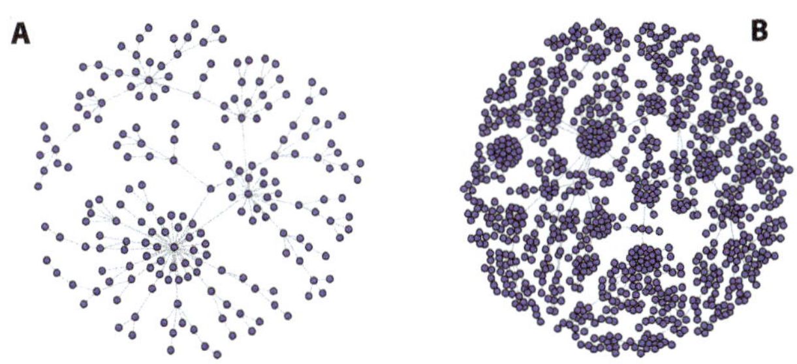

Figure 16.22: Scale-free networks with $n = 200$ (left) and $n = 1000$ (right).

16.6 Further reading

For a general introduction to graph theory, we recommend [88, 141]. For graph algorithms the book by [38] provides a cornucopia of useful algorithms that can be applied to many graph structures. An introduction to the usage of networks in biology, economics, and finance can be found in [67, 74]. As an initial reading about network science, the article [75] provides an elementary overview.

16.7 Summary

Despite the fact that graph theory is a mathematical subject, similar to linear algebra and analysis, it has a closer connection to practical applications. For this reason many real-world networks have been studied in many disciplines, such as chemistry, computer science, economy [64, 65, 143]. A possible explanation for this is provided by the intuitive representation of many natural networks, e. g., transportation networks of trains and planes, acquaintance networks between friends or social networks in twitter or facebook. Also many attributes of graphs, e. g., paths or the degrees of nodes, have a rather intuitive meaning. This motivates the widespread application of graphs and networks in nearly all application areas. However, we have also seen in this chapter that the analysis of graphs can be quite intricate, requiring a thorough understanding of the previous chapters.

16.8 Exercises

1. Let $G = V, E$ be a graph with $V = \{1, 2, 3, 4, 5\}$ and $E = \{\{1, 2\}, \{2, 4\}, \{1, 3\}, \{3, 4\}, \{4, 5\}\}$. Use R to obtain the following results:
   - Calculate all vertex degrees of G.
   - Calculate all shortest paths of G.
   - Calculate $\mathrm{diam}(G)$.
   - Calculate the number of circles of G.
2. Generate 5 arbitrary trees with 10 vertices. Calculate their number of edges by using R, and confirm $E = 10 - 1 = 9$ for all 5 generated trees.
3. Let $G = V, E$ be a graph with $V = \{1, 2, 3, 4, 5, 6\}$ and $E = \{\{1, 2\}, \{2, 4\}, \{1, 3\}, \{3, 4\}, \{4, 5\}, \{5, 6\}\}$. Calculate the number of spanning trees for the given graph, G.
4. Generate scale-free networks with the BA algorithm. Specifically, generate two different networks, one for $n = 1000$ and $m = 1$ and one for $n = 1000$ and $m = 3$. Determine for each network the degree distribution of the resulting network and compare them with each other.
5. Generate small-word networks for $n = 2500$. Determine the rewiring probability p_{rw} which separates small-word networks from random networks. Hint: Investigate the behavior of the clustering coefficient and the average shortest paths graphically.
6. Identify practical examples of generalized trees by mapping real-world observations to this graph structure. Are the directories in a computer organized as a tree or a generalized tree? Starting from your desktop and considering shortcuts, does this change this answer?

17 Probability theory

Probability theory is a mathematical subject that is concerned with probabilistic behavior of random variables. In contrast, all topics of the previous chapters in Part III were concerned with deterministic behavior of variables. Specifically, the meaning of a probability is a measure quantifying the likelihood that events will occur. This significant difference between a deterministic and probabilistic behavior of variables indicates the importance of this field for statistics, machine learning, and data science in general, as they all deal with the practical measurement or estimation of probabilities and related entities from data.

This chapter introduces some basic concepts and key characteristics of probability theory, discrete and continuous distributions, and concentration inequalities. Furthermore, we discuss the convergence of random variables, e. g., the law of large numbers or the central limit theorem.

17.1 Events and sample space

To learn about a phenomenon in science, it is common to perform an experiment. If this experiment is repeated under the same conditions, then it is called a *random experiment.* The result of an experiment is called an *outcome,* and the collection of all outcomes constitutes the *sample space*, Ω. A subset of the sample space, $A \subset \Omega$, is called an *event.*

Example 17.1.1. If we toss a coin once, there are two possible outcomes. Either we obtain a "head" (H) or a "tail" (T). Each of these outcomes is called an elementary event, ω_i (or a sample point). In this case, the sample space is $\Omega = \{H, T\} = \{(H), (T)\}$, or abstractly $\{\omega_1, \omega_2\}$. Points in the sample space $\omega \in \Omega$ correspond to an outcome of a random experiment, and subsets of the sample space, $A \subset \Omega$, e. g., $A = \{T\}$, are *events.*

Example 17.1.2. If we toss a coin three times, the sample space is $\Omega = \{(H, H, H), (T, H, H), (H, T, H), \ldots, (T, T, T)\}$, and the elementary outcomes are triplets composed of elements in $\{H, T\}$. It is important to note that the number of triplets in Ω is the total number of different combinations. In this case the number of different elements in Ω is $2^3 = 8$.

From the second example, it is clear that although there are only two elementary outcomes, i. e. H and T, the size of the sample space can grow by repeating such base experiments.

https://doi.org/10.1515/9783110796063-017

17.2 Set theory

Before we proceed with the definition of a probability, we provide some necessary background information about set theory. As highlighted in the examples above, a set is a basic entity on which the following rests on.

Definition 17.2.1. A set, A, containing no elements is called an *empty set*, and it is denoted by $\emptyset$.

Definition 17.2.2. If for every element $a \in A$ we also have $a \in B$, then A is a *subset* of B, and this relationship is denoted by $A \subset B$.

Definition 17.2.3. The *complement* of a set A with respect to the entire space Ω, denoted A^c or $\overline{A}$, is such that if $a \in A^c$, then $a \in \Omega$, but not in A.

There is a helpful graphical visualization of sets, called *Venn diagram*, that allows an insightful representation of set operations. In Figure 17.1 (left), we visualize the complement of a set A. In this figure, the entire space Ω is represented by the large square, and the set A is the inner circle (blue), whereas its complement $\overline{A}$ is the area around it (white). In contrast, in Figure 17.1 (right), the set A is the outer shaded area, and $\overline{A}$ is the inner circle (white).

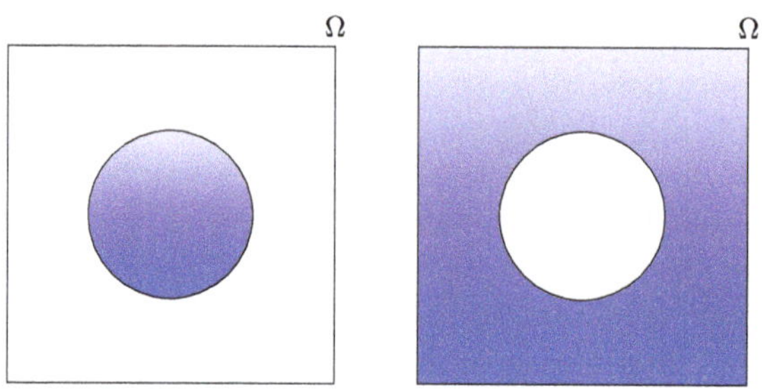

Figure 17.1: Visualization of a set A and its complement $\overline{A}$. Here $\Omega = A \cup \overline{A}$.

Definition 17.2.4. Two sets A and B are called *equivalent* if $A \subset B$ and $B \subset A$. In this case $A = B$.

Definition 17.2.5. The *intersection* of two sets A and B consists only of the points that are in A and in B, and such a relationship is denoted by $A \cap B$, i. e., $A \cap B = \{x \mid x \in A \text{ and } x \in B\}$.

Definition 17.2.6. The *union* of two sets A and B consists of all points that are either in A or in B, or in A and B, and this relationship is denoted by $A \cup B$, i. e., $A \cup B = \{x \mid x \in A \text{ or } x \in B\}$.

Figure 17.2 provides a visualization of the intersection (left) and the union (right) of two sets A and B.

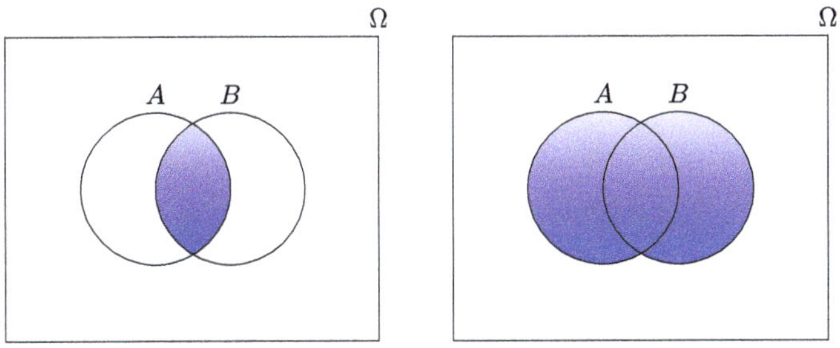

Figure 17.2: Venn diagrams of two sets. Left: Intersection of A and B, $A \cap B$. Right: Union of A and B, $A \cup B$.

Definition 17.2.7. The *set difference* between two sets, A and B, consists of the points that are only in A, but not in B, and this relationship is denoted by $A \setminus B$, i. e., $A \setminus B = \{x \mid x \in A \text{ and } x \notin B\}$.

Using R, the four aforementioned set operations can be carried out as follows:

Listing 17.1: Set operations

```
setequal(A, B)  #Equivalence
intersect(A, B) #Intersection
union(A, B)     #Union
setdiff(A, B)   #Difference
```

These commands represent the computational realization of the above Definitions 17.2.4 to 17.2.7, which describe the equivalence, intersection, union, and set difference of sets.

Theorem 17.2.1. *For three given sets A, B, and C, the following relations hold:*

1. *Commutativity:* $A \cup B = B \cup A$, *and* $A \cap B = B \cap A$.
2. *Associativity:* $A \cup (B \cup C) = (A \cup B) \cup C$, *and* $A \cap (B \cap C) = (A \cap B) \cap C$.
3. *Distributivity:* $A \cup (B \cap C) = (A \cup B) \cap (A \cup C)$, *and* $A \cap (B \cup C) = (A \cap B) \cup (A \cap C)$.
4. $(A^c)^c = A$.

For the complement of a set, a bar over the symbol is frequently used instead of the superscript "c", i. e., $\overline{A} = A^c$.

Definition 17.2.8. Two sets A_1 and A_2 are called *mutually exclusive* if the following holds: $A_1 \cap A_2 = \emptyset$.

If n sets A_i with $i \in \{1, \ldots, n\}$ are *mutually exclusive*, then $A_i \cap A_j = \emptyset$ holds for all i and j with $i \neq j$.

Theorem 17.2.2 (De Morgan's Laws). *For two given sets, A and B, the following relations hold:*

$$\overline{(A \cup B)} = \overline{A} \cap \overline{B}, \tag{17.1}$$

$$\overline{(A \cap B)} = \overline{A} \cup \overline{B}. \tag{17.2}$$

From, the above relationship, a negation of a union leads to an intersection, and vice versa. Therefore, De Morgan's Laws provides a mean for interchanging a union and an intersection via an application of a negation.

17.3 Definition of probability

The definition of a probability is based on the following three axioms introduced by Kolmogorov [48]:

Axiom 17.3.1. For every event A,

$$\Pr(A) \geq 0. \tag{17.3}$$

Axiom 17.3.2. For the sample space Ω,

$$\Pr(\Omega) = 1. \tag{17.4}$$

Axiom 17.3.3. For every infinite set of independent events $\{A_1, \ldots, A_\infty\}$,

$$\Pr(A_1 \cup A_2 \cup \ldots A_\infty) = \sum_{i=1}^{\infty} \Pr(A_i). \tag{17.5}$$

Definition 17.3.1. We call $\Pr(A)$ a *probability of event A* if it fulfills all the three axioms above.

Such a probability is also called a *probability measure* on sample space Ω. For clarity, we repeat that Ω contains the outcomes of all possible events. There are different conventions to denote such a probability and frequent choices are "Pr" or "P". In the following we use for brevity the latter one.

These three axioms form the basis of probability theory, from which all other properties can be derived.

From the definition of a probability and the three above axioms, follow a couple of useful identities, including:

1. If $A \subset B$, then $P(A) \leq P(B)$.
2. For every event A, $0 \leq P(A) \leq 1$.
3. For every event A, $P(A^c) = 1 - P(A)$.
4. $P(\emptyset) = 0$.

5. For every finite set of disjoint events $\{A_1, \dots, A_k\}$,

$$P(A_1 \cup A_2 \cup \dots A_k) = \sum_{i=1}^{k} P(A_i). \tag{17.6}$$

6. For two events A and B,

$$P(A \cup B) = P(A) + P(B) - P(A \cap B). \tag{17.7}$$

Probabilities are called *coherent* if they obey the rules from the three axioms above. Examples for the contrary will be given below.

We would like to note that the above definition of probability does not give a description about how to quantify it. Classically, Laplace provided such a quantification for *equiprobable elementary outcomes*, i. e., for $p(\omega_i) = 1/m$ for $\Omega = \{\omega_1, \dots, \omega_m\}$. In this case, the probability of an event A is given by the number of elements in A divided by the total number of possible events, i. e., $p(A) = |A|/m$. In practice, not all problems can be captured by this approach, because usually the probabilities, $p(\omega_i)$, are not equiprobable. For this reason a frequentist quantification or a Bayesians quantification of probability, which hold for general probability values, is used [91, 161].

17.4 Conditional probability

Definition 17.4.1 (Conditional probability). For two events A and B with $P(B) > 0$, the conditional probability of A, given B, is defined by

$$P(A|B) = \frac{P(A \cap B)}{P(B)}. \tag{17.8}$$

In the case $P(B) = 0$, the conditional probability $P(A|B)$ is not defined.

Definition 17.4.2 (Partition of the sample space). Suppose that the events $\{A_1, \dots, A_k\}$ are disjoint, i. e., $A_i \cap A_j = \emptyset$ for all i, and $j \in \{1, \dots, k\}$ and $\Omega = A_1 \cup \dots \cup A_k$. Then, the sets $\{A_1, \dots, A_k\}$ form a partition of the sample space Ω.

Theorem 17.4.1 (Law of total probability). *Suppose that the events $\{B_1, \dots, B_k\}$ are disjoint and form a partition of the sample space Ω and $P(B_i) > 0$. Then, for an event $A \in \Omega$,*

$$P(A) = \sum_{i=1}^{k} P(A|B_i)P(B_i). \tag{17.9}$$

Proof. From the identity

$$A = A \cap \Omega \tag{17.10}$$

we have

$$A = A \cap (B_1 \cup \cdots \cup B_k), \tag{17.11}$$

since $\{B_1, \ldots, B_k\}$ is a partition of Ω.

From De Morgan's Laws, it follows that

$$A = (A \cap B_1) \cup \cdots \cup (A \cap B_k). \tag{17.12}$$

Since every pair of terms in equation (17.12) is disjoint, i. e., $(A \cap B_i) \cap (A \cap B_j) = \emptyset$, because of $A \cap (B_i \cap B_j) = A \cap \emptyset = \emptyset$, the probability expression in equation (17.12) can be deduced as follows:

$$\begin{aligned} P(A) &= P\big((A \cap B_1) \cup \cdots \cup (A \cap B_k)\big) && (17.13)\\ &= P(A \cap B_1) + \cdots + P(A \cap B_k) && (17.14)\\ &= P(A|B_1)P(B_1) + \cdots + P(A|B_k)P(B_k) && (17.15)\\ &= \sum_{i=1}^{k} P(A|B_i)P(B_i). && (17.16) \end{aligned}$$

□

17.5 Conditional probability and independence

The definition of joint probability and conditional probability allows us to connect two or more events. However, the question is, when are two events said to be independent? This is specified in the next definition.

Definition 17.5.1. Two events A and B are called *independent*, or *statistically independent*, if one of the following conditions hold:
1. $P(AB) = P(A)P(B)$
2. $P(A|B) = P(A)$ if $P(B) > 0$
3. $P(B|A) = P(B)$ if $P(A) > 0$

Theorem 17.5.1. *If two events A and B are independent, then the following statements hold:*
1. *A and $\overline{B}$ are independent*
2. *$\overline{A}$ and B are independent*
3. *$\overline{A}$ and $\overline{B}$ are independent*

The extension to more than two events deserves attention, because it requires independence among all subsets of the events.

Definition 17.5.2. The n events $A_1, A_2, \dots, A_n \in \mathcal{A}$ are called *independent* if the following condition holds for all subsets I of $\{1, \dots, n\}$:

$$P(A_1, \dots, A_n) = \prod_{i \in I} P(A_i). \tag{17.17}$$

17.6 Random variables and their distribution function

Definition 17.6.1. For a given sample space Ω, a *random variable* X is a function that assigns to each event $A \in \Omega$ a real number, i. e., $X(A) = x \in \mathbb{R}$ with $X : \Omega \to \mathbb{R}$. The codomain of the function X is $C = \{x \mid x = X(A), A \in \Omega\} \subset \mathbb{R}$.

In the above definition, we emphasized that a random variable is a function, assigning real numbers to events. For brevity this is mostly neglected when one speaks about random variables. However, it should not be forgotten.

Furthermore, we want to note that the probability function has not been used explicitly in the definition. However, it can be used to connect a random variable to the probability of an event. For example, given a random variable X and a subset of its codomain $S \subset C$, we obtain

$$P(X \in S) = P(\{a \in \Omega \mid X(a) \in S\}), \tag{17.18}$$

since $\{a \in \Omega \mid X(a) \in S\} \subset \Omega$.

Similarly, for a single element $S = x$, we obtain

$$P(X = x) = P(\{a \in \Omega \mid X(a) = x\}). \tag{17.19}$$

In this way, the probability values for events are clearly defined.

Definition 17.6.2. The *cumulative distribution function* of a random variable X is a function $F_X : \mathcal{R} \to [0, 1]$ defined by

$$F_X(x) = P(X \leq x). \tag{17.20}$$

In this definition, the right-hand side term is interpreted as in equation (17.18) and (17.19) by

$$P(X \leq x) = P(\{a \in \Omega \mid X(a) \leq x\}). \tag{17.21}$$

Frequently, a cumulative distribution function is just called a *distribution function*.

Example 17.6.1. Suppose that we have a fair coin and define a random variable by $X(H) = 1$ and $X(T) = 0$ for a probability space with $\Omega = \{H, T\}$. We can find a piecewise definition of the corresponding distribution function as follows:

$$F_X(x) = P(\{a \in \Omega \mid X(a) \leq x\}) = \begin{cases} P(\emptyset) = 0 & \text{for } x < 0; \\ P(\{T\}) = 1/2 & \text{for } 0 \leq x < 1; \\ P(\{T, H\}) = 1 & \text{for } x \geq 1. \end{cases} \quad (17.22)$$

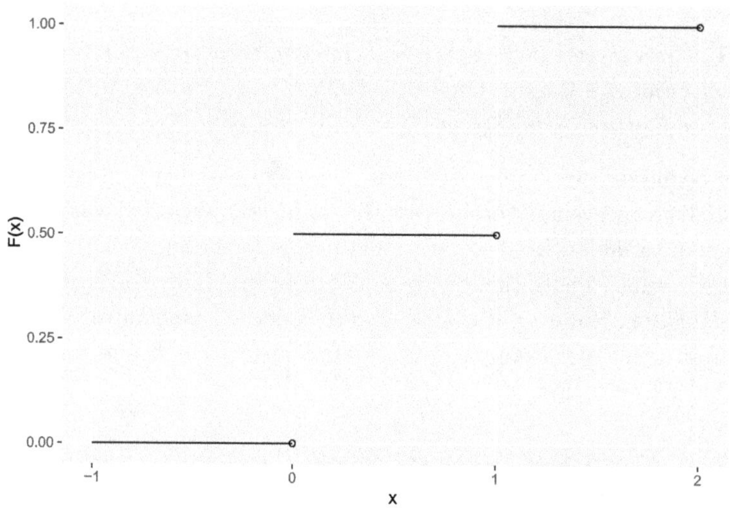

Figure 17.3: Distribution function $F(x)$ for equation (17.22).

The circle at the end of the steps in Figure 17.3 means that the end points are not included, but all points up to the end points themselves are. Mathematically, this corresponds to an open interval indicated by ")", e. g., $[0, 1)$ for the second step in Figure 17.3.

Theorem 17.6.1. *The cumulative distribution function, $F(x)$, has the following properties:*

1. $F(-\infty) = \lim_{x\to-\infty} F(x) = 0$ *and* $F(\infty) = \lim_{x\to\infty} F(x) = 1$;
2. $F(x+) = F(x)$ *is continuous from the right;*
3. $F(x)$ *is monotone and nondecreasing; if* $x_1 \leq x_2 \Rightarrow F(x_1) \leq F(x_2)$;
4. $P(X > x) = 1 - F(x)$;
5. $P(x_1 < x \leq x_2) = F(x_2) - F(x_1)$;
6. $P(X = x) = F(x) - F(x-)$;
7. $P(x_1 \leq x \leq x_2) = F(x_2) - F(x_1-)$.

17.7 Discrete and continuous distributions

From the connection between a random variable and its probability value, given by equation (17.18), we can now introduce the definition of discrete and continuous random variables as well as their corresponding distributions.

Definition 17.7.1. If a random variable, X, can only assume a finite number of different values, e. g., $x_1, \dots, x_n$, then X is called a *discrete random variable.* Furthermore, the collection, $P(X = x_i)$ for all $i \in \{1, \dots, n\}$, is called the discrete distribution of X.

Definition 17.7.2. Let X be a discrete random variable. The *probability function* of X, denoted $f(x)$, is defined for every real number, x, as follows:

$$f(x) = P(X = x). \tag{17.23}$$

Given these two definitions and the properties of probability values, it can be shown that the following conditions hold:
1. $f(x) = 0$, if x is not a possible value of the random variable X;
2. $\sum_{i=1}^{n} f(x_i) = 1$, if the x_i are all the possible values for the random variable X.

Definition 17.7.3. If a random variable, X, can assume an infinite number of values in an interval, e. g., between a and $b \in \mathbb{R}$, then X is called a *continuous random variable.* The probability of X being within an interval $[a, b]$ is given by the integral

$$P(a \leq X \leq b) = \int_a^b f(x)dx. \tag{17.24}$$

Here, the nonnegative function $f(x)$ is called the *probability density function* of X.

It can be shown that

$$\int_{-\infty}^{\infty} f(x)dx = 1. \tag{17.25}$$

It is important to note that the probability for a single point $x_0 \in \mathbb{R}$ is zero, because

$$P(x_0 \leq X \leq x_0) = \int_{x_0}^{x_0} f(x)dx = 0. \tag{17.26}$$

In Section 17.12, we will discuss some important continuous distributions. However, here we want to give an example for such a distribution.

17.7.1 Uniform distribution

The simplest continuous distribution is the *uniform distribution*. It has a constant density function within the range $[a,b]$, with $a,b \in \mathbb{R}$, and it is defined by

$$f(x) = \begin{cases} \frac{1}{b-a} & \text{if } x \in [a,b]; \\ 0 & \text{otherwise.} \end{cases} \quad (17.27)$$

The notation $\text{Unif}([a,b])$ is often used to denote a uniform distribution in the interval $[a,b]$.

17.8 Expectation values and moments

In the previous sections, we discussed discrete and continuous distributions for random variables. In principle, such distributions contain all information about a random variable X. Practically, there are specific properties of such distributions that are of great importance, and these are related to *expectation values*.

17.8.1 Expectation values

The following definition specifies what is meant by an expectation value of a random variable.

Definition 17.8.1. The *expectation value* of a random variable X, denoted $\mathbb{E}[X]$, is defined by

$$\mathbb{E}[X] = \sum_i x_i f(x_i), \quad \text{for a discrete random variable } X, \quad (17.28)$$

$$\mathbb{E}[X] = \int x f(x) dx, \quad \text{for a continuous random variable } X. \quad (17.29)$$

The expectation value of X is also called the *mean* of X.

A generalization of the above definition can be given, leading to the expectation value of a function $g(X)$ for a random variable X:

$$\mathbb{E}[g(X)] = \sum_i g(x_i) f(x_i), \quad \text{for a discrete random variable } X, \quad (17.30)$$

$$\mathbb{E}[g(X)] = \int g(x) f(x) dx, \quad \text{for a continuous random variable } X. \quad (17.31)$$

From the definition of the expectation values of a random variable follows several important properties that hold for discrete and continuous random variables.

Theorem 17.8.1. *Suppose that X and $X_1, \dots, X_n$ are random variables. Then the following results hold:*

$$\mathbb{E}[Y] = a\mathbb{E}[X] + b, \tag{17.32}$$

for $Y = aX + b$, with a and b finite constants in $\mathbb{R}$.

$$\mathbb{E}[X_1 + \dots + X_n] = \sum_{i=1}^{n} \mathbb{E}[X_i]. \tag{17.33}$$

If $X_1, \dots, X_n$ are independent random variables and $\mathbb{E}[X_i]$ is finite for every i, then

$$\mathbb{E}\left[\prod_{i=1}^{n} X_i\right] = \prod_{i=1}^{n} \mathbb{E}[X_i]. \tag{17.34}$$

17.8.2 Variance

An important special case for an expectation value of a function is given by

$$g(x) = (X - \mu)^2 \tag{17.35}$$

with $\mu = \mathbb{E}[X]$. In this case, we write

$$\mathrm{Var}(X) = \mathbb{E}\big[g(x)\big] = \mathbb{E}\big[(X - \mu)^2\big]. \tag{17.36}$$

Due to the importance of this expression, it has its own name. It is called the *variance* of X. If the mean of X, μ, is not finite, or if it does not exist, then $\mathrm{Var}(X)$ does not exist.

There is a related measure, called the *standard deviation*, which is just the square root of the variance of X, denoted $sd(X) = \sqrt{\mathrm{Var}(X)}$. Frequently, the Greek symbol σ^2 is used to denote the variance, i. e.,

$$\sigma^2(X) = \mathrm{Var}(X). \tag{17.37}$$

In this case, the standard deviation assumes the form, $sd(X) = \sqrt{\mathrm{Var}(X)} = \sigma$.

The variance has the following properties:

1. For $Y = a + bX$: $\mathrm{Var}(Y) = b^2\,\mathrm{Var}(X)$.
2. If $X_1, \dots, X_n$ are independent random variables: $\mathrm{Var}(X_1 + \dots + X_n) = \mathrm{Var}(X_1) + \dots + \mathrm{Var}(X_n)$.
3. If $\bar{X} = \frac{1}{n}\sum_{i=1}^{n} X_i$ and $\mathrm{Var}(X_i) = \mathrm{Var}(X)$ for all i: $\mathrm{Var}(\bar{X}) = \frac{\mathrm{Var}(X)}{n}$.

Property (3) has important practical implications, because it says that the variance of the mean of a sample of size n for random variables that have all the same variance has a variance that is reduced by the factor $1/n$. If we take the square root of $\mathrm{Var}(\bar{X}) = \frac{\mathrm{Var}(X)}{n}$, we get the standard deviation of $\bar{X}$ given by

$$SE = sd(\bar{X}) = \frac{sd(X)}{\sqrt{n}}. \tag{17.38}$$

This is another important quantity called the *standard error* (SE).

A frequent error observed in applications is the usage of $sd(X)$ when the standard error, SE, should be used. For instance, if one performs a repeated analysis leading to ten error measures, E_i for $i \in \{1, \ldots, 10\}$, e. g., when performing a 10-fold cross validation [68], one is interested in the standard error of $E_{\text{tot}} = \frac{1}{10}\sum_{i=1}^{10} E_i$, and not in the variance of the individual errors E_i.

17.8.3 Moments

Along the same principle, as for the definition of the variance of a random variable X, one can define further expectation values.

Definition 17.8.2. For a random variable X and a function

$$g(x) = (X - \mu), \tag{17.39}$$

with $\mu = \mathbb{E}[X]$, the kth *central moment* of X, denoted m'_k, is defined by

$$m'_k = \mathbb{E}[g(x)^k] = \mathbb{E}[(X - \mu)^k]. \tag{17.40}$$

For $k = 2$, the central moment of X is just the variance of X. Analogously, one defines the kth *moment* of a random variable.

Definition 17.8.3. For a random variable X and a function

$$g(x) = X, \tag{17.41}$$

the kth *moment* of X, denoted m_k, is defined by

$$m_k = \mathbb{E}[g(x)^k] = \mathbb{E}[X^k]. \tag{17.42}$$

17.8.4 Covariance and correlation

The covariance between two random variables X and Y is defined by

$$\mathrm{Cov}(X, Y) = \mathbb{E}[(X - \mathbb{E}[X])(Y - \mathbb{E}[Y])]. \tag{17.43}$$

The covariance has the following important properties:

1. Symmetry: $\mathrm{Cov}(X, Y) = \mathrm{Cov}(Y, X)$;
2. If $Y = a + bX$: $\mathrm{Cov}(X, Y) = b\,\mathrm{Var}(X)$;
3. $\mathrm{Cov}(X, Y) \leq \sqrt{\mathrm{Var}(X)\,\mathrm{Var}(Y)}$.

Definition 17.8.4. The linear *correlation*, often referred to as simply correlation, between two random variables X and Y is defined by

$$\mathrm{Cor}(X, Y) = \mathbb{E}\big[\big(X - \mathbb{E}[X]\big)\big(Y - \mathbb{E}[Y]\big)\big] / \sqrt{\mathrm{Var}(X)\,\mathrm{Var}(Y)} \tag{17.44}$$

$$= \mathrm{Cov}(X, Y) / \sqrt{\mathrm{Var}(X)\,\mathrm{Var}(Y)}. \tag{17.45}$$

The linear correlation has the following properties:

1. It is normalized: $-1 \leq \mathrm{Cor}(X, Y) \leq 1$;
2. $\mathrm{Cov}(X, Y) \leq \sqrt{\mathrm{Var}(X)\,\mathrm{Var}(Y)}$.

We call X and Y positively correlated if $\mathrm{Cor}(X, Y) > 0$, and negatively correlated if $\mathrm{Cor}(X, Y) < 0$. When $\mathrm{Cor}(X, Y) = 0$, X and Y are said to be linearly uncorrelated. Frequently, the correlation is denoted by the Greek letter $\rho(X, Y) = \mathrm{Cor}(X, Y)$.

The above correlation has been introduced by Karl Pearson. For this reason it is also called Pearson's correlation coefficient.

17.9 Bivariate distributions

Now we generalize the distribution of one random variable to the joint distribution of two random variables.

Definition 17.9.1 (Discrete joint distributions). The *joint cumulative distribution function* $F : \mathbb{R}^2 \to [0, 1]$ for the discrete random variables X and Y is given by

$$F(x, y) = P(X \leq x \text{ and } Y \leq y). \tag{17.46}$$

The corresponding *joint probability function* $f : \mathbb{R}^2 \to [0, 1]$ is given by

$$f(x, y) = P(X = x \text{ and } Y = y). \tag{17.47}$$

Theorem 17.9.1. *Let X and Y be two discrete random variables with joint probability function $f(x, y)$. If (x_a, y_a) is not in the definition range of (X, Y), then $f(x_a, y_a) = 0$. Furthermore*

$$\sum_{\forall\, i} f(x_i, y_i) = 1, \tag{17.48}$$

and

$$P\big((X,Y)\in Z\big)=\sum_{(x,y)\in Z} f(x,y). \tag{17.49}$$

For evaluating such a discrete joint probability function, the corresponding probabilities can be presented in a form of table. In Table 17.1, we present an example of a discrete joint probability function $f(x,y)$ with $X\in\{x_1,x_2\}$ and $Y\in\{y_1,y_2,y_3\}$.

Table 17.1: An example of a discrete joint probability function $f(x,y)$ with $X\in\{x_1,x_2\}$ and $Y\in\{y_1,y_2,y_3\}$.

		Y		
		y_1	y_2	y_3
X	x_1	$f(x_1,y_1)$	$f(x_1,y_2)$	$f(x_1,y_3)$
	x_2	$f(x_2,y_1)$	$f(x_2,y_2)$	$f(x_2,y_3)$

17.10 Multivariate distributions

For multivariate distributions, i. e., for $f(x_1,\dots,x_n)$ with $n>2$, the above definitions generalize naturally. However, the practical characterization of such distributions, e. g., in form of tables like Table 17.1 causes problems, because 3, 4, or 100-dimensional tables are not manageable. Fortunately, for random variables that have a dependency structure that can be represented by a directed acyclic graph (DAG), there is a simple representation.

By application of the chain rule, one can show that every joint probability distribution factorizes in the following way:

$$P(X_1,\dots,X_n)=\prod_{i=1}^{n} p\big(X_i|\operatorname{pa}(X_i)\big). \tag{17.50}$$

Here, $\operatorname{pa}(X_i)$ denotes the "parents" of variable X_i. In Figure 17.4 (left), we show an example for $n=5$. The joint probability distribution $P(X_1,\dots,X_5)$ factorizes in

$$P(X_1,\dots,X_5)=p(X_1)p(X_2)p(X_3|X_1)p(X_4|X_1,X_2)p(X_5|X_1,X_2). \tag{17.51}$$

Similarly, the joint probability distribution, for Figure 17.4 (right), can be written as follows

$$P(X_1,\dots,X_5)=p(X_1)p(X_2)p(X_3)p(X_4|X_1,X_2,X_3)p(X_5|X_4). \tag{17.52}$$

The advantage of such factorization is that the numerical specification of the joint probability distribution is distributed over the terms $p(X_i|\,\mathrm{pa}(X_i))$. Importantly, each of these terms can be represented by a simple table, similar to Table 17.1.

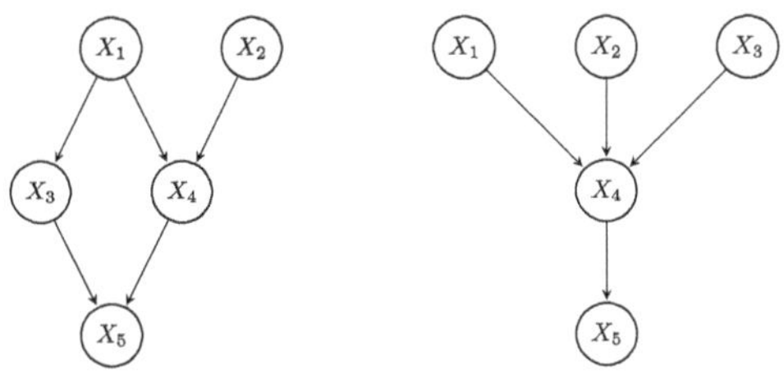

Figure 17.4: Examples of factorization of a joint probability distribution that can be represented by a DAG.

The shown DAGs in Figure 17.4, together with the factorizations of their joint probability distributions, are examples of so called *Bayesian networks* [149, 114]. Bayesian networks are special examples of probabilistic models called *graphical models* [116].

17.11 Important discrete distributions

In this section, we discuss some important distributions that arise from random variables that are discrete, which can be found frequently in data science applications. For example, flipping a coin or tossing a dice leads to discrete outcomes. In the case of a coin, we observe either a "head" or a "tail". For a dice, we observe different faces with the number 1 to 6 on them. In general, a random variable, X, has a discrete distribution if the sample space of X is either finite or countable. For convenience, in the following, we label these discrete values by integers. For instance, by defining "head" $= 1$ and "tail" $= 0$.

17.11.1 Bernoulli distribution

One of the most simple discrete distributions and yet very important is the Bernoulli distribution. For this distribution, the sample space consists of only two outcomes $\{0, 1\}$. The probabilities for these events are defined by

$$P(X = 1) = p, \tag{17.53}$$

$$P(X = 0) = 1 - p. \tag{17.54}$$

As a short notation, we write $X \sim \mathrm{Bern}(p)$ for a random variable, X, drawn from a Bernoulli distribution with parameter p. Hence, the symbol $\sim$ means "is drawn from" or "is sampled from". The R-package `Rlab` provides the Bernoulli distribution. With the help of the command *rbern*, we can draw 10 random variables from a distribution with $p = 0.5$.

Listing 17.2: Generate Bernoulli random variables

```
rbern(10, 0.5)
 [1] 1 1 0 1 0 1 1 1 1 0
```

An alternative is to use the *sample* command. Here it is important to sample with replacement.

Listing 17.3: Alternative way to sample from a Bernoulli distribution

```
sample(c(0,1), size=10, replace = TRUE, prob = c(0.5,0.5))
 [1] 1 0 0 0 0 1 0 0 1 0
```

A simple example for a discrete random variable with a Bernoulli distribution is a coin toss.

17.11.2 Binomial distribution

A Binomial distribution is based on Bernoulli distributed random variables. Suppose that we observe N independently drawn random variables $X_i \sim \text{Bern}(p)$ with $i \in \{1, \dots, N\}$ and $P(X_i = 1) = p$. Then the probability to observe n "1s" (e. g. heads) from the N tosses is given by

$$P(X = n) = \binom{N}{n} p^n (1-p)^{N-n}. \tag{17.55}$$

As a short notation, we write $X \sim \text{Binom}(N, p)$. For example, $\text{Binom}(6, 0.2)$ is obtained in R as shown in Listing 17.4.

Listing 17.4: Binomial distributions, see Figure 17.5

```
rbinom(10, size=6, prob=0.2)
 [1] 1 2 0 0 2 3 1 1 0 1
```

In Figure 17.5, we visualize two Binomial distributions with different parameter. Each bar corresponds to $P(X = n)$ for a specific value of n.

For $N \to \infty$ and large values of p, the Binomial distribution can be approximated by a normal distribution (discussed in detail in Sec. 17.12.4). In this case, one can set the mean value to $\mu = Np$, and the standard deviation to $\sigma = \sqrt{Np(1-p)}$ for the normal distribution. The advantage of such approximation is that the normal distribution is computationally easier to handle than the Binomial distribution. As

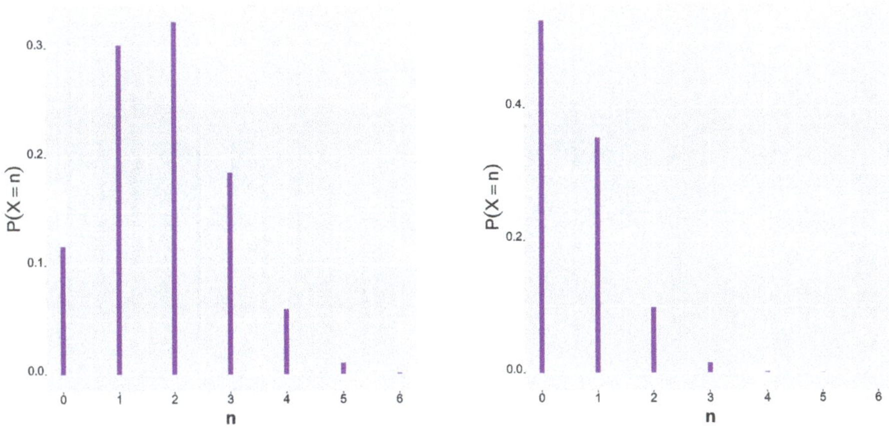

Figure 17.5: Binomial distribution, $\text{Binom}(N = 6, p = 0.3)$ (left) and $\text{Binom}(N = 6, p = 0.1)$ (right).

a rule of thumb, this approximation can be used if $Np(1 - p) > 9$. Alternatively, it can be used if $Np > 5$ (for $p \leq 0.5$) or $N(1 - p) > 5$ (for $p > 0.5$).

To illustrate how to generate figures such as Figure 17.5 (right), we provide below a listing, using `ggplot`, for producing such figure.

Listing 17.5: Plot for a Binomial distributions, see Figure 17.5 (right)

```
n <- 0:6
d <- dbinom(n, size=6, prob=0.3)

df <- data.frame(n = n, prob = d)
p <- ggplot(df, aes(x = n, y = prob))
p + geom_segment(aes(xend = n, yend = 0), size=4, color="blue") +
    ylab(expression(P(X == n))) + theme(axis.text.x =
    element_text(colour="grey20",size=10,face="plain"),
axis.text.y = element_text(colour="grey20", size=10, angle=0,
hjust=1, vjust=0, face="plain"),
axis.title.x = element_text(colour="grey20", size=15, angle=0,
    hjust=.5,
vjust=0, face="bold"),
axis.title.y = element_text(colour="grey20", size=15, angle=90,
    hjust=.5,
 vjust=.5, face="bold"))
 + theme(legend.position="none")
```

In the following, we do not provide the scripts for the visualizations of similar figures, but only for the values of the distributions. However, by following the example in Listing 17.5, such visualizations can be generated easily.

So far we have seen that `R` provides for each available distribution a function to sample random variables from this distribution, and a function to obtain the corresponding probability density. For the Binomial distribution, these functions

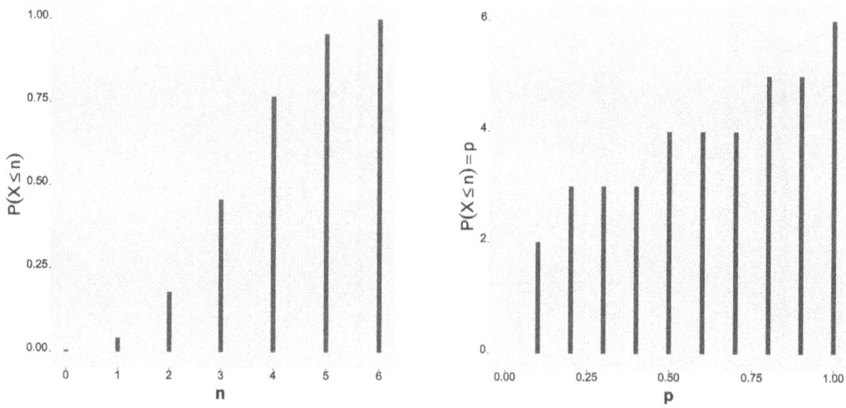

Figure 17.6: Binomial distribution, *pbinom(n,* `size`=*6,* `prob`=*0.6)* (left) and *qbinom(p,* `size`=*6,* `prob`=*0.6)* (right).

are called *rbinom* and *dbinom*. For other distributions, the following pattern for the names apply:

- `r'name-of-the-distribution'`: draw random samples from the distribution;
- `d'name-of-the-distribution'`: density of the distribution.

There are two more standard functions available that provide useful information about a distribution. The first one is the *distribution function*, also called cumulative distribution function, because it provides $P(X \leq n)$, i. e., the probability up to a certain value of n, which is given by

$$P(X \leq n) = \sum_{m=0}^{m=n} P(X = m). \tag{17.56}$$

The second function is the *quantile function*, which provides information about the value of n, for which $P(X \leq n) = p$ holds. In `R`, the names of these functions follow the pattern:

- `p'name-of-the-distribution'`: distribution function;
- `q'name-of-the-distribution'`: quantile function.

17.11.3 Geometric distribution

Suppose that we observe an infinite number of independent and identically distributed (iid) random variables $X_i \sim \text{Bern}(p)$. Then, the probability to observe in the first n consecutive observations a tail, is given by the geometric distribution defined by

$$P(X = n) = (1 - p)^n p. \tag{17.57}$$

For example, if we observe 0001... then the first $n = 3$ observations show consecutively tail, and the probability for this to happen is given by $P(X = 3) = (1 - p)^3 p$.

Using R, sampling from $X \sim \text{Geom}(p = 0.4)$ is obtained as shown in Listing 17.6.

Listing 17.6: Generation of Geometric random variables

```
rgeom(10, 0.4)
 [1] 0 0 7 5 2 2 9 0 0 0
```

17.11.4 Negative binomial distribution

Suppose that we observe an infinite number of independent and identically distributed random variables $X_i \sim \text{Bern}(p)$. Then the probability to observe n tails before we observe r "heads" is given by the negative binomial distribution, defined by

$$P(X = n) = \binom{r + n - 1}{n} p^r (1 - p)^n. \tag{17.58}$$

For instance, sampling from $X \sim \text{nbinom}(r = 6, p = 0.2)$ using R can be done as follows:

Listing 17.7: Generation of Negative Binomial random variables

```
rnbinom(10, size=6, prob=0.2)
 [1] 22 23 41 36 12 32 42 39 12 18
```

17.11.5 Poisson distribution

The Poisson distribution expresses the probability of a given number of independent events occurring in a fixed time interval. The Poisson distribution is defined by

$$P(X = n) = \frac{\lambda^n \exp(-\lambda)}{n!}. \tag{17.59}$$

For example, sampling from $X \sim \text{pois}(\lambda = 3)$ using R can be done as follows:

Listing 17.8: Generation of Poisson random variables

```
rpois(10, lambda = 3)
 [1] 1 4 2 4 3 1 2 1 4 5
```

Figure 17.7 provides some visualization of some Poisson distributions.

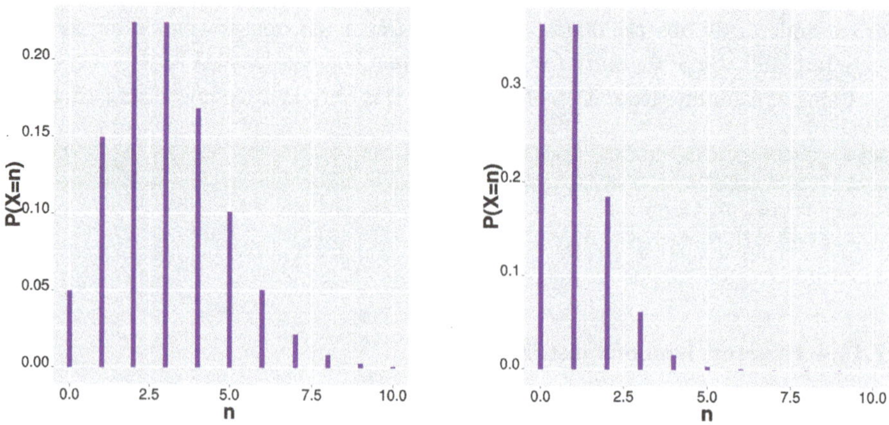

Figure 17.7: Poisson distribution, $\text{pois}(\lambda = 3)$ (left) and $\text{pois}(\lambda = 1)$ (right).

Listing 17.9: Poisson distribution, see Figure 17.7

```
n <- 0:10
d <- dpois(n, lambda = 3)    #Figure17.7 Left

d <- dpois(n, lambda = 1)    #Figure17.7 Right
```

It is worth noting that the Poisson distribution can be obtained from a Binomial distribution for $N \to \infty$ and $p \to 0$, assuming that $\lambda = Np$ remains constant. This means that for large N and small p we can use the Poisson distribution with $\lambda = Np$ to approximate a Binomial distribution, because the former is easier to handle computationally. Two rules of thumb say that this approximation is good if $N \geq 20$ and $p \leq 0.05$, or if $N \geq 100$ and $Np \leq 10$.

This approximation explains also why the Poisson distribution is used to describe rare events that have a small probability to occur, e. g., radioactive decay of chemical elements. Other examples of rare events include spelling errors on a book page, the number of visitors of a certain website, or the number of infections due to a virus.

17.12 Important continuous distributions

Similar to discrete distributions, there are also important continuous distributions, i. e. for continuous random variables, which will be discussed in the following.

17.12.1 Exponential distribution

The density or the probability function of the exponential distribution is defined by

$$f(x) = \begin{cases} \lambda \exp(-\lambda x) & \text{if } x \geq 0 \\ 0 & \text{otherwise.} \end{cases} \tag{17.60}$$

The parameter λ of the exponential distribution must be strictly positive, i. e., $\lambda > 0$.

Listing 17.10: Exponential distribution, see Figure 17.8

```
x <- seq(0,6,0.1)
d <- dexp(x, rate = 1)    #Figure17.8 Left

p <- pexp(x, rate = 1)    #Figure17.8 Right
```

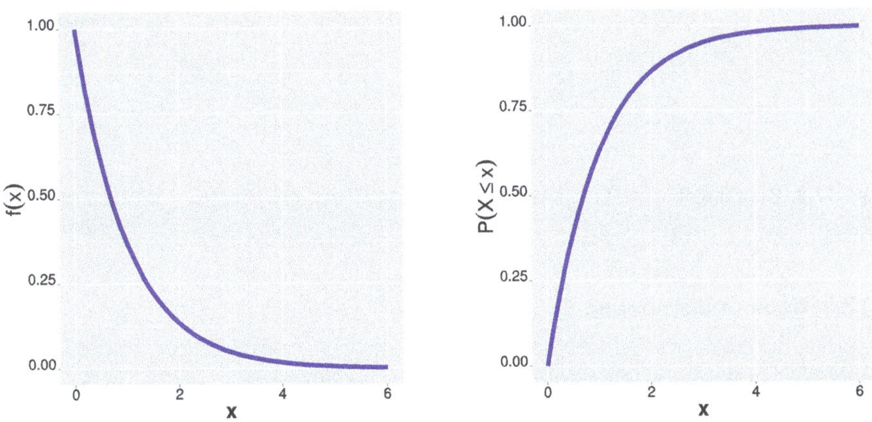

Figure 17.8: Exponential distribution. Left: dexp(rate = 1) (left) and pexp(rate = 1) (right).

17.12.2 Beta distribution

The density or the probability function of the Beta distribution is defined by

$$f(x) = \frac{1}{B(\alpha,\beta)} x^{\alpha-1}(1-x)^{\beta-1}, \quad x \in]0,1[. \tag{17.61}$$

In the denominator of the definition of the Beta distribution appears the *Beta function*, which is defined by

$$B(\alpha,\beta) = \int_0^1 x^{\alpha-1}(1-x)^{\beta-1} dx. \tag{17.62}$$

The parameters α and β in the Beta function must be strictly positive.

Listing 17.11: Beta distribution, see Figure 17.9

```
x <- seq(0.015, 0.985,length.out=1000)
d <- pbeta(x, shape1=1, shape2=3)  #Figure17.9 Left

p <- pbeta(x, shape1=1, shape2=3)   #Figure17.9 Right
```

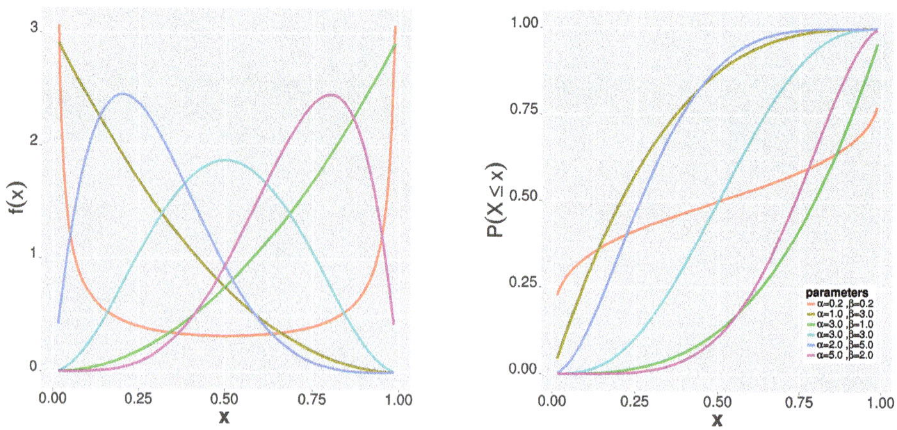

Figure 17.9: Beta distribution. Left: $\text{dbeta}(\alpha = 2, \beta = 2)$ (left) and $\text{pbeta}(\alpha = 2, \beta = 2)$ (right).

17.12.3 Gamma distribution

The density function of the gamma distribution is defined by

$$f(x) = \begin{cases} \frac{1}{\Gamma(\alpha)\beta^{\alpha}} x^{-\alpha-1} \exp(-x/\beta) & \text{if } x \geq 0 \\ 0 & \text{otherwise} \end{cases} \tag{17.63}$$

The parameters α and β must be strictly positive. In the denominator of the density appears the *gamma function*, Γ, which is defined as follows:

$$\Gamma(\alpha) = \int_{0}^{\infty} t^{\alpha-1} \exp(-t) dt. \tag{17.64}$$

Listing 17.12: Gamma distribution, see Figure 17.10

```
x <- seq(0,7.5,0.1)
d <- dgamma(x,shape = 1, rate = 2)  #Figure17.10 Left

p <- pgamma(x,shape = 1, rate = 2)   #Figure17.10 Right
```

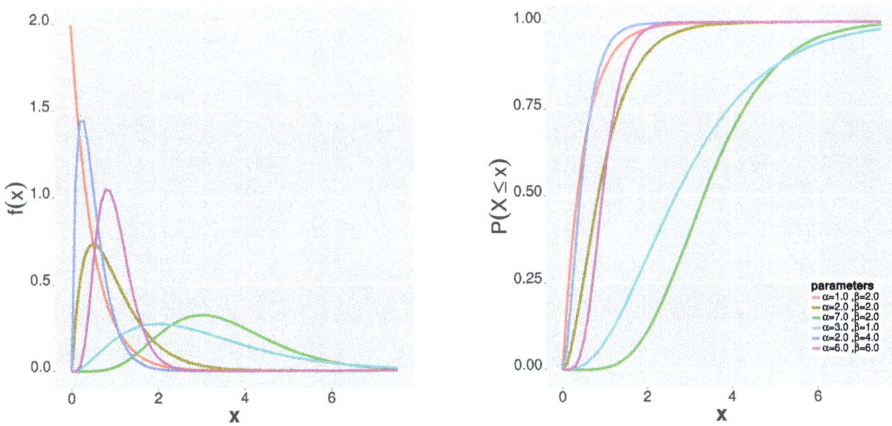

Figure 17.10: Gamma distribution. Left: $\text{dgamma}(\alpha = 2, \beta = 2)$ (left) and $\text{pgamma}(\alpha = 2, \beta = 2)$ (right).

17.12.4 Normal distribution

The normal distribution is the most important probability distribution in statistics, because it is the appropriate way to describe many natural phenomena. The normal distribution is also known as the Gaussian distribution or the bell-shape distribution.

17.12.4.1 One-dimensional normal distribution

The density function of the one-dimensional normal distribution is defined by

$$f(x) = \frac{1}{\sqrt{2\pi}\sigma} \exp\left(-\frac{(x-\mu)^2}{2\sigma^2}\right), \quad -\infty \leq x \leq \infty. \tag{17.65}$$

An important special case of the normal distribution is the standard normal distribution defined by

$$f(x) = \frac{1}{\sqrt{2\pi}} \exp\left(-\frac{x^2}{2}\right), \quad -\infty \leq x \leq \infty. \tag{17.66}$$

The standard normal distribution has a mean of 0, and a variance of 1.

Listing 17.13: One-dimensional normal distribution, see Figure 17.11

```
x <- seq(-10,10,0.1)
d <- dnorm(x, mean=0, sd=1/2) # Figure17.11 Left

d <- dnorm(x, mean=-1, sd=2)    # Figure17.11 Right
```

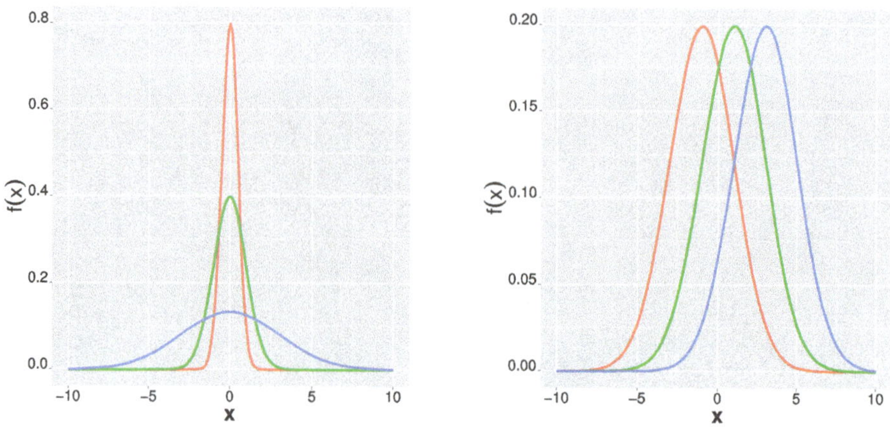

Figure 17.11: One-dimensional normal distribution. Left: Different values of $\sigma \in \{0.5, 1, 3\}$ for a constant mean of $\mu = 0$. Right: Different values of $\mu \in \{-1, 1, 3\}$ for a constant standard deviation of $\sigma = 2$.

17.12.4.2 Two-dimensional normal distribution

The density function of the normal distribution in $\mathbb{R}^2$ is defined by

$$f(x) = c \exp\left(-\frac{1}{2(1-\rho^2)}\left[\frac{(x_1-\mu_1)^2}{\sigma_1^2} + \frac{(x_2-\mu_2)^2}{\sigma_2^2} - 2\rho\frac{(x_1-\mu_1)(x_2-\mu_2)}{\sigma_1\sigma_2}\right]\right),$$
$$x = (x_1, x_2) \in \mathbb{R}^2, \tag{17.67}$$

whereas ρ is the correlation between X_1 and X_2 and the factor c is given by

$$c = \frac{1}{2\pi\sigma_1\sigma_2\sqrt{(1-\rho^2)}}. \tag{17.68}$$

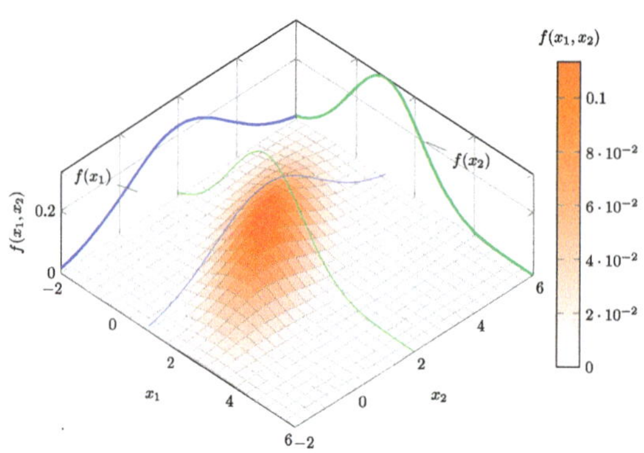

Figure 17.12: Two-dimensional normal distribution. In addition, projections on the x_1- and x_2-axis are shown presenting a perspective view.

A visualization of a two-dimensional normal distribution is shown in Figure 17.12. This figure shows also projections on the x_1- and x_2-axis resulting in one-dimensional projections. In contrast, Figure 17.13 shows a contour plot of this distribution. Such a plot shows parallel slices of the x_1–x_2 plane.

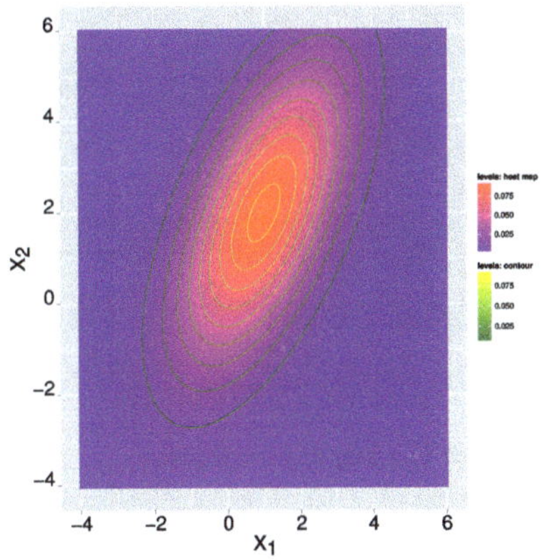

Figure 17.13: Two-dimensional normal distribution: heat map and contour plot.

17.12.4.3 Multivariate normal distribution

The density function of the multivariate normal distribution is defined by

$$f(x) = \frac{1}{\sqrt{(2\pi)^n|\Sigma|}} \exp\left(-\frac{(x-\mu)\Sigma^{-1}(x-\mu)^t}{2}\right), \quad x \in \mathbb{R}^n. \tag{17.69}$$

Here, $x \in \mathbb{R}^n$ is a n-dimensional random variable and the parameters of the density are its mean, $\mu \in \mathbb{R}^n$, and the $n \times n$ covariance matrix Σ. $|\Sigma|$ is the determinate of Σ. For $n = 2$, we obtain the two-dimensional normal distribution given in Eqn. (17.67).

17.12.5 Chi-square distribution

The density function of the chi-square distribution is defined by

$$f(x) = \frac{1}{2^{k/2}\Gamma(k/2)} x^{\frac{k}{2}-1} \exp\left(-\frac{x}{2}\right), \quad 0 \le x < \infty. \tag{17.70}$$

It is worth noting that for k iid random variables $X_i \sim N(0,1)$, $Y = \sum_{i+1}^{k} X_i^2$ follows a chi-square distribution with k degrees of freedom, $Y \sim \chi_k^2$.

Listing 17.14: Chi-square distribution – for one parameter pair, see Figure 17.14

```
x <- seq(0,30,0.1)
d1 <- dchisq(x, df=2)    #Figure17.14 Left
```

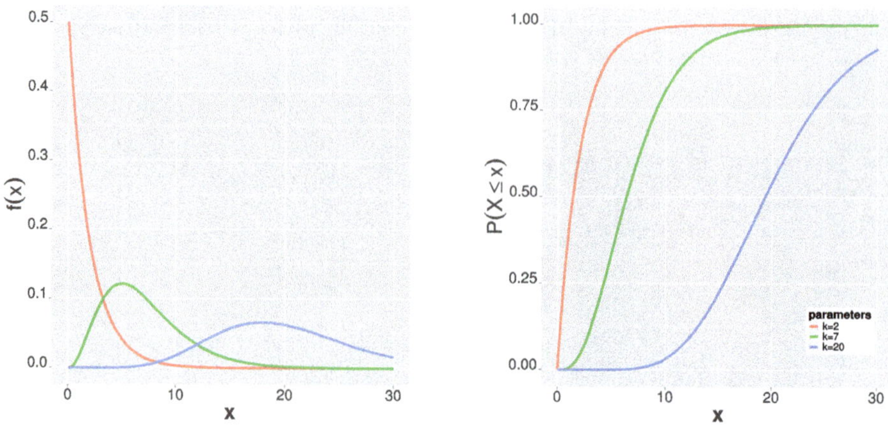

Figure 17.14: Chi-square distribution. Left: Different values of the degree of freedom $k \in \{2, 7, 20\}$. Right: Cumulative distribution function.

An example of the application of the Chi-square distribution is the sampling distribution for a Chi-square test, which is a statistical hypothesis test that can be used to study the variance or the distribution of data [171].

17.12.6 Student's t-distribution

The density function of the t-distribution with ν degrees of freedom is defined by

$$f(x) = \frac{\Gamma((\nu+1)/2)}{\sqrt{\nu\pi}\Gamma(\nu/2)} \left(1 + \frac{x^2}{\nu}\right)^{-\frac{\nu+1}{2}}, \quad -\infty \leq x \leq \infty. \tag{17.71}$$

Here ν can assume integer values.

If $Z \sim N(0, 1)$ and $Y \sim \chi^2_\nu$ (Chi-square distribution with ν degrees of freedom) are two independent random variables, then

$$X = \frac{Z}{\sqrt{\frac{Y}{\nu}}}, \tag{17.72}$$

follows a Student's t distribution, i. e., $X \sim t_\nu$.

Listing 17.15: Student's t-distribution – for one parameter pair, see Figure 17.15

```
x <- seq(-5,5,0.1)
d <- dt(x, df=2) #Figure17.15 Left
```

The Student's t-distribution is also used as a sampling distribution for hypothesis tests. Specifically, it is used for a t-test that can be used to compare the mean value

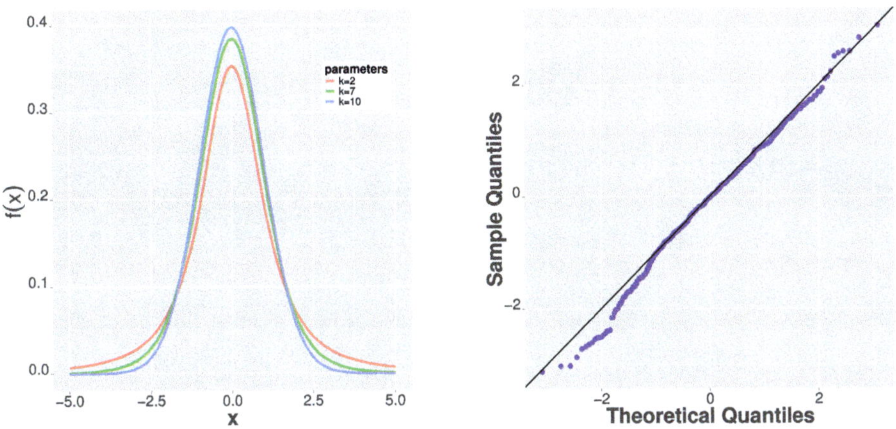

Figure 17.15: Student's t-distribution. Left: Different values of the degree of freedom $k \in \{2, 7, 20\}$. Right: QQnormal plot for t-distribution with $k = 100$.

of one or two populations, i. e., groups of measurements, each with a certain number of samples [171].

17.12.7 Log-normal distribution

The log-normal distribution is defined by

$$f(x) = \frac{1}{\sqrt{2\pi}\sigma x} \exp\left(-\frac{(\ln x - \mu)^2}{2\sigma^2}\right), \quad 0 < x < \infty. \tag{17.73}$$

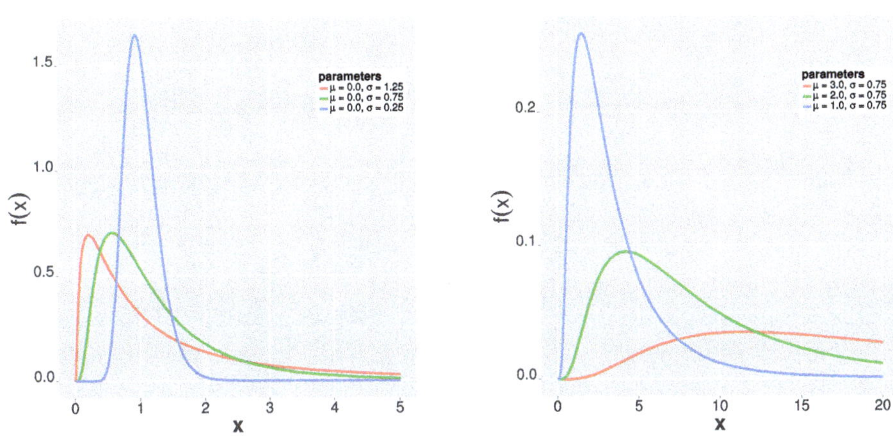

Figure 17.16: Log-normal distribution. Left: Constant $\mu = 0.0$ and varying $\sigma \in \{1.25, 0.75, 0.25\}$. Right: Constant $\sigma = 0.75$ and varying $\mu \in \{3.0, 2.0, 1.0\}$.

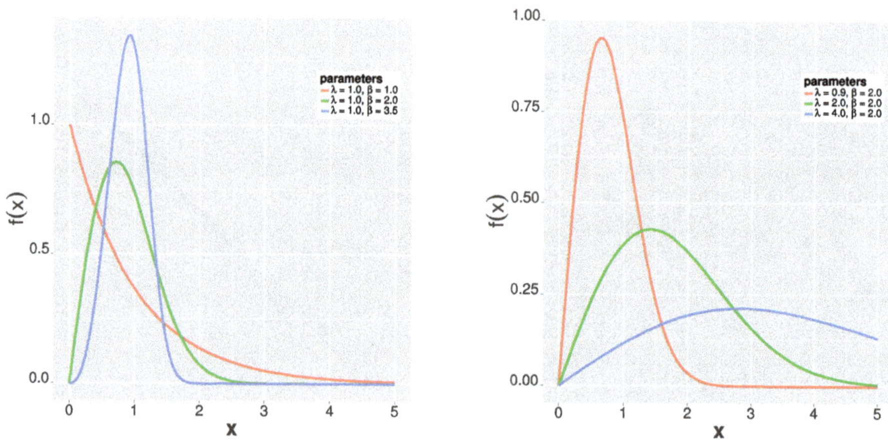

Figure 17.17: Weibull distribution. Left: Constant value of $\lambda = 1.0$ and varying $\beta \in \{1.0, 2.0, 3.5\}$. Right: Constant value of $\beta = 2.0$ and varying $\lambda \in \{0.9, 2.0, 4.0\}$.

The log-normal distribution, shown in Figure 17.16, has the following location measures:

$$\text{mean:} \quad \exp\left(\mu + \frac{\sigma^2}{2}\right), \tag{17.74}$$

$$\text{variance:} \quad \exp(2\mu + \sigma^2)\left(\exp(\sigma^2) - 1\right), \tag{17.75}$$

$$\text{mode:} \quad \exp(\mu - \sigma^2). \tag{17.76}$$

17.12.8 Weibull distribution

The Weibull distribution is defined by

$$f(x) = \frac{\beta}{\lambda}\left(\frac{x}{\lambda}\right)^{\beta-1} \exp\left(-\left(\frac{x}{\lambda}\right)^{\beta}\right), \quad 0 < x < \infty. \tag{17.77}$$

The Weibull distribution, shown in Figure 17.17, has the following location measures:

$$\text{mean:} \quad \lambda\Gamma(1 + 1/\beta), \tag{17.78}$$

$$\text{variance:} \quad \lambda^2\left[\Gamma(1 + 2/\beta) - \left(\Gamma(1 + 1/\beta)\right)^2\right], \tag{17.79}$$

$$\text{mode:} \quad \lambda\left(\frac{\beta - 1}{\beta}\right)^{1/\beta}, \quad \beta > 1, \tag{17.80}$$

where Γ denotes the *Gamma* function.

In biostatistics, the log-normal distribution and the Weibull distribution find their applications in survival analysis [112]. Specifically, these distributions are used as a parametric model for the baseline hazard function of a Cox proportional hazard model, which can be used to model time-to-event processes by considering covariates.

17.13 Bayes' theorem

The Bayes' theorem provides a systematic way to calculate the inverse for a given conditional probability [114]. For instance, if the conditional probability $P(D|H)$ for two events D and H is given, but we are interested in $P(H|D)$, which can be viewed as the inverse conditional probability of $P(D|H)$; and Bayes' theorem provides a way to achieve this.

In its simplest form, the *Bayes' theorem* can be stated as follows:

$$P(H|D) = \frac{P(D|H)P(H)}{P(D)}. \tag{17.81}$$

Its proof follows directly from the definition of conditional probabilities and the commutativity of the intersection.

The terms in the above equation have the following names:
- $P(H)$ is called the prior probability, or prior.
- $P(D|H)$ is called the likelihood.
- $P(D)$ is just a normalizing constant, sometimes called marginal likelihood.
- $P(H|D)$ is called the posterior probability or posterior.

The letters denoting the above variables, i. e., D and H, are arbitrary, but by using D for "data" and H for "hypothesis", one can interpret equation 17.81 as the change of the probability for a hypothesis (given by the prior) after considering new data about this hypothesis (given by the posterior).

Bayes' theorem can be generalized to more variables.

Theorem 17.13.1 (Bayes' theorem). *Let the events $B_1 \dots B_k$ be a partition of the space S such that $P(B_i) > 0$ for all $i \in \{1, \dots, k\}$ and $P(A) > 0$. Then, for $i \in \{1, \dots, k\}$, we have*

$$P(B_i|A) = \frac{P(A|B_i)P(B_i)}{\sum_{j=1}^{k} P(A|B_j)P(B_j)}. \tag{17.82}$$

To understand the utility of the Bayes' theorem, let us consider the following example: Suppose that a medical test for a disease is performed on a patient, and this test has a reliability of 90 %. That means, if a patient has this disease, the test will be positive with a probability of 90 %. Furthermore, assume that if the patient does not have the disease, the test will be positive with a probability of 10 %. Let us assume that a patient tests positive for this disease. What is the probability that this patient has this disease? The answer to this question can be obtained using Bayes' theorem.

In order to make the usage of Bayes' theorem more intuitive, we adopt the formulation in equation (17.82). Specifically, let us denote a positive test by $A = T^+$, a sick patient that has the disease (D) by $B_1 = D^+$, and a healthy patient that does not have the disease by $B_2 = D^-$. Then, equation (17.82) becomes

$$P(D^+|T^+) = \frac{P(T^+|D^+)P(D^+)}{P(T^+|D^-)P(D^-) + P(T^+|D^+)P(D^+)}. \tag{17.83}$$

Note that D^+ and D^- provide a partition of the sample space, because $P(D^+) + P(D^-) = 1$ (either the patient is sick or healthy). From the provided information about the medical test, see above, we can identify the following entities:

$$P(T^+|D^+) = 0.9, \tag{17.84}$$

$$P(T^+|D^-) = 0.1. \tag{17.85}$$

At this point, the following observation can be made: the knowledge about the medical test is not enough to calculate the probability $P(D^+|T^+)$, because we also need information about $P(D^+)$ and $P(D^-)$.

These probabilities correspond to the prevalence of the disease in the population and are independent from the characteristics of the performed medical test. Let us consider two different diseases: one is a common disease and one is a rare disease. For the common (c) disease, we assume $P_c(D^+) = 1/1000$, and for the rare (r) disease $P_r(D^+) = 1/1000000$. That means, for the common disease, one person from 1000 is, on average, sick, whereas, for the rare disease, only one person from 1000000 is sick. This gives us

$$\text{Common disease } P_c(D^+) = 1/10^3, P_c(D^-) = 1 - 1/10^3, \tag{17.86}$$

$$\text{Rare disease } P_r(D^+) = 1/10^6, P_r(D^-) = 1 - 1/10^6. \tag{17.87}$$

Using these numbers in equation (17.83) yields

$$\text{Common disease } P_c(D^+|T^+) = 0.0089, \tag{17.88}$$

$$\text{Rare disease } P_r(D^+|T^+) = 8.99 \cdot 10^{-6}. \tag{17.89}$$

It is worth noting that although the used medical test has the exact same characteristics, given by $P(T^+|D^+)$ and $P(T^+|D^-)$ (see equation (17.84) and (17.85)), the resulting probabilities are different from each other. More precisely,

$$P_c(D^+|T^+) = 991.1 \cdot P_r(D^+|T^+), \tag{17.90}$$

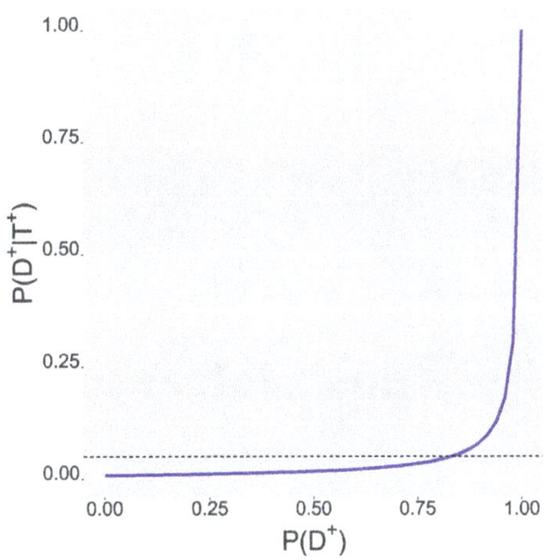

Figure 17.18: $P(D^+|T^+)$ as a function of the prevalence probability $P(D^+)$ for a common disease. The horizontal lines corresponds to 5 %.

which makes it almost 1000 times more likely to suffer from the common disease than the rare disease, if tested positive.

The above example demonstrates that the *context*, as provided by $P(D^+)$ and $P(D^-)$, is crucial in order to obtain a sensible result.

Finally, in Figure 17.18, we present some results for repeated analysis of the above example, using different values for $P(D^+)$ from the full range of possible prevalence probabilities, i. e., from $[0, 1]$. We can see that for any probability value of $P(D^+)$ below 80 %, the probability to have a disease, if tested positive, is always below 5 %. Furthermore, we can see that the functional relation between $P(D^+)$ and $P(D^+|T^+)$ is strongly nonlinear. Such a functional behavior makes it difficult to make good guesses for the values of $P(D^+|T^+)$ without doing the underlying mathematics properly.

After this example, demonstrating the use of the Bayes' theorem, we will now provide the proof of the theorem.

Proof. From the definition of a conditional probability for two events A and B,

$$P(A|B) = \frac{P(A \cap B)}{P(B)}, \tag{17.91}$$

follows the identity

$$P(A \cap B_i) = P(B_i|A)P(A) = P(A|B_i)P(B_i), \tag{17.92}$$

since $P(A \cap B_i) = P(B_i \cap A)$.

Rearranging equation (17.92) leads to

$$P(B_i|A) = \frac{P(A|B_i)P(B_i)}{P(A)}. \tag{17.93}$$

Using the law of total probability and assuming that $\{B_1, \ldots, B_k\}$ is a partition of the sample space, we can write

$$P(A) = \sum_{j=1}^{k} P(A|B_j)P(B_j). \tag{17.94}$$

Substituting this in equation (17.93) gives

$$P(B_i|A) = \frac{P(A|B_i)P(B_i)}{\sum_{j=1}^{k} P(A|B_j)P(B_j)}, \tag{17.95}$$

which is Bayes' theorem. □

It is because of the simplicity of this "proof" that the Bayes' theorem is sometimes also referred to as the Bayes' rule.

17.14 Information theory

Information theory is based on the application of probability theory concerned with the quantification, storage, and communication of information. It builds upon the fundamental work of Claude Shannon [169]. In this chapter, we introduce the key concept of entropy and related entities, e. g., conditional entropy, mutual information, and Kullback–Leibler divergence.

17.14.1 Entropy

Shannon defined the entropy for a discrete random variable X, assuming values in $\{X_1, \ldots, X_n\}$ with probability density $p_i = P(X_i)$, as follows:

Definition 17.14.1 (Entropy). The *entropy*, $H(X)$, of a discrete random variable X is given by

$$H(X) = \mathbb{E}\big[-\log\big(P(X)\big)\big] = -\sum_{i=1}^{n} p_i \log(p_i). \tag{17.96}$$

Usually, the logarithm is base 2, because the entropy is expressed in bits (that means its unit is a bit). However, sometimes, other bases are used, hence, attention to this is required.

The entropy is a measure of the uncertainty of a random variable. Specifically, it quantifies the average amount of information needed to describe the random variable.

Properties of the entropy

The entropy has the following properties:

- Positivity: $H(X) \geq 0$.
- Symmetry: Let Π be a permutation of the indices $1, \dots, n$ of the probability mass function $P(X_i)$ in the form that $P(X_{\Pi(i)})$ is a new probability mass function for the discrete random variable $X_i' = X_{\Pi(i)}$. Then,

$$H(X) = H(X'). \tag{17.97}$$

- Maximum: The maximum of the entropy is assumed for $P(X_i) = 1/n = \text{const.}$ $\forall i$, for $\{X_1, \dots, X_n\}$.

The definition of the entropy can be extended to a continuous random variable, X, with probability mass function $f(X)$ and $X \in D$ as follows:

$$H(X) = \mathbb{E}\big[-\log\big(f(X)\big)\big] = -\int_{x \in D} f(x)\log\big(f(x)\big)dx. \tag{17.98}$$

In this case, the entropy is also called *differential entropy.*

In Figure 17.19, we present an example of the entropy for a random variable X that can assume two values, i. e.,

$$X = \begin{cases} 0, & \text{with probability } 1-p \\ 1, & \text{with probability } p \end{cases} \tag{17.99}$$

Clearly, the entropy is positive for all values of p, and assumes its maximum for $p = 0.5$ with $H(p = 0.5) = 1$ bit. In order to plot the entropy, we used $n = 50$ different values for p obtained with the R command `p <- seq(from=0, to=1, length.out=n)`.

Similar to the joint probability and the conditional probability, there are also extensions of the entropy along these lines.

Definition 17.14.2 (Joint entropy). Let X and Y be two random variables assuming values in $X_1, \dots, X_n$ and $Y_1, \dots, Y_m$. Furthermore, let $p_{ij} = P(X_i, Y_j)$ be their joint probability distribution. Then, the *joint entropy* of X and Y, denoted $H(X, Y)$, is given by

$$H(X, Y) = -\sum_{i=1}^{n}\sum_{j=1}^{m} p_{ij}\log(p_{ij}). \tag{17.100}$$

Definition 17.14.3 (Conditional entropy). Let X and Y be two random variables assuming values in $X_1, \dots, X_n$ and $Y_1, \dots, Y_m$ with probability distribution $p_i = P(X_i)$ for X.

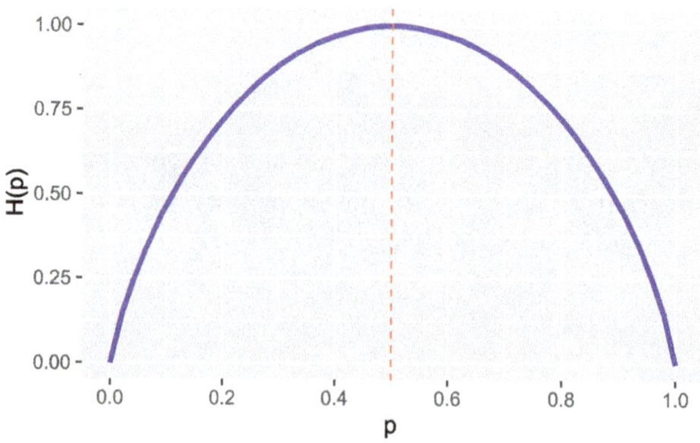

Figure 17.19: Visualization of the entropy $H(p)$ for different values of p. The vertical dashed line (red) indicates the maximum of $H(p)$.

Furthermore, let $p_{ji} = P(Y_j|X_i)$ be their conditional probability distribution and $H(Y|X = x_i)$ the entropy of Y, conditioned on $X = x_i$. Then, the *conditional entropy* of Y given X, denoted $H(Y|X)$, is given by

$$H(Y|X) = \sum_{i=1}^{n} p_i H(Y|X = x_i) = \sum_{i=1}^{n}\sum_{j=1}^{m} p_i p_{ji} \log(p_{ji}). \qquad (17.101)$$

Properties of the conditional entropy

The joint and conditional entropy have the following properties:

- Chain rule: $H(Y|X) = H(X, Y) - H(X)$;
- Symmetry: $H(X, Y) = H(X) + H(Y|X) = H(Y) + H(X|Y)$

17.14.2 Kullback–Leibler divergence

The Kullback–Leibler divergence, also called relative entropy, is a measure of the distance between two probability distributions [39].

Definition 17.14.4 (Kullback–Leibler divergence). Let X and Y be two random variables assuming values in $X_1, \ldots, X_n$ and $Y_1, \ldots, Y_n$ with the probability distributions $p_i = P(X_i)$ and $q_j = P(Y_j)$. Then the *Kullback–Leibler divergence* for X and Y, denoted $\mathrm{KL}(P \parallel Q)$, is given by

$$\mathrm{KL}(P \parallel Q) = \sum_{i=1}^{n} p_i \log\left(\frac{p_i}{q_j}\right). \qquad (17.102)$$

Properties of the Kullback–Leibler divergence

The Kullback–Leibler divergence has the following properties:

- The Kullback–Leibler divergence $\mathrm{KL}(P \parallel Q)$ is nonsymmetric;
- Gibbs' inequality: $\mathrm{KL}(P \parallel Q) \geq 0$;
- $\mathrm{KL}(P \parallel Q) = 0$ if and only if both distributions are identical, i. e., $P = Q$.

Figure 17.20 presents an example of the Kullback–Leibler divergence. On the left-hand side is depicted the probability distribution $p(x)$, which is a gamma distribution, and $q(x)$ which is a normal distribution. On the right-hand side is shown only the logarithm, $\log(\frac{p}{q})$, of both distributions. The vertical dashed lines indicate the intersection points between both distributions. At these points the sign of the logarithm changes, as shown on the right-hand side, since for $\log(x)$ with $x > 1$ the logarithm is positive, and for $x < 0$ the logarithm is negative.

17.14.3 Mutual information

Another measure, called mutual information, follows from the definition of the Kullback–Leibler divergence by the transformation $p(x) \to p(x, y)$ and $q(x) \to p(x)p(y)$. It measures the amount of information of one random variable, X, from another random variable Y.

Definition 17.14.5 (Mutual information). Let X and Y be two random variables assuming values in $X_1, \ldots, X_n$ and $Y_1, \ldots, Y_m$ with the probability distributions $p_i = P(X_i)$ and $q_j = P(Y_j)$.

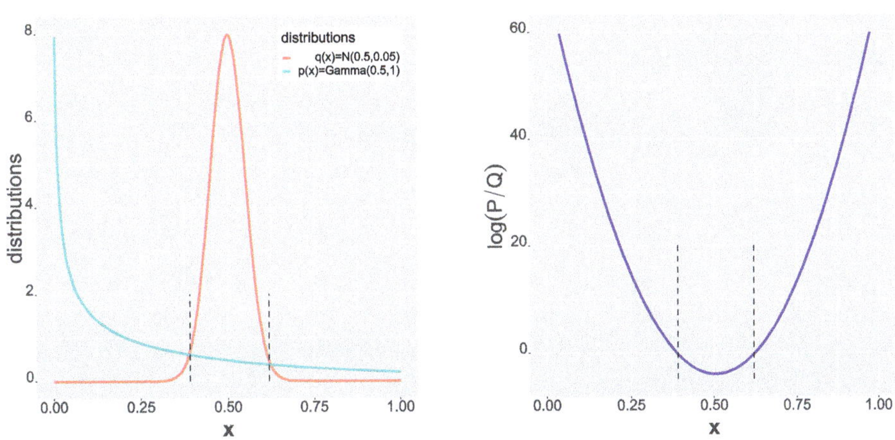

Figure 17.20: An example for the Kullback–Leibler divergence. On the left-hand side, we show the probability distribution $p(x)$ (a gamma distribution) and $q(x)$ (a normal distribution). On the right-hand side, we show only the logarithm, $\log(\frac{p}{q})$, of both distributions.

Furthermore, let $p_{ij} = P(X_i, Y_j)$ be their joint probability distribution. Then, the *mutual information* of X and Y, denoted $I(X, Y)$, is given by

$$I(X,Y) = \sum_{i=1}^{n}\sum_{j=1}^{m} p_{ij} \log\left(\frac{p_{ij}}{p_i q_j}\right). \tag{17.103}$$

Properties of the mutual information

The mutual information has the following properties:

- Symmetry: $I(X, Y) = I(Y, X)$
- If X and Y are two independent random variables, $I(X, Y) = 0$
- $I(X, Y) = H(X) + H(Y) - H(X, Y)$
- $I(X, Y) = H(X, Y) - H(X|Y) - H(Y|X)$
- $I(X|X) = H(X)$
- $I(X, Y) = H(X) - H(X|Y)$

From the last relationship above follows a further property of the conditional entropy:

$$H(X|Y) \leq H(X). \tag{17.104}$$

In Figure 17.21, we visualize the relationships between entropies and mutual information. This graphical representation of the abstract relationships helps in summarizing these nontrivial dependencies and in gaining an intuitive understanding.

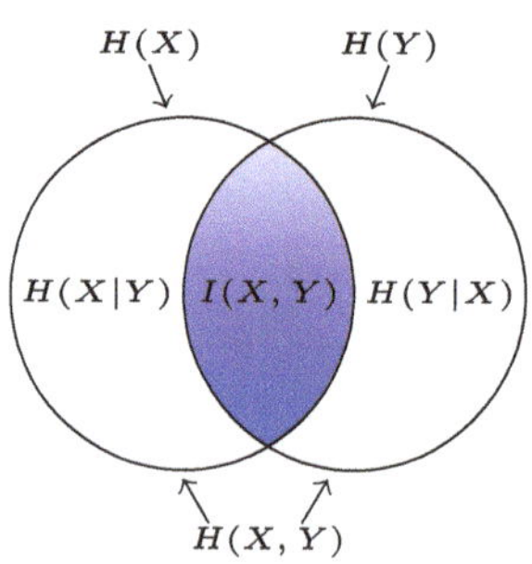

Figure 17.21: Visualization of the nontrivial relationships between entropies and mutual information.

In contrast with the correlation discussed in Section 17.8.4, mutual information measures linear and nonlinear dependencies between X and Y. This extension makes this measure a popular choice for practical applications. For instance, the mutual information has been used to estimate the regulatory effects between genes [44] to construct gene regulatory networks [139, 69, 72]. It has also been used to estimate finance networks representing the relationships between stocks from, e. g., the New York stock exchange [66] or investor trading networks [7].

17.15 Law of large numbers

The *law of large numbers* is an important result, because it provides a systematic connection between the sample mean from a distribution and its population mean. In other words, the law of large numbers provides a theoretical foundation for using a finite sample from a distribution to make a statement about the underlying (unknown) population mean. However, before we are in a position to state and prove the law of large numbers, we need to introduce some inequalities between probability values and expectation values.

Theorem 17.15.1. *For a given random variable X with $P(X \geq 0)$ and every real $t \in \mathbb{R}$ with $t > 0$, the following inequality holds:*

$$P(X \geq t) \leq \frac{\mathbb{E}[X]}{t}. \tag{17.105}$$

This inequality is called the Markov inequality.

Theorem 17.15.2. *For a given random variable X with finite* $\mathrm{Var}(X)$ *and every real $t \in \mathbb{R}$ with $t > 0$, the following inequality holds:*

$$P(|X - \mathbb{E}[X]| \geq t) \leq \frac{\mathrm{Var}(X)}{t^2}. \tag{17.106}$$

This inequality is called the Chebyshev inequality.

Proof. To prove the Chebyshev inequality, we set $Y = |X - \mathbb{E}[X]|^2$. This guarantees $P(Y \geq 0)$, because Y is nonnegative. Furthermore, $\mathbb{E}[Y] = \mathrm{Var}(X)$ per definition of the variance. Now, application of the Markov inequality and setting $s = t^2$ gives

$$P(|X - \mathbb{E}[X]| \geq t) = P(|X - \mathbb{E}[X]|^2 \geq t^2), \tag{17.107}$$

$$= P(Y \geq s) \leq \frac{\mathbb{E}[Y]}{s}, \tag{17.108}$$

$$= \frac{\mathrm{Var}(X)}{s}. \tag{17.109}$$

□

It is important to emphasize that the two above inequalities hold for *every* probability distribution with the required conditions. Despite this generality, it is possible to make a specific statement about the distance of a random sample from the mean of the distribution. For example, for $t = 4\sigma$, we obtain

$$P(|X - \mathbb{E}[X]| \geq 4\sigma) \leq \frac{1}{16} = 0.063. \tag{17.110}$$

That means, for every distribution, the probability that the distance between a random sample X and $\mathbb{E}[X]$ is larger than four standard derivations is less than 6.3 %.

At the beginning of this chapter, we stated briefly the result of the law of large numbers. Before we formulate it formally, we have one last point that requires some clarification. This point relates to the mean of a sample. Suppose that we have a random sample of size n, given by $X_1, \dots, X_n$, and each X_i is drawn from the same distribution with mean μ and variance σ^2. Furthermore, each X_i is drawn independently from the other samples. We call such samples independent and identically distributed (iid) random variables.[1] Then,

$$\mathbb{E}[X_1] = \cdots = \mathbb{E}[X_n] = \mu, \tag{17.111}$$

and

$$\operatorname{Var}(X_1) = \cdots = \operatorname{Var}(X_n) = \sigma^2. \tag{17.112}$$

The question of interest here is the following: what is the expectation value of the sample mean?

The sample mean of the sample $X_1, \dots, X_n$ is given by

$$\bar{X}_n = \frac{1}{n} \sum_{i=1}^{n} X_i. \tag{17.113}$$

Here, we emphasize the dependence on n by the subscript of the mean value. From this, we can obtain the expectation value of $\bar{X}_n$ by applying the rules for the expectation values discussed in Section 17.8, giving

$$\mathbb{E}[\bar{X}_n] = \mathbb{E}\left[\frac{1}{n} \sum_{i=1}^{n} X_i\right] = \frac{1}{n} \sum_{i=1}^{n} \mathbb{E}[X_i] = \mu. \tag{17.114}$$

Similarly, we can obtain the variance of the sample mean, i. e., $\operatorname{Var}(\bar{X}_n)$, by

$$\operatorname{Var}(\bar{X}_n) = \operatorname{Var}\left(\frac{1}{n} \sum_{i=1}^{n} X_i\right), \tag{17.115}$$

$$= \frac{1}{n^2} \operatorname{Var}\left(\sum_{i=1}^{n} X_i\right), \tag{17.116}$$

$$= \frac{1}{n^2} \sum_{i=1}^{n} \operatorname{Var}(X_i), \tag{17.117}$$

$$= \frac{1}{n^2} n\sigma^2 = \frac{\sigma^2}{n}. \tag{17.118}$$

1 When we speak about a random sample, we mean an iid sample.

These results are interesting, because they demonstrate that the expectation value of the sample mean is identical to the mean of the distribution, but the sample variance is reduced by a factor of $1/n$ compared to the variance of the distribution. Hence, the sampling distribution of $\bar{X}_n$ becomes more and more peaked around μ with increasing values of n, and also having a smaller variance than the distribution of X for all $n > 1$.

Furthermore, application of the Chebyshev inequality for $X = \bar{X}_n$, gives

$$P(|\bar{X}_n - \mathbb{E}[\bar{X}_n]| \geq t) \leq \frac{\mathrm{Var}(\bar{X}_n)}{t^2}. \tag{17.119}$$

Hence,

$$\Pr(|\bar{X}_n - \mu| \geq t) \leq \frac{\sigma^2}{nt^2}. \tag{17.120}$$

This is a precise probabilistic relationship between the distance of the sample mean $\bar{X}_n$ from the mean μ as a function of the sample size n. Hence, this relationship can be used to get an estimate for the number of samples required in order for the sample mean to be "close" to the population mean μ.

We are now in a position to finally present the result known as the law of large numbers, which adds a further component to the above considerations for the sample mean. Specifically, so far, we know that the expectation of the sample mean is the mean of the distribution (see equation (17.114)) and that the probability of the minimal distance between $\bar{X}_n$ and μ, given by t, decreases systematically for increasing n (see equation (17.120)). However, so far, we did not assess the opposite behavior of equation (17.120), namely what is $P(|\bar{X}_n - \mu| < t)$?

Using the previous results, we obtain

$$P(|\bar{X}_n - \mu| < t) = 1 - P(|\bar{X}_n - \mu| \geq t) \geq 1 - \frac{\sigma^2}{nt^2}. \tag{17.121}$$

Taking the limit $n \to \infty$, the above equation yields

$$\lim_{n\to\infty} P(|\bar{X}_n - \mu| < t) = 1. \tag{17.122}$$

This last expression is the result of the law of large numbers. That means, the law of large numbers provides evidence that the distance between $\bar{X}_n$ and μ stays with certainty, i. e., with a probability of 1, below any arbitrary small value of $t > 0$.

Formally, in statistics there is a special symbol that is reserved for the type of convergence presented in equation (17.122), which is written as

$$\bar{X}_n \xrightarrow{p} \mu. \tag{17.123}$$

The "p" over the arrow means that the sample mean converges *in probability* to μ.

Theorem 17.15.3 (Law of large numbers). *Suppose that we have an iid sample of size n, $X_1, \ldots, X_n$, where each X_i is drawn from the same distribution with mean μ and variance σ^2. Then, the sample mean $\bar{X}_n$ converges in probability to μ,*

$$\bar{X}_n \xrightarrow{p} \mu. \tag{17.124}$$

17.16 Central limit theorem

In the previous section, we saw that the expected sample mean and the variance of a random sample are μ and σ^2/n, respectively, if the distribution from which the samples are drawn has a mean of μ and a variance of σ^2. What we did not discuss, so far, is the distributional form of this random sample. This is the topic addressed by the central limit theorem.

Theorem 17.16.1 (Central limit theorem). *Let $X_1, \ldots, X_n$ be an iid sample from a distribution with mean μ and variance σ^2. Then,*

$$\lim_{n\to\infty} \Pr\left(\frac{\bar{X}_n - \mu}{\sqrt{\sigma^2/n}} \leq x\right) = F(x). \tag{17.125}$$

Here, F is the cumulative distribution function of the standard normal distribution, and x is a fixed real number.

To understand the importance of the central limit theorem, we would like to emphasize that equation (17.125) holds for a large sample from any distribution, whether discrete or continuous. In this case, $\frac{\bar{X}_n - \mu}{\sigma/n^{1/2}}$ can be approximated by a standard normal distribution. This implies that $\bar{X}_n$ can be approximated by a normal distribution with mean μ and variance σ^2/n.

The central limit theorem is one of the reasons why the normal distribution plays such a prescind role in statistics, machine learning, and data science. Even when individual random variables do not come from a normal distribution (i. e., they are not sampled from a normal distribution), their sum is normally distributed.

17.17 Concentration inequalities

In Section 17.15, we discussed already the Markov and Chebyshev inequalities, because they are needed to prove the law of large numbers. In general, such inequalities, also called concentration inequalities or probabilistic inequalities, are playing an important role in proving theorems about random variables, since they provide bounds on the behavior of random variable and their deviates, e. g., for expectation values. However, aside from this, they provide also insights into the laws of probability theory. For this reason, we present, in the following, some additional concentration inequalities.

17.17.1 Hoeffding's inequality

Theorem 17.17.1 (Hoeffding's inequality). *Let $X_1, \dots, X_n$ be some iid random variables with finite mean, $a_i \leq X_i \leq b_i$ $\forall i$, sample mean $\bar{X} = 1/n \sum_{i=1}^{n} X_i$ and $\mu = \mathbb{E}[\bar{X}]$. Then, for any $\epsilon > 0$, the following inequalities hold:*

$$P(\bar{X} - \mu \geq \epsilon) \leq \exp\left(-\frac{2n^2\epsilon^2}{\sum_{i=1}^{n}(b_i - a_i)^2}\right), \tag{17.126}$$

$$P(|\bar{X} - \mu| \geq \epsilon) \leq 2\exp\left(-\frac{2n^2\epsilon^2}{\sum_{i=1}^{n}(b_i - a_i)^2}\right). \tag{17.127}$$

By setting $\epsilon' = n\epsilon$, one obtains inequalities for $S = \sum_{i=1}^{n} X_i$,

$$P(S - \mathbb{E}[S] \geq \epsilon') \leq \exp\left(-\frac{2\epsilon'^2}{\sum_{i=1}^{n}(b_i - a_i)^2}\right), \tag{17.128}$$

$$P(|S - \mathbb{E}[S]| \geq \epsilon') \leq 2\exp\left(-\frac{2\epsilon'^2}{\sum_{i=1}^{n}(b_i - a_i)^2}\right). \tag{17.129}$$

As an application of Hoeffding's inequality, we consider the following example:

Example 17.17.1. Suppose $X_1, \dots, X_n$ are independent and identically distributed random variables with $X_i \sim \text{Bernoulli}(p)$ and $a \leq X_i \leq b$, $\forall i$. Then, from the Hoeffding's inequality we obtain the following inequality:

$$P(|\bar{X} - p| \geq \epsilon) \leq 2\exp(-2n\epsilon^2). \tag{17.130}$$

The Hoeffding's inequality finds its applications in statistical learning theory [192]. Specifically, it can be used to estimate a bound for the difference between the in-sample error E_{in} and the out-of-sample error E_{out}. More generally, it is used for deriving learning bounds for models [138].

17.17.2 Cauchy–Schwartz inequality

Let us define the scalar product for two random variables X and Y by

$$X \cdot Y = \mathbb{E}[XY]. \tag{17.131}$$

Then, we obtain the following probabilistic version of the Cauchy–Schwartz inequality for expectation values

$$\mathbb{E}[XY]^2 \leq \mathbb{E}[X^2]\mathbb{E}[Y^2]. \tag{17.132}$$

Using the Cauchy–Schwartz inequality, we can show that the correlation between two linearly *dependent* random variables X and Y is 1, i. e.,

$$\left|\rho(X,Y)\right| = 1 \quad \text{if } Y = aX + b \quad \text{with } a, b \in \mathbb{R}. \tag{17.133}$$

17.17.3 Chernoff bounds

Chernoff bounds are typically tighter than Markov's inequality and Chebyshev bounds, but they require stronger assumptions [137].

In a general form, Chernoff bounds are defined by

$$P(X \geq a) \leq \frac{\mathbb{E}[\exp(tX)]}{\exp(ta)} \quad \text{for } t > 0, \tag{17.134}$$

$$P(X \leq a) \leq \frac{\mathbb{E}[\exp(tX)]}{\exp(ta)} \quad \text{for } t < 0. \tag{17.135}$$

Here, $\mathbb{E}[\exp(tX)]$ is the moment-generating function of X. There are many different Chernoff bounds for different probability distributions and different values of the parameter t. Here, we provide a bound for Poisson trails, which is a sum of iid Bernoulli random variables, which are allowed to have different expectation values, i. e., $P(X_i = 1) = p_i$.

Theorem 17.17.2. *Let $X_1, \ldots, X_n$ be iid Bernoulli random variables with $P(X_i = 1) = p_i$, and let $\bar{X}_n = \sum_{i=1}^{n} X_i$ be a Poisson trial with $\mu = \mathbb{E}[\bar{X}_n] = \sum_{i=1}^{n} p_i$. Then $\forall \delta \in (0,1]$*

$$\Pr\bigl(X \leq (1-\delta)\mu\bigr) < \left(\frac{\exp(-\delta)}{(1-\delta)^{(1-\delta)}}\right)^{\mu}, \tag{17.136}$$

whereas for $\delta > 0$

$$\Pr\bigl(X \geq (1+\delta)\mu\bigr) < \left(\frac{\exp(\delta)}{(1+\delta)^{(1+\delta)}}\right)^{\mu}. \tag{17.137}$$

Example 17.17.2. As an example, we use this bound to estimate the probability when tossing a fair coin $n = 100$ times to observe $m = 40$, or less heads. For this $\mu = 50$, and from $(1-\delta)\mu = 30$ follows $\delta = 0.2$. This gives $P(X \leq m) = 0.34$.

17.18 Further reading

For readers interested in advanced reading material about the topics of this chapter, we recommend for probability theory [18, 17, 48, 87, 105, 147, 150], Bayesian analysis [84, 101, 180], and for information theory [39, 83]. An excellent tutorial on Bayesian analysis can be found in [173], and a thorough introduction to information theory, with focus on machine learning, is provided by [123]. For developing a better and intuitive understanding of the terms discussed in this chapter, we recommend the textbooks [118, 145]. Finally, for a historical perspective on the development of probability, the book by [91] provides a good overview.

17.19 Summary

Probability theory plays a pivotal role when dealing with data, because essentially every measurement contains errors. Hence, there is an accompanied uncertainty that needs to be quantified probabilistically when dealing with data. In this sense, probability theory is an important extension of deterministic mathematical fields, e. g., linear algebra, graph theory and analysis, which cannot account for such uncertainties. Unfortunately, such methods are usually more difficult to understand and require, for this reason, much more practice. However, once mastered, they add considerably to the analysis and the understanding of real-world problems, which is essential for any method in data science.

17.20 Exercises

1. In Section 17.11.2, we discussed that under certain conditions a Binomial distribution can be approximated by a Poisson distribution. Show this result numerically, using `R`. Use different approximation conditions and evaluate these. How can this be quantified?
   Hint: See Section 17.14.2 about the Kullback–Leibler divergence.
2. Calculate the mutual information for the discrete joint distribution $P(X,Y)$ given in Table 17.2.

Table 17.2: Numerical values of a discrete joint distribution $P(X,Y)$ with $X \in \{x_1, x_2\}$ and $Y \in \{y_1, y_2, y_3\}$.

		Y		
		y_1	y_2	y_3
X	x_1	0.2	0.3	0.1
	x_2	0.1	0.1	0.2

3. Use `R` to calculate the mutual information for the discrete joint distribution $P(X,Y)$ given in Table 17.3, for $z \in S = [0, 0.5)$, and plot the mutual information as a function of z. What happens for z values outside the interval S?

Table 17.3: Numerical values of a discrete joint distribution $P(X, Y)$ with $X \in \{x_1, x_2\}$ and $Y \in \{y_1, y_2, y_3\}$ in dependence on the parameter z.

		Y		
		y_1	y_2	y_3
X	x_1	z	$0.5 - z$	0.1
	x_2	0.1	0.1	0.2

4. Use the Bayes' theorem for doping tests in sports. Specifically, suppose that we have a doping test that identifies with 99 % someone correctly who is using doping, i. e., $P(+|\text{doping}) = 0.99$, and has a false positive probability of 1 %, i. e., $P(+|\text{no doping}) = 0.01$. Furthermore, assume that the percentage of people who are doping is 1 %. What is the probability that someone who tests positive is doping?

18 Optimization

Optimization problems consistently arise when we try to select the best element from a set of available alternatives. Frequently, this consists of finding the best parameters of a function with respect to an optimization criterion. This is especially difficult if we have a high-dimensional problem, meaning that there are many such parameters that must be optimized. Since most models, used in data science, essentially have many parameters, then optimization (or optimization theory) is necessary to devise these models.

In this chapter, we will introduce some techniques used to address unconstrained and constrained, as well as deterministic and probabilistic optimization problems, including Newton's method, simulated annealing and the Lagrange multiplier method. We will discuss examples and available packages in `R` that can be used to solve the aforementioned optimization problems.

18.1 Introduction

In general, an optimization problem is characterized by the following:
- a set of alternative choices called *decision variables*;
- a set of parameters called *uncontrollable variables*;
- a set of requirements to be satisfied by both decision and uncontrollable variables, called *constraints*;
- some measure(s) of effectiveness expressed in term of both decision and uncontrollable variables, called *objective-function(s)*.

Definition 18.1.1. A set of decision variables that satisfy the constraints is called a *solution* to the problem.

The aim of an optimization problem is to find, among all solutions to the problem, a solution that corresponds to either
- the maximal value of the objective function, in which case the problem is referred to as a *maximization* problem, e. g. maximizing the profit;
- the minimal value of the objective-function, in which case the problem is referred to as a *minimization* problem, e. g. minimizing the cost; or
- a trade-off value of many and generally conflicting objective-functions, in which case the problem is referred to as a *multicriteria* optimization problem.

Optimization problems are widespread in every activity, where numerical information is processed, e. g. mathematics, physics, engineering, economics, systems biology, etc. For instance, typical examples of optimization applications in systems biology include *therapy treatment planning and scheduling*, *probe design and selection*, *genomics analysis*, etc.

https://doi.org/10.1515/9783110796063-018

18.2 Formulation of an optimization problem

Optimization problems are often formulated using mathematical models. Let $x = (x_1, x_2, \ldots, x_n)$ denote the decision variables; then a general formulation of an optimization problem is written as follows:

$$\begin{aligned} &\underset{x \in \mathbb{R}^n}{\text{Optimize}} \quad f(x), \\ &\text{subject to: } x \in S \subseteq \mathbb{R}^n, \end{aligned} \tag{18.1}$$

i. e., the problem is to find the solution $x^* \in S$, if it exists, such that for all $x \in S$, we have

- $f(x^*) \leq f(x)$, if "Optimize" stands for "minimize";
- $f(x^*) \geq f(x)$, if "Optimize" stands for "maximize".

The function f denotes the objective function or the cost-function, whereas S is the feasible set, and any $x \in S$ is called a feasible solution to the problem.

Definition 18.2.1. A solution $\bar{x}$ to the problem (18.1) is called a local optimum if

- $f(\bar{x}) \leq f(x)$ for all x in a neighborhood of $\bar{x}$, for a minimization-type problem, or
- $f(\bar{x}) \geq f(x)$ for all x in a neighborhood of $\bar{x}$, for a maximization-type problem.

Definition 18.2.2. A solution x^* to the problem (18.1) is called a global optimum if

- $f(x^*) \leq f(x)$ for all $x \in S$, for a minimization-type problem, or
- $f(x^*) \geq f(x)$ for all $x \in S$, for a maximization-type problem.

If $S = \emptyset$, then the problem (18.1) has no solution, otherwise,

1. if $f(x^*)$ is finite, then the problem (18.1) has a *finite optimal solution*;
2. if $f(x^*) = -\infty$ (for a minimization-type problem) or $f(x^*) = \infty$ (for a maximization-type problem), then the problem (18.1) is *unbounded*, i. e., the optimal value of the objective function is not a finite number and, therefore, cannot be achieved.

When $S = \mathbb{R}^n$ then, the optimal solution, x^*, can be any *stationary point* of f over $\mathbb{R}^n$, such that $f(x^*) \leq f(x)$ (respectively $f(x^*) \geq f(x)$) for a minimization-type problem (respectively for a maximization-type problem) for all $x \in \mathbb{R}^n$. In this case, the problem (18.1) is termed an *unconstrained optimization problem*. On the other hand, if $S \subset \mathbb{R}^n$, then the problem (18.1) is called a *constrained optimization problem*, in which case, S is determined by a set of constraints. Typically, one can distinguish three types of constraints:

- Equality constraints: $g(x) = c$, where $g : \mathbb{R}^n \longrightarrow \mathbb{R}$ and $c \in \mathbb{R}$, e. g.,

$$4x_1 + 25x_2 - 7x_3 + \cdots - 5x_n = 59.$$

- Inequality constraints: $h(x) \leq c$ or $h(x) \geq c$, where $h : \mathbb{R}^n \longrightarrow \mathbb{R}$, and $c \in \mathbb{R}$, e. g.,

$$\begin{aligned} 4x_1 + 25x_2^2 - 7x_3 + \cdots - 5x_n &\leq 59 \\ 4x_1 + 25x_2 - 7x_3 + \cdots - 5x_n &\geq 59. \end{aligned}$$

- Integrality constraints: e. g., $x \in \mathbb{Z}^n$, $x \in \mathbb{N}^n$.

Remark 18.2.1. If all the decision variables, x_i, in the problem (18.1) take only discrete values (e. g. $0, 1, 2, \ldots$), then the problem is called a *discrete optimization* problem, otherwise it is called a *continuous optimization* problem. When there is a combination of discrete and continuous variables, the problem is called a *mixed optimization* problem.

Remark 18.2.2. Any minimization problem can be rewritten as a maximization problem, and vice versa, by substituting the objective function $f(x)$ with $z(x) = -f(x)$.

Therefore, from now, we will focus exclusively on minimization-type optimization problems.

18.3 Unconstrained optimization problems

Unconstrained optimization problems arise in various practical applications, including data fitting, engineering design, and process control. Techniques for solving unconstrained optimization problems form the foundation of most methods used to solve constrained optimization problems. These methods can be classified into two categories: gradient-based methods and derivative-free methods.

Typically, the formulation of an unconstrained optimization problem can be written as follows:

$$\underset{x \in \mathbb{R}^n}{\text{Minimize}} \quad f(x). \tag{18.2}$$

18.3.1 Gradient-based methods

Gradient-based algorithms for solving unconstrained optimization problems assume that the function to be minimized in (18.1) is twice continuously differentiable, and are based upon the following conditions: a solution $x^* \in \mathbb{R}$ is said to be a local optimum of f if

1. the gradient of f at the point x^*, $\nabla f(x^*)$, is zero, i. e., $\frac{\partial f(x^*)}{\partial x_j} = 0$, $j = 1, \ldots, n$, and
2. the Hessian matrix of f at the point x^*, $\nabla^2 f(x^*)$, is positive definite, i. e., $\eta \nabla^2(f(x^*))\eta > 0$ for all nonzero $\eta \in \mathbb{R}^n$.

The general principle of the gradient-based algorithms can be summarized by the following steps:

- Step 1: Set $k = 0$, and choose an initial point $x^{(k)} = x^{(0)}$ and some convergence criteria;
- Step 2: Test for convergence: if the conditions for convergence are satisfied, then we can stop, and $x^{(k)}$ is the solution. Otherwise, go to Step 3;
- Step 3: Computation of a search direction (also termed a descent direction): find a vector $d_k \neq 0$ that defines a suitable direction that, if followed, will bring us as close as possible to the solution, x^*;
- Step 4: Computation of the step-size: find a scalar $\alpha_k > 0$ such that

$$f(x^{(k)} + \alpha_k d_k) < f(x^{(k)}).$$

- Step 5: Updating the variables: set $x^{(k+1)} = x^{(k)} + \alpha_k d_k$, $k = k + 1$, and go to Step 2.

The main difference between the various gradient-based methods lies in the computation of the descent direction (Step 3) and the computation of the step-size (Step 4).

In R, various gradients-based methods have been implemented either as standalone packages or as part of a general-purpose optimization package.

18.3.1.1 The steepest descent method

The steepest descent method, also called the gradient descent method, uses the negative of the gradient vector, at each point, as the search direction for each iteration; thus, steps 3 and 4 are performed as follows:

- Step 3: the descent direction is given by $d_k = -\frac{\nabla f(x^{(k)})}{\|\nabla f(x^{(k)})\|}$;
- Step 4: the step-size is given by $\alpha_k = \arg\min_\alpha f(x^{(k)} - \alpha d_k)$.

In R, an implementation of the steepest descent method can be found in the package `pracma`.

Let us consider the following problem:

$$\min_{(x_1,x_2)\in\mathbb{R}^2} f(x_1, x_2) = x_1^2 + x_2^2; \tag{18.3}$$

The contour plot of the functions $f(x_1, x_2)$, depicted in Figure 18.1 (left), is obtained using the following script:

Listing 18.1: Contour plot of $f(x_1, x_2)$ in (18.3) (see Figure 18.1 (left))

```
require(grDevices)
fxy<-function(x, y) x^2+y^2
x1 <- x2 <- seq(-1.5, 1.5, length=200)
f <- outer(x1, x2, fxy)
rgb.palette <-
    colorRampPalette(c("firebrick2","lightsalmon1","oldlace"
    ),space = "rgb")
image(x1, x2, f, xlab=expression(x[1]), ylab=expression(x[2]),
    col=rgb.palette(256))
contour(x1, x2, f, levels = seq(-2, 2, by = 0.1), add=TRUE)
```

Using the steepest descent method, the problem (18.3) can be solved in R as follows:

Listing 18.2: Solving the problem (18.3) using the Steepest Descent method

```
#The package pracma is required here
library(pracma)
#Defining the function f(x1, x2); its only minimum is reached at
    x1=0 and x2=0
fx <- function(x) x[1]^2 + x[2]^2
#Defining an initial solution
x0<-c(-1.2,1)
#Calling the Steepest Descent method
sol<-steep_descent(x0, fx)
sol$xmin
[1] 2.220446e-16  0.000000e+00  #These are the obtained optimal
    values of x1 and  x2, respectively
sol$fmin
[1] 4.930381e-32   #This is the obtained optimal value of f
#Using a new initial solution
x0 <- c(10,10)
sol<-steep_descent(x0, fx)
sol$xmin
[1] 0  0   #These are the obtained optimal values of x1 and  x2,
    respectively
sol$fmin
[1] -0.6880447  #This is the obtained optimal value of f
#Thus, for any initial solution the method converges towards the
    only minimum of  f
```

Let us consider the following problem:

$$\max_{(x_1,x_2)\in\mathbb{R}^2} g(x_1, x_2) = e^{(x-2x^2-y^2)} \sin\big(6\big(x + y + xy^2\big)\big). \tag{18.4}$$

The contour plot of the functions $g(x_1, x_2)$, depicted in Figure 18.1 (right), is obtained using the following script:

Listing 18.3: Contour plot of $g(x_1, x_2)$ in (18.4), (see Figure 18.1 (right))

```
require(grDevices)
gxy<-function(x, y) exp(x-2*x^2-y^2)*sin(6*(x+y+x*y^2))
x1 <- x2 <- seq(-1.5, 1.5, length=200)
g <- outer(x1, x2, gxy)
rgb.palette <-
    colorRampPalette(c("firebrick2","lightsalmon1","oldlace"
    ),space = "rgb")
image(x1, x2, g, xlab=expression(x[1]), ylab=expression(x[2]),
    col=rgb.palette(256))
contour(x1, x2, g, levels = seq(-2, 2, by = 0.25), add=TRUE)
```

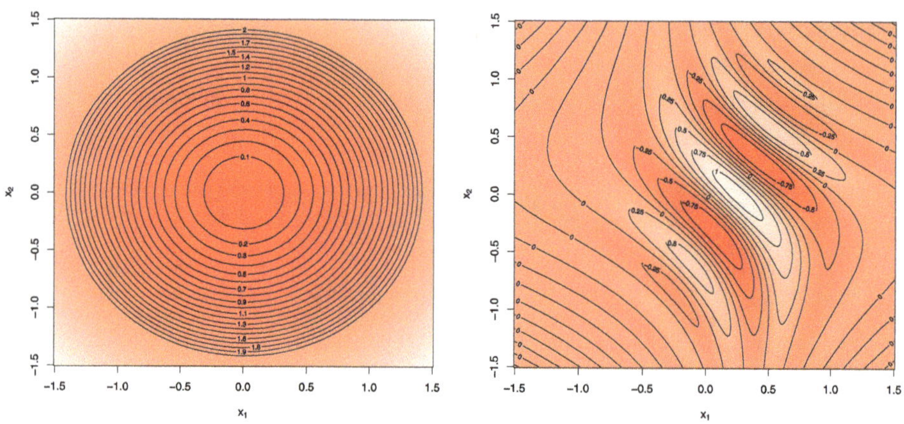

Figure 18.1: Left: contour plot of the function $f(x_1, x_2)$ in (18.3) in the (x_1, x_2) plane; right: contour plot of the function $g(x_1, x_2)$ in (18.4) in the (x_1, x_2) plane.

Most of the optimization methods available in R, including the steepest descent, are implemented for minimization problems. Since the solution that maximizes a function $h(x)$ minimizes the function $-h(x)$, we can solve the problem (18.5) to find the solution to (18.4), and then multiply the value of the objective-function of (18.5) by -1 to recover the value of the objective-function of (18.4).

$$\min_{x_1,x_2} g(x_1, x_2) = -e^{(x-2x^2-y^2)} \sin\big(6\big(x + y + xy^2\big)\big) \tag{18.5}$$

Using the steepest descent method, implemented in R, the problem (18.5) can be solved as follows:

Listing 18.4: Solving the problem (18.5) using the steepest descent method

```
#The package pracma is required here
library(pracma)
#Defining the function -g(x1, x2); its global minimum is reached at
    x1=0.2538, x2=0.0076
```

```
mgx<-function(x) -
    exp(x[1]-2*x[1]^2-x[2]^2)*sin(6*(x[1]+x[2]+x[1]*x[2]^2))
#Defining an initial solution
x0<-c(1, 1)
#Calling the Steepest Descent method
sol<-steep_descent(x0, mgx)
Warning message:
In steep_descent(x0, mgx) :
Maximum number of iterations reached -- not converged.
#Using a new initial solution
x0 <- c(-1.2,1)
sol<-steep_descent(x0, mgx)
sol$xmin
[1] 0.5046936  0.6012042  #These are the obtained optimal values of
    x1 and  x2, respectively
sol$fmin
[1] -0.6880447 #This is the obtained optimal value of -g
#Using a new initial solution
x0 <- c(0, 0)
sol<-steep_descent(x0, mgx)
sol$xmin
[1] 0.253778741  0.007586204  #These are the obtained optimal
    values of x1 and  x2, respectively
sol$fmin
[1] -1.133047 #This is the optimal value of -g, hence g=1.133047
#Thus, depending on the initial solution, either the method does
    not converge at all, or  it converges towards a local or a
    global minimum of -g
```

Note that the convergence and solution given by the steepest descent method depend on both the form of the function to be minimized and the initial solution.

18.3.1.2 The conjugate gradient method

The conjugate gradient method is a modification to the steepest descent method, which takes into account the history of the gradients to move more directly towards the optimum. The computation of the descent direction (Step 3) and the step-size (Step 4) are performed as follows:

– Step 3: the descent direction is given by

$$d_k = \begin{cases} -\nabla f(x^{(k)}), & k = 0, \\ -\nabla f(x^{(k)}) + \beta_k d_{k-1}, & k \geq 0, \end{cases}$$

where several types of formulas for β_k have been proposed. The most known formulas are those proposed by Fletcher–Reeves (FR), Polak–Ribière–Polyak (PRP) and Hestenes–Stiefel (HS), and they are defined as follows:

$$\beta_k^{\mathrm{FR}} = \frac{\|\nabla f(x^{(k)})\|^2}{\|\nabla f(x^{(k-1)})\|^2}, \tag{18.6}$$

$$\beta_k^{\mathrm{PRP}} = \frac{(\nabla f(x^{(k)}))^T y_{k-1}}{\|\nabla f(x^{(k-1)})\|^2}, \tag{18.7}$$

$$\beta_k^{HS} = \frac{(\nabla f(x^{(k)}))^T y_{k-1}}{d_{k-1}^T y_{k-1}}, \tag{18.8}$$

where $\|\cdot\|$ denotes the Euclidean norm, and $y_{k-1} = \nabla f(x^{(k)}) - \nabla f(x^{(k-1)})$.

- Step 4: The step-size α_k is such that

$$f(x^{(k)}) - f(x^{(k)} + \alpha_k d_k) \geq -\delta\alpha_k(\nabla f(x^{(k)}))^T d_k, \tag{18.9}$$

$$|(\nabla f(x^{(k)} + \alpha_k d_k))^T| \leq -\sigma(\nabla f(x^{(k)}))^T d_k, \tag{18.10}$$

where $0 < \delta < \sigma < 1$.

In R, the implementation of the conjugate gradient method can be found in the general multipurpose package `optimx`. This implementation of the conjugate gradient method can be used to solve the problem (18.3) as follows:

Listing 18.5: Solving the problem (18.3) using the conjugate gradient method

```
#The package optimx is required here
library(optimx)
#Defining the function f(x1, x2), its only minimum is reached at
    x1=0 and x2=0
fx<- function(x) x[1]^2 + x[2]^2
#Defining an initial solution
x0 <- c(-1.2,1)
#Calling the Conjugate Gradient methods (CG)
sol <- optimx(x0, fx, method = "CG")
sol$par
$par
[1]  4.924372e-07, -4.103643e-07  #These are the obtained optimal
    values of x1 and  x2, respectively
> sol$fvalues
$fvalues
[1]  4.108933e-13     #This is the obtained optimal value of f
#Using a new initial solution
x0<-c(10,10)
sol <- optimx(x0, fx, method = "CG")
sol$par
$par
[1]  2.166724e-07  2.166724e-07  #These are the obtained optimal
    values of x1 and  x2, respectively
sol$fvalues
$fvalues
[1]  9.389383e-14    #This is the obtained optimal value of f
#Thus, for any initial solution the method converges towards the
    only minimum of  f
```

Now, let us use the conjugate gradient method, implemented in the package `optimx` to solve the problem (18.4).

Listing 18.6: Solving the problem (18.4) using the conjugate gradient method

```
#The package optimx is required here
```

```
library(optimx)
#Defining the function -g(x1, x2); its global minimum is reached at
    x1=0.2538, x2=0.0076
mgx<-function(x)
    exp(x[1]-2*x[1]^2-x[2]^2)*sin(6*(x[1]+x[2]+x[1]*x[2]^2))
#Defining an initial solution
x0<-c(1, 1)
#Calling the Conjugate Gradient methods (CG)
sol<- optimx(x0, mgx, method = "CG")
sol$par
$par
[1]  1.511231  2.016832  #These are the obtained optimal values of
    x1 and  x2, respectively
sol$fvalues
$fvalues
[1] -0.0008079518
#Using a new initial solution
x0<-c(-1.2,1)
sol<- optimx(x0, mgx, method = "CG")
sol$par
$par
[1]  -1.018596  1.491097 #These are the obtained optimal values of
    x1 and  x2, respectively
sol$fvalues
$fvalues
[1] -0.004766019    #This is the obtained optimal value of -g
#Using a new initial solution
x0<-c(0,0)
sol<- optimx(x0, mgx, method = "CG")
sol$par
$par
[1]  0.253778535  0.007586373  #These are the obtained optimal
    values of x1 and  x2, respectively
sol$fvalues
$fvalues
[1] -1.133047    #This is the obtained optimal value of -g
#Thus, depending on the initial solution, the method converges
    towards either a local or a global minimum of -g
```

The solution to the problem (18.4) with the initial solution $x^{(0)} = (x_1^{(0)}, x_2^{(0)}) = (1,1)$ is $\bar{x} = (1.5112, 2.016)$, and $f(\bar{x}) = -0.0008079518$, which is a local minima. However, in contrast with the steepest descent method, the conjugate gradient method converges with the initial solution $x^{(0)} = (1,1)$.

18.3.1.3 Newton's method

In contrast with the steepest descent and conjugate gradient methods, which only use first-order information, i. e., the first derivative (or the gradient) term, Newton's method requires a second-order derivative (or the Hessian) to estimate the descent direction. Steps 3 and 4 are performed as follows:

- Step 3: $d_k = -[\nabla^2 f(x^{(k)})]^{-1} \nabla f(x^{(k)})$ is the descent direction, where $\nabla^2 f(x)$ is the Hessian of f at the point x.
- Step 4: $\alpha_k = \arg\min_\alpha f(x^{(k)} - \alpha d_k)$.

Since the computation of the Hessian matrix is generally expensive, several modifications of Newton's method have been suggested in order to improve its computational efficiency. One variant of Newton's method is the Broyden–Fletcher–Goldfarb–Shanno (BFGS) method, which uses the gradient to iteratively approximate the inverse of the Hessian matrix $H_k^{-1} = [\nabla^2 f(x^{(k)})]^{-1}$, as follows:

$$H_k^{-1} = \left(I - \frac{s_k y_k^T}{s_k^T y_k}\right) H_{k-1}^{-1} \left(I - \frac{s_k y_k^T}{s_k^T y_k}\right) + \frac{s_k s_k^T}{s_k^T y_k},$$

where, $s_k = x^{(k)} - x^{(k-1)}$ and $y_k = \nabla f(x^{(k)}) - \nabla f(x^{(k-1)})$.

In R, the implementation of the BFGS variant of Newton's method can be found in the general multipurpose package `optimx`. This implementation of the BFGS method can be used to solve the problem (18.3), as follows:

Listing 18.7: Solving the problem (18.3) using Newton's method

```
#The package optimx is required here
library(optimx)
#Defining the function f(x1, x2); its only minimum is reached at
    x1=0 and x2=0
fx<- function(x) x[1]^2 + x[2]^2
#Defining the initial solution
x0<-c(-1.2,1)
#Calling the BFGS function
sol<- optimx(x0, fx, method = "BFGS")
sol$par
$par
[1]  -5.520439e-16  6.456213e-16  #These are the obtained optimal
    values of x1 and  x2, respectively
sol$fvalues
$fvalues
[1] 1.755293e-29    #This is the obtained optimal value of f
# Using a new initial solution
x0<-c(10,10)
sol<- optimx(x0, fx, method = "BFGS")
sol$par
$par
[1]  3.583324e-16  3.583324e-16 #These are the obtained optimal
    values of x1 and  x2, respectively
> sol$fvalues
$fvalues
[1] 6.42035e-30 #This is the obtained optimal value of f
#Thus, for any initial solution the method converges towards the
    only minimum of  f
```

Now, let us use the BFGS method, implemented in the package `optimx`, to solve the problem (18.4).

Listing 18.8: Solving the problem (18.4) using Newton's method

```
#The package optimx is required here
library(optimx)
```

```
Defining the function -g(x1, x2); its global minimum is reached at
    x1=0.2538 and x2=0.0076
gx<-function(x) -
    exp(x[1]-2*x[1]^2-x[2]^2)*sin(6*(x[1]+x[2]+x[1]*x[2]^2))
#Defining the initial solution
x0<-c(1, 1)
#Calling the BFGS function
sol <- optimx(x0, gx, method = "BFGS")
sol$par
$par
[1] 2.377465  2.812073 #These are the obtained optimal values of x1
    and  x2, respectively
sol$fvalues
$fvalues
[1] 2.649525e-08    #This is the obtained optimal value of -g
#Using a new initial solution
x0<-c(-1.2,1)
sol<- optimx(x0, gx, method = "BFGS")
sol$par  # This gives x1* and  x2*, respectively
$par
[1] -0.9961257  1.5270273  #These are the obtained optimal values
    of x1 and  x2, respectively
> sol$fvalues
$fvalues
[1] -0.004783334    #This is the obtained optimal value of -g
#Using a new initial solution
x0<-c(0,0)
sol<-optimx(x0, gx, method = "BFGS")
sol$par
$par
[1] 0.253780320  0.007584573 #These are the obtained optimal values
    of x1 and  x2, respectively
> sol$fvalues
$fvalues
[1] -1.133047    #This is the obtained optimal value of -g
#Thus, depending on the initial solution, the method converges
    towards either a local or a global minimum of -g
```

18.3.2 Derivative-free methods

Gradient-based methods rely upon information about at least the gradient of the objective-function to estimate the direction of search and the step size. Therefore, if the derivative of the function cannot be computed, because, for example, the objective-function is discontinuous, these methods often fail. Furthermore, although these methods can perform well on functions with only one extrema (unimodal function), such as (18.3), their efficiency in solving problems with multimodal functions depend upon how far the initial solution is from the global minimum, i. e., gradient-based methods are more or less efficient in finding the global minimum only if they start from an initial solution sufficiently close to it. Therefore, the solution obtained using these methods may be one of several local minima, and we often cannot be sure that the solution is the global minimum. In this section, we will present some commonly used derivative-free methods, which aim to reduce the limitations of the gradient-based methods by providing an alternative to the computation of the derivatives of the objective-functions. These methods can be very efficient in handling complex problems, where the functions are either discontinuous or improperly defined.

18.3.2.1 The Nelder–Mead method

The Nelder–Mead method is an effective and computationally compact simplex algorithm for finding a local minimum of a function of several variables. Hence, it can be used to solve unconstrained optimization problems of the form:

$$\min_{x} f(x), \quad x \in \mathbb{R}^n. \tag{18.11}$$

Definition 18.3.1. A simplex is an n-dimensional polytope that is the convex hull of $n+1$ vertices.

The Nelder–Mead method iteratively generates a sequence of simplices to approximate an optimal solution to the problem (18.11). At each iteration, the $n+1$ vertices of the simplex are ranked such that

$$f(x_1) \leq f(x_2) \leq \cdots \leq f(x_{n+1}). \tag{18.12}$$

Thus, x_1 and x_{n+1} correspond to the best and worst vertices, respectively.

At each iteration, the Nelder–Mead method consists of four possible operations: reflection, expansion, contraction, and shrinking. Each of these operations has a scalar parameter associated with it. Let us denote by α, β, γ, and δ the parameters associated with the aforementioned operations, respectively. These parameters are chosen such that $\alpha > 0$, $\beta > 1$, $0 < \gamma < 1$, and $0 < \delta < 1$.

Then, the Nelder–Mead simplex algorithm, as described in Lagarias et al. [207], can be summarized as follows:

- Step 0: Generate a simplex with $n+1$ vertices, and choose a convergence criterion;
- Step 1: Sort the $n+1$ vertices according to their objective-function values, i. e., so that (18.12) holds. Then, evaluate the centroid of the points in the simplex, excluding x_{n+1}, given by: $\bar{x} = \sum_{i=1}^{n} x_i$;
- Step 2:
  - Calculate the reflection point $x_r = \bar{x} + \alpha(\bar{x} - x_{n+1})$;
  - If $f(x_1) \leq f(x_r) \leq f(x_n)$, then perform a *reflection* by replacing x_{n+1} with x_r;
- Step 3:
  - If $f(x_r) < f(x_1)$, then calculate the expansion point $x_e = \bar{x} + \beta(x_r - \bar{x})$;
  - If $f(x_e) < f(x_r)$, then perform an *expansion* by replacing x_{n+1} with x_e;
  - otherwise (i. e. $f(x_e) \geq f(x_r)$), then perform a *reflection* by replacing x_{n+1} with x_r;

- Step 4:
  - If $f(x_n) \leq f(x_r) < f(x_n + 1)$, then calculate the outside contraction point $x_{\text{oc}} = \bar{x} + \gamma(x_r - \bar{x})$;
  - If $f(x_{\text{oc}}) \leq f(x_r)$, then perform an *outside contraction* by replacing x_{n+1} with x_{oc};
  - otherwise (i. e. if $f(x_{\text{oc}}) > f(x_r)$), then go to Step 6;
- Step 5:
  - If $f(x_r) \geq f(x_{n+1})$, then calculate the inside contraction point $x_{\text{ic}} = \bar{x} - \gamma(x_r - \bar{x})$;
  - If $f(x_{\text{ic}}) < f(x_{n+1})$, then perform an *inside contraction* by replacing x_{n+1} with x_{ic};
  - otherwise (i. e. if $f(x_{\text{ic}}) \geq f(x_{n+1})$), then go to Step 6;
- Step 6: Perform a shrink by updating x_i, $2 \leq i \leq n + 1$ as follows:

$$x_i = x_1 + \delta(x_i - x_1);$$

- Step 7: Repeat Step 1 through Step 6 until convergence.

In R, an implementation of the Nelder–Mead method can be found in the general multipurpose package `optimx`. The Nelder–Mead method in the package `optimx`, can be used to solve the problem (18.3) as follows:

Listing 18.9: Solving the problem (18.3) using the Nelder–Mead method

```
#The package optimx is required here
library(optimx)
#Defining the function f(x1, x2); its only minimum is reached at
    x1=0 and x2=0
fx<- function(x) x[1]^2 + x[2]^2
#Defining an initial solution
x0<-c(-1.2,1)
#Calling the Nelder-Mead method
sol<-optimx(x0, fx, method = "Nelder-Mead")
sol$par
$par
[1] 1.992835e-04, 3.659277e-05  #These are the obtained optimal
    values of x1 and  x2, respectively
sol$fvalues
$fvalues
[1] 4.105294e-08   #This is the obtained optimal value of f
```

Now, let us use the Nelder–Mead method, implemented in the package `optimx`, to solve the problem (18.4).

Listing 18.10: Solving the problem (18.4) using the Nelder–Mead method

```
#The package optimx is required here
library(optimx)
#Defining the function -g(x1, x2); its global minima is reached at
    x1=0.2538 and x2*=0.0076
```

```
mgx<-function(x) -
    exp(x[1]-2*x[1]^2-x[2]^2)*sin(6*(x[1]+x[2]+x[1]*x[2]^2))
#Defining an initial condition
x0<-c(1, 1)
sol<- optimx(x0, mgx, method = "Nelder-Mead")
sol$par
$par
[1] 0.8007997 1.2758681  #These are the obtained optimal values of
    x1 and  x2, respectively
sol$fvalues
$fvalues
[1] -0.1201183    #This is the obtained optimal value of -g
#Using a new initial solution
x0<-c(-1.2,1)
sol<- optimx(x0, mgx, method = "Nelder-Mead")
sol$par
$par
[1] -0.9960316  1.5271877  #These are the obtained optimal values
    of x1 and  x2, respectively
sol$fvalues
$fvalues
[1] -0.004783335   #This is the obtained optimal value of -g
#Using a new initial solution
x0<-c(0,0)
sol<-optimx(x0, mgx, method = "Nelder-Mead")
sol$par
$par
[1] 0.25377876  0.00758619  #These are the obtained optimal values
    of x1 and  x2, respectively
sol$fvalues
$fvalues
[1] -1.133047    #This is the obtained optimal value of -g
#Thus, depending on the initial solution, the method converges
    towards either a local or a global minimum of -g
```

18.3.2.2 Simulated annealing

The efficiency of the optimization methods, previously discussed, depends on the proximity of the initial point, from which they started, to the optimum. Therefore, they cannot always guarantee a global minimum, since they may be trapped in one of several local minima. Simulated annealing is based on a neighborhood search strategy, derived from the physical analogy of cooling material in a heath bath, which occasionally allows uphill moves.

Simulated annealing is based on the Metropolis algorithm [133], which simulates the change in energy within a system when subjected to the cooling process; eventually, the system converges to a final "frozen" state of a certain energy.

Let us consider a system with a state described by an n-dimensional vector x, for which the function to be minimized is $f(x)$. This is equivalent to an unconstrained minimization problem. Let T, denoting the generalized temperature, be a scalar quantity, which has the same dimensions as f. Then, the Metropolis algorithm description, for a nonatomic system, can be summarized as follows:

- Step 0:
  - Construct an initial solution x_0; set $x = x_0$;
  - Set the number of Monte Carlo steps $N_{\text{MC}} = 0$;
  - Set the temperature, T, to some high value, T_0.
- Step 1: Choose a transition Δx at random.
- Step 2: Evaluate $\Delta f = f(x) - f(x - \Delta x)$.
- Step 3:
  - If $\Delta f \leq 0$, then accept the state by updating x as follows:

$$x \longleftarrow x + \Delta x.$$

  - Otherwise (i. e., $\Delta f > 0$) then,
    - Generate a random number $u \in [0, 1]$;
    - If $u < e^{-\Delta f/T}$, then accept the state by updating x as follows:

$$x \longleftarrow x + \Delta x;$$

- Step 4:
  - Update the temperature value as follows: $T \longleftarrow T - \varepsilon_T$, where $\varepsilon_T \ll T$ is a specified positive real value.
  - Update the number of Monte Carlo steps: $N_{\text{MC}} \longleftarrow N_{\text{MC}} + 1$.
- Step 5:
  - If $T \leq 0$, then stop, and return x;
  - Otherwise (i. e. $T > 0$) then go to Step 1.

In **R**, an implementation of the simulated annealing method can be found in the package **GenSA**, and it can be used to solve the problem (18.3) as follows:

Listing 18.11: Solving the problem (18.3) using Simulated Annealing

```
#The package GenSA is require here
library(GenSA)
#Defining the function f(x1, x2), its only minimum is reached at
    x1=0 and x2=0
fx<- function(x) x[1]^2 + x[2]^2
#Calling the GenSA function - this function requires the definition
    of some finite boundaries of the search domain
lb<-c(-5, -5)
ub<-c(5, 5)
sol <-GenSA(fn=fx,lower=lb, upper=ub)
sol$par
[1]   0   0    #These are the obtained optimal values of x1 and
    x2, respectively
sol$value
[1]   0           #This is the obtained optimal value of f
```

Now, let us use the simulated annealing method, implemented in the package **GenSA**, to solve the problem (18.4).

Listing 18.12: Solving the problem (18.4) using Simulated Annealing

```
#The package GenSA is require here
library(GenSA)
#Defining the function - g(x1, x2), its global minimum is reached
    at x1=0.2538 and x2=0.0076
mgx<-function(x) -
    exp(x[1]-2*x[1]^2-x[2]^2)*sin(6*(x[1]+x[2]+x[1]*x[2]^2))
#Calling the GenSA function - this function requires the definition
    of some finite boundaries of the search domain
lb<-c(-5, -5)
ub<-c(5, 5)
sol <-GenSA(fn=mgx,lower=lb, upper=ub)
sol$par
[1]   0.25377876   0.00758618   #These are the obtained optimal
    values of x1 and x2, respectively
temp$value
[1]   -1.133047   #This is the obtained optimal value of -g
```

18.4 Constrained optimization problems

Constrained optimization problems describe most of the real-world optimization problems. Their complexity depends on the properties of the functional relationships between the decision variables in both the objection function and the constraints.

18.4.1 Constrained linear optimization problems

A linear optimization problem, also referred to as a linear programming problem, occurs when the objective function f and the equality and inequality constraints are all linear. The general structure of such a problem can be written as follows:

$$\begin{aligned}
\text{Optimize}\quad f(x) = &\sum_{j=1}^{n} c_j x_j \\
\text{subject to}\quad &\sum_{j=1}^{n} a_{ij} x_j \le b_i, && i \in I \subseteq \{1,\dots,m\}; \\
&\sum_{j=1}^{n} a_{kj} x_j \ge b_k, && k \in K \subseteq \{1,\dots,m\}; \\
&\sum_{j=1}^{n} a_{rj} x_j = b_r, && r \in R \subseteq \{1,\dots,m\}; \\
&l_j \le x_j \le u_j, && j = 1,\dots,n.
\end{aligned}$$

- Optimize = Minimize or Maximize;
- $x \in \mathbb{R}^n$ and $f : \mathbb{R}^n \longrightarrow \mathbb{R}$ is a linear function;

- I, K, and R are disjunct and $I \cup K \cup R = \{1, \ldots, m\}$;
- $l_j, u_j \in \mathbb{R} \cup \{\pm\infty\}$;
- The coefficients c_j, a_{ij}, a_{kj}, a_{rj}, b_j, b_k and b_r are given real constants.

Linear constrained optimization problems can be solved using algorithms, such as the simplex method or the interior point method.

In R, methods for solving linear optimization problems can be found in the package `lpSolveAPI`.

Let us consider the following constrained linear optimization problems:

$$
(P_1) \quad \begin{array}{lrcrcr}
\text{Maximize} & f(x_1,x_2) = x_1 & + & 3x_2 & & \\
\text{subject to} & x_1 & + & x_2 & \leq & 14 \\
 & -2x_1 & + & 3x_2 & \leq & 12 \\
 & 2x_1 & - & x_2 & \leq & 12 \\
 & x_1, & & x_2 & \geq & 0
\end{array}
$$

$$
(P_2) \quad \begin{array}{lrcrcr}
\text{Minimize} & f(x_1,x_2) = x_2 & - & x_1 & & \\
\text{subject to} & 2x_1 & - & x_2 & \geq & -2 \\
 & x_1 & - & x_2 & \leq & 2 \\
 & x_1 & + & x_2 & \leq & 5 \\
 & x_1, & & x_2 & \geq & 0
\end{array}
$$

$$
(P_3) \quad \begin{array}{lrcrcr}
\text{Maximize} & f(x_1,x_2) = 5x_1 & + & 7x_2 & & \\
\text{subject to} & x_1 & + & x_2 & \geq & 6 \\
 & x_1 & & & \geq & 4 \\
 & & & x_2 & \leq & 3 \\
 & x_1, & & x_2 & \geq & 0
\end{array}
$$

$$
(P_4) \quad \begin{array}{lrcrcr}
\text{Minimize} & f(x_1,x_2) = x_2 & - & x_1 & & \\
\text{subject to} & 2x_1 & - & x_2 & \geq & -2 \\
 & x_1 & - & 2x_2 & \leq & -8 \\
 & x_1 & + & x_2 & \leq & 5 \\
 & x_1, & & x_2 & \geq & 0
\end{array}
$$

Since most of the optimization methods available in R are implemented for minimization-type problems, and the solution which maximizes a function $f(x)$ minimizes the function $-f(x)$, then it is necessary to multiply the objective-functions for problems (P_1) and (P_3) by -1, and solve the corresponding minimization problems. Afterwards, we multiply the values of the objective-functions by -1 to recover the value of the objective functions of (P_1) and (P_3).

The problem (P_1) can be solved using the lpSolveAPI package as follows:

Listing 18.13: Solving the problem (P_1)

```
#The package lpSolveAPI is required here
library(lpSolveAPI)
#Building the model
P1 <- make.lp(0, 2) #Setting the number of variables
set.objfn(P1, c(-1, -3)) #Setting the objective-function -f
add.constraint(P1, c(1, 1), "<=", 14) # Adding the constraints
add.constraint(P1, c(-2, 3), "<=", 12)
add.constraint(P1, c(2, -1), "<=", 12)
#Visualizing the model
P1
Model name:
                C1    C2
Minimize        -1    -3
R1               1     1    <=  14
R2              -2     3    <=  12
R3               2    -1    <=  12
Kind           Std   Std
Type          Real  Real
Upper          Inf   Inf
Lower            0     0
#Solving the model
solve(P1)
[1] 0  #This indicates that the problem has a finite optimal
    solution
get.variables(P1)
[1] 6 8  #These are the obtained optimal values of x1 and  x2,
    respectively
get.objective(P1)
[1] -30  #This is the obtained optimal value of -f, thus f=30
```

The problem (P_2) can be solved using the lpSolveAPI package as follows:

Listing 18.14: Solving the problem (P_2)

```
#The package lpSolveAPI is required here
library(lpSolveAPI)
#Building the model
P2 <- make.lp(0, 2)
set.objfn(P2, c(-1, 1))
add.constraint(P2, c(2, -1), ">=", -2)
add.constraint(P2, c(1, -1), "<=", 2)
add.constraint(P2, c(1, 1), "<=", 5)
#Solving the model
solve(P2)
[1] 0  #This indicates that the problem has a finite optimal
    solution
get.variables(P2)
[1] 2  0  #These are the obtained optimal values of x1 and  x2,
    respectively
get.objective(P2)
[1] -2  #This is the obtained optimal value of  f
```

The problem (P_3) can be solved using the **lpSolveAPI** package as follows:

Listing 18.15: Solving the problem (P_3)

```
#The package lpSolveAPI is required here
library(lpSolveAPI)
#Building the model  P3
P3 <- make.lp(0, 2)
set.objfn(P3, c(-5, -7))
add.constraint(P3, c(1, 1), ">=", 6)
#The second constraint is just a lower bound on x2
set.bounds(P3, lower = 4, columns = 1)
#The third constraint is just an upper bound on x1
set.bounds(P3, upper = 3, columns = 2)
#Solving the model
solve(P3)
[1] 3  #This indicates that the problem is unbounded i.e the
    optimal solution of P3 is not finite
```

The problem (P_4) can be solved using the **lpSolveAPI** package as follows:

Listing 18.16: Solving the problem (P_4)

```
#The package lpSolveAPI is required here
library(lpSolveAPI)
#Building the model
P4 <- make.lp(0, 2)
set.objfn(P4, c(-1, 1))
add.constraint(P4, c(2, -1), ">=", -2)
add.constraint(P4, c(1, -2), "<=", -8)
add.constraint(P4, c(1, 1), "<=", 5)
#Solving the model
solve(P4)
[1] 2 # This indicates that the problem is infeasible i.e there are
    contradicting constraints in the problem
```

Suppose that, in the problem (P_1), x_1 is a binary variable (i. e., it takes only the value 0 or 1), and x_2 is an integer variable, then it is necessary to set them to the appropriate type before solving the problem ($P1$). This can be done as follows:

Listing 18.17: Solving a binary version of the problem (P_1)

```
set.type(P1, 1, "binary")
set.type(P1, 2, "integer")
solve(P1)
[1] 0  #This indicates that the problem has a finite optimal
    solution
get.variables(P1)
[1] 1 4  #These are the obtained optimal values of x1 and  x2,
    respectively
get.objective(P1)
[1] -13  #This is the obtained optimal value of  -f, thus f=13
```

18.4.2 Constrained nonlinear optimization problems

In its general form, a nonlinear constrained optimization problem, with n variables and m constraint, can be written as follows:

$$\begin{array}{llcll} \text{Optimize} & f(x) & & & \\ \text{subject to} & g_i(x) & = & b_i, & i \in I \subseteq \{1,\dots,m\}; \\ & h_j(x) & \leq & d_j, & j \in J \subseteq \{1,\dots,m\}; \\ & h_k(x) & \geq & d_k, & k \in K \subseteq \{1,\dots,m\}; \\ & x & \leq & u, & \\ & x & \geq & l, & \end{array} \tag{18.13}$$

where

- Optimize = Minimize or Maximize;
- $f : \mathbb{R}^n \longrightarrow \mathbb{R}$, $g_i : \mathbb{R}^n \longrightarrow \mathbb{R}$, $\forall\, i \in I$, $h_r : \mathbb{R}^n \longrightarrow \mathbb{R}$, $\forall\, r \in J \cup K$, with at least one of these functions being nonlinear;
- I, J, and K are disjunct and $I \cup J \cup K = \{1,\dots,m\}$;
- $b_i, d_j, d_k \in \mathbb{R} \cup \{\pm\infty\}$, $\forall\, i,\ j,\ k$;
- $l, u \in (\mathbb{R} \cup \{\pm\infty\})^n$.

The solution to constrained nonlinear optimization problems, in the form of (18.13), can be obtained using the Lagrange multiplier method.

18.4.3 Lagrange multiplier method

Without loss of the generality, assume that the problem (18.13) is a minimization problem, and let us multiply the inequality constraints of type "$\geq$" by -1; then the problem can be rewritten as:

$$\begin{array}{llcll} \text{Minimize} & z & = & f(x) & \\ \text{subject to} & g_i(x) & = & b_i, & i = 1,\dots,p, \ \text{with}\, p \leq m; \\ & h_j(x) & \leq & d_j, & j = 1,\dots,m-p. \end{array} \tag{18.14}$$

The Lagrangian of the problem (18.14), denoted L, is defined as follows:

$$L(x,\lambda,\mu) = f(x) + \sum_{i=1}^{p} \lambda_i \big(g_i(x) - b_i\big) + \sum_{j=1}^{m-p} \mu_j \big(h_j(x) - d_j\big), \tag{18.15}$$

where λ_i, and μ_j are the Lagrangian multipliers associated with the constraints $g_i(x) = b_i$, and $h_j(x) \leq d_j$, respectively.

The fundamental result behind the Lagrangian formulation (18.15) can be summarized as follows: suppose that a solution $x^* = (x_1^*, x_2^*, \dots, x_n^*)$ minimizes the function $f(x)$ subject to the constraints $g_i(x) = b_i$, for $i = 1, \dots, p$ and $h_j(x) \le d_j$, for $j = 1, \dots, m-p$. Then we have one of the following:

1. Either there exist vectors $\lambda^* = (\lambda_1^*, \dots, \lambda_p^*)$ and $\mu^* = (\mu_1^*, \dots, \mu_{m-p}^*)$ such that

$$\nabla f(x^*) + \sum_{i=1}^{p} \lambda_i^* \nabla g_i(x^*) + \sum_{j=1}^{m-p} \mu_j^* \nabla h_j(x^*) = 0; \tag{18.16}$$

$$\mu_j^* \big(h_j(x^*) - d_j\big) = 0, \quad j = 1, \dots, m-p; \tag{18.17}$$

$$\mu_j^* \ge 0, \quad j = 1, \dots, m-p; \tag{18.18}$$

2. Or the vectors $\nabla g_i(x^*)$, for $i = 1, \dots, p$, $\nabla h_j(x^*)$ for $j = 1, \dots, m-p$ are linearly dependent.

The result that is of greatest interest is the first one, i. e., case 1. From the equation (18.17), either μ_j is zero or $h_j(x^*) - d_j = 0$. This provides various possible solutions and the optimal solution is one of these. For an optimal solution, x^*, some of the inequalities constraints will be satisfied at equality, and others will not. The latter can be ignored, whereas the former will form the second equation above. Thus, the constraints $\mu_j^*(h_j(x^*) - d_j) = 0$ mean that either an inequality constraint is satisfied at equality, or the Lagrangian multiplier μ_j is zero.

The conditions (18.16)–(18.18) are referred to as the Karush–Kuhn–Tucker (KKT) conditions, and they are necessary conditions for a solution to a nonlinear constrained optimization problem to be optimal. For a maximization-type problem, the conditions (KKT) remain unchanged with the exception of the first condition (18.16), which is written as

$$\nabla f(x^*) - \sum_{i=1}^{p} \lambda_i^* \nabla g_i(x^*) - \sum_{j=1}^{m-p} \mu_j^* \nabla h_j(x^*) = 0.$$

Note that the KKT conditions (18.16)–(18.18) represent the stationarity, the complementary slackness and the dual feasibility, respectively. Other supplementary KKT conditions are the primal feasibility conditions defined by constraints of the problem (18.14).

In `R`, an implementation of the Lagrange multiplier method, for solving nonlinear constrained optimization problems, can be found in the package `Rsolnp`.

Let us use the function `solnp` from the `R` package `Rsolnp` to solve the following constrained nonlinear minimization problem:

$$(P)\quad \begin{array}{lrcl} \text{Minimize} & f(x_1,x_2) & = & e^{x_1}(4x_1^2+2x_2^2+4x_1x_2+2x_2+1) \\ \text{subject to} & & & \\ & x_1+x_2 & = & 1 \\ & x_1x_2 & \geq & -10 \end{array}$$

Listing 18.18: Solving the problem (P)

```
#The package Rsolnp is required here
library(Rsolnp)
#Building the model
#Setting the objective function
fobj <- function(x)
    exp(x[1])*(4*x[1]^2+2*x[2]^2+4*x[1]*x[2]+2*x[2]+1)
#Setting the left hand side of equality constraints
lhseq <- function(x){
     eq1=x[1]^2 + x[2]
     return(eq1)
}
#Setting the right hand side of equality constraints
rhseq <- 1
#Setting the variable term in the inequality constraints
vtineq <- function(x){
     ineq1=x[1]*x[2]
     return(ineq1)
}
#Setting the lower bound of inequality constraints
lbineq <-  -10
#Setting the upper bound of inequality constraints: if an
    inequality constraint has no upper bound its corresponding
    upper bound is set to infinity
ubineq <- Inf
#Solving the model
sol<-solnp(x0, fun = fobj, eqfun = lhseq, eqB =rhseq, ineqfun =
    vtineq, ineqLB = lbineq, ineqUB = Iubineq,
    control=list(trace=0))
sol$convergence
[1] 0  #This indicates that the problem has a finite optimal
    solution
sol$par
[1] -0.7528791  0.4331731   #These are the obtained optimal values
    of x1 and  x2, respectively
fobj(sol$pars)
[1] 1.509311 #This is the obtained optimal value of f
```

18.5 Some applications in statistical machine learning

Most of the statistical theory, including statistical machine learning, consists of the efficient use of collected data to estimate the unknown parameters of a model, which answers the questions of interest.

18.5.1 Maximum likelihood estimation

The likelihood function of a parameter ω for a given observed data set, $\mathcal{D}$, denoted by $\mathcal{L}$, is defined by

$$\mathcal{L}(\omega) = \kappa P(\mathcal{D}, \omega), \quad \omega \in \Omega; \tag{18.19}$$

where κ is a constant independent of ω, $P(\mathcal{D}, \omega)$ is the probability of the observed data set and Ω is the feasible set of ω.

When the data set, $\mathcal{D}$, consists of a complete random sample $x_1, x_2, \dots, x_n$ from a discrete probability distribution with probability function $p(x/\omega)$, the probability of the observed dataset is given by

$$P(\mathcal{D}, \omega) = P(X_1 = x_1, X_2 = x_2, \dots, X_n = x_n|\omega), \tag{18.20}$$

$$= \prod_{i=1}^{n} P(X_i = x_i) = \prod_{i=1}^{n} p(x_i|\omega). \tag{18.21}$$

When the data set $\mathcal{D}$ consists of a complete random sample $x_1, x_2, \dots, x_n$ from a continuous probability distribution with probability function $f(x/\omega)$, then $x \in \mathbb{R}$ and the observation x_i falls within a small interval $[x_i, x_i + \Delta x_i]$ with approximate probability $\Delta x_i f(x/\omega)$. The probability of the observed data set is then given by

$$P(\mathcal{D}, \omega) \approx \prod_{i=1}^{n} \Delta x_i f(x_i|\omega) = \prod_{i=1}^{n} \Delta x_i \prod_{i=1}^{n} f(x_i|\omega). \tag{18.22}$$

Definition 18.5.1. Without loss of generality, the likelihood function of a sample is proportional to the product of the conditional probability of the data sample, given the parameter of interest, i. e.,

$$\mathcal{L}(\omega) \propto \prod_{i=1}^{n} f(x_i|\omega), \quad \omega \in \Omega. \tag{18.23}$$

Definition 18.5.2. The value of the parameter ω, which maximizes the likelihood $\mathcal{L}(\omega)$, hence the probability of the observed dataset $P(\mathcal{D}, \omega)$, is known as the maximum likelihood estimator (MLE) of ω and is denoted $\hat{\omega}$.

Note that the MLE $\hat{\omega}$ is a function of the data sample $x_1, x_2, \dots, x_n$. The likelihood function (18.23) is often complex to manipulate and, in practice, it is more convenient to work with the logarithm of $\mathcal{L}(\omega)$ ($\log \mathcal{L}(\omega)$), which also yields the same optimal parameter $\hat{\omega}$.

The MLE problem can then be formulated as the following optimization problem, which can be solved using the numerical methods, implemented in `R`, presented in the previous sections.

$$\underset{\omega\in\Omega}{\text{Maximize}} \quad \log \mathcal{L}(\omega). \tag{18.24}$$

18.5.2 Support vector classification

Suppose that we are given the following data points: $(x_1, y_1), \ldots, (x_n, y_n)$, where $x_i \in \mathbb{R}^m$ and $y \in \{-1, +1\}$. The fundamental idea, behind the concept of support vector machine (SVM) classification [191], is to find a pair $(w, b) \in \mathbb{R}^m \times \mathbb{R}$ such that the hyperplane defined by $\langle w, x\rangle + b = 0$ separates the data points labeled $y_i = +1$ from those labeled $y_i = -1$, and maximizes the distance to the closest points from either class. If the points (x_i, y_i), $i = 1, \ldots, n$ are linearly separable, then such a pair exists.

Let (x_1, y_1) and (x_2, y_2), with $y_1 = +1$ and $y_2 = -1$, be the closest points on either sides of the optimal hyperplane defined by $\langle w, x\rangle + b = 0$. Then, we have

$$\begin{cases} \langle w, x_1\rangle + b = +1, \\ \langle w, x_2\rangle + b = -1. \end{cases} \tag{18.25}$$

From (18.25), we have $\langle w, (x_1 - x_2)\rangle = 2 \Longrightarrow \langle \frac{w}{\|w\|}, (x_1 - x_2)\rangle = \frac{2}{\|w\|}$. Hence, for the distance between the points (x_1, y_1) and (x_2, y_2) to be maximum, we need the ratio $\frac{2}{\|w\|}$ to be as maximum as possible or, equivalently, we need the ratio $\frac{\|w\|}{2}$ to be as minimum as possible, i. e.

$$\underset{w\in\mathbb{R}^m}{\text{minimize}} \quad \frac{1}{2}\|w\|^2. \tag{18.26}$$

Generalizing (18.25) to all the points (x_i, y_i) yields the following:

$$\begin{cases} \langle w, x_i\rangle + b \geq +1, & \text{if } y_i = +1 \\ \langle w, x_i\rangle + b \leq -1, & \text{if } y_i = -1 \end{cases} \Longrightarrow y_i\big(\langle w, x_i\rangle + b\big) \geq 1. \tag{18.27}$$

Thus, to construct such an optimal hyperplane, it is necessary to solve the following problem:

$$\begin{aligned} &\underset{w\in\mathbb{R}^m,\, b\in\mathbb{R}}{\text{minimize}} \quad z(w) = \frac{1}{2}\|w\|^2 \\ &\text{subject to} \quad y_i\big(\langle w, x_i\rangle + b\big) \geq 1, \quad \text{for } i = 1, \ldots, m \end{aligned} \tag{18.28}$$

The above problem is a constrained optimization problem with a nonlinear (quadratic) objective function and linear constraints, which can be solved using the Lagrange multiplier method.

The Lagrangian associated with the problem (18.28) can be defined as follows:

$$L(w,b,\lambda) = \frac{1}{2}\|w\|^2 - \sum_{i=1}^{m} \lambda_i\big(y_i\big(\langle w, x_i\rangle + b\big) - 1\big), \tag{18.29}$$

where $\lambda_i \geq 0$, for $i = 1, \dots, m$ denote the Lagrange multipliers.

The Lagrangian (18.29) must be minimized with respect to w and b, and maximized with respect to λ.

Solving

$$\begin{cases} \frac{\partial}{\partial b} L(w,b,\lambda) = 0 \\ \frac{\partial}{\partial w} L(w,b,\lambda) = 0 \end{cases} \tag{18.30}$$

yields

$$\sum_{i=1}^{m} \lambda_i y_i = 0, \tag{18.31}$$

$$w = \sum_{i=1}^{m} \lambda_i y_i. \tag{18.32}$$

Substituting w into the Lagrangian (18.29) leads to the following optimization problem, also known as the dual formulation of support vector classifier:

$$\begin{aligned} \underset{\lambda \in \mathbb{R}^m}{\text{maximize}} \quad & Z(\lambda) = \sum_{i}^{m} \lambda_i - \frac{1}{2}\sum_{i=1}^{m}\sum_{j=1}^{m} \lambda_i\lambda_j y_i y_j \langle x_i, x_j\rangle \\ \text{subject to} \quad & \sum_{i=1}^{m} \lambda_i y_i = 0, \\ & \lambda_i \geq 0, \quad \text{for } i = 1, \dots, m. \end{aligned} \tag{18.33}$$

Both problems (18.28) and (18.33) can be solved in `R` using the package `Rsolnp`, as illustrated in Listing (18.18). However, since the constraints of (18.28) are relatively complex, it is computationally easier to solve the problem (18.33) and then recover the vector w through (18.32).

18.6 Further reading

For advanced readings about numerical methods in optimization, we recommend the following references: [13, 16, 144]. For stochastic optimization, the textbook [162] provides a good introduction and overview.

18.7 Summary

Optimization is a broad and complex topic. One of the major challenges in optimization is the determination of global optima for nonlinear and high-dimensional problems. Generally, optimization methods find applications in attempts to optimize a parametric decision-making process, such as classification, clustering, or regression of data. The corresponding optimization problems either involve complex nonlinear functions or are based on data points, i. e., the problems include discontinuities. Knowledge about optimization methods can be helpful in designing analysis methods, since they usually involve difficult optimization solutions. Hence, a parsimonious approach for designing such analysis methods will also help to keep optimization problems tractable.

18.8 Exercises

1. Consider the following unconstrained problem:

$$\max_{(x_1,x_2)\in\mathbb{R}^2} f(x_1,x_2) = -(x_1-5)^2-(x_2-3)^2. \tag{18.34}$$

   Using R, provide the contour plot of the function $f(x_1, x2)$ and solve the problem (18.34) using
   - the steepest descent method;
   - the conjugate gradient method;
   - Newton's method;
   - the Nelder–Mead method;
   - Simulated annealing;
2. Consider the following unconstrained problem:

$$\min_{(x_1,x_2)\in\mathbb{R}^2} z(x_1,x_2) = -2x_1-3x_2+\frac{1}{5}x_1^2+2x_2^2-3x_1x_2. \tag{18.35}$$

   Using R, provide the contour plot of the function $z(x_1, x2)$ and solve the problem (18.35) using
   - the steepest descent method;
   - the conjugate gradient method;
   - Newton's method;
   - the Nelder–Mead method;
   - Simulated annealing;

3. Using the R package `lpSolveAPI`, solve the following linear programming problems:

$$(A)\quad \begin{array}{llcrcrcl} \text{Minimize} & f(x_1,x_2) = & 2x_1 & + & 3x_2 & & \\ \text{subject to} & & \frac{1}{2}x_1 & + & \frac{1}{4}x_2 & \leq & 4 \\ & & x_1 & + & 3x_2 & \geq & 20 \\ & & x_1 & + & x_2 & = & 10 \\ & & & x_1, & x_2 & \geq & 0 \end{array}$$

$$(B)\quad \begin{array}{llcrcrcl} \text{Maximize} & f(x_1,x_2) = & 3x_1 & + & x_2 & & \\ \text{subject to} & & x_1 & + & x_2 & \geq & 3 \\ & & 2x_1 & + & x_2 & \leq & 4 \\ & & x_1 & + & x_2 & = & 3 \\ & & & x_1, & x_2 & \geq & 0 \end{array}$$

4. Using the function `solnp` from the R package `Rsolnp`, solve the following nonlinear constrained optimization problems:

$$(A)\quad \begin{array}{lrcl} \text{Minimize} & f(x_1,x_2) & = & (x_1-1)^2+(x_2-2)^2 \\ \text{subject to} & & & \\ & -x_1+x_2 & = & 1 \\ & x_1+x_2 & \leq & 3 \end{array}$$

$$(B)\quad \begin{array}{lrcl} \text{Minimize} & f(x_1,x_2) & = & -x_1^2-x_2^2+3x_1+5x_2 \\ \text{subject to} & & & \\ & x_1+x_2 & \leq & 7 \\ & x_1 & \leq & 5 \\ & x_2 & \leq & 6 \end{array}$$

Bibliography

[1] H. Abelson, G. J. Sussman, and J. Sussman. *Structure and Interpretation of Computer Programs*, 2nd edition. MIT Press, 1996.

[2] L. Adamic and B. Huberman. Power-law distribution of the world wide web. *Science*, 287:2115a, 2000.

[3] W. A. Adkins and M. G. Davidson. *Ordinary Differential Equations*. Undergraduate Texts in Mathematics. Springer New York, 2012.

[4] R. Albert and A. L. Barabási. Statistical mechanics of complex networks. *Rev. Mod. Phys.*, 74:47–97, 2002.

[5] G. R. Andrews. *Foundations of Multithreaded, Parallel, and Distributed Programming*. Addison-Wesley, 1999.

[6] M. Ashburner, C. A. Ball, J. A. Blake, D. Botstein, and H. Butler et al. Gene ontology: tool for the unification of biology. The Gene Ontology Consortium. *Nat. Genet.*, 25(1):25–29, May 2000.

[7] K. Baltakys, J. Kanniainen, and F. Emmert-Streib. Multilayer aggregation of investor trading networks. *Sci. Rep.*, 1:8198, 2018.

[8] A. L. Barabási and R. Albert. Emergence of scaling in random networks. *Science*, 206:509–512, 1999.

[9] A. L. Barabási and Z. N. Oltvai. Network biology: understanding the cell's functional organization, *Nat. Rev. Genet.*, 5:101–113, 2004.

[10] Albert-László Barabási. Network science. *Philos. Trans. R. Soc. Lond. A*, 371(1987):20120375, 2013.

[11] M. Barnsley. *Fractals Everywhere*. Morgan Kaufmann, 2000.

[12] R. G. Bartle and D. R. Sherbert. *Introduction to Real Analysis*. Wiley Publishing, 1999.

[13] Mokhtar S. Bazaraa, Hanif D. Sherali, and Chitharanjan M. Shetty. *Nonlinear Programming: Theory and Algorithms*. John Wiley & Sons, 2013.

[14] R. A. Becker and J. M. Chambers. *An Interactive Environment for Data Analysis and Graphics*. Wadsworth & Brooks/Cole, Pacific Grove, CA, USA, 1984.

[15] M. Behzad, G. Chartrand, and L. Lesniak-Foster. *Graphs & Digraphs*. International Series. Prindle, Weber & Schmidt, 1979.

[16] D. P. Bertsekas. *Nonlinear Programming*. Athena Scientific Optimization and Computation Series. Athena Scientific, 2016.

[17] Dimitri P. Bertsekas and John N. Tsitsiklis. *Introduction to Probability*, Vol. 1, 2002.

[18] Joseph K. Blitzstein and Jessica Hwang. *Introduction to Probability*. Chapman and Hall/CRC, 2014.

[19] D. Bonchev. *Information Theoretic Indices for Characterization of Chemical Structures*. Research Studies Press, Chichester, 1983.

[20] D. Bonchev and D. H. Rouvray. *Chemical Graph Theory: Introduction and Fundamentals*. Mathematical Chemistry. Abacus Press, 1991.

[21] D. Bonchev and D. H. Rouvray. *Complexity in Chemistry, Biology, and Ecology*. Mathematical and Computational Chemistry. Springer, New York, NY, USA, 2005.

[22] G. S. Boolos, J. P. Burgess, and R. C. Jeffrey. *Computability and Logic*, 5th edition. Cambridge University Press, 2007.

[23] S. Bornholdt and H. G. Schuster. *Handbook of Graphs and Networks: From the Genome to the Internet*. John Wiley & Sons, Inc., New York, NY, USA, 2003.

[24] U. Brandes and T. Erlebach. *Network Analysis*. Lecture Notes in Computer Science. Springer, Berlin Heidelberg New York, 2005.

[25] A. Brandstädt, V. B. Le, and J. P. Sprinrad. *Graph Classes. A Survey*. SIAM Monographs

https://doi.org/10.1515/9783110796063-019

on Discrete Mathematics and Applications, 1999.

[26] L. Breiman. Random forests. *Mach. Learn.*, 45:5–32, 2001.

[27] O. Bretscher. *Linear Algebra with Applications*, 3rd edition. Prentice Hall, 2004.

[28] Sergey Brin and Lawrence Page. The anatomy of a large-scale hypertextual Web search engine. *Comput. Netw. ISDN Syst.*, 30(1–7):107–117, 1998.

[29] M. Brinkmeier and T. Schank. Network statistics. In U. Brandes and T. Erlebach, editors, *Network Analysis*, Lecture Notes of Computer Science, pages 293–317. Springer, 2005.

[30] I. A. Bronstein, A. Semendjajew, G. Musiol, and H. Mühlig. *Taschenbuch der Mathematik*. Harri Deutsch Verlag, 1993.

[31] F. Buckley and F. Harary. *Distance in Graphs*. Addison Wesley Publishing Company, 1990.

[32] P. E. Ceruzzi. *A History of Modern Computing*, 2nd edition. MIT Press, 2003.

[33] S. Chiaretti, X. Li, R. Gentleman, A. Vitale, M. Vignetti, F. Mandelli, J. Ritz, and R. Foa. Gene expression profile of adult t-cell acute lymphocytic leukemia identifies distinct subsets of patients with different response to therapy and survival. *Blood*, 103(7):2771–2778, 2003.

[34] W. F. Clocksin and C. S. Mellish. *Programming in Prolog: Using the ISO Standard*. Springer, 2002.

[35] S. Cole-Kleene. *Mathematical Logic*. Dover Books on Mathematics. Dover Publications, 2002.

[36] B. Jack Copeland, C. J. Posy, and O. Shagrir. *Elements of Information Theory*. The MIT Press, 2013.

[37] T. H. Cormen, C. E. Leiserson, and R. L. Rivest. *Introduction to Algorithms*. MIT Press, 1990.

[38] T. H. Cormen, C. E. Leiserson, R. L. Rivest, and C. Stein. *Introduction to Algorithms*. MIT Press, 2001.

[39] T. M. Cover and J. A. Thomas. *Information Theory*. John Wiley & Sons, Inc., 1991.

[40] T. M. Cover and J. A. Thomas. *Elements of Information Theory*. Wiley Series in Telecommunications and Signal Processing. Wiley & Sons, 2006.

[41] N. Cristianini and J. Shawe-Taylor. *An Introduction to Support Vector Machines*. Cambridge University Press, Cambridge, UK, 2000.

[42] Gabor Csardi and Tamas Nepusz. The igraph software package for complex network research. *InterJournal*, Complex Systems:1695, 2006, http://igraph.sf.net.

[43] L. da F. Costa, F. Rodrigues, and G. Travieso. Characterization of complex networks: a survey of measurements. *Adv. Phys.*, 56:167–242, 2007.

[44] R. de Matos Simoes and F. Emmert-Streib. Influence of statistical estimators of mutual information and data heterogeneity on the inference of gene regulatory networks. *PLoS ONE*, 6(12):e29279, 2011.

[45] R. de Matos Simoes and F. Emmert-Streib. Bagging statistical network inference from large-scale gene expression data. *PLoS ONE*, 7(3):e33624, 2012.

[46] Pierre Lafaye de Micheaux, Rémy Drouilhet, and Benoit Liquet. The R software. 2013.

[47] J. Debasish. *C++ and Object Oriented Programming Paradigm*. PHI Learning Pvt. Ltd., 2005.

[48] Morris H. DeGroot and Mark J. Schervish. *Probability and Statistics*. Pearson Education, 2012.

[49] M. Dehmer. *Die analytische Theorie der Polynome. Nullstellenschranken für komplexwertige Polynome*. Weissensee-Verlag, Berlin, Germany, 2004.

[50] M. Dehmer. On the location of zeros of complex polynomials. *J. Inequal. Pure Appl. Math.*, 7(1), 2006.

[51] M. Dehmer. *Strukturelle Analyse web-basierter Dokumente*. Multimedia und

Telekooperation. Deutscher Universitäts Verlag, Wiesbaden, 2006.

[52] M. Dehmer, editor. *Structural Analysis of Complex Networks*. Birkhäuser Publishing, 2010.

[53] M. Dehmer and F. Emmert-Streib, editors. *Analysis of Complex Networks: From Biology to Linguistics*. Wiley-VCH, Weinheim, 2009.

[54] M. Dehmer, K. Varmuza, S. Borgert, and F. Emmert-Streib. On entropy-based molecular descriptors: statistical analysis of real and synthetic chemical structures. *J. Chem. Inf. Model.*, 49:1655–1663, 2009.

[55] M. Dehmer, K. Varmuza, S. Borgert, and F. Emmert-Streib. On entropy-based molecular descriptors: statistical analysis of real and synthetic chemical structures. *J. Chem. Inf. Model.*, 49(7):1655–1663, 2009.

[56] R. Devaney and M. W. Hirsch. *Differential Equations, Dynamical Systems, and an Introduction to Chaos*. Academic Press, 2004.

[57] J. Devillers and A. T. Balaban. *Topological Indices and Related Descriptors in QSAR and QSPR*. Gordon and Breach Science Publishers, Amsterdam, The Netherlands, 1999.

[58] E. W. Dijkstra. A note on two problems in connection with graphs. *Numer. Math.*, 1:269–271, 1959.

[59] S. N. Dorogovtsev and J. F. F. Mendes. *Evolution of Networks. From Biological Networks to the Internet and WWW*. Oxford University Press, 2003.

[60] J. Duckett. *Beginning HTML, XHTML, CSS, and JavaScript*. Wrox, 2009.

[61] F. Emmert-Streib and M. Dehmer. Defining data science by a data-driven quantification of the community. *Mach. Learn. Knowl. Extr.*, 1(1):235–251, 2019.

[62] F. Emmert-Streib. Exploratory analysis of spatiotemporal patterns of cellular automata by clustering compressibility. *Phys. Rev. E*, 81(2):026103, 2010.

[63] F. Emmert-Streib and M. Dehmer. Topological mappings between graphs, trees and generalized trees. *Appl. Math. Comput.*, 186(2):1326–1333, 2007.

[64] F. Emmert-Streib and M. Dehmer, editors. *Analysis of Microarray Data: A Network-based Approach*. Wiley VCH Publishing, 2010.

[65] F. Emmert-Streib and M. Dehmer. Identifying critical financial networks of the djia: towards a network based index. *Complexity*, 16(1), 2010.

[66] F. Emmert-Streib and M. Dehmer. Influence of the time scale on the construction of financial networks. *PLoS ONE*, 5(9):e12884, 2010.

[67] F. Emmert-Streib and M. Dehmer. Networks for systems biology: conceptual connection of data and function. *IET Syst. Biol.*, 5:185–207, 2011.

[68] F. Emmert-Streib and M. Dehmer. Evaluation of regression models: model assessment, model selection and generalization error. *Mach. Learn. Knowl. Extr.*, 1(1):521–551, 2019.

[69] F. Emmert-Streib, M. Dehmer, and B. Haibe-Kains. Untangling statistical and biological models to understand network inference: the need for a genomics network ontology. *Front. Genet.*, 5:299, 2014.

[70] F. Emmert-Streib, M. Dehmer, and O. Yli-Harja. Against Dataism and for data sharing of big biomedical and clinical data with research parasites. *Front. Genet.*, 7:154, 2016.

[71] F. Emmert-Streib and G. V. Glazko. Network biology: a direct approach to study biological function. *Wiley Interdiscip. Rev., Syst. Biol. Med.*, 3(4):379–391, 2011.

[72] F. Emmert-Streib, G. V. Glazko, Gökmen Altay, and Ricardo de Matos Simoes. Statistical inference and reverse engineering of gene regulatory networks from observational expression data. *Front. Genet.*, 3:8, 2012.

[73] F. Emmert-Streib, S. Moutari, and M. Dehmer. The process of analyzing data is the emergent feature of data science. *Front. Genet.*, 7:12, 2016.

[74] F. Emmert-Streib, S. Tripathi, O. Yli-Harja, and M. Dehmer. Understanding the world economy in terms

of networks: a survey of data-based network science approaches on economic networks. *Front. Appl. Math. Stat.*, 4:37, 2018.

[75] Frank Emmert-Streib and Matthias Dehmer. Network science: from chemistry to digital society. *Front. Young Minds*, 2019.

[76] P. Erdös and A. Rényi. On random graphs. I. *Publ. Math.*, 6:290–297, 1959.

[77] P. Erdös and A. Rényi. On random graphs. *Publ. Math. Inst. Hung. Acad. Sci.*, 5:17, 1960.

[78] G. Fichtenholz. *Differentialrechnung und Integralrechnung*. Verlag Harri Deutsch, 1997.

[79] R. W. Floyd. The paradigms of programming. *Commun. ACM*, 22(8):455–460, 1979.

[80] L. C. Freeman. A set of measures of centrality based on betweenness. *Sociometry*, 40, 1977.

[81] L. C. Freeman. Centrality in social networks: conceptual clarification. *Soc. Netw.*, 1:215–239, 1979.

[82] Thomas M. J. Fruchterman and Edward M. Reingold. Graph drawing by force-directed placement. *Softw. Pract. Exp.*, 21(11):1129–1164, 1991.

[83] R. G. Gallager. *Information Theory and Reliable Communication*. Wiley, 1968.

[84] A. Gelman, JB. Carlin, HS. Stern, and DB. Rubin. *Bayesian Data Analysis*. Chapman & Hall/CRC, 2003.

[85] C. Gershenson. Classification of random boolean networks. In R. K. Standish, M. A. Bedau, and H. A. Abbass, editors, *Artificial Life VIII*, pages 1–8. MIT Press, Cambridge, 2003.

[86] G. H. Golub and C. F. Van Loan. *Matrix Computation*. The Johns Hopkins University, 2012.

[87] Geoffrey Grimmett, Geoffrey R. Grimmett, and David Stirzaker. *Probability and Random Processes*. Oxford University Press, 2001.

[88] Jonathan L. Gross and Jay Yellen. *Graph Theory and Its Applications*. CRC Press, 2005.

[89] Grundlagen der Informatik für Ingenieure, 2008. Course materials, School of Computer Science, Otto-von-Guericke-University Magdeburg, Germany.

[90] I. Gutman. The energy of a graph: old and new results. In A. Betten, A. Kohnert, R. Laue, and A. Wassermann, editors, *Algebraic Combinatorics and Applications*, pages 196–211. Springer Verlag, Berlin, 2001.

[91] Ian Hacking. *The Emergence of Probability: A Philosophical Study of Early Ideas About Probability, Induction and Statistical Inference*. Cambridge University Press, 2006.

[92] P. Hage and F. Harary. Eccentricity and centrality in networks. *Soc. Netw.*, 17:57–63, 1995.

[93] R. Halin. *Graphentheorie*. Akademie Verlag, Berlin, Germany, 1989.

[94] F. Harary. *Graph Theory*. Addison Wesley Publishing Company, Reading, MA, USA, 1969.

[95] R. Harrison, L. G. Smaraweera, M. R. Dobie, and P. H. Lewis. Comparing programming paradigms: an evaluation of functional and object-oriented programs. *Softw. Eng. J.*, 11(4):247–254, 1996.

[96] T. Hastie, R. Tibshirani, and J. H. Friedman. *The Elements of Statistical Learning*. Springer, Berlin, New York, 2001.

[97] D. C. Hoaglin, F. Mosteller, and J. W. Tukey. *Understanding Robust and Exploratory Data Analysis*. Wiley, New York, 1983.

[98] R. E. Hodel. *An Introduction to Mathematical Logic*. Dover Publications, 2013.

[99] A. S. Householder. *The Numerical Treatment of a Single Nonlinear Equation*. McGraw-Hill, New York, NY, USA, 1970.

[100] T. Ihringer. *Diskrete Mathematik*. Teubner, Stuttgart, 1994.

[101] Edwin T. Jaynes. *Probability Theory: The Logic of Science*. Cambridge University Press, 2003.

[102] J. Jost. *Partial Differential Equations*. Springer, New York, NY, USA, 2007.
[103] G. Julia. Mémoire sur l'itération des fonctions rationnelles. *J. Math. Pures Appl.*, 8:47–245, 1918.
[104] B. Junker, D. Koschützki, and F. Schreiber. Exploration of biological network centralities with centibin. *BMC Bioinform.*, 7(1):219, 2006.
[105] Joseph B. Kadane. *Principles of Uncertainty*. Chapman and Hall/CRC, 2011.
[106] Tomihisa Kamada, Satoru Kawai, et al. An algorithm for drawing general undirected graphs. *Inf. Process. Lett.*, 31(1):7–15, 1989.
[107] M. Kanehisa and S. Goto. KEGG: Kyoto Encyclopedia of Genes and Genomes. *Nucleic Acids Res.*, 28:27–30, 2000.
[108] Daniel Kaplan and Leon Glass. *Understanding Nonlinear Dynamics*. Springer Science & Business Media, 2012.
[109] S. A. Kauffman. *The Origin of Order: Self Organization and Selection in Evolution*. Oxford University Press, USA, 1993.
[110] S. V. Kedar. *Programming Paradigms and Methodology*. Technical Publications, 2008.
[111] U. Kirch-Prinz and P. Prinz. *C++. Lernen und professionell anwenden*. mitp Verlag, 2005.
[112] D. G. Kleinbaum and M. Klein. *Survival Analysis: A Self-Learning Text*. Statistics for Biology and Health. Springer, 2005.
[113] V. Kontorovich, L. A. Beltrň, J. Aguilar, Z. Lovtchikova, and K. R. Tinsley. Cumulant analysis of Rössler attractor and its applications. *Open Cybern. Syst. J.*, 3:29–39, 2009.
[114] Kevin B. Korb and Ann E. Nicholson. *Bayesian Artificial Intelligence*. CRC Press, 2010.
[115] R. C. Laubenbacher. *Modeling and Simulation of Biological Networks*. Proceedings of Symposia in Applied Mathematics. American Mathematical Society, 2007.
[116] S. L. Lauritzen. *Graphical Models*. Oxford Statistical Science Series. Oxford University Press, 1996.
[117] M. Z. Li, M. S. Ryerson, and H. Balakrishnan. Topological data analysis for aviation applications. *Transp. Res., Part E, Logist. Transp. Rev.*, 128:149–174, 2019.
[118] Dennis V. Lindley. *Understanding Uncertainty*. John Wiley & Sons, 2013.
[119] E. N. Lorenz. Deterministic nonperiodic flow. *J. Atmos. Sci.*, 20:130–141, 1963.
[120] A. J. Lotka. *Elements of Physical Biology*. Williams and Wilkins, 1925.
[121] K. C. Louden. *Compiler Construction: Principles and Practice*. Course Technology, 1997.
[122] K. C. Louden and K. A. Lambert. *Programming Languages: Principles and Practice*. Advanced Topics Series. Cengage Learning, 2011.
[123] D. J. C. MacKay. *Information Theory, Inference and Learning Algorithms*. Cambridge University Press, 2003.
[124] D. Maier. *Theory of Relational Databases*, 1st edition. Computer Science Press, 1983.
[125] B. B. Mandelbrot. *The Fractal Geometry of Nature*. W. H. Freeman and Company, San Francisco, 1983.
[126] E. G. Manes and A. A. Arbib. *Algebraic Approaches to Program Semantics*. Monographs in Computer Science. Springer, 1986.
[127] M. Marden. *Geometry of Polynomials*. Mathematical Surveys of the American Mathematical Society, Vol. 3. Rhode Island, USA, 1966.
[128] O. Mason and M. Verwoerd. Graph theory and networks in biology. *IET Syst. Biol.*, 1(2):89–119, 2007.
[129] N. Matloff. *The Art of R Programming: A Tour of Statistical Software Design*. No Starch Press, 2011.
[130] B. D. McKay. Graph isomorphisms. *Congr. Numer.*, 730:45–87, 1981.
[131] J. M. McNamee. *Numerical Methods for Roots of Polynomials. Part I*. Elsevier, 2007.
[132] A. Mehler, M. Dehmer, and R. Gleim. Towards logical hypertext structure. A

graph-theoretic perspective. In *Proceedings of I2CS'04*, Lecture Notes, pages 136–150. Springer, Berlin–New York, 2005.

[133] N. Metropolis, A. W. Rosenbluth, M. N. Rosenbluth, and A. H. Teller. Equations of state calculations by fast computing machines. *J. Chem. Phys.*, 21(6):1087–1092, 1953.

[134] C. Meyer. *Matrix Analysis and Applied Linear Algebra.* SIAM, 2000.

[135] M. Mignotte and D. Stefanescu. *Polynomials: An Algorithmic Approach.* Discrete Mathematics and Theoretical Computer Science. Springer, Singapore, 1999.

[136] J. C. Mitchell. *Concepts in Programming Languages.* Cambridge University Press, 2003.

[137] Michael Mitzenmacher and Eli Upfal. *Probability and Computing: Randomization and Probabilistic Techniques in Algorithms and Data Analysis.* Cambridge University Press, 2017.

[138] Mehryar Mohri, Afshin Rostamizadeh, and Ameet Talwalkar. *Foundations of Machine Learning.* MIT Press, 2018.

[139] D. Moore, R. de Matos Simoes, M. Dehmer, and F. Emmert-Streib. Prostate cancer gene regulatory network inferred from RNA-Seq data. *Curr. Genomics*, 20(1):38–48, 2019.

[140] C. Müssel, M. Hopfensitz, and H. A. Kestler. Boolnet—an R package for generation, reconstruction and analysis of Boolean networks. *Bioinformatics*, 26(10):1378–1380, 2010.

[141] M. Newman. *Networks: An Introduction.* Oxford University Press, Oxford, 2010.

[142] M. E. J. Newman. The structure and function of complex networks. *SIAM Rev.*, 45:167–256, 2003.

[143] M. E. J. Newman, A. L. Barabási, and D. J. Watts. *The Structure and Dynamics of Networks.* Princeton Studies in Complexity. Princeton University Press, 2006.

[144] Jorge Nocedal and Stephen Wright. *Numerical Optimization.* Springer Science & Business Media, 2006.

[145] Peter Olofsson. *Probabilities: The Little Numbers That Rule Our Lives.* John Wiley & Sons, 2015.

[146] G. O'Regan. *Mathematics in Computing: An Accessible Guide to Historical, Foundational and Application Contexts.* Springer, 2012.

[147] A. Papoulis. *Probability, Random Variables, and Stochastic Processes.* McGraw-Hill, 1991.

[148] Lothar Papula. *Mathematik für Ingenieure und Naturwissenschaftler Band 1: Ein Lehr-und Arbeitsbuch für das Grundstudium.* Springer-Verlag, 2018.

[149] J. Pearl. *Probabilistic Reasoning in Intelligent Systems.* Morgan-Kaufmann, 1988.

[150] J. Pitman. *Probability.* Springer Texts in Statistics. Springer New York, 1999.

[151] V. V. Prasolov. *Polynomials.* Springer, 2004.

[152] T. W. Pratt, M. V. Zelkowitz, and T. V. Gopal. *Programming Languages: Design and Implementation*, Vol. 4. Prentice-Hall, 2000.

[153] R, software, a language and environment for statistical computing. www.r-project.org, 2018. R Development Core Team, Foundation for Statistical Computing, Vienna, Austria.

[154] R Development Core Team. *R: A Language and Environment for Statistical Computing.* R Foundation for Statistical Computing, Vienna, Austria, 2008. ISBN 3-900051-07-0.

[155] Q. I. Rahman and G. Schmeisser. *Analytic Theory of Polynomials. Critical Points, Zeros and Extremal Properties.* Clarendon Press, Oxford, UK, 2002.

[156] J.-P. Rodrigue, C. Comtois, and B. Slack. *The Geography of Transport Systems.* Taylor & Francis, 2013.

[157] O. E. Rössler. An equation for hyperchaos. *Phys. Lett.*, 71A:155–157, 1979.

[158] W. Rudin. *Real and Complex Analysis*, 3rd edition. McGraw-Hill, 1986.

[159] G. Sabidussi. The centrality index of a graph. *Psychometrika*, 31:581–603, 1966.

[160] A. Salomaa. *Formal Languages.* Academic Press, 1973.

[161] Leonard J. Savage. *The Foundations of Statistics.* Courier Corporation, 1972.

[162] J. Schneider and S. Kirkpatrick. *Stochastic Optimization*. Scientific Computation. Springer Berlin Heidelberg, 2007.

[163] Uwe Schöning. *Algorithmen—kurz gefasst*. Spektrum Akademischer Verlag, 1997.

[164] Uwe Schöning. *Theoretische Informatik—kurz gefasst*. Spektrum Akademischer Verlag, 2001.

[165] H. G. Schuster. *Deterministic Chaos*. Wiley VCH Publisher, 1988.

[166] K. Scott. *The SQL Programming Language*. Jones & Bartlett Publishers, 2009.

[167] M. L. Scott. *Programming Language Pragmatics*. Morgan Kaufmann, 2009.

[168] R. W. Sebesta. *Concepts of Programming Languages*, Vol. 9. Addison-Wesley Reading, 2009.

[169] C. E. Shannon and W. Weaver. *The Mathematical Theory of Communication*. University of Illinois Press, 1949.

[170] L. Shapiro. Organization of relational models. In *Proceedings of Intern. Conf. on Pattern Recognition*, pages 360–365, 1982.

[171] D. J. Sheskin. *Handbook of Parametric and Nonparametric Statistical Procedures*, 3rd edition. RC Press, Boca Raton, FL, 2004.

[172] W. Sierpinśki. On curves which contains the image of any given curve. *Mat. Sb.*, 30:267–287, 1916. In Russian. French translation in Oeuvres Choisies II.

[173] Devinderjit Sivia and John Skilling. *Data Analysis: A Bayesian Tutorial*. OUP Oxford, 2006.

[174] V. A. Skorobogatov and A. A. Dobrynin. Metrical analysis of graphs. *MATCH Commun. Math. Comput. Chem.*, 23:105–155, 1988.

[175] P. Smith. *An Introduction to Formal Logic*. Cambridge University Press, 2003.

[176] K. Soetaert, J. Cash, and F. Mazzia. *Solving Differential Equations in R*. Springer-Verlag, New York, 2012.

[177] K. Soetaert and P. M. J. Herman. *A Practical Guide to Ecological Modelling. Using R as a Simulation Platform*. Springer-Verlag, New York, 2009.

[178] D. Ştefănescu. Bounds for real roots and applications to orthogonal polynomials. In *Computer Algebra in Scientific Computing, 10th International Workshop, CASC 2007, Bonn, Germany*, pages 377–391, 2007.

[179] S. Sternberg. *Dynamical Systems*. Dover Publications, New York, NY, USA, 2010.

[180] James V. Stone. *Bayes' Rule: A Tutorial Introduction to Bayesian Analysis*. Sebtel Press, 2013.

[181] S. H. Strogatz. *Nonlinear Dynamics and Chaos: With Applications to Physics, Biology, Chemistry, and Engineering*. Addison-Wesley, Reading, 1994.

[182] K. Sydsaeter, P. Hammond, and A. Strom. *Essential Mathematics for Economic Analysis*, 4th edition. Pearson, 2012.

[183] S. Thurner. Statistical mechanics of complex networks. In M. Dehmer and F. Emmert-Streib, editors, *Analysis of Complex Networks: From Biology to Linguistics*, pages 23–45. Wiley-VCH, 2009.

[184] J. P. Tignol. *Galois' Theory of Algebraic Equations*. World Scientific Publishing Company, 2016.

[185] Mary Tiles. Mathematics: the language of science? *Monist*, 67(1):3–17, 1984.

[186] N. Trinajstić. *Chemical Graph Theory*. CRC Press, Boca Raton, FL, USA, 1992.

[187] S. Tripathi, M. Dehmer, and F. Emmert-Streib. NetBioV: an R package for visualizing large-scale data in network biology. *Bioinformatics*, 30(19):2834–2836, 2014.

[188] S. B. Trust. *Role of Mathematics in the Rise of Science*. Princeton Legacy Library. Princeton University Press, 2014.

[189] J. W. Tukey. *Exploratory Data Analysis*. Addison-Wesley, New York, 1977.

[190] V. van Noort, B. Snel, and M. A. Huymen. The yeast coexpression network has a small-world, scale-free architecture and can be explained by a simple model. *EMBO Rep.*, 5(3):280–284, 2004.

[191] V. Vapnik. *Statistical Learning Theory.* J. Willey, 1998.

[192] Vladimir Naumovich Vapnik. *The Nature of Statistical Learning Theory.* Springer, 1995.

[193] V. Volterra. Variations and fluctuations of the number of individuals in animal species living together. In R. N. Chapman, editor, *Animal Ecology.* McGraw-Hill, 1931.

[194] J. von Neumann. *The Theory of Self-Reproducing Automata.* University of Illinois Press, Urbana, 1966.

[195] Andreas Wagner and David A. Fell. The small world inside large metabolic networks. *Proc. R. Soc. Lond. B, Biol. Sci.*, 268(1478):1803–1810, 2001.

[196] J. Wang and G. Provan. Characterizing the structural complexity of real-world complex networks. In J. Zhou, editor, *Complex Sciences*, volume 4 of Lecture Notes of the Institute for Computer Sciences, Social Informatics and Telecommunications Engineering, pages 1178–1189. Springer, Berlin/Heidelberg, Germany, 2009.

[197] S. Wasserman and K. Faust. *Social Network Analysis: Methods and Applications.* Structural Analysis in the Social Sciences. Cambridge University Press, 1994.

[198] D. J. Watts and S. H. Strogatz. Collective dynamics of 'small-world' networks. *Nature*, 393:440–442, 1998.

[199] A. Weil. *Basic Number Theory.* Springer, 2005.

[200] Hadley Wickham. *ggplot2: Elegant Graphics for Data Analysis.* Springer, 2016.

[201] Hadley Wickham. *Advanced R*, 2nd edition. Chapman and Hall/CRC, 2019.

[202] R. Wilhelm and D. Maurer. *Übersetzerbau: Theorie, Konstruktion, Generierung.* Springer, 1997.

[203] Thomas Wilhelm, Heinz-Peter Nasheuer, and Sui Huang. Physical and functional modularity of the protein network in yeast. *Mol. Cell. Proteomics*, 2(5):292–298, 2003.

[204] Leland Wilkinson. The grammar of graphics. In *Handbook of Computational Statistics*, pages 375–414. Springer, 2012.

[205] S. Wolfram. Statistical mechanics of cellular automata. *Phys. Rev. E*, 55(3):601–644, 1983.

[206] S. Wolfram. *A New Kind of Science.* Wolfram Media, 2002.

[207] J. A. Wright, M. H. Wright, P. Lagarias, and J. C. Reeds. Convergence properties of the Nelder-Mead simplex algorithm in low dimensions. *SIAM J. Optim.*, 9:112–147, 1998.

Index

www.ingramcontent.com/pod-product-compliance
Lightning Source LLC
Chambersburg PA
CBHW080932240926
51849CB00003BA/433
* 9 7 8 3 1 1 0 7 9 5 8 8 2 *